The Gardens of Flora Baum

III

The Gardens of Flora Baum

Book One: By the Tree of Life
   Part 1   Sum
   Part 2   The Path Approaching
   Part 3   Epiphany
   Part 4   The Waves Receding
   Part 5   Difference

Book Two: Towards a Greek Garden
   Part 1   The Program
   Part 2   Iliad
   Part 3   The History
   Part 4   Odyssey
   Part 5   The Diagram

Book Three: Rome
   Part 1   Urbiculture
   Part 2   Floralia
   Part 3   Umbrageous Vision

Book Four: Towards Farthest Thule
   Part 1   Lay of the Last Monk
   Part 2   Sibyl
   Part 3   Lyre, Harp, Violin

Book Five: By the Tree of Knowledge
   Part 1   By the Tree
   Part 2   The Tree of Knowledge
   Part 3   Knowledge
   Part 4   Of Knowledge by the Tree
   Part 5   Tree
   Part 6   Knowledge of the Tree
   Part 7   Of the Tree

BOOKS	PARTS	PARTS
Book One	5	
		10
Book Two	5	
Book Three	3	3
Book Four	3	
		10
Book Five	7	

Foreword

THIS IS A posthumous publication, but Julia Budenz had meticulously prepared her five-book poem and had overseen the process of digitization and proofing, and so it has the stamp of authorial approval. It rests on the author's typed version. Only the few pieces written within a week of her death on December 11, 2010, are from manuscript, and these are inserted at the points she indicated. They are "September" and "And January" (Book Three, pages 718–720, 722) and "How shall I say this?" (Book Five, page 570).

Her long poem addresses a wide range of readers, and she would have wished this first contact to be an unmediated one. So no attempt is made here to categorize, other than to indicate, as the poet did herself, that there is a different focus in each of the five books. In a short essay called "Query Re One's Work," which appeared online in the *Poetry Porch* in 1997, she said:

> The gardens are five, comprising the five books. The first garden is the garden of the holy; its book explores transcendence, is located partially in Eden, and draws upon imagery from the Bible and the liturgy. Its title, "By the Tree of Life," indicates that despite its strong center this book may be considered a Paradise Lost, as is suggested also by the names of its five parts: "Sum," "The Path Approaching," "Epiphany," "The Waves Receding," and "Difference."
>
> The second garden is the garden of the beautiful; its book contemplates the aesthetic, is situated partially in Greece, and makes use of Greek literature, mythology, and geography. This second book, which is called "Towards a Greek Garden," has a midpoint as well as a final destination and also consists of five parts, whose names intimate both the patterned centering and the linear progression: "The Program," "Iliad," "The History," "Odyssey," "The Diagram." Since Flora Baum reaches the Greek garden, the second book may be designated a Paradise Regained.
>
> The third garden is that of the true, specifically of academic

knowledge, of scholarship, of learning. Its book, entitled "Rome," uses material from Roman literature, history, and topography. This is the pivotal book in the design and development of the poem; its three parts — "Urbiculture," "Floralia," and "Umbrageous Vision" — mark not only a center which is both city and garden but also a difficult struggle to pass through pedantry to erudition and insight.

The fourth garden is that of the good and blooms with human relations. Its book, "Towards Farthest Thule," is set partly in Britain, finally in Shetland. As might be expected, it utilizes English and Scottish literature, folklore, and geography. The book begins with a long ballad, "The Lay of the Last Monk," continues with an epyllion called "Sibyl," and concludes with a sequence of lyrics, "Lyre, Harp, Violin."

The fifth and final garden is the garden of the whole. Its book, "By the Tree of Knowledge," is the philosophical book, the one most fully placed in Flora's native America but also situated in her native world, in her homeland the earth, in her home the universe. It is the book of the elm, rooted and reaching. It grounds itself not only in a meditation upon philosophy but also in social science and physical science, in culture and nature, in the microcosm and the mesocosm and the macrocosm, in the final paracosm, the final paradigm and paradise. It is the book which I will write if I can live long enough and become wise enough to do it. "O mihi tum longae maneat pars ultima vitae," I find myself crying out with Virgil, hoping to touch this great beginning or end or center or edge.

Although no critical assessment is offered here, it can be anticipated that, in due course, *The Gardens of Flora Baum* will find a place in the history of American literature once readers have had a chance to absorb its author's new and distinctive voice and to respond fully to it.

Julia's life and writing were intertwined and the following biographical sketch may prove helpful. She was the eldest daughter of Louis Budenz and Margaret Rodgers Budenz and had three sisters. She was born on May 23, 1934, in New York City. The first break in her life came in 1945 when her father renounced the Communist party and rejoined the Roman Catholic church. The family moved briefly to South Bend, Indiana, before returning to New York. The year 1956 marked Julia's graduation with an A.B. summa cum laude from the College of New Rochelle and also the beginning of the period she spent as an Ursuline nun. In 1962, she was awarded a Master of Arts degree at Catholic University and became an instructor in classics at the College of New Rochelle.

In 1966, after leaving the convent, she studied briefly at New York University in the spring and began graduate studies in comparative literature (Greek, Latin and English) at Harvard University in the fall. She graduated A.M. in 1972 and continued working towards a Ph.D. for a time, but the pull of scholarship in isolation became less compelling than the desire to create in the light of her scholarship and her vision. She began writing *The Gardens of Flora Baum* in about 1969 and received a fellowship at the Radcliffe Institute in 1974–75 for the purpose of developing it.

For the rest of her working life, she undertook paid employment with an eye always to the opportunities offered for the combination of scholarly facilities and leisure essential for her writing. Widener Library at Harvard University had the central place in her life that she speaks of in her poem. In 1972, she had begun working in Harvard's History of Science Department with I. Bernard Cohen and Anne Whitman on their new English translation of Isaac Newton's *Principia*, and, although she left Cambridge twice to teach classics — at Colby College in 1980–81 and at Berea College in 1987–88 — she was mainly engaged on History of Science Department projects until her retirement freed her to concentrate on her poetry. She suffered from ill health in her closing years and died of cancer at the age of seventy-six.

Parts of *The Gardens of Flora Baum* have been published previously in books and periodicals. *From the Gardens of Flora Baum*, Wesleyan University Press, Middletown, Connecticut, 1984, contained "The Fire Escape" and "The Sheen" (Book Two, pages 173–250), and *Carmina Carmentis*, Pivot Press, Brooklyn, New York, 2005, contained a sequence from "January" (Book Three, pages 635–673). Shorter pieces from *The Gardens of Flora Baum* were included in these edited books: *Anthology of Magazine Verse and Yearbook of American Poetry*, ed. Alan F. Pater, Monitor Book Company, Beverly Hills, California, 1980; *A Formal Feeling Comes: Poems in Form by Contemporary Women*, ed. Annie Finch, Story Line

Press, Brownsville, Oregon, 1994; *Catullus in English*, ed. Julia Haig Gaisser, Penguin Books, London, 2001; *Emily Lyle: The Persistent Scholar*, ed. Frances J. Fischer and Sigrid Rieuwerts, WVT Wissenschaftlicher Verlag Trier, Trier, 2007; *Petrarch & Dante*, ed. Zygmunt G. Baranski and Theodore J. Cachey, Jr., University of Notre Dame Press, Notre Dame, Indiana, 2009.

Other excerpts from the work appeared between 1971 and 2010 in the following periodicals: *Akros, American Arts Quarterly, The American Voice, Amphora, Arion, Bits, Bitterroot, Boston Review, Bunting Institute Newsletter, Chapman, Cloelia, Cosmos, Crazyhorse, The Cream City Review, Cross Currents, Epos, Four Quarters, La Fusta, Harvard Advocate, Harvard Review, Italian Americana, The Kenyon Review, Lines Review, The Lyric, Mati, NEeuropa, New England Classical Journal, North Stone Review, Notre Dame Review, Other Poetry, Persephone, Poet Lore, The Poetry Porch, Radcliffe Quarterly, Rhino, Scottish Literary Journal, Society of Fellows News* (American Academy in Rome), *The Society of Institute Fellows Newsletter* (The Bunting Institute of Radcliffe College), *Southwest Review, Sparrow, Studia Mystica, The Tennessee Quarterly, The Tennessee Review, Vergilius, The Wallace Stevens Journal, William and Mary Review*, and *YIP: Yale Italian Poetry*.

Very warm acknowledgement should be made in conclusion to those bodies that, through residencies, fellowships, visiting scholar appointments, and funding, gave support to this long-term poetic project. I shall instance with gratitude the American Academy in Rome, the Authors League, the Bellagio Study and Conference Center of the Rockefeller Foundation, the Djerassi Foundation, Harvard University's Departments of Comparative Literature and English, the National Endowment for the Arts, the Radcliffe Institute, and Yaddo.

EMILY LYLE
University of Edinburgh

Publisher's Note

WHEN JULIA BUDENZ began writing *The Gardens of Flora Baum* in about 1969, she prepared master sheets on a manual typewriter. By 2005 she had switched to a laptop computer, which provided digital files. The arduous task of scanning the older material (roughly 1,700 pages), processing it with optical-character-recognition software, and proofreading it was overseen by Emily Lyle. For questions that arise, readers should consult the original typescript included among Julia's papers, which have been placed on deposit in the Houghton Library, Harvard University.

Over the years Julia told friends the schedule she'd mapped out for herself, intending to finish *The Gardens of Flora Baum* in 2015, when she would have been 81. But in January 2008 she asked me to explore the idea of an "introductory edition" of the material written to that point, much of which had not yet appeared in print. She continued work on unfinished sections, mainly in Book Four and Book Five. By late 2010, with her health in sharp decline, she identified those places in the poem where she'd intended to insert further material.

In the last few months of her life she did make sure that the start and finish of every book were completed. She also discussed her preferences as to the layout and presentation of the books.

Layout and style. In preparing this set of five books for publication, my aim has been to follow the original typescript to the greatest extent possible. In most cases short titled pieces begin on a new page, or are run on with preceding pieces. The decision whether to center a title or place it flush left also follows the original. But a typewriter does not offer the stylistic variation possible in a typeset book, and we have varied heading styles to suggest the importance of each piece in the hierarchy implied by the table of contents of each book. The scheme varies somewhat from book to book.

The author's practice of having complete stanzas on a page, whenever possible, explains why some pages end short even though the piece continues on the next page. In the case of very long stanzas and other layout problems, we occasionally did break stanzas. This is indicated by the quaint device of a "catchword," set flush right at the bottom of the page. The catchword repeats the first word or two on the next page and tells the reader that the stanza has not ended yet. (To prevent anyone from mistaking a catchword for the second part of a broken line in the poem's meter, the catchword is printed in smaller type.) No catchwords were needed in Book One, but they do occur often in later books. On pages without a catchword, the page does end in a stanza break.

Occasionally the poem contains insertions that may appear to have been added by someone other than the author. One example is the use of "[sic]" in two places on page 79 of Book Two. Another is the inclusion of several footnotes in Book Five about a missing word or illegible date in a personal letter. There are a few other cases of partially bracketed dates at the tops of personal letters. All these insertions were made by Julia Budenz herself; she clearly intended them to be considered part of her poem.

Three asterisks (* * *) centered on a line denote a *lacuna,* or gap, where Julia had intended to write more material. On several occasions she commented that the asterisks could represent one stanza, one piece, or a long section of many pieces — there's no telling.

But the poem in five books appears to be at least 90 percent finished to her satisfaction. For the record, it contains about 303,700 words in 2,254 printed pages. The original typescript has 2,282 pages (owing to some differences in the locations of page breaks).

For advice and suggestions on specific issues during the preparation of these volumes, I am grateful to Virginia Furtwangler, Rebecca and Douglas Karo, Hope Mayo, Arthur Mortensen, Cynthia Thompson, and Frederick Turner. Without the monumental effort of Emily Lyle over many years, including repeated proofreading at various stages of production, this edition would not have been possible.

ROGER W. SINNOTT
Carpathia Press

Contents

Foreword   v
Publisher's Note   ix

Book Three: Rome

Part One: Urbiculture   3
   1. Amor   5
   2. Flora Baum, Thinker   6
   3. Flora Baum, Historian   6
   4. Flora Baum, Botanist   9
   5. Flora Baum, Mathematician   11
   6. Spring Fever   12
   7. Exile   29
   8. Epodes   63
   9. Flora Baum's Thesis Proposal   70
   10. Epistles   73
   11. Entry   87
   12. Winter Bud   109
   13. Flora Baum, Astronomer   110
   14. Flora Baum, Archaeologist   113
   15. Flora Baum, Geographer   114
   16. Flora Baum, Student   115
   17. Roma   115

Part Two: Floralia   135

Part Three: Umbrageous Vision   263
  Chapter 1: VMBRA   265
  Chapter 2: ARDOR   415
  Chapter 3: VIA   417

Chapter 4: ARBOR ... 418
  Article 1: Again Bright, Gray ... 418
  Article 2: A Brief Grammar ... 418
    Point One ... 418
    Point Two ... 419
  Article 3: Anne, Bronze, Gold ... 419
Chapter 5: VISIO ... 423
  Section 1: Question and Address ... 424
    Division 1: Gate ... 424
      His Vision ... 424
      Benediction ... 424
      Unnamed ... 424
      Blessing ... 426
      Halley's Poem ... 427
      LOCUS LOCANDUS ... 427
      October Twelfth ... 428
      October Fifteenth ... 428
      PORTA ... 429
    Division 2: Conversations with the Italian ... 430
      Comedy ... 430
      STUDI LEOPARDIANI ... 430
        1. PER POCO IL COR NON SI SPAURA ... 430
        2. INTERMINATI SPAZI DI LÀ DA QUELLA ... 431
        3. S'ANNEGA IL PENSIER MIO E IL NAUFRAGAR M'È DOLCE ... 431
      EPPUR SI MUOVE ... 432
      Heartwood ... 432
      ROMOLO PROFUMATISSIMO ... 434
      UNA COSA VERA, BUONA, BELLA ... 434
      Sonnets to the Italian ... 435
      SONETTI PETRARCHESCHI ... 435
        1. POCO MANCÒ CH'IO NON RIMASI IN CIELO ... 435
        2. LAURO ... 436
        3. ET ALLARGÒ LA MANO ... 436
        4. SE 'L DESIR NON ERRA ... 437
        5. LEVOMMI IL MIO PENSER ... 437
        6. ARBOR VICTORIOSA ... 438
        7. VEDEVA A LA SUA OMBRA ... 438

8. A PARLAR DE' SUOI SEMPRE VERDI RAMI	439
9. DISSI 'L VER	439
10. FACENDOMI D'UOM VIVO UN LAURO VERDE	440
11. ULMUS-OLMO	440
12. A FERRAGOSTO LA ROBINIA DEL GIAPPONE A CAMBRIDGE NEL MASSACHUSETTS	441
13. LAURORA SCRIPSIT	441
14. LAUREOLA	442
15. LA DISIATA VOSTRA FORMA VERA	442
16. PRESSO A L'EXTREMO	443
17. NOTE AI SONETTI 1–16	443
18. INDICE	444
19. BIOGRAFIA	444
20. SOFFIETTO EDITORIALE	445
21. FASCETTA	445
22. CONGEDO	446
23. ECO	446
24. RECENSIONE	447
25. SCIENZA NUOVA	447
26. SAGGIO DI FLORA BAUM	448
27. APPENDICE: LEONARDO OLSCHKI E L'USIGNUOLO DI COLOMBO	448
28. AL SUON DE' DETTI	449
29. IL MIO BEL VELO	449
30. FRA LOR CHE 'L TERZO CERCHIO SERRA	450
31. LAUREA	450
32. IN PARTE OV' ERA	451
VITA NUOVA O MONDO NUOVO	452
1. ROMEA	452
2. BIBLIOTECA COLOMBIANA	453
3. L'UCCELLO MOTTEGGIATORE	453
4. IL TIGLIO	454
5. L'INVITO	454
6. ALLA SALUTE	455
7. LA CENA	455
8. LA COLOMBA	456
9. O L'INFERNO	456
10. LA VEDUTA	457

11. IL PURGATORIO	457
12. IL BIGLIETTO	458
13. IL LUSSO	458
14. L'ALBERO GENEALOGICO	459
15. DALLA COROLLA AL CALICE	459
16. DAGLI ALBERI ALLE CASE	460
17. NOTE AI SONETTI 1–16	460
18. SEMPRE	461
19. IL POETA	461
20. LA POETESSA	462
21. LA VITA	462
22. IL COLPO E LA COLPA	463
23. LA POESIA	463
24. MONNA INNOMINATA	464
25. QUESTIONI NOMINALI	464
26. QUESTIONI FAMILIARI	465
27. QUESTIONI RELIGIOSE	465
28. QUESTIONI MONDIALI	466
29. QUESTIONI VITALI	466
30. LA LETTERATURA	467
31. TROVARE, SCOPRIRE	467
32. ROMA	468
SONETTI PREROMANI	469
1. VIRGILIO	469
2. UDRALLO IL BEL PAESE	470
3. IL ROMANZO DI CORINNA	470
4. CORINNA, O L'ITALIA	471
5. CORINNA O PINDARO	471
6. LA MEMORIA	472
7. IL PARTITO	472
8. IL PARADISO	473
9. IL PATRIMONIO	473
10. ROMEO	474
11. SUGGERIRE, ISPIRARE	474
12. MONNA NOMINATA	475
13. CHIARA MATRAINI	475
14. TUTTI LI FEDELI D'AMORE	476
15. UN SECONDAMENTO	476

16. CHIAROSCURO	477
17. NOTE AI SONETTI 1–16	477
18. LO SVILUPPO	478
19. TRASLATO	478
20. LA RICERCA	479
21. L'OCCASIONE	479
22. IL DISCORSO	480
23. O VOI CHE PER LA VIA D'AMOR PASSATE	480
24. IN SETTEMBRE LE ROBINIE DEL GIAPPONE A CAMBRIDGE NEL MASSACHUSETTS	481
25. PIANGETE, AMANTI, POI CHE PIANGE AMORE	481
26. DEH PEREGRINI CHE PENSOSI ANDATE	482
27. IN QUELLE PAROLE CHE LODANO	482
28. L'8 SETTEMBRE: LA NATIVITÀ DI MARIA	483
29. POETA FUI	483
30. IL 12 SETTEMBRE: IL SANTISSIMO NOME DI MARIA	484
31. DAL 13 AL 14 SETTEMBRE	484
32. VIRGILIA	485
FIORI TOSCANI	485
LETTERA AL PROFESSOR FONTANELLA	486
Macaronic	486
MACCHIATO	487
VIAGGIO-VILLAGGIO	487
BUON VIAGGIO	487
PARCA-VILLAGGIO	487
Trans World	489
UMBRA-OMBRA	489
Division 3: Bridge	490
Television	490
Grace	490
Vergil/Virgil	490
Thanksgiving	491
Thesis	491
LUCUS A NON LUCENDO	491
October Thirteenth	492
November Fourth	492
PONS	492

Section 2: Question and Answer	493
Question and Answer	493
Versed Sine	493
To Bruce Bennett, Richard Rorty, Quintus Horatius Flaccus, et al.	494
A. Sounds out of Season	494
B. Rhymes and/or Reason	496
C. Rounds If Not Treason	499
D. Times with the Tease in	503
E. Bounds that Let Breeze in	508
Martial 8.69	517
Question and Question	518
Section 3: Vision	519
January	519
February	673
Intercalary	674
March	684
April	687
May	703
June	703
Roman Sonnets	704
The Libraries	717
The Myth of Scipio	717
Quintile	717
Sextile	717
September	718
October	721
November	721
December	721
And January	722

Book Three

Rome

Part One

Urbiculture

Urbiculture

The city has three names: secret, sacred, and civic. The secret name is Amor, or Desire . . . ; the sacred name is Flora, or Flowering . . . ; the civic name is Roma.

Lydus, *The Months*.

1. Amor

If you will not come down to me from the sky,
Your chariot drawn by sparrows all aflutter
Flung from a palace of gold,

                    I will take flight
Over the deepest purple velvets of earth
Bejewelled with bright necklaces and brooches;

My great gray wings, without any flutter,
Will darken and grow pale;
Sunset, yellow and red, will yield

To sunrise, red and yellow, streak upon streak,
Like the roses, cheek to cheek,
There in the patch of garden.

The folds of the toga of the snow
Hang over the flat roof.

A summer dawn. The roses hang
Over the wall, glistening of dawn
And dew.

      A winter night.
Snow grows along the branches
And over the cars in the parking lot
Quietly as roses.

These modern wings do not quiver,
Only this old-fashioned heart,

For the rose may open, yellow and red,
Or orange, or peach, or nectarine,

Or apricot, like the horizon
Beyond that stretch of silver pinion.

2. Flora Baum, Thinker

There is a rock in my head.
It is wedged just under the skull.
My mind, getting ready to move,
Envies Sisyphus.

3. Flora Baum, Historian

The vina gulps,
The vina burps
Through the floors.

There were flowers, for the wings
Of gigantic weeds are spinning
In the Thanksgiving wind.

There were flowers, for the mops
Upended between brick fortresses
Will seed the dust.

There were flowers, for the tan
Tatters rustling on maple and ailanthus
Poles are such as once were nearly gold.

Two recorders squeak.
The recorders leak
Through the doors.

There will be flowers, for the sun
Decembering among the fruity tops
Of the four-story weeds,

Although too unbending to stoop
To panes that stare at fortresses
And fortress-encompassed

Fruiters, folds the fruits
In gleam. There will be flowers
Growing green-gold as the tan-gold gleam.

Deep in my ears,
Deep deep in my ears,
The drill ddrrillll dddrrrillllll dddrrrrillllllll bores.

When I called the transit authority
To complain about the drilling for the new subway
They promised not to start before seven.

When I knocked on the door of the vina player
She told me I should go live in the country.
When I stamped on the floor I shocked my knee.

When I knocked on the door of the recorder players
They were surprised. They didn't think
The sound would carry. I said I thought I could take it

If it weren't for the vina downstairs and that nameless electronic
Keyboard next door. In one vina note
You can hold all knowledge, the player said.

In the country you can find peace and flowers.
The hollow gourds of the vina —
Were they flowers? If you could find

The flowers flowering, if you could find
The flowering trees, if you could find
The trees, if in December you could find

The trees in flower, if you could hear
Them quietly flowering, couldn't you note them,
Couldn't you hold them in your note, in your notion,

Your dendriform gnosis, your anthological
Knowing, your simple knowing of them,
Your simple knowing? All knowing

Is complicated. Trees shoot between
Sterile brick buildings. There were flowers.
Flowering named the city. The city

(What shall I say of the city? The city
Is here? was Rome? is civilization?
Will kill the flowers? will kill?) .... The city

Was Rome. Real city. Breathing. Burgeoning.
Gulping the shining sea. If only
You could breathe you could find the shining.

Upstairs that's not stamping. That's walking.
That's not all Hannibal's elephants crossing
The Alps. That's walking in two stockinged feet.

An island across the Alps (white
Are the weedy trees, the fire escapes,
The sooty screens) is besieged by oceans

Surging from the long strings of the vina, battered
By blizzards of metaphor whitening red
Walls and diving through slim apertures

As ailanthus fruits have wormed their way in
Like winged worms, assaulted by lightning
Like the Carthaginian dragon's, here, there, here.

That's not a whistling tea kettle. That's
No cup of tea. That's not a signal
For battle. That's the coming of the heat.

Rome, trembling as a brick building trembles
At subway blasting, pulls her white
Cloak about her and waits it out.

Well she knows how to stride forth. She has
Traversed the peninsula. She has essayed
To bestride the sea. She will stride forth

Once more, breasting eternity. Carthage,
Gazing across the waters, cannot
Hear the song that belongs to tomorrow.

That's not rocks thrown through the windows.
That is rock. They've a right
To find their flowers on the rocky beat.

4. Flora Baum, Botanist

Beyond the rocky beach
They found new flowers
And founded a new city—
On rock, let us hope.
Can cities flourish on sand?

Can flowers flourish on rock?
Can trees root in the rock?
Can trees root in the sand?
The city, rooted in rock, expanded
Banyanwise to a sandy place

Where, not far from Hell Gate,
Behind the ramparts (habitations)
Encircling, or rather enrectangling
(They lined the four sides of the block
As their clones did block after block),

Gardens Babylonian,
The vast willow grew in the vast
Sandpile, flanked by castles,
Battles, chants
Of sundry inviolable laws:

Finders keepers,
Losers weepers.
Sticks and stones
May break my bones
But names will never hurt me.

First by day,
Last by night.
Red and yellow,
Catch a fellow.
Pink for girls. O Hammurabi.

Castles rose and fell, battles waxed and waned,
The tree stood firm and flexible,
Golden into winter, golden ahead of spring.

O land of lotus and of asphodel,
O land of moly and of amaranth,

O salix admiranda — though then,
Except for an altar boy or two,
We were all pretty innocent of Latin,
If not of Greek, Hebrew, Polish,
Italian, Yiddish, Czech, Chinese,
Russian. Tavarish! The tree stood silent,
Silent, admirable, and strong
Until the storm. We ran out like ants
And stopped before the revolution.
So lay the pillars of Olympian Zeus.

So a white breaking beauty
Fills the world, and then the shovels begin.

So a purer pulchritude, a truer
Treeness, a flowering
Less abruptly finite is admired.

Admiror, admirari, admiratus sum:
I gaze at with passion, desire to obtain,
Strive after from admiration of. Nil
Admirari — to marvel at nothing —
Alone makes you happy. If you could find

The trees, if in December you could find
The trees in flower, if in December
You found, marveled at, admired
Willow? acacia, callistemon,
Hibiscus, or butterfly tree

Bright with yellow, bright with red,
With pinks, with purples among green wings,
With filaments of lemon drop,
With filaments of cherry ice,
With petals of pink of dawn and purple of sunset

Up the stream and down the sky,
If you could look through a louvered window
And watch through the sun-steeped breeze
Beyond the ficus, beyond the palm,
The green spray against the white wall

Like a green ocean on a white beach
Without the boom, with only
A lapping and a pink plenitude,
If only you could map from edge to center
White pink, light pink, deep pink, deepest

Pink, five dots of red,
You would break the graying boundaries of December
Without a boom.
I mean what I say.
I can't say I say what I mean.

5. Flora Baum, Mathematician

She stood looking down the path
Through green trees. The lawns
Caught, blade by blade, the prime
Gold streaks of sun. Was this the third
Garden or, as she once thought, the second,
Or was it not, after all, the first?

She walks quickly down the path
Over the ice, by the broken trees,
Up the wooden snow-steps, through the heavy door,
Onto the red carpet, onto the marble floor.
She has wiped her feet on the red carpet.

It is not the red carpet, not the marble,
Not the pillars, not the arches, not the dome,
Not the wide stairways,
Not the burnished banisters,
Not the laqueate ceilings,
Not the heroic murals
That have drawn her through the drumlins of the snow.

She skims the stairs to paneled rooms,
Pulls out certain worn wooden drawers,
Fingers certain well-fingered cards,
Jots down certain occult notations,
Claps the drawers to,

Fumbles for a small magic pass,
Enters through a narrow guarded door,
Noses her way along maze upon maze
Of occult notations. Here, and here,
And here, triumph, the treasures, the books.
She clasps them to her.
She carries them off.

She walked slowly down the path
Through red trees. The lawns
Held, blade by blade, the late
Gold streaks of sun. This was the third
Garden or, as she once thought, the second
Or, after all, the first. In the end
Would it not be, if she should reach the end,
The fifth, where parallels bend?

6. Spring Fever

You see things when it thaws —
Say, the big barred owl in Harvard Yard.

His big brown frontal eyes look down.
My frontal eyes look up.
It is a confrontation.

It is

It is an encounter.
Knowingly, we exchange glances.
No looks barred.

Standing there, the library looks
On. Let me get back to my books.

Knowingly. No, they wrote in the margins.
Yes, get back to your books.

Andante.

At the tramp's goal,
Sunlets scent dull February's cold.
Snowdrops live. They do not melt
In the witchhazelshine.

Back at home, sun
Is draped over the edge of the roof. Snow
Is draped over the edge of the roof. Ice
Fringes the windows.

                    Tears
Of joy soon drip from the lidded lashes.
This has happened
For years.

Ambling along.

You don't know all the things I've said
About the crocuses that shine
In the glory of the brick apartment house
On a February afternoon.

They're packed into my files.
I shall not tug them out,
Cutting a finger on the edge
Of some acute observation.

I don't live in their neighborhood now.
By the time I'm home my hands are numb
Or my numb mind has forgotten
Their sharp small purpureality.

But
March is coming in.
Here the nubs of buds rub
The brick. But

Cambridge, Mass., is not New York,
Except in your efficiency apartment
Whenever the officiously efficient
Heat rattles in and vanishes
As it is in the nature of metal and steam
To conduct and come, to let go and go
(Warranty: always far too hot
Except when far too cold),
Or when the neighboring brick walls
Are far too close, or when your own,
Your very own, your rented cracking
Plaster walls of eggshell white
Tighten (do at least not crack
Open) on your books and you.

Is there only the one city?
Why in the Amtrak pane
Had Boston become a toy?
Is there only the implacable, the irrefutable,
Rubbing, galling, grating the gray hopes
Of more than ailanthus, sharpening the golden
Dreams to pierce through clamorous echoes
And write on the sky? Is it a city
If you can walk two blocks and see
Silver maples bright March red,
Dull March gold?

And in Harvard Yard the large wise owl
Sleeps in the pine while a silly squirrel
Runs up and down the pine boughs
Feathering his large nest.

Urban: of a city, of the city?
Articulation may be reductive.
At least, Latin is cultivated here,
Even if with hints of Grecity
And oriental importations
Accommodating occidental specifications.
Vernal ardor flames.
Ambulation inspects
Acer saccharum,
Acer saccharinum,
Acer rubrum,
Acer negundo.
Fenestral vision accepts
Acer pseudoplatanus,
Acer platanoides,
And, of course,
Ailanthus altissima.

The owl sits by the drey
Asleep. The squirrel is gone.
Was there a confrontation
While I sat in the library
Awake? How do I know?
Now there's a demonstration
Circling on the library steps.
Now the loudspeaker spouts
Something, no doubt right and true.
Now the chapel bell showers
Something, no doubt right and good.
Sacrifice. Communion.
Between, in the pine, the owl is sleeping.
Tonight, when the trains stop, quietly, in the subway
He'll do his killing and his eating.

What are those little yellow or purple
Ones there seem to be a lot of? asked
The man from California. Where
Have you been? They are spring, I answered.

Bigger, no doubt, but small,
Ailanthus gray,
Norway maple brown,
Sycamore maple green,
While the jangle and boop that shoot from a window
Below blow up through the branches —
Here, besides stereophony
Butting into tender calyxes
(Ears, your quivering ears) —
Here there are but buds,
Not guns, butts of buds,
The unobtrusive butts of buds, but

Over the southern wall
And through the western window
Slants in, comes in,
Briefly, really,
Into the room, really,
Not reflected, really,
The sun,

                        while out and away,
Above small saffron or lavender cups,
The modest silver maples finely fluffily flower.

If I lived on the front of my building
I'd have a brighter Weltanschauung
Looking east and south out over lights:

Street lights, stop lights, car lights, shop lights —
Crimson Cleaners in crimson, Bence Pharmacy in green,
Green pepper steak, red pizza, and blue grinders,

White shishkebab, and turning turning turning
Old-fashioned stripes of red and white and blue,
Disappearing, ever revenant.

Back here the gray day darkens on the black
Gleam of fire escapes, the brownish glint
Of unfledged boughs, the gleamless brick.

Checking on the box elders, those maples
Incogniti, that lack the name and — this is worse —
The maple leaf, I found them still
To be waited for, with gilt hints of a break-out,
Not much more, yet, one must say,
More than just buds. Checking maples, I found
Budding's shadows all over the elms,
The color of shadow in shade, of copper in sun.
I found and read the purple patches
Of crocuses, the blue ink spots
(Spurted from an outmoded pen) of the first
Siberian squills, some cheery (what's in a name?)
Gold coins of winter aconite,
And smudged on its royal purple scrap
The gold line of each iris
Sturdy and small enough for March.
What, however, of maples?
I found the dark green cutlery
Of daffodils — the many knives, few spoons.
I spied the imminent hatching of one white star
Among the furred magnolia eggs.
But what of maples?
The silver maples, now less fine
Perhaps, more fluff, yet once, in sun,
And once again, refined and shining gold.

Spring's pentameters! How they fade
On Massachusetts Avenue
Despite its yellow buses
And its lights, red, white, and blue.

But the city and green Flora
Are one, says the ancient book.
Today? Tomorrow? The light is green.
Let's see, by hook or by crook.

I go in to read Latin.
I read of Rome in Greek.
The death of our dear codex
Is what our new scrolls squeak.

Lo! The whale's mittened fingers
Hold her baby to her breast.
Things hold, retrograde,
Move on from rest.

It is cold. The crocuses are closed.
The squirrel is hasting to the drey in the pine.
The owl is sleeping in the breeze in the elm.

Squire squirrel looks across — Borders not secure! — ,
Rushes down the pine,
Rushes up the elm,
Purposeful, undeviating,

Confronts (nudges? or nips?) professor owl,
Who, swelling, magnified, whitening, aerial, flies

Away, in another elm sits tight,
His eyes black holes, his head a-swivel,
The doll whose eyes have fallen in,
Whose head will soon fall off.

He keeps his head. No doubt he sees
Professor squirrel, white-mouthed, file
Reading matter in his renovated den.

Or in her nursery. Here?
But this is no Mount Athos.

The crocuses are a purple huddle.
Chill and dull, March shuffles along,
With bits of exposed magnolia browned in the bud,
The sprinkled squills the only (if very) blue,
Red maples and box elders ever
Indistinctly about to flower, the cardinal —
Dark, reddish wedge
Toward the chill, dull sky —
Vibrant, vibrating, calling warm and bright.

Finally it's true. It's April first.
It's the reddest red, noticeably,
A flowering not to be doubted,
If, though undoubted, generally unnoticed,
Remarkable if mainly unremarked.

Thus of the red maples, in the flush
Of spring. And even
Young thin street trees, even
Urchins inhabiting Massachusetts Avenue,
Rubied, flourish in the unbreathable breeze.

Last year it was bluest blue.
This year it is reddest red.
Next year — who thinks of future Aprils
With this not yet unswaddled?

Jewel red bugs stretch antennae
On the silver Byzantine boughs.

And what can be said of the acer negundo?
A castle where every petite Rapunzel,
Debonair,
Lets down shining hair.
I forbear.

Will she of the flowery, fairy-tale mind
Ever bloom into a serious scholar?
If she could find
The precise anthesis (a dillar a dollar)
Before the sun wholly declined.

The space in the painting
Gets us from then to now.
Blessed be windows.
More blessed be legs.

Walk, and it is not December.
Walk, and there are daffodils.
Walk, and you need not remember
How the robin thrills.

Here, through the panes,
No April echo
Blossoms in my
Narcissistic gaze.

Primavera.

Andante.

Fioritura.

Adagio.

Alla finestra.

There are flowers — three,
Four, five small posies
April-green against the brick-red bricks
On leafless sticks.

The wind rocks the wintry ailanthus.
The vina swirls and booms.
A tall weed blooms.

And so, before April ended, the acer platanoides
Here, right here, through the dirty panes, made it.
As has been indicated above, no native trees, whether maple
Or otherwise, flourish or even exist in the soil
Adjacent to this building. Yet, since as with
The first thoughts of Copernicus (cf. Kant)
The observer is mobile, if the observed is not,
Note:
For blooming of acer saccharum see especially
Book Two, Part One, Section Three, Subsection One, Segment One,
Of "The Gardens of Flora Baum," and, generatim,
Sensing omissions in the immediate treatment of the period
Circa February 1 to June 21, consult
Books One, Two, and Four supra et infra,
Passim.

It is May. The five bouquets
Of the maple are sunny under the newly
Opened umbrellas of leaves, and even
Ailanthus twigs now push toward spring.
Why can't you breathe here? Is it the sooty air
That slips through the inefficient filter
Of the sooty screens? Is it that smell
That has settled in the refrigerator, the milk, the cottage cheese?
Is it the smothering tomorrow
Standing above you as you gasp on your pillow,
Holding the gag, dragging the vinculation

To be applied on the stroke of nine?
Elsewhere the lilacs and the dogwoods
Verge on luminous explication.
Elsewhere — his splash of color
Splashing utterance — the cardinal at high lectern

Lectures

Lectures brilliantly. Elsewhere, with their white sheets
Flying, flashing in the wind,
Magnolias gleam in pages
Redolent of scientia. Breathing
Deeply the scholars stroll with their volumes.

There are almost flowers. They hang like fresh
Green grapes from the sycamore maple
Which serves as chair and breakfast table
For the rash

Furred hulk that sits on his rocking chair
Devouring. They are delicious
Obviously. He needs no dishes,
For the ware

Would crash on concrete, iron, brown
Hard sod. He needs no cup
As he digests his breakfast up-
Side down.

They are fluffed out now, and yellow,
Turned into flowers.
(A few are missing, of course,
Turned into squirrel.)
They dangle to be discovered
By the indefatigable bees.
They are flowers, among green leaves, and almost gold.
Like bees the sunbeams steal between the fortresses.
Elsewhere the pendent blossoms of the laburnum
Are real gold at the edge of a wide green lawn.

At the end of breakfast she went on reading,
Holding the book — it was less heavy than usual — easily in one hand.
She rested the other hand comfortably up behind her head.
Between the words of the book an idea began to peer.
Moisture. Water. Her hair was wet.
Behind her, three wide windowsills, wooden floor,

                                                                     Beside

Beside her, piles of papers and books on Woolworth tables
Drooled. Yes, the windows were closed. The generous precipitation
Seeped, dripped, poured, it seemed, through the lintels.
How damp were last night's paragraphs?
This is the graduate student's life, where rain,
As the world turns, as pages turn,
Falls in through vertical walls.

Flowering order of six maples
Throughout Cambridge, Massachusetts,
Twentieth century, March, April, May:
Silver maples first,
Red maples second,
Box elders third,
Norway maples fourth,
Sugar maples fifth,
Sycamore maples sixth,
In general. Anschauung. Erkenntniss.
(Again see Kant.) Verstand.
So far the revolution continues.

Don't cry, graduate student.
Some day you'll be a professor

With a study at the top of Widener,
Your personal key to the stacks below,

Smyth and Child full of books at the ends of halls
Of pink and baby blue to compare with the sky,

Views of the sky, views of the copper-splendid
Roof (or will it again be green of Greece?),

Warm aromas emerging into the halls (will they still smoke pipes?),
And views out over the surviving Harvard elms.

Or if you end up on welfare
You'll fare well:

You won't need a television set
As one does in the mud shacks of Yemen;

You'll have your own farsight
Deep in your eyes.

A robin passed into the stand of ailanthus
Guarding the dusk of the parking lot,
Sang a few measures,
Drew open a window,
Drew open more than a window,
And, unheard under the supervention
Of dark, went not unsung.

If he had perched among the magical groves
Of pearl-dripping virgilias,
If he had sung high in the tulip tree
Cups, cups, cups, cups,
Lifted and lifted,
All full of sun, of sun,
We would have heard banquets and palaces.

He passed between the brick buildings.
The televisions were silent.
Cold though it was, we could no longer
Stare at a pane of glass.
We lifted the window,
Looked out into trees,
Heard June.

Knew June?

Finally there's some sun.
The floods are receding.
The radiators (were they ever on in June before?)
Have stopped their steaming.
The long days of tarnished silver
Are blown into a day of gold,
The untarnishable.

Beyond

Beyond these long soft stretches of green
The reddish fetal tips
Keep reaching,
And terminal panicles, hard and green,
Keep reaching, too.
Soon the sun will light
Green lamps on the ailanthus trees.

The sun merits special mention.
It seems that in our twisted, elliptical way
We're reaching toward that gold focus,
Hearth to our very mobile home,
In the long run perhaps un feu de paille
But surely at this turning un feu de joie
Before the oppression of sumptuous summer,
Junoesque or dictatorial or imperial,
Turns us to straw indeed.

But now, still young,
Mysterious Etruscan June
Comes with her pearls, her cups,
Her lamps, her troubadours.

Pearls? Lace? Say flowers,
Clusters of flowers,
Flower after opening lifting flower,
Cluster on thick dripping glistening cluster.
Read them in the light of the sun.

There is light on the gray smooth trunks.
There is light in the white frilly flowers.
Read them — the glint, the gleam of the trunks,
The gleam, the glitter of the flowers,
In a green context.

Do not neglect the context.
The graduands are walking among the trees,
Their blue books behind them, looking toward commencement.
The trees stand around like benign alumni
Or proud parents or dazzled siblings.

The trees stand around like indifferent trees
Above the crowd, like self-assured divinities
Knowing themselves, willing to be admired,
Willing to be known. Acceptable, it seems,
Are glances, stares, interjections, names.

I'll always call them virgilias.
That fits their magicalness,
Ever of the Virgil of the virge.

It's hard to imagine them hidden in a new-world forest
In all their ornamentalness,
Unknown to Virgilians, unplanted, unmentioned

By tongues tamed to dictionaries.
Their names were living on the sweet, fresh breeze
And fell deader than Latin.

It's hard to imagine them prized for a yellow dye
By the tough, pushy supplanters
Who saw through their smooth gray suits

And found yellowwood a proper denomination
Or, though not prepared for a new deluge
In this new rainbowed land,

Thought gopherwood an appropriate appellation.
After all, there were gophers about them.
Cladrastis lutea appealed to others,

Who explored the terete branchlets, pinnate leaves,
Rhombic-ovate terminal leaflet, cylindric-
Campanulate calyx, obliquely obconic at base,

Cupuliform disk, petals unguiculate and white.
But when the nearly orbicular standards rise
I prefer the obsolete, epic designation.

Virgilias. The groves of June,
The urban groves,
Like clouds collect the sweet white rain
Which slowly moves

(Watch) over sidewalks, over roads,
And into seas
Of traffic churning up the suds
Each breathes and blows.

We cut you down on Garden Street
To let the line
Of cars speed off without a thought
Of white and green.

But there and there you stand alight
With precious fuel,
Shining for a non-infinite
Bejewelled while.

Virgilias. The groves of June,
The urban groves,
Like clouds collect the sweet white rain
Which slowly moves.

I can't help it. It is as it was.
But have I always
Observed precisely, told the truth?
Wasn't
The ailanthus altering even in April?
Weren't
There fresh brown twiglets oddly protruding
Alongside buds a bit less flat?
And did
I accurately track the wings of the owl
Flying off softly at dusk?
Analysis may untie
Some of the multiple bands that thwart our sight,
But what of comparison?
                                            What

What of, say, the contemporaneous
Dawn of magnolia suddenly tugging
Off scarves, tearing veils?
File this among the observations,
Among the truths, against apology.

Ease it along.

Not noticing, on their trellises,
Before the brick apartment house,
The first red, blood-red roses,
Does one know June? Before July,
Virgilia, luxuriance unrestrained,
Mountain laurel, delicacy unbridled,
Are future perfect. The perfect roses
Are present into December.

Adagio.

No, no, no, they wrote in the margins.
Stop. And sometimes why.

The light is green. One cannot stop.
Beyond any twentieth-century decorum,
Beyond twentieth-century hallucination,
Beyond riot or restraint,
Beyond violence or sophistication,
Beyond the ugliness and the urbanity of this city
Gleams the exuberance of the unmentionable — beauty.

At evening one cannot stop.
Despite that unevenness in one's breathing,
Driven, one visits the enchanted places.
Someone is dragging his feet on the bulging hillside.
Someone is shielding his fist in his bulging pocket.
Stop. Here one must stop
Before a lavishness utterly refined.

The virgilias rose and set.
The delirium rose and subsided.

How many stars are there to know in the sky?
Which are fixed? Which flame new?
Which, agèd, fade and fall?
How is our own Pegasus progressing,
Flapping his safe and waxless wings
As the merry-go-round in its nearly orbicular circuit
Tilts toward the fire?

The light is still green. Candelabra
Shine hard and green on ailanthus.
The linden lamps shine hard and green.
Hardly a hard, green bulb is seen
Yet on the just-burgeoning catalpa.
Who are we to see red
Unless the roses whirl us to centers?

7. Exile

Desidero enim
Non mea solum neque meos
Sed me ipsum.

This is the edge.
This is the west of the west.
This is the evening of eveningland.
The sun fell into the ocean.

The sun fell and the fog came in,
But she stood on Dark Mountain
Above Dark Gulch, below
Lighting moon and moving star.

And the unmoving stars came on
Here and there about the dome
Just as in a planetarium
Except for the names,

Singing their songs from the night
As the birds had sung from the day
Beneath the yellow grasses of the crest
Where she stared long at the long straw,

Not knowing the signals' meaning,
Not knowing the signals' source,
Asking to see what she could hear
As now she asked to hear what she could see,

Asking not even the meanings,
Asking only the names
As she asked in which green trees
She heard the unremitting wind

When it called and shouted all day
And blew the crest of the Steller's jay
Into black tresses above the black eyes.
She knew the jay's name no more than the stellar skies.

It was not Australia, only the Outer Coast Range
Along the blue Pacific. Cattle gleamed
Black or orange by day, by night stars gleamed
To the Kyrie of coyotes. Between the night and the day,
On acutest evenings, under the stripe of orange,
Which blue bands were mist and which were ocean?
But the orange of sun-permeated poppies gleaming in the grass,
The blue and orange of the swallows twisting in the air,
The blue and orange of the scrub jays plopping on the porch
By the catfood, the blue and orange on the resting wing
Of the monstrous slumbrous ocean all turned black.

If she knew the stars
How far could she fly
And be at home each night

And be at home with the stars,
Not wandering blind alleys
On mountains edged with night

Under stars that fly the alleys of night?

She flew the paths of day
Westward, ahead of the sun.
It was a long way to the edge:
Boston, Scranton, Cleveland, Columbus, Indianapolis —
But there are no cities in the air.
Earthways and airways diverge.
Airways do not draw the right
Roman lines, straight superhighway lines.
It is airy arcs that they describe,
It is bits of circle in the sky.

That last day: heat, open windows,
Someone's music, someone's blasting entertainment,
Heat, a walk, a newsstand, a bookstore,
A map, a drugstore, a mountain laurel, a virgilia.
That last night: heat, open windows,
A nighthawk, a TV resounding from the brick,
Summer's unsheeted tossing. Day:
The whale of the ocean of air. And what
Is ahead? There's Bunker Hill behind.
She looks out over the silver fin, smells gasoline,
Sees stiff red triangles waving no,
Adjusts her ears to cetacean growl,
And weans her eyes from the harbor starred
With the June sun sprung from the Atlantic.

This whale with stripes of red is white,
This sea with stripes of white is blue,
Unfathomed upward, spacious out
From sea to sea, and bottomed now
By rectangled soil and now, and now,
By an islanded Mississippi. Down
The silver-finned white beast must dive,
Billowed, bellowing, over the green-edged
River mapped as a middle on the mind,
Pillowed, mellowing, just past the river-edged
City mapped on the airport wall
                                        As center

As center of the earth, and then ascend
Into undulations of wind and cloud
Above great rocky waves of mountain,
Past a large pink land, past a small blue lake,
And on, on towards an endless length
Of snow-etched sierra. Then out of the whale
She can clamber to the clamor of the other ocean.

This ocean, though the sky is blue,
Is not blue. It is gray.
But unlike the gray doves
It does not whistle away upon her step,
And unlike the timorous agile bulks of cows
It does not gallop away under her gaze.
It is agile but unafraid.
Is she afraid
As out there sierra evolves upon sierra?
Is she afraid,
Glancing behind her for a back-up
On the petrified waves of the shore
While the grayness, whitening, throws itself into her arms
To marinate her with its gray self,
To retract her blackward?

Is her banishment
An annotation
Of the Pacific?

Is this dark edge
The darkening edge
Of an ocean's night?

Is there some green
Or sometimes green
Up the burnt slopes

Or down the damp gulch?
Is there some watery green
Under each crest?

Rivers are not intermittent
Here, westbound to the sea.
They are perennial,

They run on as the ocean — whether
Blue or green or gray or white or black —
Runs all year and year after year,
As the dishlike ship,
Busy with signals,
Keeps running out past Neptune.
Is this the edge,
Past the perils of the circling rocks,
Past Jupiter's whip, past Pluto's long
Elliptical trail, past the final trident
Held by the sea-lord, out to that sea
Where — does a dark tenth planet roam,
Pulling at planets? —
Where — do the waves of gravity roar,
A billion miles long? —
Where — no question — the sun
Becomes another twinkling star?

Out here, is this the edge,

Or is she at home
Strolling among galactic cows
Or galloping along the Milky Way,
However big, however much
Bigger than one thought
If one thought
Dozens or thousands of light years thinkable?

Is she at home
Ambling along the ridge
Toward skies ripped by dark vultures
Or skipping among two hundred billion stars,
However little they give
To the big sphere weighted at the rim
By dark perplexities?

                  Is this the edge,
At the shell of the galaxy's
Globe crusted by dark bulks
Moving, massing, massive, more massive than one thought
If one thought
Those-two-hundred-billion-luminous-stars-now-suspected-of-
    constituting-merely-a-fifth-or-so-of-the-total-mass-of-the-
    Milky-Way
Massive enough?

                Is she at home
Where the dark things far outweigh the bright?

What kind of edge?
Massed on the subway platform
Waiting for the train.
Two hundred billion galaxies to go.

The orange sun collapsing into the ocean.
The orange moon ballooning up from the mountain.

Coyotes screeching for the round moon.
The round moon bitten by the black earth.

The black cow loud in her grassy dream.
The black gulch silent in milky mist.

The vulture asleep.
The rattlesnake asleep.

The fog coming closer.
The edge moving in.

It is not this evening of which I speak
But of another,
Darker, larger, longer —

More obscure, voluminous, perpetual.
Terror, sinuous and latinate,
Touches the effort to explain.

It must be explained.

I've lost
Not just my possessions,
Not only my family and friends,
But my self.

That's how Cicero wrote from Thessalonica
To his dear friend Titus Pomponius in Rome
On the fourteenth day before the Kalends of September
(Let's call it, not counting backward, the seventeenth of August),
In the year when Lucius Calpurnius Piso Caesoninus
And Aulus Gabinius — both unfriendly — were consuls
(Let's call it, now counting backward, the year 58 B.C.).
He had been five months in exile, was to be twelve months more,
Forbidden fire and water.

                      Sicca took him in
At Vibo when he still thought he might go south
Through Sicily to Malta. When the second law was amended
To force him at least four hundred miles overseas,
Marcus Laenius Flaccus, risking his own fortunes and his head
(Not literally his head, but in the Roman fashion),
Was not afraid to be both friend and host
And harbored him for thirteen days at Brundisium.
So Cicero sailed east, wanting but not daring
To go to Athens. He would find enemies there,
And the distance might be interpreted as not sufficiently far
From Italy. He would go to Asia, he wrote,
To Cyzicus preferably. Did Cyzicus seem fit
For a man whose property now had been confiscated?
They were banging down his grand house on the Palatine —
The one he had built and of which he was terribly proud —
To make place for a temple to Freedom; they were vandalizing his
    villas —
The ones he so cherished, at Tusculum and Formiae,
Where he sat and thought and talked and wrote — for spite.
His wife and daughter and six-year-old son faced a city —
The city — that now had rejected him, once its leader,
Its savior. He had lost so much. He had lost Rome.

At nightfall . . . Coriolanus.

BOOK THREE | PART ONE

On that dark March evening,
Whether they could not or would not,
Neither gods nor men had protected him,
Not Caesar, not Pompey, not Crassus,
Not Titus Pomponius Atticus,
Not Cato, not Varro, not Hortensius,
Obviously not the consuls, of whom
Calpurnius Piso was father-in-law to Caesar
(Caesar wouldn't go to Gaul
Till Cicero was out of Rome),
And Minerva, that great guardian
Of wisdom and of the city,
Ignored her image, long honored in his house,
Brought to her father's house on the Capitol.
Cicero must have offered it at the Quinquatrus,
Her festival on the nineteenth day of March.
He was still unexiled. He could still seem wise.

He had lost so much. He had lost . . .

Not homeward. Past the wandering rocks . . .

Knowing nothing. Only nostalgia . . .

In an essay, as philosopher, Cicero said,
There is no exile for the wise.
In a letter, as one exiled, Cicero said,
I've lost . . . my self.

Too much has been prolusory.
Too much has been apophatic.
The cow's honks thunder through the mountains.
The hawk's screech wheezes from the sky.

As the winds slither through the long tawny grass,
Reptilian mists approach me, Flora said.

Yet some things were the same. The mourning doves,
More urbano, drew in the evening, though
The jays were deeper blue, the ocean deeper.

Too much has been pseudepical.
Too much has been asthenopic.

She walked up the slope.

Big, bovine eyes
Looked out from the edge of her brain,
Saw, under her nose, the gold of straw,
The regal purple puffs of a few multistellar thistles,
Saw, beyond this, mist,
Soundless, unsounded, except for, now and then,
A twitter, a tinkle,
Monochromatic, achromatic, simple, single
Grayish shade, except for, now and then,
Hardly darker, intimation of mountain.

If the point of vision and desire were the same
For her, the difficulties would be different.
But I have admitted to an upward slant,
I have admitted that she did see stars,
I may have suggested even a sideration.
You only need to see the one star once.
The mist is thicker if just once you glimpsed
That which it demolishes.

      For her
Vision was mist, star was desire, desire
Was constellation, net of somethings, thistles
Graying in the straw between the fog
And her, between the center and the edge,

No, wanted, not seen, past the misty known,
The unknown thistles beyond the fog.

There were thistles.
There were flowers.
What was the matter?
The gray matter

> Stayed gray.
> She might call the white calf silver in the early sun,
> She might call the grass tips silver at the tip of dusk,
> No aprication, no Mediterranean night
> Sharpened the gray edge of sight,
> No silvery glints diminished mist,
> Its limitings, its imprecisions, its invisibilities.
> Will the wind blow in some clarities?
> The wind blew her hair across her eyes and into her mouth.

Then to be a connoisseur of fog?
Fog stampeding across the road,
Fog as ocean at the edge of the slope,
Fog as the disarming of the sun?

Do I have to start over and over?
Fog stampeded across her retina,
Laved the edge of her brain, unmanned
Her mind. Fog is no knowing.

Mist is that minimum: knowing
That you don't know. Again
O Socrates! What if a Plato
Beat his wings at her brain,

What if an Aristotle called
As cow calls calf, what if the thistles
Bespoke analysis, not disintegration,
Not the gray blowing in?

Her principal experience was mist. The thistles
Eluded specification, the thistle tribe
Generification, the floristic field
More than blunt nudges as by cows' noses.

If one could only ruminate, she thought,
Travel with the herd,
Discriminate the grasses,
Live a life in the mountains under the sky.

Were these sidereal longings
As, in another context, books and time
For books, colleagues and leisure for colleagues,
Most of all, mind itself, impossible star,

Or weren't her yearnings those of the cow
That pined to jump over the moon?
The moon shimmered in the trough.
She licked at mist.

She called then for a telescope.
She called then for a rocket.
At best there was a blur
And a gravity most grievous.

Her field was degenerate stars. Her field?
Straw gilded by mist,
Starred by a few thistles,
Jarred by a gray road sharply sloping

In a terrain that has never known crocuses.
All men by nature desire to know,
And all women, too. In a terrain
With a slope in a mist.

When sometimes some sun breaks through
On the steep yellowish slant
Is that a cow and her calf
Or is that a cow and her shadow?

She stepped into her shadow.
Up here there was just one tree,
A small pepper tree and a pepper tree's
Fragile shadow. Her shadow was larger.

The shadow of fog is larger
Than the shadows of sun,
Than the hawk's shadow circling the loud,
The roaring grass, than the vulture's shadow.

She strained to catch the markings on the wailing circling hawk.
She strained to catch the markings on the wailing circling sentence.
What else? The fog came in.
If the snake curling on the bars

Of the cattle guard startled but did not wake
The somnambulist drawn ever on
Toward the strokable tawny mane of the mountain,
The kingly region of merely straw and sky,

To be squinted at even in sleep,
So blinding was the briefly imperial sun,
And if, half waking, she was cowed
By a cow or by the daedal image

Of a cow or by a likeness to a cow
Munching or disgustedly staring her down,
And if, tiring, she thought,
If I could just lie down in my own shadow,

But kept ascending on the gray-paved path
Though sensing the waves of the fog,
Though sensing how the preferred path of the fog
Lay through her mind,

Though sensing that the floscules of the fog
Were not even thistles, that the rocks,
Not stars, were not even asteroids,
She would grow uneasy.

Why are you afraid, they would ask.
Because in sun
I am always in shadow.
Because under the sun
I am always under a cloud.
Because the sun is always over there.
The windy grass
Has a misty sound.
The sun that dazzles me,
The mist that shadows me,
The fog that edges me,

The hinted

The hinted peak that held me, that kept me ascending—
All these obiter dicta
Placed me on the rocky shore
Of the gray inabordable ocean,
Blinding, obfusc, teratoid, lacunose
Receptacle of suns and constellations,
Serrate waves waving at best no.
I see shadows flying.
I cannot see my left hand or my right.

She sat at the desk.

Her left hand held the book,
Her right hand wrote.

She sat at the flat desk,
Deciphering, scratching.

What's wrong with my glasses, she asked,
Not, what's wrong with my eyes.

For Greeks the vowels have tended to turn into i's.
For her the vowels were tending to turn into o's.

So Cocoro wrote,
Mea moo boo book books,

Meos moos boos boor boon
Colleagues of collogue or colloquy,

Me mo -mo mono- no
O o o o o,

Like clashing rocks before the passage,
Before the Bosporus, before the Black Sea.

She heard the cow rustling the grass
As the cow heard her rustling her page

Through the screen door. Or was the cow seeing
The green grass on her side of the fence?

Through the window she glimpsed, glancing
The red-winged blackbirds. Like a bee

She couldn't see red. Red was black.
There is a black evening after the red sun

Like a hat has sat on the ocean.
There is the evening of the nyctalope.

She might call the grass tips silver at the tip of dusk,
She might call argentine the rattlesnake's silver slough,

After the gray edges came the black
Gulch, the black hole, the dense

Empty center. De-orbiting, she did not reach
The unseen beating heart of the Milky Way

Hidden by stars and dust; she did not see
Those secrets; concentrating, she heard,

Internal exile: the sentence;
Your own dark center: the condemnation;
Your own black labyrinth: the prison.

She walked down the slope.

One can always go deeper,
Can't one? There were trees,
Big trees: curlicue oaks,

Ramrod redwoods — the redwoods, like her,
Confined to the fog belt. I speak
Thus plainly, with complete candor. The white

Fog — oceanic — filled the valley
And she sauntered at the bottom of the sea,
Among the pearls, the masts,

The bullion, the bones. There are voids
That are cluttered. The cat had followed
On little fog feet; the gate, at which she fumbled,

Had clanged; she had heard the traffic of the trees
In wind; she had stirred a few bushtits
And stones; the deer, outside a universe

Of cows, went leaping like dolphins,
Like men on the moon; she was in the white wood;
The voluminous moonlight fell through — no,

I have called it the fog.
She might call the ocean silver as the day declined,
It was the afternoon's white ocean,

It was the dark's white light,
It was the mind's blank night.
Mist moistened her lenses.

The marble groves of her city
Are hard
And hard to remember.

Memory is soft.
There bright colors waft from books.
Splendid sounds there warble from conversations.

Steps ascend to the marble halls
Of dream. She dwelt
In those high halls, not dreamed.

There are no cities in the air.
Moonlight, frail, cool, secondary,
Hides the self-consuming brilliance — distant — of the stars.

The ludicrous sphinx
Alludes, colludes,
Eludes, illudes, deludes,

Questions. Who is she
That becomes four-footed by night?
She doesn't know.

There are degrees of obscuration.
Can one speak plainly about confusion,
Or does one, reckless, pour together

The murky wets, the dry pages
Of the album, the negatives:
Distraction, lackluster lack,

Scartissued failure, unfathomable shallows
Of not quite pulling one's thoughts together,
Of pulling together what just are not quite thoughts?

I can speak very plainly: there is a profound negation,
A negation so profound it is the negation of profundity,
An emptiness so empty it is empty even of emptiness

(You've heard that before?
Of this? Someone
Has said that of this before?),

A being replete with non-being albeit licensed to be:
Isthi, isthi, it heard, before it went back to the sea,
Be, know, be, it heard, as it went slipping down on the v,

Vanquished, sappy, insipient, hominid,
Hominoid, wrecked in the ocean,
Not to be rescued by any whale or porpoise or dolphin.

Is this deeper? Is this an explanation?
Only a teratology can plumb the heart
That turns from Avernus to the stars —

Such stars:
Study; talk;
Above all, mind —

Beating always, although in the depths, with the surf,
The tidal not yet, not quite, never, ever
Beating on the vacuous deep drum.

Is this an explanation? There is a whole
That is a part. There is a part
That is the whole. I speak not just of the world,

Not just of the others, but (Can there be no candor?
Do I shift from the albumen to the vitellus?
Do I slide from the sun to the candle?

Do I merge the nocturne with the aubade?
Before she reached the sempervirent redwoods
Did she apprehend the nondescript plumage

Of the common bushtits as diagnostic?
Discern — distant — the white calf blue
As the moon? Did she blink at a blaze

Or at a bleak bleaching, did she blush
Or blanch or was she blind?)
I speak of the self as the mind.

I search for abstraction. Incensed, she descries,
Where the fire-resistant evergreens rise,
Etiolation, alphosis, blank sky.

I strive for abstraction. Daubed, she sees,
Deep, deep among the tall trees,
White takes a long time to dry.

Io, the white cow,
Found herself first in a field of cows,
Long before reaching the cliff at the edge of the world,
Found herself sitting, frightened, watching,
Among the deep summer grasses of Lerna.
How could she get up? She watched
As the others sensed Jove's vertical anthropomorphic nearness.
The black one looked around, her black mouth stopped,
Her black nose may have sniffed or snorted slightly.
There. Watch. That's what you do. Shift
A bit in the front, unfold the hind legs, now
You're up in the back, unfold the forelegs, now
You're up, then stare a little, then get moving,
Not too much worried about where or how you're proceeding,
Conscious only of what or whom you are fleeing.

How did she find herself there and where did she come from
And where would she go now? Please tell me, ancient Muses,
For I fear this story. Tell me,

Tell me, Apollodorus,
Ignoring powerful Rome,
Treasuring learned books,
In your good plain prose,

Tell me, laughing Ovid,
Laughing if not weeping,
Peering into chambers of hearts,
In rushing embroidered streams,

Tell me, O grand Aeschylus,
Goldendappledfireflowerfountained,
Let me steal from you
As Prometheus stole from heaven,

Knowing ahead,
Green hope,
Red fire.

Io was born, not a calf but a baby girl,
To Melia, ashen beauty, queen of Argos,
And Inachus, son of Ocean and Argos' king.
At five, indulged by her father, she learned to read
From the ancient priestess of Juno. When she was six
She would sit for hours with the princes under their tutors,
Conning the stories of heroes, the stories of gods,
Studying numbers and measures and movements of waters,
Placements of cities and placements and movements of stars.
Then she would run to the sanctuary of Juno
And ask of the priestess the ways of each glittering goddess:
Juno herself, Jove's consort, guardian of Argos;
Diana, virgin goddess of the moon;
Minerva, virgin too, fountain of wisdom.
Serve Juno, the priestess said; admire Diana;
Beg of Minerva the purest, brightest gift.
Thus was she schooled for six years. Then one spring morning,
Summoned into the great hall of the palace,
She found the king and queen on their golden thrones.
Io, her mother said, you are twelve years old.
You have learned what men learn, now you must learn to be
                                        A woman,

A woman, learn to spin and weave and sew,
To bake, to sweep, to launder, to carry keys,
To supervise, to plan, to manage a palace.
Io, her father said, you're a big girl now.
You must be betrothed to a prince from far away.
I will send out ships today to Attica, Crete,
And gleaming islands strewn throughout the sea —
To Melos, Paros, Naxos, Tenos, Andros,
Lesbos, Lemnos, Imbros, Samothrace.
You must start preparing to leave your home, to find
Your home where I find your husband. Don't cry, dear,
My dear, don't cry, you must learn, all daughters must learn
To leave . . . Her arms were about his knees, her face
Was streaked, her hair unbound. Her father stroked
The disheveled head. Now, Io, now, he was saying.
Behind her she heard a voice. All turned toward the door.
Lying on a litter, the aged priestess of Juno
Was carried in. Lord Inachus, she said,
This is my deathbed. From it I address you.
Argos must have a new young priestess of Juno.
Io, your daughter, can read the ancient books,
She knows the ways of goddesses and gods.
Permit her to spend her days in the sanctuary
Studying. Let her read and talk and walk
With the scholars. Allow her to fix her eyes on the stars.
Dedicate her to bright Diana,
Dedicate her to flashing Minerva,
Dedicate her to Juno, great mistress of this city.
The priestess closed her eyes. Inachus thought,
Then nodded. His daughter rose. She smiled. He said,
I surrender you, Io. The heavens seem to have spoken.

She went to the altar of silver-horned Diana:
Goddess, may I know moon, sun, and stars.

She went to the altar of great owl-eyed Minerva:
Goddess, may I keep my eyes in my books.

She went to the altar before the white columns
Of cow-eyed Juno, guardian of Argos:
Goddess, may I remain, learning, in my city.

Thus she was free. She studied for nine years,
Sipping the clearest waters,
Tasting the purest flames,
Drawing deep within her the brightest gleams —
Until the time of the dread three nights.

On the first night she heard a whisper:

Come, come to the flowery pastures of Lerna.
Come, lie in the fragrant and lengthening grasses.
See, I am Jove.
I will smile upon your flesh.

He seemed to stand there, a gentleman, distinguished,
With glinting silver curling hair and beard.

She felt a shiver in her heart, then said:

O grandeur,
You are too much better than I.
I must shrink away. I have feared
To love what must be revered.

On the next night she heard a deep voice:

Come, come to the flowery pastures of Lerna.
Come, lie in the fragrant and lengthening grasses.
Look, I am Jove.
I will draw you close to me.

He seemed to stand there, tall, strong, soft,
With golden waves of hair, smooth-shaven cheek.

She felt a quiver in her heart, then said:

O splendor,
You have a dear regal wife.
I must crawl away. I must seek
To be her handmaiden, meek.

On the third night she heard the thunder:

Come, come to the flowery pastures of Lerna.
Come, lie in the fragrant and lengthening grasses.
Lo, I am Jove.
I will fill you with my power.

He seemed a flash, a gleam, a flame,
A flaming column, blazing, hurling fire.

She felt a shimmer in her heart, then said:

O ruler,
It is not power that I crave.
I must turn away. I desire
A burning deeper and higher.

On the following morning her father, deeply disturbed
By nights of noise and brightness, quickly dispatched
Heralds to the oak groves of Dodona:
Jove, grandeur, greatest, best,
What are these portents that glimmer and bang
About our high halls and what must we do?

In a month the heralds returned with the message:
Her who is called out send out.
Puzzled, Inachus renewed the legation:
Jove, splendor, greatest, best,
What are you telling us? What must we do?

In a month the heralds returned with the command:
Her who is pulled out push out.
Anxious, Inachus repeated the embassy:
Jove, ruler, greatest, best,
What do you ask of us? What must we do?

In a month the heralds returned with the proclamation:
Exile Io. Banish her from the city.
Take her under guard to the meadows of Lerna.
Leave her there alone at the edge of the field.
Otherwise Jove's thunderbolts will level
Argos, blast the Argives forever.

The king's duty was clear.
Weeping, he saved the city.
Io, clutching one book, was escorted
On that very day in the glint of sunset
To the fragrant pasture by soldiers in armor.

She saw him when they left her there alone.
She began to run. But suddenly she was dizzy.
She could only crouch abruptly on the grass, a blackness
Before her eyes, a lightness in her head,
A heaviness in her neck and arms and legs.
When her eyes had started to clear, she saw the woman,
Tall, tiaraed, majestic, angry, gleaming,
Standing beside him on the grass and coldly speaking:
My dear, who is this? Jove smiled and easily replied:
Not who but what, my love. A pretty cow.
— Get her out of here. And from her shining hand
Flew a fireless monstrous winged and stinging thing.

How could she get up? She watched,
She was up. She was stepping. But her book.
She looked behind her. Jove and Juno were standing
Motionless, ignoring her, conversing.
She dared to slip between two cows.

The book was lying on the ground.
She pushed it open with her hoof.
She could not read.

O save me, she tried to cry
To Juno. I have not sinned.
She could not speak.

By now it was night. She looked up
At the stars to plan her route.
She could not think.

Turning their backs, glimmering, calm,
The deities strolled off together.

Io could not even sigh,
Io, io, popoi.
Out came the horrifying mugitus.

Luckily the fences were broken.
She couldn't open gates.
She had to get into motion.

The sting-thing stung.
A lone cow looks lost,
But Io alone would run.

Stung, she rushed right past Delphi,
Center of the earth, as eagles, hawks,
And vultures orbited the peaks
And the god sat ready to give answers.
She rushed by, seeing nothing, naming
Nothing, mapping nothing, asking
Not names, not responses, nothing.

She came to the groves of dread Dodona.
Above her the oak leaves rustled loudly.
She could not speak, but the trees
Could and did: Hail, chosen
Of Jove. She shuddered, running . . .

Stung, she plunged into the waters
Of the long blue Ionian gulf,
Discerning no colors, asking no names,
Incapable of naming, naming
Nothing, becoming eponymous.

She galloped through the land of the Gauls
To the northwest edge of the earth
(Naming nothing, mapping nothing),
Coming to the circle of her grandfather, Ocean.
There gaunt Prometheus, the forethinker, stood,
Vulture-carved and pinned to the cliff
By a bolt of Jove. Io, I know
Your name, your history, your journey. You must try to comprehend
What I tell you. As you wander through the world,
                                                                         Hope

Hope to reach the city of Minerva.
There you must climb a temple-crested hill,
Ascend the steps, enter the white marble temple
Of Jove, the best, the greatest (do not tremble),
Of Juno, wife of Jove (but do not fear),
Of wise Minerva, guardian of the city,
Honored at the Quinquatrus above stout Mars
(The owl is honored above the woodpecker-wolf).
It is not the martial city of lupine Mars,
The powerful city of Juno, angered or appeased,
The triumphal city of ever-triumphant Jove,
But the city of Minerva you must seek.
Low there, heifer, don't be afraid, but hope
She will turn her glaucal eyes upon you, grant
Memory, words, names, knowledge, understanding.

Alas, no stichomythia
(High on that cliff,
Over that gulch)
Was possible for them now.
Upon this paraenesis
Followed her mooed monody
Bellowed in blackest B-minor.

And, still stung, she ran on and on
Through the chilly unplowed acres of the Scythians,
Whose homes are wagons.

She swam the Bosporus, water in her eyes,
Again eponymous, etio-etymological,
Monstrously now.

Crossing the Caucasus' starneighboring crest,
The white cow on the horizon like a low cloud
Was the horizon.

She came to the land of the one-eyed Arimaspians,
Who live on horseback along the river of gold,

She came to the land of Cisthene, east of east,
Where you see neither sun by day nor moon by night,

Where to see the snake-haired Gorgons is to turn to stone,
Where the three thin swan-haired sisters pass their sole eye.

Having swum the starless, roarless seas,
She used a modest litotes,

As she turned in an ellipse
And ran on west toward Cyzicus,

And like Cicero she said
(So I translate that mooed dread),

I miss
Not just my possessions,
Not only my family and friends,
But my self.

Minerva,

Minerva, memorable, remembering,
Bright-armored custodian of Rome,
Sprung armed and wise from the mind of Jove,
Sexless virginal androgynous mind,
Virile not appetitive,
Potent not hungry for power,
Seminal not intent on influence,
Armed not in violence but with light,

Sibylla,
Eyeing present, future, and past,
Shrieking of war,
Speaking of peace,
Writing on leaves,
Opening books,
Opening woods
Gleaming
With the gold that cannot be constrained,
Leading down to Avernus,
Leading upward to Rome,
Leading to something greater,
A somewhat greater song,

Athena,
Who quipped with the witty seeker, who give your name
To the city of the park, the walk, the porch,
The garden, the school,

Glaucopis,
Of the seeing eyes
Of the owl,

Sophia,
To whom mother earth or the earthshaker god of the sea
Offered the tumbled marbles of Cyzicus
In the new Rome,

Madonna,
Of the birch-bole Byzantine eyes,
Moon-slippered,
Dawn-gowned,
Sky-cloaked,
Star-crowned,
Sun-armored,
Nicē,
Nicopoea over darkness,
Hodegetria into light,
Sedes Sapientiae revered,
Rosa Mystica and meek,
Virgo Mater high deep,

Minerva, remembered in marble,
The waves of your hair like the ripples of sea,
Your hard cheeks ever soft
As your blank eyes ever see,

Minerva, admonishing in bronze,
With flashing of eyes on a sun-thunder scene,
Wreathed in shining olive,
Ageless goddess aging green,

Minerva in the Norway spruce,
Existing in mist,
Growing green and three-dimensioned

Into

Into the rain, under the rain,
Lifting into the downpour,
Falling with the folds of the rain
Falling silver, falling silver-green
And silver-green rising,

Picea excelsa,
Excellently named,

If one asks a name,
Or, if one requests the accepted denomination,
Less elegant, more up-to-date,
Picea abies, which must be accepted
Though it would seem to a Roman neither abies nor picea,
This tree of the European north,
Spruce from encounters in Prussia,
Norway from a reaching of that northern way,

A species at home in the Alps,
Brought here, so the story, from the old Black Forest,
Planted in the new State of New York
In the new life here just after the Revolution,
A transplant that took,

That flowered, for there are flowers,
Monoecious, solitary, growing in conical aments
On the new shoots,

For there are new shoots on this aging tree
Whose green folds fall
With the gray fall of the rain,
Fall in rain or in sun
In black, white, green,

An old green, a weathered green,
Of which one could ask sapientia,

A moderate, a modest green,
Of which one can modestly ask scientia,

Saving the hope of sapience for one's own old age,
Craving science, asking names,

Examining angles, for spruce leaves are quadrangular,
Norway spruce leaves flattened to triangular,

Leaves the names of these stiff green needles,
Flowers those entities that grow into long thin cones,

Though I don't really know them, am trying to know them,
Desiring

A green
Dangling from branches

Like huge medieval sleeves from arms outstretched,
With hands that bless, with fingers lifted

Pointing, instructing,
Like the fingers of the mother,

Like the fingers of the child, held, reaching,
Clutching the scroll, touching the curl, teaching

How to discover, how to learn, leaning
On the shoulder where the light veil, drooping

Lightly like the spruce's leafage draping
Air, whitely greening, lining

Circumambient spaces, declines
To back and breast, above

The folds cascading down the dress, around
The powerful knees, to the carpeted floor

Where they trail and surge
Like surf on the shore, where you almost see

The sheathing slippers rest, step on the sand,
On the moon, advancing, dancing, azure

As the bluejays, scarlet as the cardinals, silver
As the glassy whiteness of the spruce's foliage

Of verre, vert
As its verdancy, soft and furred as its vair

Descendings where the slim birds flitter
Out and in, dipping in like dolphins, slipping out

Like ethereal rumors, where the breeze
Lifts and drops, where the sun comes and goes,

Where, like the shadow of cloud on cloud,
The leafy shadow of bough on bough

Dripping virid sun and viridian shadow
In truth is ultimately cerulean-backed,

As the hangings, whatever their shade
Or solar tint, are frontlets

Fixed before me, though flexible, mediating
Between the eye and the sky, the old

Green of evergreen, sky-blued in the morning,
Sun-bleached at noon, golden-boughed at evening,

Lighting into the sable waves of night,
Its hells, its dark heavens, its cities of constellations,

Unless there are no cities in the air,
Its constellated, castellated Rome

Involving earth and ocean in her shade
As the tree involves my tiny microcosm,

Shadows me, shows me the sun
Burning through the shadower, burning

On branches, shows me the moon
Staring through boughs, and shows

An ochre, gold, a Gorgon's head as aegis,
A Medusa visage turning not to stone

But toward the rocks of roots and toward the stars
And possible planets accreting from stellar debris

And possibles accreting from actuals
And other possibles, revealing swords

Green-draped, the hope-hung scimitars that slash
Through emptiness as plowshares cut through soil

And green grows as the green tree grows, a green
Of dawning dewy blue, of sunny gold,

Of blacks and whites, no, grays and grays, no, green
And viridescence and viridity,

An ordinary green, gray-shaded green,
Black-shadowed green, a heightened, whitened green,

A darkened, deeper, greener green, a green
Not just for spring but for two hundred winters,

The blue skirt dragging on the grass
As blue hills are green, are yon Vermont,

As gray stone steps in oil turn violet,
As brown dirt earthy rocky banks become

A casein incarnation of purple and gold,
As the fleece beneath the enchantment of the virge

Learns of itself a crimson, scarlet, saffron,
As the black bunting in sun bursts into blue

Hues for a brush, not for names, for a hanging canvas,
For a great blue painting into which you can enter

As you enter the spruce, as you stand in its blue-green cavern,
For the greater painting which enters into you,

Its emanations penetrating your pores,
Its films pushing and pushing into your flesh,

Your bones, your muscles, your memory, thought,
If you think, mind, if you have a mind, its lights

Almost making a mind, its luminous stimulations
Accreting your mental debris, although you know

Little of color, less of the colors' names,
Least of this green that seeks your understanding

By merely standing outstretched, under which you stand
As under the mother's blue mantle, before which you stand

Merely seeing until you call out names,
The names voiced by the form of that great green,

The greenness of that form, formosa, lux,
Verdant lumination, lady, whom

Reverent blue-white clouds salute from the sky
Like courtly angels doffing their three-cornered hats,

Like attendant blue-white lions lying in the sky,
Like attentive blue-green lions lying at the knees

Of Cybele, taut but fawning, bristly but soft,
Whose blue-green manes you can stroke, whose force you can feel,

Whose voicings you hear, first murmurings and hums,
Then mumblings, rumblings, rushing thunders, roars

Oceanic, aquilonian,
Volcanic vocables and vocatives,

Vociferating, voluble, dissolving,
Resolving not into words but into notes

For strings, angelic oboes, celestial horns
Played upon the advent of the queen

For coronation, emerald-diademed
Regina, seen sun-crowned from her shadow,

Seen sun-enthroned from a yet longer shadow,
Seen from my shadow sun-green-garmented,

Green-regal-robed, sun-royal-raimented,
Densely, amply, massively, ponderously garbed,

With the massiveness of the mother, encompassing,
The amplitude of the pregnant human brain,

The ponderousness of the thinker, the density
Without inflexibility of mind,

A stature, stateliness without stagnation
Or stasis — thought —, the subtle grand, the grand

Subtle of the princess, delicate,
Slim, slender, about to curtsy, loveliness

And lightness, trim abstraction, fingering
The slips of breeze, the ductile vina strings

Of most ethereal air, which my dull digits
Cannot distinguish, cannot enumerate,

Can, squeezing needles, but scale down: vermilion,
Alizarin crimson, mars violet, mars black,

Nought's black, without a single overtone
Or undertone of red, blue, yellow, green,

Blackness Ovidian, tristive, beside the Black Sea, in the long dark
Frozen nights of the wild hiemal distance from Rome,

Far from Ausonian lights and beyond the Ionian waters,
Past the Corinthian gulf, past the Corinthian shore,

Past the bright temple of Neptune, who guides men over the swart flood
Through each islanded sea, through seas islandless, past

Imbros, Zerynthian Samothrace, Hecate's lusterless cave, past
Cyzicus, sticking there fast, fixed on Propontiac sand,

Cyzicus, famed work, founded by famous Haemonian questers
Questing along the dim coasts, seeking a barbarous gleam,

The golden fleece that hung in a wood,
Mars' wood, farther than Cyzicus, farther than Tomis,

Incult exile's edge cut into a Scythian winter,
Ultimate habited orb, land from my land too remote,

Place so abhorred that even the named place-name is abhorrent,
Tomis, a barbarous clime marred by a barbarous crime,

Murder and mayhem of brother by terrible sister, the small limbs
Cut into chunks to be sowed over the harvestless sea,

Past which are Bosporus, Don, and the Scythian marshes, and hard cold,
Past which are names so few, places so vast and unknown

Only the exile, the banished, will try them, for even the questers
Seeking the fabulous fleece sought it as searchers condemned

At the Euxine's end, where it hung in the wood
Gleaming, as here a civilized gleam

Grows toward evening on the spruce,
Not like the blatant goldenrod of August,

Subtler, more grand, as a gleam
That will civilize grows in the wood

Of Cumae, ready to light
To hell, to Rome, to the helmeted

Goddess, eagle-plumed like the spruce,
Eagle-minded, mind soaring, searching

Skies, and circling earth, earthy, touching
Earth, rooted like the spruce

Step by step from mud and dust and stone
Like steps ascending into a transcendence,

Titanic arrowhead pointing to a star,
Tipped by a star, stretching to heaven, forming

A Jacob's ladder with your verdant form,
Your formuled verdancy, studied, learned, till

Finally there is or almost is
A vision formed by green, formed by its greens,

Intrinsic these, these insite by the sun,
Day-gilded these, these full-moon-blue, and these

Lightlessly livid, and these, in flashlight, green,
And these, day after day, the streaks or strokes

Marking invisible air, out of blank air
Verdurously fashioning facts and fictions,

Unfeigned factual pigments fictile with figments,
Formal, formative, morphogenetic, almost,

Hence, immaculate form itself, staining
The varied vitrail eye, the brushy tongue,

And therefore surely viridigenous,
Not something drawn but something growing, great

With lightsome child like great Jove's massive brow,
Not something still but something flowing, fleet

With fallings, this way, that way, over rocks,
Enormous, roaring, rushing, left and right,

Direct and slanted, over, under, down,
Descending, tumbling, foaming, spuming, up

On the shore where the ship, wave-battered, Pallas-prowed,
Spews the future Roman, progenitor
Of future Rome, into the cavernous past,
Not the cadaverous, into the fathering past,
Led by the hag, led by the buxom mother's

Two mourning doves, wind-winged, mist-distant-voiced,
Closer than you think, calling you, you, you
To enter the opening cave, to pluck the supple

Bough, self-re-creating, to tempt the birdless
Lake, to drown, ascend like a dolphin, fly
Back where the woman stands, magistra, seer,
The Jewish girl, dark-eyed, envisioning,
The owl-eyed goddess, long-seen, green-seen tree,

The virgin returned, the return
Of a time before the tyranny of Jove,
The orbit of an unforced revolution
Of Saturn's anarchy, an order
Of centered minds that can fly
To edges, past edges, and return
To the burning roseate hearth,
To the central dark,

The central heavy dark,
The light light edges,

The central rosy trunk,
A scroll, a gigantic taper, a flame,
The fountain in the center of the rose garden,
Like the rose center,
The fountain in the center of the rock garden,
Like a rising star,
Like the long rose fingers of dawn,
Like dawn's red center,

Minerva,

A central self,
A mind,
Is my desire.

8. Epodes

(1) Verbosity

Words like falling leaves
Heaping mortal shadows,

Words like falling snows
Piling sterile shadows,

Shadows of gold,
Shadows of marble,

Raked words, shoveled words,
Wind-swept gold, marble

At length melting
Down to the guarded spring.

(2) Silence

The gold of the gold leaves
Against wet fire escapes' black glitter
In a dendrolatrous moment on the stair.

The silvers of the silver waves
Of voracious wing and indifferent water
Beyond the convivial restaurant on the pier.

The glass pane
That muzzles November and drizzle
If not the rain.

The brass clang
That trumpets: Remember the dazzle
But not the pang.

(3) Communication

Why was it the gods she loved,
Distant, hidden by the sky's blank boards?

They came through, they came close,
They shone bright, they spoke without words.

(4) Words

> Verba tantum adfero, quibus abundo.
>
> Cicero, in a letter to Atticus,
> May 21, 45 B.C.

She walks through her inheritance, this garden
Of vegetables and flowers, through this Eden
Where blossoms plucked redouble like friendly beheaded
Dragons' heads. So this is paradise.
This is the playground where you romp forever
Fresh. This is eternal play, eternal
                                                               Jump

Jump rope, catch, jacks, marbles, hide-and-seek,
Blowing bubbles, contemplation, heaven.
This is the hell whose grapes like the early skies
Of evening dawn and tantalize.

(5) Restraint

When it seems to her that she says
Nothing he surely agrees,
For what is the sputtering waterfall
To unuttered seas?

(6) Rhyme and Reason

Not background. Dangling in deep space, in deep air.
A color for which the name must be gold.
Indian summer. The elm.
Not solid, not film.
Warm. No, cold.
Far from his golden hair.

(7) Demonstrative

A paradigm of the Beatific Vision.
Only in such terms could she describe
That foliation. It was the perfection
Of that shade of gold, falling that way
Through the afternoon below the dark bough
Of the elm, falling that not cheaply, that
Richly, completely, exactly, essentially
Golden way that could have satisfied
Richly, completely, exactly, essentially
Forever if they had been fixed there,
She staring, the elm sustaining
Its gold, her stare.
This was life, this the world, that was waning,
That more than one could bear.

She

She went home slowly through November, complaining,
He doesn't love me, he doesn't love me, he doesn't care.

(8) Modification

Descending the descending stair.
First, without blasphemy, the balcony
Of white-hot heaven. One does not forget
Endless, far-past-flame-fresh sight,
Something unadulterated, sharp, and rare.
Then the oaks, the hyacinths, the roses,
Green leaves, gold leaves, white leaves read.
Then something warm, aromatic, delicious,
Earthy, common, adulterous, and bare.

(9) The Story

Only a heart of marble can be cold
On this November afternoon.
Leaves hang hammered on the air,
Stroked gold on this emptiness,
Slipped into the molds of ethereality.
Theories, whether new or old,
Are secondary, folds of materiality
Brushed gold by this sunniness.
The breathless tension of the leaves,
The breathful tensions of the heart
Are chapters in the story told.

(10) Return

To be close to your golden hair, your golden-
Ness — aureole, aura
Penetrating miles, thousands
Of nocturnal miles.

I will close my eyes. I will fend it off.
It is in my mind. I will squeeze my
Penetrated mind, my rejecting
And ejecting mind.

There is a different gold, in a different
Old direction. I return
Yours to your loves and I turn
To that gold of mine.

(11) Shot

I got it out — that Parthian arrow
Shot not by you

But by the mischievous divinity to whom such pranks
Are natural. And it was likewise natural for me,

Feeling the deepening golden pangs,
To think them from you,

For though the point that went straight to the mark and the narrow
Gleaming shaft had not been aimed at me

By you they were yours.

(12) Heart and Mind

Guard me, Apollo, in whose golden hands
Lies the lyre of my heart. It is not gold
Or marble; on its strings, however, you
Alone shall play. Guard me, Glaucopis, who
See with marmoreal eyes my slackening hold
Upon Parnassian cliffs in golden lands.

(13) The Sycamore Maple

Beside the fire escape, the weedy maple's gold
Was worn now. Where the gold had gone,
Before the snow came, there were, clearly seen, the great
Green buds, November's edge on spring.
And though this has been said before, can that have spoiled
The outburst's freshly common spate?

(14) Passion

> Non dici potest quam flagrem desiderio urbis.
>
> Cicero, in a letter to Atticus,
> July 6, 51 B.C.

He wrote from Athens to Rome, a Rome
About to become wholly other.
Though Forum and Capitol and Senate might pretend,
The public thing would die.
His private house on the Palatine would succumb
Eventually to a veritable palace,
Imperial (of a Tiberius? of a Caligula?).
I do not mention the more eventual gardens
(Planted where his roof rose high and fell?).
Philosophy was upside down in Athens,
But not on that account did Cicero burn
For Rome. Why do we burn?
Not because the gods had gone away,
Not because the trees remained unreached,
Not because a touch was momentary
Did she long for the books to open, for the words to live,
For the black lines to grow green in her mind,
For the black lines to grow gold in her soul.

(15) Antihorace

If, though books love her pillow,
She reminds you of a cow,

The black tooth
May chew truth.

(16) A Rome

What is digression in epic
Is distraction in graduate school;
What is a simile in epic
In school is a dereliction;
The long first line with which the epode rings its bell,
A call to class against the pull
Not just of dreams like leaves golden upon the beech,
Then bronze, then slowly yielding like
All history to bared iron, clasped by heroes called
Comrades of Mars, the Mars who laid
His shield before the feet of Venus, her who loved
A mortal and gave birth to Rome,
A Rome not just of dreams,
But of the half-read volume lying on the desk,
But of the half-scrawled tablet fallen to the floor.

(17) Theory

Sterile marble.
Mortal gold.
White leaves in a book,
Yellow leaves in books beckoning,
Golden groves of books
Among the marble mountains
Beneath a gold and marble sky,
Books with leaves speaking,
Beech leaves of Dodona,

Golden

Golden oak leaves of Dodona,
Jove, maybe gold, maybe marble, opening his mouth
From trees and mountains and the sky.

9. Flora Baum's Thesis Proposal
Roads to Rome, January 11, 49 B.C.

Chapter One: Roads to Rome

They stretch, direct, paved, lined
With cypresses and tombs —
Grand tombs, monumental.
They are monumental.
But some are rougher, unmarked, perilous.

Chapter Two: Gaius Julius Caesar (100–44 B.C.)

The creak of the little bridge.
Across! The city's gleam.

Map of his progress.

Chapter Three: Marcus Tullius Cicero (106–43 B.C.)

Unfortunately, there is no letter of January 11
Extant, but we have his letter of the 12th to Tiro,
Those of the 18th and (probably) 21st and 22nd to Atticus,
Those of the 22nd and 23rd to his wife and daughter,
Those of the 23rd and 24th and 25th and 26th to Atticus,
That of the 27th to Tiro, that of the 28th to Atticus.
We must keep in mind that January — four years before the Julian
    reform —
Did not yet have thirty-one but only twenty-nine days.
We must keep in mind that news of what happened at the Rubicon
As the sun rose over the edge of Gaul on the eleventh
And news of what happened later that day at Ariminum,
                                                            Though

Though carried to Rome by the most excellent roads,
Lacked telegraph, lacked radio,
Lacked satellite. We must always keep in mind
What happened before and after. The roads were long.
There is all that thirsting for Rome in all those letters
Written on his way to Cilicia in 51
And then from Cilicia in 51 and 50
And on the way back to Rome, still in 50, from August through
    December.
He arrived outside the city on January 4, 49,
Counseling peace,
But did not cross the pomerium, the sacred boundary line,
Hoping for a triumph. You would forfeit your triumphal entry
If you first went into the city, since you had to keep your imperium, your
    power of provincial command,
Until you celebrated your triumph, but you were never to be in the city
While holding your provincial command. He had governed
    conscientiously
In Cilicia and had conquered — this would merit the triumph —
Fierce if tiny strongholds in the mountains on the Syrian border,
Even, for a few days in October, 51,
Camped on the spot where, in the contest with Darius,
Two hundred eighty-two years before,
Had stood the camp of Alexander — though Cicero did not pretend
To be Alexander. That was a dream
For Pompey, for Caesar. Cicero dreamed his own dreams.
There are his letters of February and March, 49,
Notably that of March 28, the day when, still in Italy himself,
He told Caesar, who, Italy having been won
(Beginning on January 11 with the surrender of Ariminum)
And Pompey with most of the government having sailed off for the East,
Was still on his way to Rome, having called a meeting of the Senate
For the first of April, having by deputy and letter
Urged Cicero in particular to attend,
Having visited Cicero's villa at Formiae
On the 28th of March, when Cicero told him
That under Caesar's conditions he would not go to Rome.

Caesar continued on his way and entered the city —
We know that in April he crossed the line of the pomerium,
For our evidence clearly shows him in the area of the forum
    and the Capitol —
Although he held or claimed to hold imperium
And although three years later, for victories on three
    continents — over Gaul, Egypt, Bosporus, Numidia — he
    would celebrate a fourfold triumph.
Cicero would never see his own triumph.

Cicero, who in 74, after a year as quaestor in Sicily, had
    resolved that he would never leave Rome,
Cicero, who in 63 had avoided the usual proconsular
    assignment to a province,
Cicero, whose exile even, in 58–57, had lasted only that terrible
    year and a half,
Cicero, who, unwillingly appointed governor of Cilicia and
    therefore holding imperium for this province,
Was obliged to stay outside the city boundary from perhaps as
    early as February, 51,
And who left even the neighborhood of Rome for the months
    of eastward journeying about May 1, 51,
Would not be inside the city again until October, 47.

Years, then, of absence.

Chapter Four: Marcus Terentius Varro (116–27 B.C.)

Already legate in Spain?
The knower, not the known.

Known, though, for two ways.

Chapter Five: Rubicon

Paulo maiora. The civic name is Roma.
Render unto Caesar. Romanize.
Julian. Kaiser. Czar. The Ides of March.

                                                              Citizens.

Citizens. Res publica. Urbane.
Imperial. Io io triumphe.
Letters. Latin. Liberty. And peace.
Oligarchy. Tyranny. Those Greek terms.
Red stream. Flows to Ionian Gulf.
Conclude. Era of Varro. Ciceronian. July.

10. Epistles

(1) To Joseph Orcome.
From Cambridge, Massachusetts, December 17, 1983.

        Sat., Dec. 17

Dear Joe,

Tell Suzanne,
If she should ever wonder,
That my desire was only hypothetical,
Subject to some unimaginable
Supposition, twist
In reality itself, whereby we all became
Angels that stay, face, lock, merge, and part
Ethereally, without the body's hurt,
Exclusion, or exclusiveness. Tell her
My body was excluded, though it hurt.

        Love,
        Flora

(Not sent.)

(2) To Francis Petrarch.
From over the western Atlantic, December 20, 1983.

Flora Baum to Francis Petrarch greetings.

I don't like to boast,
But as I write I'm looking down on clouds.
        They

They look, I think, like the Apennines feather-bedded in snow.
From them no snow
Is likely to feather the ocean
At a latitude of thirty-two degrees
Even near our far point from the sun. You've heard
Of Copernicus? Galileo? Newton? But wait,
That might be an avalanche. Remember the Alps?

I'm sitting in a ship that flies with large gray wings.
We're impatient. This head wind
Constitutes an obstruction. More than three hours
For not much more than fifteen hundred miles!
I'm blushing. How silly it will seem
If six hundred years from now there is anyone who reads Latin,
Or anyone who reads English (I'm supplying a translation),
Or anyone who reads, or anyone.
That's what comes of looking down on clouds.

You know from Mont Ventoux. More than six hundred
Years have elapsed since you were writing epistles
Not just to fourteenth-century correspondents
But to Cicero (who died more than twice six hundred
Years before you wrote two letters to him
After searching for, finding, and avidly reading, you said,
His letters), Seneca, Varro, Quintilian, Livy,
Asinius Pollio, Horace, Vergil, Homer.
You see, therefore, why I must write to you.

What is from here abysmal
Is sunlight to a non-flying ship.
If one abyss is filled with blinding gold,
In a wider one we glimpse down there
What up here we don't fear all day:
Shadow, shade, umbra, call it what you will
Down there among the shades or up
In higher worlds of which we have lost sight.
Now we start plunging. I'll fasten my seat belt and get ready to go down.

Dated among those above, the 13th day before the Kalends of January.

(3) To Marcus Terentius Varro.
From Miami, Florida, December 24, 1983.

Flora Baum to Marcus Terentius Varro greetings.

Though not quite the rustic thing,
This would interest you — would draw
Your scholar's mind. I wish you could see
And smell this garden. These flakes,
White in winter, not snow, are petals for fragrant
Flowers, their scent sensed on the breeze
Before they are glimpsed on their Costa Rican shrub,
Euphorbia leucocephalia, which, of course, will mean
Something to you, whether or not the binomial system
Means something to you,
Or before they are seen on their little East Indian tree,
Pittosporum Moluccanum, which, I think, will mean
Something, as will leguminous lemon-peel-blossomed
Cassia polyphylla from Puerto Rico, or as will
Arikuryroba schizophylla from Brazil.

Swift on the breeze
Sifting through the fan palms,
Shifting through the feather palms,
Odoriferous words and half-words wisp.

The 9th day before the Kalends of January.

(4) To Joseph Orcome.
From the air, December 28, 1983.

> Wed., Dec. 28

Dear Joe,

There is always someone else or something else —
In the garden one slim copernicia gleaming behind another,
One slim bird of paradise gleaming behind the first,
In the sky one plump soft cloud rising above another,
> Another

Another hard sun rising above the one
We see and know. I saw you before I knew Suzanne
Existed. She existed. I saw you

(Not completed or sent.)

(5) To Marcus Tullius Cicero.
From Cambridge, Massachusetts, January 2, 1984.

Flora Baum to Marcus Tullius Cicero greetings.

I admit that my language is barbarous,
Though I'm no slave. Half Celt, half German,
I live farther than Gaul, farther than Britain, far over Ocean, in a
    land of myth,
A land Homeric, Ulixean,
Quixotic, if you know what I mean.
I want you to know how much you mean to me.

First let me apologize expressly
For my Latin style. Surely once, before your time,
The Romans seemed barbarian to the Greeks.
If now Americans (that's our name) seem savage and uncouth
To you Romans, think that other men will seem
Barbarous to them unless — until —
Barbarity has ceased to be or ceased
To be felt or to be named. We abound at least in names.

I'm writing for your birthday, which I know is tomorrow,
When I think you'll be 2089.
Oh, all of a sudden, that computation
Distances you from this whitish day
As snowflakes studiously descend, collect
Cuneate in the wedges of slender trees
And decipherable as hieroglyphs of braille
On that fire escape's slender, slanting rail.

I don't want you to seem so far away.
Can't you be close again? I've been reading over
Your letters from the end of 50 B.C.,
Remembering and reflecting as I read
How after an absence of more than a year and a half
You were planning in the middle of December
To reach Rome on your birthday, staying over
At Pompey's Alban place the night before.
But later in December, when you found
That in 49 Compitalia would be observed
On January 2, not wishing to inconvenience
Pompey's household, you thoughtfully changed your plans
And reached Rome on the fourth. Everyone
Went out to meet you on the road. Nothing
Could have given you greater honor. But, as you said, you fell
Into the very flame of civil discord or rather war.

You urged peace. What if they had listened?
What if they had listened? What if spring,
Fresh with reconciliation, not wintry war,
Had been breathed by Pompey; Caesar; Cato;
Mark Antony; Quintus Cassius; Curio; Caelius;
Messalla; Gabinius; Gnaeus Domitius Calvinus;
Tiberius Claudius Nero, your daughter's suitor
(Whom Livia married since Tullia chose Dolabella,
As you will recall, but do you know that the son
Of Livia and Tiberius Claudius Nero
Became the second emperor?); Dolabella,
Your son-in-law; Pompey's father-in-law,
Metellus Scipio; Lentulus Crus, the consul;
Lentulus Spinther; Domitius Ahenobarbus;
The Marcelli; Bibulus; Brutus; Gaius Cassius;
Appius Claudius Pulcher? Who were the twenty-two
That voted no on December 1, 50,
When three hundred seventy senators voted yes,
That both Caesar and Pompey should disarm?
What if they now had listened to counsels of peace?

What if? No Rubicon? No Pharsalus?
No veni vidi vici? No Actium?
What if? No Antony and Cleopatra?
No Maecenas? No *Aeneid*? No *Roman Odes*?
No *Tristia*? No *Letters from the Black Sea*?
Neither any July nor any August?
No leap year? No December 31?
No palace and no prince? No emperor?
Never a Christian offered to the lions?
No Nero? No Domitian? No Constantine?
Never, never your severed head and hands
Bolted to the rostrum from which you had thundered?

I haven't been able to say what I wanted to say,
But what if I want you to get this letter tomorrow?
I'd better pull on my boots and try to catch
The next collection. Undoubtedly you can guess
How everywhere the mail is slowing down.

The 4th day before the Nones of January, there being no consuls.

(6) To Marcus Tullius Cicero.
From Cambridge, Massachusetts, January 10, 1984.

Flora Baum to Marcus Tullius Cicero greetings.

I should be writing to Caesar tonight.
I'm writing, however, to you.
What ancient historians said about
The general's hesitation
Cannot compare with what could be said
Of ours. It is quiet tonight,
In quietly whitening dark, as snow
Forecast all day, feared
All day, felt all day, effects
All night its inexorable descent.
It has been quiet except for my voice
On the phone for hours. Should I?
Should I not? Should I? Would I? Will I?

On this evening in 49 B.C.
Caesar attended a banquet in Ravenna,
Then left quietly, climbed into a mulecart,
And rode off through the darkness. When his lights
Went out and mules and muleteers lost their way,
He walked by narrowest footpaths to the river,
Where he met his men. Then, says Suetonius, he hesitated.
Then, says Plutarch, he kept changing his mind.
Then, says Lucan (the poet), fresh from the Alps
He trembled before a vision of Rome. Then,
Say all, he crossed. The stream, which creeps through summer,
Surged with melting Alps, the poet says.

What was the crossing of a little river
To him, first of Romans to bridge the Rhine?
To one who rowed onto unknown Ocean?

Lucan, Plutarch, Suetonius: after your time.
But maybe Asinius Pollio was their source,
And maybe you heard the things that he reported.
Caesar himself, you'll recall, in his book on the war
Never mentions the Rubicon at all.

Is this a Roman general, you asked
In a letter of that January, 49,
Or is it a Hannibal? What had you said
In that speech of June, 56? Caesar
Has freed Rome from the terror of Gaul. The Alps,
Italy's ramparts — let them collapse. Between
These heights and Ocean nothing will be feared
By Italy if Caesar is allowed
Only a summer or two to finish the job.
By 50 he finished. Winter was coming. What then?

What is that story of the Alpine village where Caesar
Preferred being first to being second in Rome?
What did you say you learned on your way back to Rome
From your first provincial assignment? Roman ears
Are poor but Roman eyes are very good.
                                                                      If one

If one leaves, the Romans will never hear of the good
Accomplished. Never leave. Stay and be seen.

To be a slave in Rome or to be free
(In the mountains, there you are free,
By great rivers, there you are free,
By resounding oceans, there you are free),
To be a citizen in Switzerland,
To be a burgher by the flowing Rhine,
To be a native across the ocean,
To be a citizen beside the Mississippi
Ice-stilled or, near the dam, steaming
Like Phlegethon, eagle-starred like Delphi,
There, where a railroad bridge first crossed,
Entrance, center. The center is Rome.
Here are all your works in the best editions.
Freedom is all one needs. Here are his, too.

Did he, the unhesitating, hesitate?
He, the man of celerity, stop?
It is we, you and I, who ask all night, Should I?
Should I not? Should I? Shall I? Will I?

                                                    Yet,
Hearing Sirens, does one delay?

Did you mean what you said about the Sirens
Or were you recording Antiochus' conviction
That Ulysses wouldn't stop for a song?
Knowledge, you said, that was their promise.

I have heard the Sirens, then silence, then Sirens again.
I think I broke from the ropes, jumped from the ship,
Beat my way across the water, heard, forgot.
I forget. Did I hear for twice nine years or pass
On a snowy night and stick in the ice far
From locust-sweet enchantment? I remember,

Sometimes the Sirens say, Sing,
Sometimes the Sirens say, Listen.

Sometimes the Sirens say, Stay,
Sometimes the Sirens say, Go.

Sometimes they seem all tune,
Sometimes they seem all information.

The book opens. We know, we know,
They cry. Delight and know.

The pages shimmer. To know, to know,
I cry. Alight — but, no,

The wind rises, the pages blow
Into ice and silencing snow.

There are two Sirens. One sings,
Rome. The other sings, Freedom.

There are two Sirens. One says,
It is here. One says, It is there.

There are two Sirens. One sings,
Beauty. The other sings, Knowledge.

They sing, they say,

You know nothing. Look into your mind.
What do you find? What have you to offer?

We offer company in giving.
Our coffer fills as it empties.
Soft, softer, sing with us on the shore,

Loud, louder, with us speak
To all who come to sit at our feet

Looking into our eyes, asking
More, asking, What
Do you see, asking, asking, Look at me,

With me, look, below the dam,
Above the Mississippi, eagles.

They say, they sing,

You know too much. Not in ignorance,
Not in witlessness, will you respond.

Hither! Wither on the shore.
Haste! Waste among the flowers.
Here! Hear the unwearying wingbeats of words

Worth your wearying wait, your watch
Day and night, your dwindling, not

Like Narcissian dwindling, fixed
On self, but a fading as you gaze
On ultimate flowering, summits of aquiline flight,

The flower orange and blue of sunrise,
The blue flight aureate after sunset.

So they speak and so they spoke,
Unless they were silent.
So they spoke and so they speak.
What shall I answer?
Answer, my Cicero, what shall I answer?

The 4th day before the Ides of January.

(7) To Gaius Julius Caesar.
From Cambridge, Massachusetts, February 3, 1984.

Flora Baum to Gaius Julius Caesar greetings.

To one not carried away by words
(Republic, liberty, ideal)
This is the way things are:

Sparrows, strong-toned, persistent, insistent in the trees,
Sunlight, weak-toned, vacillating, vapid on the bricks,
Weak trees by strong bricks,

Streams to cross everywhere,
Running strong from weakening snow
Not Alpine but new-town Cantabrigian

As the old-swamp ground of Cambridge reverts to swamp
And under a wind of March in a January light
The sunbeams of the witchhazel, almost ready to stream

From their small winter's caves
Like a little daymusic just for strings
From hollow of wood, from cave of brain,

From bud of mind, seem ready to sally forth
Boldly like you, bright reckless sun,
But may withdraw, Pompeian, flexible, enigmatic,

With a near smile. If Pompey's cheeks
Are puffy, yours drawn in,
That matters little. I see him running.

Our candidates are already running.
We, too, have politics, rhetoric, threats of war —
War, unlike yours (just, dignified, and clement),

Untriumphant, triumphless, hurtling us back,
After the flame, beyond the uncivilized ash,
To our huge winter's caves.

The 3rd day before the Nones of February.

(8) To Joseph Orcome.
From Cambridge, Massachusetts, February (?), 1984 (?).

Sunday

Dear Joe,

What happened today?
The sun came out.
What happened today?

Something moved above the snow.
Something breathed above the ice.

Witchhazel hinted of golden spring
To a marble winter.

The witchhazel's reverie of sweet spring
Scented crystal winter.

Last night I knew I could think the thought with happiness:
He is lying now with Suzanne as they fall asleep.

He and Suzanne abide together in happiness:
I seemed purified as I lay there half asleep.

His sneakers standing on the floor: I lost no happiness.
His blue jeans folded on the chair: I fell asleep.

Suzanne Beausoleil: How could you not
Have loved her,

Her soft green eyes, her gleaming thick
Black hair

Hanging to her waist, her smile — her mind —
Of sun?

I would not pluck —
I would not touch —
A bough, a petal.

                                        Love,
                                        Flora

(Not sent.)

(9) To Marcus Tullius Cicero.
From Cambridge, Massachusetts, March 5, 1984.

Flora to Cicero greetings.

March has come, that lion,
Roaring, rising, whitening,
Full of fight.

Alps, solemn, siren,
Oceans, martial, myelin,
Years, thundrous thousands, lie

Between us, roll or rise
Between us. Vale atque vale, my
Cicero, good-by.

The 3rd day before the Nones of March.

(10) To Marcus Tullius Cicero.
From Rome, December 17, 50 B.C.

Flora to Cicero greetings.

I remember seeing crocuses
In their fresh pale purple patches
And hearing the red song, fresh but far from pale,
Of the exultant cardinal high
In the ruddying silver maple. Then it snowed.

Then Tullia came running into the guest bedroom,
Calling, Wake up! Wake up! My father will be back
For his birthday! His letter has just arrived.
I'm glad that you'll be back,
Even though times are bad.

If Caesar runs for consul he'll be elected.
Can't he return? How I hope you can do
Something. You must have heard that Caesar always
Writes praising you. Pompey knows you've always
Been Pompey's friend.

A letter has come from Varro in Spain.
He says he has ties to Caesar and Pompey both,
Although he's Pompey's legate, of course. Some
Of the books he needs have not yet arrived from Rome.
Still, he says, the mixed life is the highest,

Not the active or, what I'd expect,
The leisured contemplative scholarly. He keeps working
On his "Ancient History," especially on the part
That treats the calendar. How I wish he could do
Something if he's a friend to both Pompey and Caesar.

Tullia seems very well. I'm certainly happy
To have this chance of talking and reading with her.
Terentia seems well, too. And Dolabella.
I'm looking forward to seeing you very soon —
No later than the 3rd day before the Nones.

The 14th day before the Kalends of January, Rome.

(11) To Joseph Orcome.
From Cambridge, Massachusetts, March 7, 1984.

Wednesday

Dear Joe,

Thank you for your card.
I'm sorry I've been a poor correspondent.
The ancients are becoming so real to me
I seem to be writing them letters,
I find myself in Rome,
I seem to be waiting for answers.
I hope your work is going well, too.
Do let me know when your book comes out.
Remember me to Suzanne.

Love,
Flora

(Postmarked March 8, 1984.)

11. Entry

Diary of Flora Baum,
June 21.

The center —
China, Chicago,
A ship-quick, train-bridged Mississippi,
A point in Kansas,
A point in South Dakota,
A point in North Dakota,
A point on the Date Line, China.

The center —
Delphic, oracular,
Holy,
Set among mountains,
Rocks, springs, groves, caves,
Columns,
Enclosed, exploding

With answers. Therefore, come,
Dip your hands in the spring,
Fix your feet on the slope,
Enter,
Striding between the laurels,
Stepping between the piled stones
Smoothed, shaped, standing, upholding

The answering cavern.
Let the answers
Glance from Parnassus to the gulf.
Beg the answers
Even to bubble,
To trickle even,
From some central crack.

The center —
Where the eagles have flown.
The center —
Where the god has gone.
The center —
Our city, our earth,
Our sun.

New York —
Columnar.
Its columns scratched the sky.
Imperial,
Its biggest pillar rose,
Rooted in the rocky earth,
Reaching glittery for the sun.

Rome —
Of marble or bricks,
Of mud or sticks,
Sticking
It out, rooted, reaching
In time, through time, teaching
Home.

Nam nos in nostra urbe
Peregrinantis errantisque tamquam hospites
Tui libri
Quasi domum deduxerunt
Ut possemus aliquando
Qui et ubi essemus
Agnoscere,

As Cicero said — I render,
We were visitors, strangers, and lost
In our own city, Rome,
But your books brought us home,
And who and where we were we could tell at last —
As Cicero said, not of Caesar,
Of Varro, of the scholar.

The center —
Columned, marbled, bricked
Surely,
Where the books are piled.
Through the chilly drizzle I went
As the finch sang, cheerful in the chill,
On the eve of the Quinquatrus,

A Sunday afternoon, the eighteenth of March,
Past the beech and past the oaks,
Past the snowsuited squirrels,
Past maples, a virgilia, the ash,
In among the big-bronze-budded elms
Almost exploding into the small bronze blossoms,
Past the owlless pine,

Toward the sphinxless platforms flanking the monumental steps,
Toward the slushy steps ascending to the wettish columns,
Toward the solid Corinthian columns, wettish bricks,
Legendless friezes, godless pediments, unopened doors
Of iron, solidly locked. Not until Monday
Would scholars' feet stamp on the red carpet
And past the morning's pail inscribed: For marble floors only.

It was Sunday. It was a vigil. I was merely
Framing anew my old petition, backing
Slowly along the wet path
To where an old virgilia stands, Professor Francis Child's,
I always think — the one he loved.
Beside its silver, tarnished by the rain,
I stopped and, gazing, saying,

A bloody spouse art thou to me,
As though I had to climb the steps on my hands and knees,
Squeeze the columns, batter the bricks,
Wrench the iron doors,
Screaming: I will go in,
This is my home, I mop here,
Saying,

A spouse

A spouse thou art,
As though I could dance up the steps,
Hug the columns, caress the bricks,
Pass through iron doors
Like a body resurrected,
Like a mind
Free for the spaceless timeless

Spouse — of a slave? when
Freedom is all one needs —
Freedom: time,
Freedom: mind? —
Saying all this to a structure
Containing, imaging,
Saying to the unimaged god,

Rain the books upon me and let me be
Permeable, containing,
As a nymph is also a pool,
A dryad also a tree,
An oread also a mountain,
Saying, let more than mouse, let more than squirrel
Germinate in that rain,

I waited, afflicted
With images, monsters, and desire.
I stepped farther back
To the comforting curving arm of the grandest elm.
Is it books that will bud here or will
Little brown flowers soften, renew
The enormous tree,

The beautiful monster whose great crook'd arm
Shepherds from the west, whose solid body
Simply stands magnetic in the north,
One focus of my orbit?
The other is the lode seen in the south,
Red equatorial point,
Green equinoctial moment.

On March 22 the sun came out, a robin came out,
The elm was coming, burnished like a robin.

The point was this:
To mine the timeless metal from the ore of time.

The center —
I remember April,
I remember, by the drift of a river,
Middletown in the drizzle,
Halfway between Hartford and New Haven,
Halfway between Boston and New York,
Halfway between a winter and a spring.
A Friday. A thirteenth of April. It becomes an evening
Alone with a greasy, grainy, thin
Hamburger in Middletown,
A lone walk to a worn room
Where a turned-on lamp hisses and sparks,
A drawn-down shade slips from its roller.
A drizzled-upon magnolia
Unbinds its promises.
Steely beeches grandiosely guard
Deep-peace-blue squills.
Undiluted by the drizzle, red maples bleed
Their far from dismal, far from middling red.

Memory is less thin.
It thickens. Or does it thin?
Red memory, minute
As the maple drops and fine
As the points of the beeches, reaches, falls
Through falls, winters, Aprils, for

Nos in nostra urbe —
Us in our own city —
Your books — tui libri —
Have led — deduxerunt —
With a light curve silver beside the words
In my dead professor's copy. I see the yellow
Pencil in his fingers — one of those pencils
                                            Sharpened

Sharpened weekly by his faithful man or maid.
I see the curve of a lock of his silver hair
As he bends his head to the text — his silver hair?
When did he mark the passage?

Some dates are recorded in the book itself
(Lineation retained, punctuation added):
(Inside the back cover, on a yellow slip)
Widener book due,
Jul. 6, 1984
(The first charge, obscuring
Penciled notes in the professor's hand);
(On the back of the title page, stamped in black)
Harvard University Library,
Mar. 14, 1983;
(No date stated for his bequest or purchase,
But inside the front cover, on a white simple sticker)
From the library of
James Craig La Drière,
Society of Fellows, 1936–9, 1968–9,
Professor of Comparative Literature 1965–78,
Harvard College Library (That's what it says;
It does not say: died April '78;
It does not say: was born in 1910;
It does not say:
His teaching, like those pencil marks,
Quiet, spare, silver; like his mind,
Flowing, gold — yes, spare and flowing both —;
His mind, like the urn on the book's green spine,
Gold, holding; like the turned urn, flowing;
Knowing first what was already known,
Thinking then what had not yet been thought);
(On the facing page, in ink — once black? — now gold)
W. E. Heitland,
With the editor's kind regards,
Jan. 15, 1885.
The edition's date is 1885.
10th December, 1884,
Cambridge (the real Cambridge), is the date
Of James

Of James S. Reid's short preface, which asserts:
Important and interesting
As the *Academica* is,
It has received far less than its fair share
Of attention . . . , and concludes:
The plan of writing
The critical notes in Latin . . .
Needs no apology.

Cicero wrote to Atticus in Latin
From Tusculum in June, 45 B.C.:
Mihi Arpinum eundum est —
I have to go to Arpinum.
Mihi est in animo proficisci XI Kal. —
I plan to leave on the 21st.
(The 11th before the Kalends was the 21st,
For the long year 46 had passed, and June
Had thirty days instead of twenty-nine.)

Atticus wrote to Cicero from Rome
On, it seems, that same June 21.
Cicero answered Atticus from Arpinum
On what most scholars agree was June 23:
Quod ad me de Varrone scribis —
With regard to what you write me about Varro . . . ,

And entered upon considerations
Which ended preeminently in this:
Ergo illam Ἀκαδημικήν —
Therefore the *Academica* . . . —
Ad Varronem transferamus —
Let us transfer to Varro.

Let us — me — get it all straight.
There are certainly plenty of letters,
Often letters every day.

In the middle of January Tullia had a child.
Her marriage of four years to Dolabella
Had already broken up before their son was born.

BOOK THREE | PART ONE

By the middle of February Tullia was dead.
What was as dear to Cicero as this daughter?
Only the republic, also gone —
Nothing left except to study and write
Alone with sorrow.

                Not that, of course,
He had not studied and written for years —
Loved study; loved writing; loved Latin; loved thought;
Loved sentences, phrases, and words; studied
Greek and Roman literature, rhetoric, law,
History, philosophy. Further, the *Academics*
Had probably been begun when Tullia died.

Although during those hard three months that followed
Her death he had been working on other things
As well — begun and finished the *Consolation*,
Completed the *Hortensius* no doubt, no doubt
Begun *On Ends*, tried writing the public *Letter
Of Advice* to Caesar, who soon would return from the last
Victory in Spain — by May 13, 45,
He was able to write to Atticus from Astura
(Reid suggests it's Astúra, not Aśtura)
That the two big books of *Academics* were done.

The people who criticize me for excessive mourning,
He had said in a letter to Atticus on May 9,
Can't even read as much as I've been writing.

But writing and rewriting are the same.
Let me get it all straight — maybe not all
But something. I'm not thinking about

How the two books of the *Academics*
Completed before the middle of May
Were named "Catulus" and "Lucullus"
After those very noble Romans
Who, along with Hortensius and Cicero himself,
Spoke in them about knowledge,

Or how in that same May
These two books were sent to Rome
For copying, how the copies were made
By Cicero's, then by Atticus', scribes,

Or how before the end of the month
New prefaces had been added to these books,
One praising Catulus and the other Lucullus,

Or how the author began to worry
That he had shown the noble Romans
Catulus, Lucullus, and Hortensius —
Educated, indeed, but by no means learned,
And least of all expert in philosophy — discussing
Abstruse questions which they never could have dreamed of,

Or how as soon as he reached Arpinum
On June 22 he set to work
Taking out Catulus, Lucullus, and Hortensius
And giving roles to Cato and Brutus,

Or how when Atticus' letter of the day before
Arrived at Arpinum late that afternoon
It seemed a godsend,
Telling him that Varro hankered
To be included in a dialogue by Cicero,

Or how Varro had been laboring for two years
At books of his own work, *The Latin Language*,
Which he would dedicate, he had announced
Two years before, to Cicero,

Or how the scholarly Varro was just the right person
To expound the views of the so-called Old Academy
Headed by Antiochus, since Varro was learned in philosophy
(As in everything) and, furthermore, known to approve
Strongly of Antiochus' eclectic and non-skeptical position,

Or how Cicero had to change the *Academics*
In order to introduce Varro as a speaker,
Altering time, locale, and conversation,

Or how he worried in letter after letter
About whether Varro would like what he had done
And whether he should keep Varro in or change the speakers yet again,

Or how he expanded the work from two books into four,

Or how he thought the new version much better than the old,
Both more inclusive and more concise,
Exact and elegant and splendid,

Or how he thought it so much better
He was sure that Atticus would not mind
The waste of his copyists' time on the earlier version,

Or how the new one was sent to Rome to be copied,
Or how the copy was made on expensive paper
(I'll call those fine large sheets of papyrus paper),
Or how the copyists' errors were corrected,
Or how the volumes were bound (rolls wrapped) in parchment,
Or how a letter to Varro was composed
With special care by Cicero and dictated
Not quickly, as it might have been, to Tiro,
But syllable after syllable to Spintharus,
Or how both letter and book were sent to Atticus,

Or how, apparently toward the end of July,
Cicero finally was able to write to his friend:
So you have dared to give it to Varro!
I'm waiting to hear his reaction.
But when will he read it?

I'm not thinking about those things.
I'm thinking about how quickly it was done.
How quickly was the transfer made?
How fast did Cicero compose?
How many hours a day did he spend in writing?

Did Cicero leave Tusculum on June 21,
Two thousand twenty-eight years ago today,
Stay overnight somewhere en route,
Arrive in Arpinum on June 22,

                                                  Begin

Begin right away to transfer parts
Of the *Academics* to Cato and Brutus,
Receive Atticus' letter late on the 22nd,
Find himself struck by his friend's suggestion
That Varro would like a role in one of his works,

Write to Atticus early on the 23rd
That he planned to transfer the *Academics* to Varro,
Write to Atticus on June 24
That he had transferred the *Academics* to Varro,
Write to Atticus on June 25
That Atticus had been added as a third speaker,
Write to Atticus on June 26
That he had transferred the *Academics* to Varro,
Write to Atticus on June 28
That he had completed the *Academics* for Varro,
Write to Atticus on June 29:
Quia scripseras et desiderari a Varrone —
Because you wrote that it was wished by Varro —
Et magni illum aestimare —
And that he valued it highly —
Hos confeci et absolvi nescio quam bene —
I have composed this and have completed, I don't know how well, —
Sed ita accurate ut nihil posset supra —
But so carefully that nothing could be more careful, —
Academicam omnem quaestionem libris quattuor —
The whole Academic question in four books. —
In eis quae erant contra ἀκαταληψίαν —
In them the things that were, against uncertainty, —
Praeclare collecta ab Antiocho —
Excellently collected by Antiochus —
Varroni dedi — I have given to Varro. —
Ad ea ipse respondeo — To them I myself reply. —
Tu es tertius in sermone nostro —
You are the third in our conversation. — ?

Did he, then, do the new version
Possibly in two or three days,
At most in less than a week?

I don't know, no, I do not know.
It seems so, yes, it does seem so.
How delicately, how deeply can I dig
In such soil with my instrumental twig?
How delicately, how deeply can I see
In the light of the first century B.C.?

Us in our own city,
Augustine wrote in the *City of God*,
Your books — tui libri,
He wrote, of course, in Latin,
Have led domum — home,
He wrote that Cicero said
In the first book of the *Academics*,
In which work Cicero also said,

As we know only from Augustine,
Large parts of Cicero's treatise having been lost,
That his discussion was held with Marcus Varro,
Homine omnium facile acutissimo —
Of all men easily the most acute —
Et sine ulla dubitatione doctissimo —
And without any doubt the most learned.

And without any doubt the most learned, Augustine repeats,
Cicero said, Augustine says, in those books,
The *Academics*, where Cicero contended
That everything must be doubted. Did Augustine
Know, then, only the second, revised edition?

I don't know, no, I do not know.
It seems so, yes, it does seem so.
How delicately, how deeply can I dig
In this soil with my mediating twig?
How delicately, how deeply can I see
In the light of the fifth century A.D.?

Without any doubt, Petrarch wrote in Latin
From Rome on the first of November, 1350,
Sine ulla dubitatione — without any doubt —
In the middle of a sentence in his letter addressed to Varro:
All men of learning agree that Varro is the most learned,
As Marcus Cicero was not afraid to affirm
Without any doubt in those very books in which
He argues that nothing may be affirmed. Did Petrarch
Know, then, the *Academics* in the second edition?
Or did he not rather have this only from Augustine,
And was he not able to read, of the *Academics* itself,
Only the second book of the first edition?

I don't know, no, I do not know.
It seems so, yes, it does seem so.
How delicately, how deeply can I dig
In time's soil with my ascertaining twig?
How delicately, how deeply can I see
In the light of the fourteenth century?

The funny thing is this:
I have, we have — Reid gives, for example,
Or Plasberg in the later Teubner text —
The first book of the second edition,
The second book of the first edition.
That's it, more or less.
Much of one book of the four with Atticus and Varro,
All of one book of the two with Hortensius, Catulus, and Lucullus.
Can I dig in the soil, can I see
In the light of the twentieth century?

Sharpen the pencil.
Turn up the lamp.

The center, said Hicetas,
Is not the earth but the sun,

Or else he said the earth moves
And everything else is still,
And someone else, some other Pythagorean,

Perhaps Philolaus, displaced the moving earth
And sent it and the sun and all the rest
Circling around the universe's fire,

And Aristarchus was the first to move
The earth about the unmoved central sun.
Something presumably moves. Does something rest?

Our center —
The black earth:
Melanchthon, the classical scholar,

Wrote a letter to Burkhard Mithob in Latin
On October 16, 1541,
About those with absurd ideas

Like that Sarmatian astronomer
Who moves the earth
And stops the sun.

Our center —
The gray question,
Gray surmise:

Hicetas of Syracuse, as Theophrastus says,
Cicero wrote in the *Academics*,
Undoubtedly in both versions, though for this we have only the first,

Holds that sky, sun, moon, and stars —
All celestial bodies — stand
Still and not one thing except

Earth moves in the universe.
All such matters lie in darkness,
Occultate and circumfused.

Our center —
The white hypothesis,
Bright answer:

Ac repperi quidem
Apud Ciceronem primum
Nicetum sensisse terram moveri —

And I found indeed
In Cicero first
That Nicetus thought the earth moves,

Copernicus wrote to the pope
In his preface to the *Revolutions*,
Published, as everyone knows,

In 1543. Did his text
Of the *Academics* read Nicetus
For Hicetas? It seems so, yes.

I've got that all pretty straight. Now what line lies
To vision from the pedant's eyes?

Jacob lay
Resting his head on a stone.

A ladder rose through the night, not
A man-made animal backing up, proceeding, ascending,
Granting you a moment to view Harvard Yard below, then passing its wing
Stiffly, swiftly over buildings, buildings,
Your circling river, other people's rivers,
Bright gray geometries, June's map of blue and green,
And there a rumpled earth, with here a rumble in the sky.

Soundless, a ladder, a stairway, rose through the night.
Soundless, angels ascended and descended through the night.
Soundless, the ladder stood on the earth, and its top touched heaven.

The city had borne the name of Luz,
In the land of Canaan.
That was a certain place. The Lord
Was in that place. How terrible
Was that place. Jacob had not known
Who was in that place when he lay down.
It was no other than the house of God, the gate of heaven. He gave it a name.
This stone shall be the House of God if I come home.

He sent them all across the ford
And remained alone beside the stream
In that deep gorge east of Jordan.
And an angel came and gripped him, wrestled
With him there till dawn, begged
Him then to let him go. No,

Unless you bless me. Jacob, though,
Had to tell his name, be named anew
The Strong with God, and limp away. Although
The angel would not tell his name he blessed
The human man and gave a name to him
Who named the place the Face of God and lived.

And God told Jacob to go to Bethel,
And he came to Luz to build an altar.
It might have been a stained-glass city,
Gold, blue, green, red-flame.
And Jacob named Luz Bethel,
And God named Jacob Israel,
And God said, I am El Shaddaï,
And spoke with him.

And God said, I am God Almighty,
And spoke with him and gave a name
And gave him all that land.

God then left him in the place
Where he spoke with him, and he
Put a sacred pillar there,
Where God spoke, a piece of stone,
Poured out drink, and poured on oil,
Said the book.
He called the name of that place Bethel.

Appellavit nomen loci illius Domus Dei,
Wrote Jerome.

Your books brought us home,
Cicero wrote in the *Academics*.

There are flowers, I said as I stared through my window
Looking for summer through June days perfect and imperfect
With humid news of heat-warped rails on the Red Line
Or sunny breeze-brought messages stirring long leaves.

There are flowers — there they are — great nosegays
Full with the fulness of June in their setting of leaves
That radiate green from the green-yellow jewels amid them,
And there are the great leaves, there are the great leaves' shadows.

When the wind blew like the spirit like the wind,
When the sun shone like the flame that made the brick
Upon the brick, great green boughs greatly heaved,
Great leafy shadows pranced upon the wall.

I saw the pointing panicles of the ailanthus
Bump green into the red wall.

Yet the panicles fattened, the clusters fluffed
Into yellow — I cannot call it gold —
Into fresh, fair yellow on green, on red, on blue.
There are flowers — greenish, say the books,
Greenish, greenish yellow, yellow, green.

Your books . . . Back I had to go
Toward where the books are piled, first savvily
Fording the storm-vast stone-lashed flow
Of savage Massachusetts Avenue,
Leaving behind the blink, the roar,
The stupidly revengeful boar,
Leaving behind the whirl, the whir,
The utterly unsubtle stir.

Lucus in urbe fuit media —
A grove there was in the midst of the city —
That was Carthage, but it led ineluctably to Rome.
In, selecting a path
Amid the clover and grass,
Through the sun and shadow I went
As the finch sang, happy in the heat,
Breezy in the breeze,

Past the June-leaved beech with its bellying beechnuts —
Green-leaved beech with remnants and newborns of red,
Underlying remains, neonates outcrying —
Through the big-leaved, whispering oaks of the grove —
Jove-leaved oaks, Dodonian susurrants,
Clung to by yellowish acorns, infant as yet —
Met by no mountain lion, bear, boar, wolf,
Sighting the summering squirrels, the mountain laurel
Bright-cloud-white, minutely umbracular, past
A recently June-wedding-white virgilia, saying
Fated or fatuously,
Guide me, Virgil, through the grove,
Bring me, Varro, to the books,
Lead me, Cicero, through the white-frilled lessons of the catalpa,

Past the great wrestling elm
Grappling with space and time,
Rugged as age,
Soft as summer,
Fresh as rain —
The elm ascending and descending —
Ascending strong and brown,
Flowing back down, fragile, free,
Fertile, fervid, full, and green
As the tide of the twenty-first of June.

Brown as the Ohio it glided to the sky,
Green as Kentucky it galloped back to earth,
Meeting deeper brown and highest blue.

Met by brown or blue I begged:
If I could come with Rembrandt's rabbi's eyes.
I saw myself in the glass
Of — gasping for sight with gaping mouth —
That wide-eyed blind man of Picasso.

Eagles, I cried, as green wings tipped blue sky.
Green, blue, purple, the necks of the pigeons
Flickered and glittered beneath the tree.

Quid ergo est quod percipi possit—
What then is there that can be perceived —
Si ne sensus quidem vera nuntiant—
If not even the senses report the truth?
De collo columbae — About the pigeon's neck . . .
On pigeons' necks the many colors seen
Are only one. Cicero. *Academics.*

And was that Rembrandt's rabbi in the hall?

I called them green leaves, then.
They were so neatly ruled
That straight answers surely could be given.
When the Sibyl's color changed and neat hair wilded
And stature stretched and voice rang louder than mortal
And she shook and shouted: The god, behold, the god,
Aeneas pleaded: Don't put the answers on the leaves.

Oh, the leaves are free, they float and fly,
They do not toil or slave.
Oh, the tree is bound, stuck in the mud,
Fettered to earth. To move
Is not permitted. Power it has to bid
The sun within, to leave
It rolling freely through the summer sky.

Solstice, I called it; I called it then
Titanic spring, gigantic geyser, green
Niagara laving senses, soul . . . Suddenly
On came a little automatic sprinkler.
Alarmed, a pigeon flapped away.

                                        I took out my list.

Varro's *Latin Language, Rustic Things,*
Ancient History, Menippean Satires,
Urban Things, Epistolary Questions,

Tyrannio's book on accentuation in Homer,
Of which Cicero wrote to Atticus from Tusculum
On, perhaps, May 31, 45:

Me non magis ipse liber delectabit —
The book itself will not delight me more —
Quam tua admiratio, delectavit —
Than your admiration has delighted, —
Amo enim πάντα φιλειδήμονα —
For I love the lover of all knowledge —
Teque istam tam tenuem θεωρίαν —
And that you so specialized a scholarship —
Tam valde admiratum esse gaudeo —
So greatly have admired I rejoice, —
Etsi tua quidem sunt eius modi omnia —
Although yours indeed are of that sort all things, —
Scire enim vis, quo uno animus alitur —
For you want to know, by which alone the mind is fed, —
Sed, quaeso — But, I ask, —
Quid ex ista acuta et gravi refertur ad τέλος —
What have these acute and grave accents to do with the End?

Summer's green screened the red building
At the end of the path, but past another elm,
Past Child's virgilia clad in nuptial rags,
Past girlish honeylocusts, past a young elm,
My eye cleared the branch that hangs over the path.

Above the white columns, above the white frieze, in the central
    panel of red,
Something flickered on the brick,
Something stretched or ascended, stretched and ascended,
Glittered in the pediment of the sky.
Something? A scintillation,
Gowned, armed, helmeted — something? — someone?
Who else than glittering Minerva?

The wise affirm nothing,
I gather from the *Academics.*
My heart flickered. I continued along the path.

I set my right foot on the first wide step.
I set my left foot on the second.
An owllike sound jarred my right ear: Who?
On a gray rock of Cambridge I suddenly saw
The sphinx that lashed her tail and asked me: Who?
I . . . Why? I heard from the left.
I set my right foot on the third wide step.

On a gray rock of Cambridge I suddenly saw
The buddha, full, immobile, boding: Why?
So . . . Go! A voice from above
Between two columns to the right, a light, sweet voice,
But stern, compelling, a sweet siren voice
Commanded: Go.
The Alps are bright with snow
Upon the peaks. The Alpine flowerets grow
Bright on the slopes. No qualm
Must hold you here alone.
If Caesar had not gone
Would he have ruled in Rome?
Um . . . Come! A voice from above
Between two columns to the left, a honied voice
(I climbed a few steps), a honied siren voice
Entreated: Come
To the top, continue in
To the center where the bright rose must begin.
In a darkness deep and dumb
And musty, letters bud.
If Cicero had not stayed
Would he be read?

              Afraid,

Looking higher, glimpsing something new,
I said, What are these women who stand in stone
Within those scrolls above the open door,
Holding torches, girded, gowned, cloaked, veiled,
And winged? What are these two stone women with wings?
Angels? furies? liberties? victories? veritates?
                                      Their

Their veils pushed back, their cloaks pushed back, their wings
Lifted high above their heads, they stood
Identical, not furious, unmoved,
Unmoving, chiseled into quietness.

Unquiet, I kept questioning:
Urnlike maidens, if you spread
Those long stone wings and flew
Up to the long stone friezes,
What shaped legend
In what verdant Tempe
Before what erubescent sacrificial fire
Might be read?

Our twinship. Each looked out.
Each stood straight, left knee advanced,
Left hand clasping cloak,
Right hand clutching torch.
This fire burns with artifice.
This fire burns with light.
Where? Where the sun stops. Where?

I looked above them. TRUTH in Latin.
Below it, on the ledge, a pigeon
Murmured an incomprehensible warning,
Raised her wings, flew down, attacked —
An indirect attack,
A quite significant flap,
A very comprehensible admonition.
How could I have seen her child
Hiding behind the solid square container by the door?
How could I not have heard that peep, peep, peep?
The blue-gray mother soothed the black-and-white chick.

I saw that the baby was safe,
Then, under TRUTH in stone,
Entered the brick-red rose
This green-leaved June 21,

Midsummer or
The beginning of summer.

12. Winter Bud

The ancient dark and verdurous linden
With its fresh sweet golden bloom—
What has that to do with this ancient dark?

Once there was warmth.
Once there was heat.
We walked along a burning Massachusetts Avenue,
Looked up at red letters on snow emergency signs,
Said: There never was and never will be cold
To tick the sweat from the brow,
To tingle sweetly on the reddened cheek.
We went walking after supper on the side streets and we said:
It never was and never will be dark at four,
We will saunter on forever, on in the age-old light of evening,
Breathing rose and linden,
Weaving tones of robin
Into purple clematis ascending and descending the white fence,
Wreathed by green treetops beneath a softening sky.

The sky must be hard now, must be frozen
Like the dark earth. Maybe some snow would warm us.

Here a temple.
Here Sidonian Dido was building Juno a great
Temple. Here
First, his fear
Assuaged, Aeneas dared to hope, in hope await
Pebble's ripple.

Was it the huge June linden,
Rising mighty like a Jove,
Calling sweetly through the air,
Wafting gold dust to the drive?

Was it — not Danae — Daphne,
Standing maidenly, straight, and slim,
With slender lifted arms outstretched,

Dainty

Dainty fingers opened wide,
Soft green sleeves — of leaves (she is a tree,
Golden rain tree golden in July) —
Green leafy leaves, inclined a bit toward blue
At times, or pure green, pointed, well-sketched leaves,
Etched blossoms, yellow, yellow, bright, oh, bright,
Gleaming, reaching,
Feeling the breeze,
Felt by the bees,
Fingering spaces yet not inclined to seize
Anything, openhanded, open, most
Yellow except, upon inspection, now
And then dabbed with a bit of red, but yellow,
Yellow, nature's living outstretched gold?

Was it an immense December prison?
Locked in the chill of marble, what shall she do
About this unexpected gold —
Dust or rain — descending slowly,
Warm and friendly, on her hair,
Brow, cheeks, lips, friendly, caressing?
What shall she do but sink to the floor slowly
Under this assuaging weight of gold?

I ask only to make
My footnotes accurate. The bulking
Dark of the leafless tree in the hulking
Dark of the warmthless night is budding
All winter red.

13. Flora Baum, Astronomer

Not only but also —
Not only the relief
But also the excitement of the sky,
Not only the warmth
But also the desire of the stars,
Not only the far that comes near

                                                                                   But also

But also the near that leaps onto the light waves and is off
Answers her ache.

              The wet
Avenue is enormously crimson.
She doesn't go out much at night.
It's just a sign. The street
Is thoroughly lighted with yellow light.
You don't know whom you'll meet
Wandering up from the Square or the Common.
Maybe it will be golden
Faces and crimson feet.
Maybe you'll look the other way.
Maybe, given the celestial red of the night,
Something will pierce the urban murkiness of the sky.

The allurement of the stars
Catches at the heart as much here
As in Delphi's pointed nightly clarity.
Certainly the lyre that drew the trees
Rings here among the incalculable stars.

This new catalogue displays
Constellations of books as in a planetarium
Or, for that matter, in a sky, as white on deep blue,
Swims before your eyes, wobbles on the waves,
Makes you seasick, is called a duck,
Learns to obey your fingers,
Heavens moving,
Oceans stopping,
At the rudder's command.
The lights go off: it goes off, too.
You never can read it by the sun.
But you want to go off far beyond the sun.

Where blue squills grew, orange lilies rise
In undulating seas.
Where the hyacinth was beaten by the snow,
The hollyhock lies prostrate in the rain.
Blackout, whiteout: without any lights

                                                Traversing

Traversing Massachusetts Avenue,
River choppy-slick with white and black,
Portholes darkly thick with white. Along
At least some of the prettier byways
Yellow honeysuckle and purple
Bittersweet nightshade coexist.
Winter may be of marble or of bronze.

She takes her books out to read at home.
Unless she tunes in the artificial,
Her room all winter like a moon once removed
Is lit at most by the glassy reflection
Of a sun from which it is receding or has receded.
Donne put Copernicus into hell.
Whose fault is it that we recede

Or have receded, lost track of the epic
That we knew? The sparrows chip away
In the weedy trees, the bluejay rages,
Bright in brown life.

                    One way to go
Is, like the twins, the sons of Jove,
To live with stars, to metamorphose
Forever or in alternation
Into stars. An instellation
May come down to particles or waves. The muddied
Future of the book will now be studied,
Says the *Chronicle of Higher Education*.

Through the slit a sky
Eases the prisoner. If the slave
Gazes upon the heavenly bodies
Can they be counted upon?
The eerie and mysterious nighthawk
Sounds, after all, much like a sparrow.
The astigmatic, myopic mind
May, after all, look at a truth.
Among authentic witticisms
Of Cicero did Caesar register this:
                                    Someone:

Someone: Lyra will rise tomorrow.
Cicero: Yes, by decree.
Or can one ask: Is it better
To call March June and be free?

Through murkiness, the mind
Creeps to the garden of the stars.
Past muddiness, the mind
Leaps to the edges of quintessence.
It can be stuck.
It can be scared.
It is ready to fall.
It is ready to fly.
It is ready to build its ladder rung by hammered rung atilt
    through the sky.

14. Flora Baum, Archaeologist

> Latent ista omnia, Luculle, crassis occultata et circumfusa tenebris, ut nulla acies humani ingeni tanta sit quae penetrare in caelum, terram intrare possit.
>
> Cicero, *Academica* 2.122.

When you dig a new subway
You turn up many old things.

The vestal virgin climbs
The Capitol and finds
Gibbon, Henry Adams, the Blue Guides.

I will fly over with my shovel.

Venus is drawn down by a swan.
The focused roses are not yet wan.
The books have not yet up and gone.

I will fly over on my shovel.

The classicist ascends
The Capitol and bends
To what a god or goddess sends.

When we test our new weapons
In the sky or under the earth . . .

15. Flora Baum, Geographer

From Carthage then he came.

Make it a desert. Make it a jungle
Where deeds sprout without words,
Words without meanings, meanings
That don't hold water. And yet
The aqueous glisten!

                Rome
Is my watery theme, a city
Of aqueducts, beside a river,
Not far from a sea, encompassing
That sea.

        Crossing the water,

On from Carthage he came,
Crossing the cold Alps,
Burning for Rome,

From Gaul he came —
Across the cold Alps —
Burning,

From Athens —
Not yet near Cilicia —
He burned,

Burning for Rome.

16. Flora Baum, Student

20 G is the score —
Twenty years as a graduate student: to live
For twenty years fetching the freshest drops
Of learning in a Danaid sieve.

17. Roma

> Scito enim me, postea quam in urbem venerim, redisse cum veteribus amicis, id est, cum libris nostris, in gratiam.
>
> Cicero to Varro from Rome,
late 47 or early 46 B.C.

Where are all the images?
The owl has gone from the pine.
The blossoms have gone from the Norway maple, the sycamore
    maple, the ailanthus.
The vina has been sold.
The recorder players have moved away.
The drilling has stopped.
The subway has not started.

On a noon in July the fire escape
Is lined with mica, diamonds, ice,
Such is the sun.

Among Cicero's letters to his friends
Is the one which he wrote to Varro from Tusculum
On July 10 or 11 in the year 45 B.C.
With it he sent his present,
The four books of the *Academics*,
In which, as the letter explains,
Varro and Cicero talk.
In the future we will talk, the letter adds
(I translate or, at least, I paraphrase),
And would that we could carry on our studies
                                           In peaceful

In peaceful times, though then we would be called
To other, public duties. As it is,
Why do we wish to live except for study?

By July 14 some ailanthus fruits
Are bright green, some brick red,
Some, closer, gently brushed with rose
Between their elegant twists.

The month of Quintile was called July
Even in the announcement of the games
Given by Brutus for the Romans in 44.
I went to Nesis on the 8th before the Ides,
Cicero wrote to Atticus two days later.
Brutus was there. How unhappy he was
About the Nones of July. He was terribly upset.

Who inserted July
Where Brutus intended Quintile?

The tyrant is dead,
The tyranny lives,
Cicero had written in April.

Come to our help, by the gods, as soon as you can,
He would write to Brutus the next year, 43,
On July 14 (the 2nd Ides of Quintile),
And persuade yourself that on the Ides of March,
When you freed your countrymen from slavery,
You did not help your country any more
Than you will help if you come quickly now.

Brutus could not come.
Antony and the new Caesar
Could not let Cicero live.
Cicero would never see his own triumph.

Is Cicero a man or a god,
Petrarch asked the old scholar.
Without delay, A god, the old man answered,
And realizing what he had said, A god,
He added, of utterance. Petrarch tells the story
In a letter to a friend.

                    Cicero's letters to his friends,
Melanchthon wrote (I translate or paraphrase),
Should never be out of the student's hands. No other
Book in Latin is more helpful to the young.
First, in an age when Latin is not a vernacular,
This book of letters is helpful for learning Latin.
Second, it is helpful for forming style.
Third, it is helpful in fashioning manners and morals,
For in Cicero the civility with which he treats his friends
Is wonderful. Fourth, these letters contain
The history of their times — the important times
Of Caesar's civil war. And, finally,
Since letters from Cicero's friends are also included,
Variety of character and talent
Can be displayed.

              Can any kind of prose
Be helpful to the poem? Into the lines
Rise flowers: snapdragons with their familiar strange
Blends of mauve and red and orange and yellow,
Lilies looking up through depths of sheen,
Unearthly lilies looking down. You stoop
For the blessing that gleams from their celestial faces.

Desire stirs. They resemble
Nothing so much as the goddess
Of desire. They do not move
But, motionless, still move.

Between the tune and the information
Flows a stream which touches both,
Descending from the mountains, shining
Silver, pink, and blue as the sun
Descends, catching the sun and the sky.

Desire and vision merge and separate.
Desire for vision stretches toward the hem
Of vision in ascent, desire ascends
Wildly far above the bittersweet
Point where cloud closed vision off or in.
The violin ascends, then flats and squeaks,
Then trembles higher, higher.
       Something may come
Down in the rain, some tune or information,
Sometimes the cloud itself.
       Aeneas walked
In cloud. Ulysses walked
In cloud.

   You stoop.
The scent of the lilies
Catches at the heart as much here
As an effluence from the stars.

The darkening prelude of the robin
Flows above the gleaming of the lilies
Before the evening star
      steps forth.

Aeneas did not recognize her
Until, as she was turning away,
She was lily, rose.
What does it do to your soul
To have Venus for a mother?
Why can't I see you, he cried.
She could have replied,
Because I've been up with Jove,
Making your way safe through Carthage,
Making your path sure to Rome.
       She told

She told him what he needed to know.
She put a cloud around him through which he could see.

Let me see him as I saw him,
As I saw him send him now.

Then he came,
Drawn by a tame
Swan. A game?
I asked his name.
The swan — the same —
Left me to blame,
Left me to shame.

Why should I not have asked?
Why should I not have known?

When I called
There was a silence
So quiet it was loud upon the air
Like a thunder of negation. Then he came.

When I asked
There was a silence.
He answered. It was thunder in the air,
The thunder of negation. Now you know.

Ulysses did not recognize her.
What is it like if Minerva is your friend?

I prayed in a grove outside the city —
A poplar grove sacred to Minerva.
Minerva threw about me a protective
Mist. And when I entered the city
She came as a young girl holding a pitcher
And told me how to accomplish my journey
Home. And when I reached my island
She threw a protective mist about me.
No one would know me. I did not know her.
We spoke. She told me it was my island.
She came as a shepherd holding a spear.

And then she was a goddess. Clever
You are, she said, and I am clever.

We stored my treasure in the cave by the harbor
And sat down under the sacred olive
Together to make our subtle, complicated plans.

She was splendid, tall, and strong — a goddess.
I prayed to the mighty owl-eyed goddess.
Together we sat beneath the tree and laughed.

She was held by warm Amor himself.
How could she coldly limit her desire?
If he could pass from ecstasy to sleep,
She, imbued with him, could not. She lit
The lamp. If he, seen, had to leave, what more
Than vision is the true end of desire?

Yet to reach Rome!
Yet to touch home!
Still to take flight!
Are these all sight?

In summertime the tyranny of brick
Recedes. The leaves of weedy trees enlarge,
By filling, space with greens that play, that live,
And shadows make a mirror of each wall.
At night a forest looms beyond the screens.
The nighthawk, a rare eagle in the skies,
Echoes hollow mountains in his cries.

I asked only to make
My notes exact,
My tune or information
What I wanted.
I wanted the notes of the vina
That swirled beneath
To draw me in. I asked
The sun to draw
Me up. High or low,
I wanted to know.

Just as scholia disappeared,
Notes are on their way out.

If I could find
Minute red petals.
If I could find
Great towering trees.
Can one seek the acorn and the oak?
Can one see the forest and . . .

                                       But can
I even see, let's say, the elm in July,
Its great streams spotted with gold
(Can I mine — can I pan — that gold?),
Or, say, the golden rain tree, now
Green-lanterned (it is still July),
Or, say, the stocky silver maple, green
And argent soaring from its sturdy base,
Aloof, aloft in rocketing ascent,

Or, say, the pin oak, glittering green gift
Of symmetry, or, say, the fern-leaf beech,
A cavern, a green temple, the cathedral
Ringing with verdant unheard hymns? And can
I hear just one green hymn or mouth
That psalmody or draw it deep
Within my ribcage or expand
To the elephant's grand summer trumpeting,
To the megalith's resounding ferny life?

On the berries of the mountain ash
A tinge of orange (it is only July),
A sunset, a night's melancholy,
A white taste of the snow
That is slowly breaking the trees
Was what I found. A robin
Stood attentive on the lawn,
Orange-breasting the heat of the evening.

I went further. I slipped my hands
Into long soft foxgloves. But when I came
To the bittersweet nightshade on its chain-link fence
I shrank from the yellow hypodermic needles.
Swifts flatted and squeaked among the roses of the sky.

Urbem, urbem, mi Rufe, cole et in ista luce vive —
The city, the city, my Rufus, cherish and in that light live,
Or should one say,
The city, the city, my Rufus, inhabit and in its light live,
Or should one say,
Rome, Rome, Rufus . . . , or say,
Rome, Rufus, Rome . . . , or say,
Rome, Rufus, cherish Rome and live in the light there,
Or maybe,
Rome, Rufus, live in Rome and really live,
Or maybe,
Rome is the place, Rufus,
Stay there and live in its light,
Or maybe,
Rufus, what matters is Rome,
Stay there and live in the light,
As Cicero said, writing from Cilicia,
To Marcus Caelius Rufus in Rome?
It was June in the year 50.
The same letter worried about disturbances in the city
At the time of the Quinquatrus. Cicero's most recent news
From Rome was three months old.

As I've often said in my letters, peace
Can't last even a year,
Caelius Rufus wrote from Rome
To Cicero in August.
The closer the inevitable conflict comes,
The clearer is the danger.
What those who are in power are going
To fight about is this:
Pompey won't consent to Caesar's
Becoming consul without giving up

                                                  His army

His army and provinces. Caesar is sure
He can't be safe if he leaves his army;
Nevertheless, he makes the proposal
That both of them give up their armies.
I don't think it escapes you, Caelius says
Later in the letter, that when there are opposing sides
On domestic issues, as long as force is not used,
People should adhere to the better side,
But when it comes to war they should choose the stronger.
If it could be without danger, the letter ends,
What fortune is preparing would be
A great and fascinating show.

Si ille Romam modeste venturus est —
If HE to-Rome modestly going-to-come is:
If Caesar is going to use restraint
When he gets to Rome
It is all right for you to stay home
At present, but if
He is going to act like a madman and give
The city over to plunder
I'm afraid that Dolabella himself
Won't be able to help us,
Cicero wrote to Terentia, his wife,
And Tullia, his daughter,
From Minturnae, January 23,
In the year 49.

I hope you'll be at Rome when I get there,
Caesar wrote to Cicero in March,
So that as always I may make use
Of your advice and influence in everything.
Know that nothing is more congenial
To me than your Dolabella.
The letter arrived on March 26,
And Cicero sent Atticus a copy.

Caesar arrived in person two days later.
In eo   mansimus   ne   ad urbem —
In this   remained-we   not   to the-city:
I held firm in my determination
Not to go to Rome,
Cicero wrote to Atticus that same day.

More than a year had passed.
It was May of 48,
Three months before Pharsalus,
When Dolabella wrote from Caesar's camp
To Cicero in Pompey's.
Since Pompey's situation now is hopeless,
He said (more lengthily and elegantly),
I beg you at long last to be a friend
To yourself rather than to anyone else.
You have done enough already
For duty and for friendship.
You have done enough also for your party
And that republic which seemed best to you.
It remains for us to be where the republic is now
Rather than, while we adhere to the old one, to be in none.

Scito enim me, postea quam in urbem venerim —
For know that I, after I came into the city, —
Redisse cum veteribus amicis, id est, cum libris nostris, in gratiam —
Was reconciled with my old friends, that is, with my books,
Cicero wrote to Varro from Rome
In late 47 or early 46,
After the years away.
Varro had not yet returned,
But Cicero said a bit later in the letter:
They summon me back to the old intimacy
And say that you, because you held to it,
Were wiser than I.

Musa, mihi causas memora — Muse, tell me the reasons
Why the desirer of flowers and trees, the desirer of gardens —
Why my heroine must undergo such terrible dangers,
Why my heroine must undertake such burdensome labors,
Why my heroine must struggle so toward Rome.

Marble to her was white
Except for faint pink inlays on the landings
And columns of Siena stuff that stood
Large and benign between the ranks of the old
Clacking card catalogue and the long
Clicking circulation desk — columns
Which were marble of gold.

A temple must be built —
Not just cut of sky,
Not just marked with trees (as Varro says),
Not just dedicated to this god or that —
Seething with the numen of the known,
Humble as the herm, haughty as Juno,
Fat as Priapus, slim as any dryad,

Ancient and young as golden-haired Apollo,
Fragile and young as Hyacinth disporting,
Full of desire as something touched by Venus,
Gaunt as Narcissus or as Oedipus,
Then transformed to hero or to flower,
Powerful as Jove, skilled as Minerva.

Minerva did not kill her.
Arachne hangs there weaving

Temple, ocean, forest, hero, flower,
Mountain, tumulus, or constellation,
Wishing, or the wished-for, or the wish,
Web of desire, web of the known unknown.

All those things are hidden, Lucullus,
Surrounded and concealed by thick darkness,
So that no human mind, however keen,
Is keen enough to penetrate the sky
Or enter the earth, Cicero said in Book Two
Of the earlier edition of the *Academics*.

On a noon in July the fire escape,
Though black, is snow-white, white-hot, white,
Lightning of white.

You had your golden bough.
You could pass the columns of golden marble,
Penetrate the silver stacks of volumes,
Crawl into the white or yellow pages,
Glut yourself on ink and dust.

When your infant eyes opened
On the Empire State Building
Imprinting occurred.
The sky was not hurt by the needle.
The silver pencil wrote:
The sky's the limit.
The golden pencil wrote:
The limitless sky
Begins under (above) this point.
Your eyes opened.
But you moved eight hundred miles away
Though you were only three.

Out in Chicago the doctor
Stuck you with a needle. Soon you could breathe.
You were struck. You could grow up. You could be the doctor.
But you moved eight hundred miles away
Now that you were six.

You moved — let's face it — east to Queens.
The East River flowed on the west.
Let's walk west and see the East River.
Two tremendous bridges stretched on high.
You shouldn't say hell, but one was the Hell Gate.
The Triborough

The Triborough touched three parts
Of your quinquepartite city that touched the heavens.
The twins, Mary and Despy, talked about you in Greek.
We said you're a very nice girl.
You didn't go to Greek school.
You didn't go to Hebrew school.
You didn't go to Sunday school.
You didn't go to catechism.
You didn't say your prayers.
Diligent gibberish did
For your Greek, your Hebrew, and your prayers.
Or, uncomprehending, you could sing:
Dormez-vous,
Schlaf in himmlischer Ruh.
But how big is the sky?
Science hasn't measured it yet.
Once little Susan just jumped off the see-saw and you bumped
  to the cement.
Once the wide sidewalk just jumped up to hit you and you split
  your chin.
Once the gigantic willow lay in the sand.

Your prayer was the sky.
The needle was a pencil.
You played a little violin that squeaked.
Sohna layma teena.
Everyone has a story.

Can I remember
What the vina uttered?
Willow, river, ripple, sycamore, silver,
Path, grass, a lasting
Evening, green
In summer, under
The sycamores, silver, misty
By the river. And the willow? And the ripple?
I could not hear very well.
The willow, the lilies, a sliver
Like a willow's leaf, like a lily's petal in the sky.

Can I remember
What the vina uttered?
Skies, winds, oceans —
I could not hear very well —
Clouds, storms, undulations,
Undertow, the foam, the salt,
Slow soles on racing sands —

I could not hear —
The leap, unbroken by the breakers,
In accord, the accord,
The yes, not be it so,
But, oh, so that is it.
Can I remember?
Could I hear?
Will I wait?

The fire escape is a black
Balcony in Spain, the brick
Fortress a castle, a home,
The maples lapping the brick a garden.

Urbiculture, my Rufus . . .

If I don't know what I wanted to know,
The road is too long,
The names are too many,
The monsters are too frightening.
Was even Julius Caesar a monster,
As Cicero, using the Greek word, called him?

Joe, so far, did not like at all
The chapter that I sent.
Cicero, so close, whom I heard,
Just as we were about to converse,
Heard nothing, turned
And walked off through the forum.
The forum, silenced, turned
To dust. I was holding my mop.

A sparrow sang one endlessly
Reiterated note.
The stars, after all, from here are cold,
And they give little light.
The swan that came was a mute.
I stand and sway with my mop.
The mop is meant for floors of marble.
I play one note of brazen winter.

It wasn't your chapter that I didn't like,
Joe wrote to Flora;
It was merely the title, "Utroque Calle." Your chapter
Deals much more
With Varro's political and military moves than it does
With his life as a scholar.
It's only three thousand ninety-five miles by car.
We're thinking of driving.
We have till after Labor Day. That gives
Us plenty of time.
Last night the sun lazed on the Golden Gate.
Plus ultra?

Tu notitie rerum supra fidem deditus,
Petrarch wrote to Varro,
Non ideo actuose vite semitam declinasti,
Utroque calle conspicuus,
Et illis summis viris Magno Pompeio ac Iulio Cesari
Merito tuo carus —
You, devoted beyond belief to the knowledge of things,
Petrarch wrote to Varro,
Did not therefore turn aside from the path of the active life,
Distinguished for both ways
And to those eminent men Magnus Pompey and Julius Caesar
By your merit dear.

Modo nobis stet illud, una vivere in studiis nostris,
Cicero wrote to Varro,
A quibus antea delectationem modo petebamus,
Nunc vero etiam salutem . . . ,

                                                                                    Et, si

Et, si minus in curia atque in foro,
At in litteris et libris,
Ut doctissimi veteres fecerunt, navare rem publicam —
Let us be resolved to live together in our studies,
Cicero wrote to Varro,
From which, before, we sought only delight
But now also salvation . . . ,
And, if not in the senate house and in the forum,
Yet in writing and reading,
As the most learned ancients did, to serve the republic . . . .

He wrote from Rome in April, 46.
A few days before
He had written: However wretched these times are,
And they are most wretched,
Our studies somehow seem to bear richer fruit
Than they used to bear.
But, he concluded, why do I send these musings
To you, at whose home
They are born — like sending an owl to Athens? Only,
Of course, for you
To write something back and expect me. So please do.

If light from the river kept ascending like smoke
Up the trunks, on the branches, through the leaves,
If stripes from the ripples kept marching across the cliff,
If the swan suddenly stood and shook out his wings,
If the roses slowly shook out their wings,
If I shook out my wings,
My wings were shaking.

Desire, like flight,
Not silent like the roses' winging
But loud, louder than doves' winging,
Louder than the swan's winging,
Groans all through you the vibrating groan,
The cello's, no, the airplane's groan,
Whether from without or from within
It is hard to say. It is within,

And it

And it is without like the ocean,
And you're climbing high on a violet ocean
As if a plain brown hill
Seethed suddenly, subtly with heather.
As if a mist made new shapes in the world,
As if one walked between the bright
Of heather and the cloud come close,
As if one kissed another in the mist,
Just barely kissed, and the very bright
Hid above one's cloud. The heather's bright
Was longing's bright, not brightness's.

In March of the year 43
Cicero wrote to Quintus Cornificius,
The poet, governor of Africa:
On the Quinquatrus
Before a crowded senate I pleaded your cause
Not without the good will of Minerva,
For on that very day the senate decreed
That my Minerva, guardian of the city,
Knocked down in a storm, should be restored.
Although a greater storm would knock him down
Before the end of the year, Minerva knew
What he had known. She set his image up,
Displayed his weavings. Non invita Minerva,
Others would know what Cicero had known.

In her bright eyes tears.
In his large heart cares.
Gods regarding earth.
Venus speaking: Jove,
Holder of the bolt,
Flora gapes so with desire,
Shall she go unsatisfied,
Shall she never enter Rome?
Longing so renowned will not
Meet mere mockery: Jove spoke.

I'd like you to know
That once back in the city
I got close again to my old friends,
My books, Cicero wrote to Varro from Rome.

That . . . these between us studies exercise
We could . . . together could pursue these studies . . .
These studies that we share . . . now, however,
What is without these why to live we would wish . . .
Devoted beyond belief to the knowledge of things . . .
Dedicated to the pursuit of knowledge . . .
You took both paths, conspicuous in both . . .
On both . . . for both . . . distinguished in both ways . . .
Contemplative and active . . . dear to both
Pompey and Caesar . . . why do we wish to live . . .
More beyond . . . Minerva not unwilling . . .
It cannot be said how I burn with desire for the city . . .
Live in the city . . . letters . . . books . . . to serve
Republic . . . public thing . . . the constitution . . .
The form of government . . . the state . . . affairs
Of state . . . the welfare of the state . . . admire . . .
Inhabit . . . till . . . cherish . . . court . . . desire.
You who abound in words, how would you put it?

But in the future, Varro, we will talk
At length, if it seems like a good idea . . .

Urban rose, urbane
Despite the dust and wind,
Struggling through the rain
Into the refined
Oh, the rose's oh,
Red and yellow oh, oh, oh,
Out to the hot-sunned
Ah, to comprehend —
Tantae molis erat —
Ah, the sun was hot —
Such great work it was —
Ah, the bee must buzz —
Such hard work it is to understand.

Work of fire? Fire of joy?
Fire of straw? Fire of artifice?
Fire of heaven? Fatuous fire?

To me Venus,
Daughter of Jove,
Wife of Vulcan,
Mistress of Anchises,
Mother of Aeneas,
Ancestress of Julius Caesar, said
Warmly, touching my hot mind:
The very gods must pity
This yearning and vacuity,
Your crippled rush along a pitted road,
Your unarmed battle with the armored clouds
Darkening sky, eye, hill, will, plain, and brain.

For you my husband, the ignipotent,
Who, while the cows were grazing in the forum
And thick woods bristled on gold Capitol
(The period: twelfth century B.C.),
Fashioned the gleaming arms with which my son
Won and prefigured Rome,
Has made new weapons for the ancient war,
Firebrands for the fight
Against an outer and an inner dark.
Florula, Faustula, keep burning.

Too much has been pseudepical.

Virgilias bear tatters.

The secret name is Amor, or Desire.

Yielding their secrets
The rosebuds spread
Their apricot sails,
Their peach-rose-dawn wings into the wind.
                                                They stretched

They stretched to every edge
Without uncentering.
They found without a doubt
Fulfilment not disintegration.

I arrived outside the city on January 4,
Cicero wrote to Tiro on January 12
(It was the year 49). Everyone
Went out to meet me on the road. Nothing
Could have given me greater honor. But I fell
Into the very flame . . .

The road goes on. I will go on
Through the dust plying my mop.
I will fly over on my mop.
What is this antiquated dust?

Through the exhausted air
The city is blooming, purple and blue,
And green and yellow and orange and red,
Blooming, abloom, with white and black, with books.

Part Two

Floralia

Floralia

You start in April, cross to times of May.
Ovid, *The Calendar*.

. . . the kind of thing referred to by Virgil's Aeneas when he says: We sail out of the harbor, and lands and cities recede.
Copernicus, *The Revolutions*.

But why, when white is worn for Ceres' feast,
Does Flora choose a many-colored gown?
Ovid, *The Calendar*.

Virgilias' luxuriant brown rags,
Mingling with gold leaf here and there, suppose,
Supplant, the pearls that dangled here in green
And silver. Pearls are pearls. Find them again,
September. Reinvent them, western sunset.
Among green leaves leaves are shining like flowers.

Glow: bits of red on tupelo, sassafras, red maple,
Sprinklings of orange in sugar maple's voluminous green,
Lemon on linden, on locust, honey on honeylocust,
Either on elm, box elder, tulip tree,
Crimson, purple, bronze, gold, lemon on ash — ash.
This is just the beginning, fall's spring, September.

Great Virgil died September twenty-first
(The eleventh before the Kalends of October),
19 B.C., wanting his great work burned.
He was almost fifty-one. When Caesar crossed
The Rubicon Virgil was only twenty.
He was only almost seven in 63,
When, Cicero and Antonius being consuls,
On the ninth before the Kalends of October
(Julian — the eighth, pre-Julian —

September

September twenty-third) a little before
Sunrise, Gaius Octavius was born.
Octavius, calling himself Caesar, was twenty

And Virgil, called a new poet, was twenty-seven
When Cicero, called an old enemy, was killed.
The new Caesar could not let Cicero live.
But was not Rome eternal flowering?

The thesis, the precise anthesis:
The rags, the pearls, the cultivation.
One April twenty-eighth the sugar maple
Was hung with little strings.
September twenty-third: the sugar maple
Blossomed with little sunsets.

To be autumnal is not my intent.
Why can one think of April in September
And not of mellow fall in darling May?
A mockingbird emotes among red berries.
The sowing farmer surely dreams of harvest.
Some see the future and some see the past.
Some gather and some contemplate the flowers.

Flowered lands and cities receded.
Passed by islands and shadow islands,
Passing clouds and shadow clouds,
Clearing waves reduced to ripples,
Clearing ripples immobilized by distance,
I crossed a steel ocean.
I lost a green Europe
And found a brown America.
That was the azured passage
That was a matter of hours.
That was the rippled distance
From Ireland's edge to Newfoundland's.
What is the stretch of the hours
Between new-green Massachusetts
And old-brown Rome,
Between green Rome and browning Massachusetts?

Fall's pentameters press and oppress.
If it is this fall
Is it pentametric? It is
A blaze here, a flash
There, a cool morning, a hot
Afternoon, the song
Of bugs at night, the desert-blue
Descant hovering above
Proliferating melodies of day,

Tears of things or civilization,
History or Juno's anger,
Heroism or a flower,
Green or red or orange or gold or brown,
Green and red and orange and gold and brown.

Among the not mentioned: the yellows on a red maple.
Among the not stressed: the dominance of green.
It is still September, a month
Which people wanted named August.

Augustus, born (in September)
Gaius Octavius, son of Gaius Octavius,
Made Gaius Julius Caesar Octavianus,
Adopted son of Gaius Julius Caesar,
Declared Augustus, gave his latest name
Not to the month of his birth but to the month
Of that first, invaded consulship, to the month
Of great victories, which was to be the month
Of his death. When he died in August one man proposed
That the name of August be given to the month of his birth —
What others had wanted twenty-one years before.

What if we had to speak
Of awful August as hot humid Sextile?
How could we designate
September's pleasant weathering as August's?

September stayed September. One may cross
Melodiously from gently strummed September
Into October's subtly tuned flamboyance.

October, oh, October,
Red depth, orange breadth, blue height,
October, oh, October,
All gold and fire and light,

October, momentous luminousness
Of elm and sky, bright breathing
Body, lucent spiring spirit,
Yellow, blue (say, azure, gold)
Of aerial elm, aetherial sky,
Bold, definite, indefinite, incandescent,
Gold, azure, finite, intimating only
Infinities of fiery white, gigantic
Intimate blue and yellow lambency
Perceived, felt, held, absorbed, not intimated,

October, portentous numinousness
Of pulsing color, colors, not white light,
Not one, a multitude, the many, all,
So truly brilliant-resonant the trees
With names and faces through the leaves,
Transcendent, immanent, or human,

The blue-gold marriages of branch and sky,
A Jove in oaks with hints of or and gules
And in the green-gold-bronze American beech,
Auricomous Apollo in the elm,

Corydon's Alexis,
Miles away, golden Joe,
Thomas's green-clad Anthe,
Years away, silver Will,
Amaryllis' Tityrus,

For whom the bough calls,
For whom bright foliage stays or falls,

Tityrus' Amaryllis,

Virgilias silver-boughed and golden-leaved,
Virgilias silver-limbed and golden-tressed,
Euonymus hedge like fire of rose,
Euonymus bush like rose of fire,
The variations on a theme of orange
Suffusing orbs of sugar maple, good
On gray and best on blue, shooting along
The barberry hedge, fall's frenzy taking voice
In the mockingbird's silver throat, taking wing
With the honeylocust's gold feathers, taking fire
Above the euonymus from the red sparks
Of dogwood, pin oak, red maple, bursting
Above the euonymus into flame's blossom,
The orange-rose of sugar maple,
The purple-rose of ash,

The fifteenth of October, the Ides, the birthday
Of Virgil, a Monday — which Virgil never knew.
You, Tityrus, all day, wandering,
May meditate the brilliant autumn muse
Through our famous fall, and all day we —
Some of us coupled with hard machines,
Some with soft slimy mops,
Some with sharp syllables sundered from every significance —
Must be chained in the thickest towers,
Removed from air, light, color, trees, and flowers,
Our feet fettered, our hands tied, our eyes bound,
Our backs hunched, our hearts crushed, our minds ground
Into the ground under the sub-sub-basement.
It was gray at nine as we stumbled over the threshold,
Blue at noon as we stuck out our noses a moment and munched,
Blue and white at five as a shadow
Not of cloud, of time, lay chill
And will not be evaded unless you can stand
As tall as the great gold fountain sunburst of the elm.

Yet if the sun again
Will reach meridian,
Yet if the earth, its air
Intact, will turn some more . . .

Upon an ancient instrument
You, Tityrus, may play.
The tenuous tune that you invent
Stretches into a day—

Sunday, October twenty-first.
The honeylocust glows
With golden glamor softly nursed
On air that soft through softness flows,

Floats gold through gold yet undispersed,
Yet multitudes in gold repose,
Yet one gold princess fully versed
In elegance, not yet in prose,

Not yet in winter, not in exigent
Crass Monday. What more can you say?
I, Tityrus, have gone to Rome, intent
On liberty. A god has given May.

What god, if I may ask, did you adore?
Rome was, I thought, a city like the cities that we know—
Boston, New York, Chicago, San Francisco. It is more
Like the Big Tree or Bristlecone Pine that has grown and will grow,
Buds and is ancient. Here I saw one young and old and fair
And tough and venerable that said in answer to my prayer:
Both make it new and go on as before.

October fifteenth, the Capitol, Rome.
A man sitting.
Some men singing.
A temple. Evening.
A church. Vespers.
Friars singing.
Gibbon sitting.
History. 1764,
October fifteenth, the Capitol, Rome.

Magnificat.
Deposuit.

Doth magnify.
He hath deposed.

Every October fifteenth
We would read in the Saint Andrew Daily Missal
(The one with the map of Rome in the front
Showing the forty-five stational churches)
That St. Teresa died during the night
Of October fourth to fifteenth, 1582.
What had become of October fifth to fourteenth?
The Gregorian date replaced the Julian —

At least in Italy, Portugal, France, and Spain.
The Pope had done it.
And so Teresa's heavenly birthday
Was celebrated on Virgil's earthly one.
Bright leaves above, loud leaves beneath,
We tramped off for her feast.

Exsultavit.
Hath exulted.

Exaltavit.
Hath exalted.

John Adams, second president
Of the United States of America,
Was born in Braintree (later Quincy), Massachusetts,
A two hour's walk, his great-grandson would say, from Beacon Hill,
October thirtieth, 1735,
New style; that is, Gregorian;
That is, October nineteenth, old style; that is, Julian.
Compare the better-known birth date of George Washington,
The twenty-second of February, 1732,
New style, that is, but what was called
In London, at Oxford, at Cambridge, and by Pope's Creek, Virginia,
The eleventh of February, 1731,
In a part of the year that could be designated,
More internationally, 1731/2,
The way Conduitt tells us that Newton died in 1726–7,

Newton,

Newton, who was born on Christmas day
(In England), as perhaps Augustus was
(By sun and stars) in Italy, for though
The date was, by pre-Julian reckoning,
The eighth before the Kalends of October,
We know Augustus was born under Capricorn.
But when exactly did the traveling sun,
By Julian or Gregorian reckoning,
Reach Capricorn less than a century after Hipparchus?
And was the year three months off in 63
As it was in 46? It's hard to know.
It was off, one could say, by only ten days
When Isaac Newton was born in December
Of (Julian) 1642,
The year that Galileo died
In Italy, where the year was not off, though other things were.
It was off, one could say, by eleven days
When John Adams opened his eyes on a Massachusetts October.
Were the oaks still red? Were the dogwoods ruby?

A baby. The eighteenth century. What was known
Of October's gorgeous melancholy,
Of a nation not yet born?
In October, 70 B.C.,
Pompey and Crassus held the consulship.

October twenty-third of 42:
The first battle of Philippi.
Philippi over, it was 41.
Amaryllis' Tityrus.
Miles away, golden Joe.
Tityrus' Amaryllis.
Elizabeth Sherman Cameron.
How many miles from Tahiti?
October in Paris, 1891.
Henry Adams, historian, aged fifty-three.
Elizabeth Cameron, almost thirty-four, with Martha, aged five.
Henry Adams, May 19, 1860,
Aged twenty-two, in Rome,

Reading

Reading Gibbon in Rome,
Struck by Gibbon in Rome.
October 17, 1860,
Back, back in Quincy, Massachusetts,
In time for the election of November sixth.

Flora Baum in Cambridge, Massachusetts.
Oaks red or green-gold-bronze or oaken brown,
Ginkgoes pure gold in the waning of October.
Waiting for the election of November sixth.

Kerensky planned elections in November.
Thirteen days off in 1917.
What bemused us in the seventh grade?
The October Revolution in November.

Old. November is old.
Its dawns are old.
Its noons are half dead.
At five our days commence with night.
Hurry, turn on the light.
Life is ahead,
Life begins in an old
Volume, just unrolled.

Or rush back to the treasury alone —
And there under some clouds the great old one —
The elm, leafless, lovely, before the moon.

The treasures on loan.
Open! For soon
Each leaf, each side, will be a sun.

On the evening of the first,
Wrote Cicero to Atticus on November second or third, 44 B.C.,
A letter reached me from Octavian.
He has great plans. Cicero gives details,
Then adds: His goal is clearly leadership

And war with Antony. And so I think
In a few days we'll be in arms.
But whom are we to follow?
Think of his name. Think of his age.

He was just nineteen. His name?
Cicero terms him Octavian now,
But on April twenty-second of that year
He had written to Atticus from his villa at Puteoli:
Octavius, very respectful and very friendly, is with me here.
His friends are calling him Caesar, but Philippus is not, and so I
    am not either.

Philippus was his stepfather —
Lucius Marcius Philippus, consul in 56.
His mother was Atia, daughter of Julia,
Sister of Gaius Julius Caesar,
Consul (for the first time), with Marcus Calpurnius Bibulus,
In 59, the year that people called
The consulship of Julius and Caesar,
The year when Gaius Octavius turned four.
Before he turned five his father was dead at Nola
On the way home from governing his province
Without time even to run for the consulship.
And now death had given young Gaius a third father
Consul (for the fifth time), with Marcus Antonius (Antony),
In 44, until the Ides of March.
As 44 and 43 run on
Cicero's letters call him boy, youth, young man,
Octavius, Octavian, Caesar Octavian, Caesar.
In 43, in August (that is, Sextile),
The new son will be consul as well as Caesar.

By 41 — we guess it's 41
And know it's some time after 42
And think it cannot be too long thereafter
(Compare on this the many commentators) —
Virgil's Tityrus calls him a god.

November eleventh. Noon. Lead plates the sky.
Through this third-story pane
The weedy Old World maples gleam, no, shine,
Illumine, gold in the rain.

The veterans of Philippi
Must have land for pay.
But, Tityrus, you may stay
On your land and play
Your pipe under your sky.

Floralia, or, Virgilian Notes.

Pardon me, Virgil, for my rendering,
A homage decomposing great to small,
A center that may fall to deconstruction,
A thesis that may miss interpretation.
And no songs can a Meliboeus sing.

How many days off?
November twelfth.
A free morning.
One's own afternoon.
Corydon. Flora Baum.
Sat singing in Arcady.
Went weeping through Arcady.
Not Tahiti. November. Ascending
The golden layers of the fern-leaf beech.

Corydon pursued Alexis.
Flora followed Corydon.
Drawn is each one by his pleasure.
Drawn is each one by her joy.
Corydon desired Alexis.
Flora studied Corydon.

Corydon is a piece of paper.
But what was Will? And who,
Flora Baum, were you, pursuing him
For seven years? He was May,
Violet, oak, down there purple,
                              Up there

Up there gold. You offered him
This gift: to be yourself
A piece of paper
Not in his library,
Not in his mailbox,
Not under his eyes,
Not under his feet.
His hair turned gray. Nothing
To do with you.

Corydon is a piece of papyrus.
Corydon is a pan-pipe, seven
Hemlock stalks with wax compact.
Corydon is the seven notes,
The tune bruising (perhaps) the lips.
He will not mind.
The tune is softer than a kiss,
Papyrus stronger than the long embrace.

Among the shady beeches Corydon
Addressed, alone, the mountains and the woods
Though cruel Alexis was his vocative.
Though Will once walked, urbane, among the trees,
Still, Flora's unsophisticated song
Was thrown, alone, unnoted, to the trees.

What if Flora
Stole the notes
Meant for Alexis?

In her garden, all together,
Lily, violet, and poppy,
Daffodil and dill and cassia,
Hyacinth and marigold,
Laurel (Cynthian) and myrtle (Cytherean).
In her garden violet black and violet white.

Pedantic golden wanted Flora lines.
But let her beg or borrow, let her steal,
Storm Athens, Rome, or Cambridge, she will find:

Minerva cultivates the city. I
Have let a wild wind into my flowers,
A wild boar into my springs.

Am I to think of him
And he not think of me? —
Think — is that the word? —
Of — is that the preposition?

"To" alone can govern
That object, masculine personal
Pronoun, masculine person
To whom — my throat half modulating

The air waves with the proper
Noun, his name, O Joe,
O Joe — improperly,
My molecules, ungoverned, rush.

The eighteenth of November's
Fallacious images?
Gray. Orange. Brown.
Steel fixed across the late sky.
Barberry leaves pure drops of dawn.
One beauty in the leafless
Elms, living or dead.
With Amphion. Songs that built cities.
With me. These unbuilt songs.
With me. Mud. Brick. Stone.
With me. Bugs once harmonized.
A brown beauty builds through the elms.

Noon. November twenty-second.
Thursday. Thanksgiving. Thestylis out
Chopping in the kitchen with the turkey.
Others — the holiday crowd — out
Under the tender sun
That crests a shadowless serene,
Where the purple beeches, gold
Above their thickening coppery shadows,
                                                    Thin.

Thin. The more sun. The more
We wade in their shade, dispersing
Their tangible shadows, plowing their shadows.

Delicious dinner downed, all dishes done,
There's time to play an amoebean game.
Menalcas, if you win, this cow I'll give.

Damoetas, if you win, beech cups I'll give
Carved with chronologies and calendars,
With signs of Varro and Sosigenes.

Three or four leaves look chilly on their branch.
They quiver, seem to shiver, in the wind.

The sparrow's cheep sounds chilly in the wind.
He eats the black paint on the fire escape.

I had a bird, the sparrow has a tree
To feast upon. Sparrow and I have song.

If gratitude must rule over my song,
Pity and fear must . . . There a jay glints blue.

A greater poet than a Pollio
Has rendered Pollio now doubly great.

Poor Bavius and Maevius, whom great
Poets condemned. May their lot not be mine.

To love the Muses — love their music — is
To hate both Bavius and Maevius.

To love a Bavius, a Maevius,
Means surely: love the poet, not the poem.

Jove is the inspiration of my song.
He gazes from blue skies upon gray trees.

Apollo comes himself among the trees.
He sings them into silver, into gold.

The dry, drab samaras glow gold in sun,
Burning in their celestial aperture.

Between brick walls the azure aperture
Expands the vertical to infinite.

A little greater.
Cows. Cups.
Calendars. Consuls.
Cicero: Nothing
Flowers forever.
Poems. Prophecies.
Virgil: The white
Flowers fall,
The black are gathered.
Sunday, November
Twenty-fifth: The privet
Hedges are black
On Craigie Street.
A little greater.
Something between
Now and eternally.
Something between
Here and infinity.
Greater. A little.
The gold between.

Do I trivialize the virgilias?
Here is one carved with a yellow heart,
With two yellow names.

Everyone doesn't like trees.
Some complain because they breathe
Our oxygen. What ramifications
Of oaks, of beeches, maples, elms,
Virgilias can be great enough
That their great trees
May breathe upon our arms talks, leaf
Into peace over East and West?

                              The consul
Pollio, friend of the dead Caesar,
Supporter of Antony, went to Brundisium.
Maecenas, friend of the young Caesar,
Went to Brundisium. Antony went
To Brundisium. Caesar (Octavian) went.
For Antony and Octavian war
Was likely. The conference seemed to leaf
Into peace between East and West.

                              The year
Was 40 B.C.

             Have I got it straight?
Antony sailed from the East
To Brundisium, blockaded the town.
Octavian marched from the West
To Brundisium, camped near Antony.
Mediators (Lucius Cocceius Nerva,
Gaius Asinius Pollio, Gaius Maecenas)
Arranged a peace — and a marriage, not of Octavian,
Who just recently, fearing war
With Sextus, the great Pompey's son,
Had married Pompey's son's wife's father's sister,
But of Octavian's sister with Antony.

Under your leadership, Pollio, Virgil sang
(In 40 B.C., when Pollio was consul
And mediator of that year's great peace),

The last age of Cumaean song has come.
The virgin is returning to the land
Of Saturn with the nascent child of Jove,
Bringing from deepest sky an age of gold.
Silver Diana, soothe the baby. Gold
Apollo rules the baby's world. O Jove,
Let me please live to signal to the land
The scarlet, saffron, crimson joy to come.

Or was the child the one the virgin bore,
God's son, whom Sibyl and Isaiah saw,
As Constantine, Augustine, Dante knew?
Please let me live to sing of peace come true
Reaching from heaven to earth, from earth to law,
The form of things unknown, the somewhat more.

Or was the child, the increment of Jove,
Saluted by the bowing of the round
Universe — lands, tracts of sea, profound
Skies — not a god's though chosen, but the son
That surely would be born in 39,
The Julius, the Antonius to arrive?

In 39 two children were born — not sons:
Julia to Octavian (Gaius Julius Caesar) and Scribonia,
Antonia to Antony (Marcus Antonius) and Octavia.
But who in the year of the consulship
Of Gnaeus Domitius Calvinus and Gaius Asinius Pollio
Knew what would happen in the consulship
Of Lucius Marcius Censorinus and Gaius Calvisius Sabinus?
Who in 714 A.U.C. (a year of the years
From the founding of the city as counted by Atticus and Varro)
Knew what would occur in 715?
Who in 40 B.C.
Knew what would take place in 39,
Knew it was B.C.?

In December, A.D. 1984,
Who knows . . . January 1985?

Shorn days. Sheared trees. More and less shadow.
One sees the silver maples red.
One sees the sycamore maples green.
Two weeks from now the shadow
Will contract, the day expand.
And then — just wait — the shadow
Will be good, the trees expand,
Shadiness bless.

    Will the human
Hurricane, the virile volcano,
The earthy furies even of mother and wife
(As Fulvia fomented war
In fury for her Antony)
Uproot, choke down, even merely
Chop down, merely hack
Earth's oaks, earth's beeches, maples, elms,
Virgilias?

    Sunday, December 9. There is
Something funny about the Advent light.
The sky so blue — a Hellenic blaze — you expect
Pentelic reverberation, Parian
Reply. A kind of gold on boughs, on bricks,
Thin wintry wash of goldish waiting, made
Aural by the plainchant of the sparrows,
Answers the unseasoned empyrean.
Come through that surely viable purity,
That undeniable holiness of blue,
That surely permeable connecting land,
Entrancing space abutting earth and heaven.
Come through, if there is anything to come.

Do I go beyond the evidence?
A yellow heart confronts that blue,
A wooden heart bared on the branch
Of the yellowwood, worn on the sleeve
Of Ms. Baum, who would not touch a tree
But recognizes something in the gash,
Something exposed to the sky's intensity,
Something to which something comes from the sky,
Someone to whom someone, with his hands
Outstretched, comes flaming. With his hands?

The virgin returns. Apollo reigns.
Jove's child is born. And Saturn's age,
Renascent, flourishes. Not skeletal black
On rued deep deepening blue,

          Since

Since the sun has run away
So rudely, coldly, frivolously;

Not Christmas lights like constellations
Replacing the departed leaves
On dark Commons as people trudge home
From getting and spending, holding the got
With the spent; not a restrained morning,
At brightest a quintet with strings
And eighteenth-century clarinet;
Not the sighing of samaras
In shaking bunches between the weakly sunned
Towers of brick, gold though those clusters
Hang, fat clumps of thin,
Juiceless, papery grapes, consumed
(It seems, for they persist) not even
By squirrels, whirled at intervals,
One by one, reluctantly
(It seems, so many more persist
Fixed aloft), by the north wind's will
In through the screens to nestle in corners
Of windowsills with soot and bits
Of the building's or the city's disintegration;
Not the Washington thorns' haws'
Sweet rubricity, waiting
As haws wait, small, collected,
Neatly huddled, trimly bunched,
In the gray, damp, bitter air
For the suave, portended, complementary whitening;
Not, on the morning of December twenty-first,
Winter's arrival at eleven twenty-three,
Duly announced with the winter storm watch;
Not, on the evening of December twenty-first,
Snowflakes' arrival on the Boston Common,
Duly confirmed by the *Nutcracker*'s staging
(And can you also, all you little ones,
With your ruffles or your velvet jackets, dance
In the snow that falls so softly to the stage,
And can you also, you who are mature,

Brushing

Brushing the week from shoulders, out of hair,
On Friday night, make those impassioned leaps?);
Not those impassioned leaps; not our white steps
From the hall to the subway; not the three,
One with crutches laid across our path,
Who sat grinning on the sidewalk as we came
Through the first few flakes, who were gone
As we went through the thickened visitation;

And not the sevenfold great Latin O
That resonated not so long ago,
Seventeen, eighteen, nineteen years or so,

And not the sevenfold strong Latin Come
To teach, redeem, free, lead, enlighten, come
To save, come save us, Wisdom, Root, Key, come,

Those Latin songs at dusk: O dawn
And brightness of eternal light,
Come and illumine those who sit
In darkness and death's shadow (Night

Being so close we waited for Today);
Today, American, three hours away,
Not in Tahiti, not in Samoa — not even that,

That day marked on the calendar,
Not quite today, an eve all day,
Transition, parade on the runway, procession,

With pointed orange flags flying by the yellow grass,
Without any snow, without any business, although
The Business Express precedes us on line
As we pursue huge arrows, scream,
Grumble, jump, ascend, look down
On skyscrapers, find
Ourselves at right angles to the sea,
To a sea of cloud, not going to sea,
Although we have our life jackets handy,
But straightening over a great incursion of land
Called Massachusetts–Rhode Island, guessing New York's
                                                    Glory

Glory obscured in cloud,
Not at sea, not on business, not leaving our land,
Just quasi hopping over
To Tusculum, Puteoli, Pausilypum,
Not in the nautical pine, in the aerial plastic,
The aerial aluminum, wherein
We sit partaking of our grapes and cheese
Wrapped in plastic, our coffee to which we extend
Our plastic cups, our two chocolate mints,
Not going to sea but over the sea from Cape Fear,
Where blue sky, fearless, meets blue ocean
As we sit here like the reading hero reading
And glancing from our fortress in the air
Out upon the white and blue castles of cloud
Standing motionless over the lying motionless
Blue and silver and golden ocean
And glimpsing through embrasures in the sky
A whole cloud city in the sky,
Manhattan from Brooklyn Heights,
San Francisco from Sausalito,
Marble Rome with marble walls,
Marble cloud buildings, cloud hills, cloud distant mountain ranges,
Observing clouds like motionless explosions
Above an airy nothing, gaily greeting
Florida graciously coming out to meet us
As Carolina had shied away to the west,
Knowing, when the breakers begin to stir
And the skyscrapers turn vertical, that we're close,

Knowing, when four thirty p.m. is not dark,
Not even dusk, knowing, when you see green,
When you feel that first brush of sun and heat and breeze
And pass the shadowy banyans along the road,
That you've come, the miracle has recurred, knowing,
When you hear the solemn cheer of the priest: Tank God
For his birrth in your hearrts, welcome to those from Quebec,
It's the vigil of the nativity — not that,

Not, on December 25,
The muscovies' expectant hiss,
Doves' piping wings, doves' caroling wings,
The white easy flight of the egret, that, beyond the little bridge,
Alights on the verdant bank to fish,

Not the fishtail palm, the petticoat palm, the princess palm, the silver palm, the Christmas palm,
Not the sugar palm, the date palm, the oil palm, the thatch palm, the solitaire palm,
Not the cackle of a survivor, the coconut palm,
Not cypresses or cycads, not ficuses rooted in air,
Not the shady mahoe (you long for shade as you run
In sandals after your breeze-blown big straw hat),
With the big green circular fans
And crepe-paper flowers, yellow
Before noon, red before dusk,
On that big dark rounded tree,
Not the poinsettias reddening out in the garden,
Not the spreading yellow butterfly palm,
Not the jelly palm, the royal palm, the queen palm, the king palm, the cabbage palm,
Not the bottle palm that sits on the fit, fat grass,

Not the unbottled sun
Into which have been prettily dipped
The fine scarlet fibers of bottlebrush trees,

Not the bluer sky
Behind the green-winged leaves
And flying purple flowers of the bauhinia,

Not an etherial gleam
On delicate yellow petals,
The saffron of the fragile Jerusalem thorn,

Jerusalem in this green land —

Not even that, but some particular
Idea, certain golden notion
Must I live to sing.

A little greater.
Forty years later
(As counted, one might say, by Dionysius Exiguus),
When Caesar Augustus ruled the world
(As reckoned, one might say, from the city center of Rome):
The pastoral of Western civilization.
Shepherds with angels.
God among the cows.
Come! He came,
Stayed nearly two thousand years.
Came to Rome, stayed,
Lives there, one might say, still.

Jam noli tardare.
Now do not delay.

Hodie apparuit.
He hath appeared today.

Like stars, like angels, like the very gods
Before the megalopolitan night
Pastoral pales.

Yet, nymphs of Solyma, will you begin?
But what shall be the invocation?

Calliope, or is it the white splendor of Diana,
The suavity — brown, lustrous — of Irene,
Melanie's dark dulcitude,
Aurora's peach-gold-ochre,
Or Anthe with her ivory face
And the blush of the ivory rose? —
Muse, whether Sicilian nymph,
Olympian goddess, dryad, sibyl,
Or Anthe with her green silk gown,
Soft arms, slim fingers fingering
The stops, let us sing.

But will you harp or carp, she asked.
The truth, said Thomas, is
Sweetness to my tongue,

Sonance

Sonance to my ears,
Brightening my eyes,
Carved upon my heart,
Tugging ceaselessly upon my mind,
Ceaselessly elusive, ceaselessly
Unpossessed, by which I am possessed,
Something not for me, for which I am.

Speak then, she said, and speaking sing.
And so I began.

Who is Jove's child? Monstrosity!
The virgin shall not bear but be.
Daughter Minerva's is the age
Of knowledge, of the well-read page,
Well-studied universe, when man
And woman, academic, can
Under the rule of mind be we
And not the body's he and she,
When violent lust and martial rage
Yield to the passion of the sage,
Respect for what is and has been
And will be, freedom, discipline
Of self that gaily breaks the chain
(Crown or dunce cap) that clasps the brain,
Otium: leisure, peace. Machine,
Unfeeling, do the brute's routine.
Man, oh, like Jove, bear from the keen
Intelligence. Woman, be seen
Like Jove, who when he bears is clean.
Anthropos, know, think, live, serene.

And will
The cattle, fearless, meet the lions,
The lions cease to eat the cows,
The people cease to eat the cows,
The people have enough to eat,
Earth, smiling, give enough to eat
To lions, cattle, people? Yes,

        And Mars

And Mars and Venus, too, will give
Enough.

Enough! For this is not
My song, true Thomas cried,
Essential though it is.
Each has his song, he sighed,
Greater, lesser. Each has
Her song, Anthe replied.

And what about you, Flora? Can
You forget, among your flowers, famine?
No, I can't. I forget
More than I remember. I remember
More than I can tell.
Tears of ages, millennia
Of lacrimation,
Wailing oceans, continents
Of lamentation
Are here suppressed.

But why, the poet asked the goddess, why,
The poet Ovid asked the goddess Flora,
When robes of white are given at the feast
Of Ceres, is a many-colored gown
Your preference? Is it because the fields
Whiten with the ripened ears but all
Color and appearance is in flowers?
She nodded. At the movement of her hair
The flowers fell.

    There is a truth of white
Seen with a steady unrelenting stare.
There is a rainbow truth. The crocuses
Rush into gladdening spring though some each year,
As winter turns and shoots, must fall.

        Perhaps,
Said goddess Flora, you have thought my realm
One of sweet garlands only. My divine
         And kindly

And kindly power touches all the fields.
Threshed grain, pressed grape, rich olive oil, the green
Vegetable, honey itself depend
Upon my pretty blossoming.

                        The world,
The student thought, is manifold; the truth
Must flourish from the garden of the world,
Must nourish from the garden of the world.

The roseless thorn.
The bony hand.
The half-closed eye
To which the sky
Is torture. And
To wither, die,
Curled on the sand,
Almost before you're born.

Roses and bread.
That all could heed
And all be fed
And all could read
And all be read.

The rights of all male citizens
Must be protected first.
Women must wait. Their languid turn
Is likely to be next,
But one thing at a time, they said,
Even if yours comes last.

Sojourner Truth,
American sibyl,
Addressed crowds,
Spoke with presidents,
Went to register,
Was refused,
Went to the polls,
Was turned away.

Not butterflies, not nightingales,
Not mockingbirds, not meadowlarks,
Not bluebirds, blackbirds, swans, not elves,
Not fairies, angels, women, men,
On humble wings of tamarisk
We human spirits downward flew
Into the deep skies of ourselves.

All we golden spirits flew
With emerald and roseate wings
Where saffron and where sapphire skies
Welled within us,
Where the crimson melodies
Rung from all the jasper spheres
Belled within us.

Up and down were one,
Petals, pinions, one,
Melodies and harmonies,
Conflagrations and the cool
Spacious shade of trees.

How we loved the labyrinth,
How we loved the highway,
How we loved the solitary
Grassy path, the rocky altitudinous road,
The glancing web, the dangling thread.

In civil cases
The preponderance of the credible evidence
Spilled into the golden balance
Counts.
Did Minerva
Having conceived and produced the flute
Throw it away because it puffed out her
Cheeks?

The verdict: She could weave
Tunes as well as tapestries.

If not the whole, yet nothing but,
Say what you must, truth sang.
Each has a song, piped truth.
Or songs, truth trumpeted.

If I tell my truth,
If I sing my song,

If I tell the truth that I see,
If I sing the song that I hear,

Will Orpheus move trees,
Or Linus human hearts,

Or bright Apollo all the world
With greater sweetness and precision

Than that with which I touch
Someone known or unknown

Who knew, who knows, or who will know
A ringing, flaming leaf of sky?

Whether rhetorical questions
Are permitted in dissertations
I wonder. I don't ask.
My audience, I remember,
Consists of my thesis adviser,
Professor Edward Lane.
The flaming page is Virgil's, the flaming
Trumpet is his. Limping, I try
To run like a Hamelin child, to fly.

But mustn't you rake and hoe,
Get your hands a bit dirty,
Dig, plant, mine,
Set out over the ocean,
Plus ultra, plus, plus ultra?

Sunday, December 30. Somewhere,
High against a cerulean sky,
A tulip tree is blooming scarlet,
                              A bombax

A bombax blooms vermilion. There
You turn your head and sniff. The breeze
Brings a sweetness. With precision
(Varro will recall) you run
To where white flowers on their shrub,
Euphorbia leucocephalia, shine.
And in the pool the beautiful
Nymphaea, blue and yellow, floats.
Nymphs with blue eyes and yellow hair
Clearly frolic there.

                It's time
(If there is time) to think about
A northern new year's resolution
Good for gray ice, gray trees, gray sky,
Something scarlet or vermilion
To bloom against a nival sky,
To run along a ravous page.
And does that mean to write with blood?
Images, true Thomas said,
Are vegetable; they bloom and die
And live again above the wood,
Ancient and gray, of the trusty tree,
Live again, rejuvenate,
Differing and yet the same,
At youth's fountain, age after age.

What shall I resolve
Except to welcome Apollo?

What does that mean?

                The notes
For my thesis, of course.

                      Something
Seems wrong.

              Only the proof.

And Saturn, Jove, Minerva,
Diana, what do they mean?

The same.

        Something seems wrong.

Only the demonstration.
This is, keep in mind,
Merely the second stage,
The hero reading, Achilles,
Although the oaks drip honey,
Off again to Troy.

Beyond the bronzy gumbo limbo
Across the long green mondo grass
The bees and yellow butterflies
Quaff the red euphorbia.

Tuesday, January first.
Hibiscus pink and green against the white wall.
Hibiscus yellow and orange beside the blue pool.
The walls turn into a village.
The pool becomes a country spring.
The mahogany tree spreads into a beech.
It must be June.
The virgilias must be edged with exquisite white lace.
The poinsettia is reddening out in the garden.

Forward! Courage! However wild
The long-haired pelts of the casuarinas.
On! On! However strange
The sky-blue ripples of the black stream.

However languidly the keys
Respond, however forced the sound,
Play, play, heliconist,
Copyist of Thalia, labor.

You may object that the notes
Are hardly few. I explain
That I don't play them. Who
Does? How? And why?

Who does?
Was
It Apollo,
Stretching
Out
A golden
Wing?

Was
It Diana,
Silvering
Lips,
Breasts, thighs,

Because
As Lucina
She perceived
Imaginable
Emergent

Brazen,
Maybe,
Or iron
Glitter
For better
Like a marriage
Or not?

The white African violets float
Softly above their green pool of leaves.
He's into angiosperms, I heard
As she gestured with the red bombax blossom
She had picked up on the garden path.
It was noon. The dome was blue—
That big blue airy heaven—
The edges leafily white
With hedges of cloud. The unremitting
Arrows of the sun, which the unceasing
Breezes sailing across the lake
And flying into the numberless palms tempered,
        Persuading

Persuading us to yield ourselves here
To utopia, did nothing to dissuade
Us from that surrender, as though they were
Love's. The arrows, sails, and wings
All whistled whisperingly: Never,
Never leave this never-
Never land. The palms agreed.
Still, I glanced for just a moment
Past the cement pole of the copernicia
At the guzmania lingulata, red-
Tongued, pointed-tongued, smooth-
Tongued, I thought for just a moment.

I rose through clouds, through clarity,
Shadowed smaller and smaller on land, on sea,
Saw a cloud haystack in a cloud haze,
Saw another, another, not one of Monet's,
Fell through clouds, felt on my chin
A chill that leapt to forehead, hand, and shin.
The next morning, up in the cold
Ailanthus, blue jays, not green parrots, told
Tales of heroes and of felons,
Murderous Medeas, gorgeous Helens.

Could I fly across the Alps,
Which are held by Lepidus' troops?
This question expected the answer No.
It occurred in a letter to Cicero
From Gaius Asinius Pollio
Writing from Corduba, Spain,
In 43. He went on:
Think of me as one
Who first of all wants peace and secondly
Will fight to make my land and myself free.

Pollio's triumph was held in 39.
With booty a Roman victor would do something fine.
Pollio repaired the Hall of Freedom
And built there the first public library in Rome.

In this he would have been anticipated
By Julius Caesar (helped by Varro) had not
Death, as Suetonius remarks,
Prevented Caesar from accomplishing
Many projects which he had in mind
To benefit the city, one of which
Consisted in a plan to give the public
The greatest possible Greek and Latin libraries,
Charging the learned Varro with the task
Of selection, acquisition, and classification.

Virgil, oh, what am I doing? I am afraid.
Bavius, Maevius, standing over my head!
All I want is to read and to have read,
But notes keep squeezing out of my scrannel reed.
Pan perhaps supposes he has made
A Syrinx of me, which I must concede.

The columns gleam as I climb the steps.
Inside I reach for a volume, unroll it.
Achilles weeps by the shore.
His mother, deep in the sea,
Hears, responds, climbs
As high as the throne of Jove.
I saved you once; now listen
To my son's desire. Jove hears,
Responds, nods. Is that it?

Walking into the Latin room
I gaze at the new portrait of Varro —
The only one of a living author
Allowed among the portraits of authors —
And see displayed on the new-book shelf
Bavius' latest. About to skim it,
I notice next to it a volume
By young Vergilius Maro. Standing there
Reading, I flush, uneathes can breathe, otherwise move
Only my eyes and my hands as the lines require. Do I cry:
Here is the second Homer, here

              Again

Again is Troy? It is too soon;
I do not know that yet. I hear
Menalcas say to Mopsus:
Why, since we are both good,
You at tunes and I
At verses, do we not
Sit here under the elms?
That is certainly not what I hear.
I hear the verses, I hear the tunes.

The gleam has left the columns. Evening
Shadows the steps. The Hall of Freedom
Empties. Something overwhelms
Emptiness, something sweet and sharp.
Since you harp and since I carp
Why not sit beneath the elms?

It is January. Shall we sit
In the thin snow lighting
Harvard Yard? The warrior wind
Strides tuneless through the elms.
The fair-cheeked maiden moon
Looks on in silence.
Music, words, are blown away.
Tomorrow will be Whitsun.
The white will be blankness.
The sun will be blindness
Beaming again from the snow.

It was not Whitsun. It was not June.
It is Sunday, January sixth.
The sky is an epiphany of blue.
The blue is an objective
Genitive, opaque, revealed,
Itself the eyes' excitement,
Itself perpetual rest,
Itself itself.
The blue is a subjective
Genitive, transparency, disclosing
                                         To the

To the reader, out beyond the shaking golden
Censers of the ailanthus, the ever yet,
The yet ever, the wintry frenzy rising
To suns, to other skies, to bluer blues,
To purple, scarlet, saffron atmospheres,
Vast blacks enfolding constellations, vast
Recurvatures where everything returns,
Vast straight escapes into infinity.

With Monday came snow
In which my pieced pinion
Served as well as an umbrella
Broken in a blizzard, which
Was made a mirror of my mind's swirling
Particles, pieces of paper,
Tattered tidbits of music,
Bits of meaning, falling
Flat as the collapsed
Wing. It wasn't that something
Shook that paperweight
Mind. It was only
Weather. That lightweight
Mind was heavy

Only with Monday's
Heavy cloud
Shedding upon it
Not a glory
But nevertheless
Something profoundly
Bowing it down,
Shed upon it
As upon a sidewalk
That after winter's
Rage has reigned
Must be shoveled.

Here is the blue and white of morning.
Come sit under the elms.
Under the white-sleeved elms?
Under the wooly elms
Upon the thick-fleeced ground?
I guess I could break my syrinx pipe
And lie on the white blanket.
It is thick and soft but very cold.

I'll shut myself up in Tuesday's tower.
I'll last — I'll make myself last —
Till evening, when, after, beyond
The western window the sky
Stains raspberry, the snow blue-purple,
One chooses one's book, is chosen
By one's book.

        Uncouth, unkissed
One may be, but the inhabitants
Of certain focal homes, of bright
Warm apartments with picture windows,
Rich carpets, polish, china, or
Of (must one admit it?) frail
Shrines, do not ignore, reject,
Despise one but clearly welcome
Intellectual intercourse
Within their chambers. More than this,
They come to visit, stay the night,
Share meals, seem right at home, in hut,
Garret, studio, wherever
One invites them. Even more,
They're willing to go out with one,
To take one out, into society,
Rumbling over cobblestones
To banquets, balls, salons, afternoon
Teas, symphonies, museums,

Into gardens, into deserts,
Into pastures, into forests,
Into agoras and forums,
                      Into

Into ghettoes or cathedrals,
Onto battlefields and oceans,
On May mornings, August evenings,
January afternoons,
Midnights in July or March,
To London, Paris, up the Nile,
Up rainbows, up cloud steps, and up
Rapturous ascents to seventh heavens.

They said to me:
Come under the elms
And if you are
Too cold to sing
Listen to us.
It is summer here.

They said: It is November.
In January who thinks of November?

Melpomene, although my pipe unbroken lies,
My heart is broken. If I put my pipe
To my slow lips, let the lament arise
Of which my heart's tune is the prototype,
Something as thin and shrill as a mere gripe,
As dark and dolorous as lone
Choking sobs that the ocean's moan
Loudly connotes
When someone loved is gone, and a soft hope
But lightly floats.

The personage was secret and is still unknown,
The song sung in November (though not mine),
Recalled, resung under another sign.

Is there more tangible joy
Outside the ramparts of Troy?

I did not touch her, Agamemnon swore
And gave her to Achilles, together
With seven other women, twelve horses,
Twenty gleaming cauldrons, seven
                              Tripods,

Tripods, and ten talents of gold.
She was like golden Aphrodite.

When she came to Achilles' hut she saw
The body, gashed by bronze. Dearest Patroclus,
Screamed Briseis, to me you were most cherished,
The kindest of the Greeks. I left you here
Alive, and now I find you dead. I weep
And cannot stop, for you were kind.

She weeps, and all the women groan.
Mourning Patroclus, each one mourns her own.

New, fine pearls will glow
About now on the virgilias.
Saturday, January twelfth.
The mail. Here's a new
Review of Cedric's *Heroic
Paradox*. I'll call
Anne. Anne is gone.
Cedric is longer gone.

Benjamin Franklin was born
In Boston, Massachusetts,
On January seventeenth, 1706.
Benjamin Franklin was born
At Boston in America
On January sixth, 1705.
Benjamin Franklin was born,
Said the record of his birth,
On January sixth, 1706.
Benjamin Franklin was born
On January sixth/seventeenth, 1705/6.
Saturday, January nineteenth.
A blue jay creaks through new snow.

By the eve of St. Agnes it is so cold
We can hardly dream. Agnes of old
(So young) caught sight of one
Upon whose beauty moon and sun
Gazed hot with wonder.

Monday, January twenty-first.
A chill over the inauguration.
Our nation is poised for greatness.
The chill is nothing but weather.
Nothing can be done outdoors.
In through the closed windows the wind
Slips into your muscles, your bones,
Your brain, bringing the welter of the world.
But it's a holiday. We honor —
We hope to honor — a dead man's dreams.

It is cold. It is not pearls
That trickle from your lids.
It is cold. It is not rubies
That ooze upon your fingers.
It is not a silver road
On which you slide and slip.
It is not a lawn of ivory
And gold at which you wince.
The wind that icily burns
Your eyes is not of diamond.

Let's rush to Arcady
And rest beneath a tree.

Sitting under the elms they sang
Of death. Rather they entered the cave
Under the wild vine's clustered cover,
Just beyond the elms. The coolness
Was delightful. Daphnis had died.

They sang the shepherd Daphnis, whose death
The cave sang, the elms sang —
The cave with its dark resonance,
The verdant tremulous elms — the hills,
The streams, the summer skies all sadly sang.

Sitting in the cool cave, they sang
Olympus above the clouds, apotheosis.

Mourning Patroclus, each one mourned her own.
In February who thinks of November?

As the age of gold went bronze
In November's way, a leaf
Fluttered and fell — a leaf
First rushed into by a sun.
From the envisioning face
Of Tiresias, the envisioned
Flickered and shone. And through
The translucent countenance
We knew, suddenly day
Would break from the constant sun
Within — Anne's radiance.
Outside our constraining
Time, the leaf, unfallen, gleams.

Anne Miller (Mrs. Cedric Whitman),
February sixth, 1937–
November fourth, 1984.

Hadn't we passed the beech,
The abundant willows?
Weren't we sitting in the parlor —
It was a parlor —
Fronting on Shady Hill Square?
Weren't we sitting
In the kitchen with the cookies and the tea?
At the end of our visit
Didn't we say goodbye
Among hyacinths?

Both saint and scholar, I shouted,
And others shouted, too,
In irrepressible acclamation.
Was it her mastery of Latin
That placed Anne among the stars?
                                          It was not,

It was not, but at her canonization
We heard the music glittering from her fingers,
We heard the Latin glowing on her lips.
These, too, were jewels.
These, we knew, were jewels even among the virtues of the sky.

It was a tunnel rather than a cave.
There was a place where you could go in
Like the entrance to a cave,
But there seemed to be another from which you might emerge,
And emerge into a brighter or at least a different light,
Or you might describe the tunnel as a telescope.
The difficulty was focusing.
If you sat at your end and looked down the long darkness
You felt something clarifying beyond the other end,
Something not exactly looked for in this garden,
Something not really expected in this garden.
The cave was in this garden.
Every so often, just beyond the elms, you found yourself inside the entrance.
What was that bud of light like a new star?
Perhaps you would see.

Scientia, scientiae, scientiae, scientiam, scientia.
I'm saying my beads.

Humanitas, humanitatis, humanitati, humanitatem, humanitate.
I'm praying my litanies.

Scientiae, scientiarum.
Humanitates, humanitatum.
My chants must flower into plurals.

Altertumswissenschaft.
Literaturgeschichte.
I'm planting the seeds in definite beds.
Even now in the hothouse of February
The spring semester is progressing.

Scientia
Is plural only in Vitruvius,
Humanitas
In no one, it seems.

What are violets?
What are hyacinths?
Are we no one?

But you specified
Altertumswissenschaft.

Add the plot
Wortforschung.
And even hope that some day we
Will be
Antiquity.
And Varro wrote
Antiquitates.

And you —
Do you write
English
(Finally to ask the question)?

Sicker I do.
It's sunburn —
If you underfong my meaning.
It's something like
Television
Or
Sociology
Though my main field be
Olderdom's witship.
Listen to
Bavius and Maevius
Criticizing Virgil's
Barleys.
And as for
Ars,
Even Cicero has the plural.

Anne, it's still so close —
Your life, I mean.
Would you — will you — be horrified
To hear us call you sanctified?
We did it behind your back
Even when you were living —
When Job was living —
Limping, dialyzed, believing,
Blinded, cheerful, humble, giving,
Brilliant, modest, gracious, loving,
Serving, salving, saving, laving,
Relieving, perceiving, achieving, grieving,
Leaving.

What are these adjectives?
What is all this jangle?
Truth
Bereaving.

A bright whiteness. A strangeness. Wonder. The threshold of
 Olympus.
Beneath his feet he sees the clouds and the stars. It is Daphnis.
That bright whiteness is Daphnis. The wonder is his. The strange
Location a kind of place which he has never approached before.

Daphnis, standing on the threshold
In wonderment, in admiration, sees
The stars very far below.
If this is a mountain, its great
Cone has spearheaded a projection
Out past space. If it is a palace
Its hallways lead to timeless suites
Deep in being. Thus it is that Daphnis

Without

Without distraction hears
The woods and mountains singing,
The singing of the nymphs and of the stars,
The music of mind, of immaterial
Depth and matterless elevation.

    i̇   i̇ 2̇   7. 7 6   7   i̇   i̇.
Sancta Anna, ora pro nobis.

The grand old beech
Rehearsed its new song.

Anne (I translate), if the flame of spirit
That burned in your broken body burns
Beyond it, bend to light our wicks,
And if our wax may serve preserve
It to its possible length (I interpret).

Anne, if the amaranthine bloom
(I render) truly never fades
Help us to find it for our yard
Where squills sleep in the beechen shades
Thrown by the sun as by a tomb.

Why was there something hard
About the glimmering beech?
It had to take the winter, jarred
Perhaps by its very reach
Into cloud and up toward blue.
It had to make an old song new.

You don't seem to understand, Maevius said,
How we write nowadays. Our rhythms, diction, syntax,
Images, myths, history, literal leanings,
Philosophical bents differ from yours.
It did not matter. I had to satisfy

Only Professor Lane. Eventually,
Of course, Bob Stevens and Julia Budenz, the readers,
Would see a draft, but they, most people thought,
Would be content to go along with Lane.

The uncertainty of the shadows
Drove me inside the cave.
There it was the unsureness of the light
That fired the song.
There I could not see
How some well-meaning uncaught gardener
Had pruned the great elm.
There I was not compelled
To tack back the vanquished, vanished branches
And restore the wild decorum of their adventure into the sky.

I was not startled by the shade
At the entrance to the cave. I was not surprised.
I knew, when it was there, that it had been coming.
I was distressed because just then
I had expected something else,
Yet this came naturally, not unexpected,
Not less golden in its approach
Than its reality. It glowed
In the entrance like a sunset
After a day of cloud, although it was veiling
The sky. Would it come in?
Would I admit it? And would the cave
Fill and glitter and shake and ring?
It was only — would I admit it? — Joe's
Shadow. At that phantom's passing
Would the sky uncloud?

The nymphs just laughed, but how
Could it be that the solemn cave
Of solitude encompassed
So many and such varied visitants?

The cave of February is like
The earth itself, from which the seed
Will rise into leaf and flower.
I sat there with my books
(Bought or borrowed) thick
About me like rich soil.

           The north,

The north, the dark, the cold
Cloak one in the hibernation
Known as study. February is precious
Because it is the end. The restlessness
Of hints of softening in fields and winds
Has not yet penetrated. One should stay home —
This is the natural vacation — hide
Deep beneath the humus where the human
Autochthony renews itself remembering.

Far from breme winter's wrack,
Far from the hewn elm and the hatcheted oak,
Far from the spiteful, frostbitten briar,
I sat by the cavern's fire.
The fire was very hot and crackled and spit and threw designs all over the walls.
Although as I sat there my eyes were closed, I saw the glistering fire and all its designs,
I saw the dancing fire, and although I sat there I was dancing with its flames,
I was swept into the orgy of the dance, I was dancing with my ancestors who danced there,
Their bones lay in the ground, their ashes in the earth, but their magnificent spirits visit that cave,
I took their hands, I bowed as they came before me, I called them by name,
I am afraid to name them now but I named them then, I was not ashamed, I said their names,
I greeted them, breathless as I was, while we danced designs upon the floor
And multiplied the fire's engravings, the paintings of flame, the perfect skies and towers, oaks and oceans, curling hyacinths uncurling fragrances, warriors and waving women, waiting women, spindles, spears, and thyrsi twined with vines on all the walls and ceilings of the cavern as the dancers moved.
To one, as we met and bowed and stepped along the level, lifting our feet, skipping, flying,

               Although

Although my heart pounded, although I was panting, I said very
    boldly, Homer,
Good evening. He took my hands, I was crying, I was frightened, I
    was terrified, I did not run away, I kept dancing.
Another came, another, I will not drop their names, I addressed
    them then, we kept cavorting,
I said their names and through all that confusion and all that
    beauty they said mine.

The cave grew as still as a garden of snow,
The fire was the embers' glow.
I opened my eyes. I was alone
Except for one
Who sat across from me in the strange warmth that remained.
It was a man — no, the spirit of a man — a poet, an old
    Roman — no, still young,
Still handsome, elegant, pale, with the scent of perfume faintly
Floating, I thought, from his abundant hair. Sextus Propertius,
I said politely, I hope you enjoyed this evening's dance.
Yes, he said, thank you. We all must stick together. The Muses
Themselves — did you notice? — were dancing among us. How
    did you happen
To be here just then? I was waiting, I answered, to be discovered.

In the past I feel at home,
But the future looms as blue as the ink in my Bic pen,
And my present finds me as gray as the characters that emerge
From my aged, ailing typewriter. Even Harvard Square's
Best photocopies no longer help much. He said,
Death gives renown, antiquity gives fame
Which life denies. What life denies
Is doubled in the brightness of your name
Once in the dark your body lies.

He left. I slept. An Apollonian
Form stood there. I lay awake.
That worried you, it said; you yearn
For the purity of the great abstractions.

Through

Through the night the figure lectured:
The bright bird in the senseless forest sings,
Sweet flower in the senseless desert gleams,
Deep heart's flame in the senseless universe
Blossoms for them. Yet they may be adored
Even through eyes and ears and intellects.
Then stretch out in surrender and arise
Pure with the energy of fiery day.
It left. I slept until a sparrow
Chirped the Sunday morning in.

Even the morning was a cave.
Even the sparrow was a thrush
Just beyond the entrance — a hermit thrush,
I felt. I felt eremitical myself.
The flute downstairs was played by a shepherd
On a distant hill.
The phonographs, the radios were still.

The shepherd and the thrush grew still.
I was sitting in a soundless symphony.
In it I was walking up and down.
Impalpable, the hot abstractions burned.
Invisible, the bright abstractions shot
Along my optic nerve. I was worn out,
But I tried to focus. The ancient trinity
Was two here, struggling to be one. Which one?

Under the morning's gaze

The blue flower is a fire,
The orange fire is a flower,
The world is an orange flower,
The sky is a blue fire,
The fire is a warm orange universe,
The cool blue flower is a sky.

The song
Could be wrong.
It could be a Kitelic,
As Benjamin Franklin, a lad of sixteen,
                                        Dubs

Dubs the genre in *The New-England Courant*.
It could be seething with ingredients from his recipe
For the New-England Funeral Elegy
(Best concocted with Harvardian dignity),
E.g., a Scrap of Latin,
E.g., a sufficient Quantity of double Rhimes —
Power, Flower,
Grieve us, Leave us.
Will truth
Rushing from its bower
Save us
As it ruth-
Lessly pulls us hour after hour
Along the slopes ascending above us?

The elm is not chopped.
Its grand gold branches tingle into the heavens,
Bow pleasantly in our humble direction,
Slip back solidly into the ground,
Resume their breathless elevation.
I remember how breathless
And how breath was inspired.
Brown tinges still arise,
Some into the February skies,
Some as visions, not lies.
I would not see them otherwise.
I would not behold the brown branches in their grandeur and their goldenness and their phenomenality.

I would rather describe than imagine.

Anne is smiling.
But not tapping a stick.
But not clutching a crutch.
She walks smiling, white face alight, eyes hazel bright, black hair shining, red dress satin, black shoes in fashion, delicate.
She fills a glass.
She walks smiling across the room in her long dress and her high-heeled shoes and from high on the shelf takes down the slim black book.

Still on the side of the elm
The squirrel, vertical, head downward, rests on the bark.
The Gael was a bard. To my cavernous envy he chanted caves of gold.
My cave is gray and vacant, not for sale, not for rent, but very empty.

Nothing counts except ideas.
They are not enough, but without them there is nothing.
You go home depressed from the party.
The cave is an enormous void.
The elm rises before it without a song.

There was the silvering of the pines.
There was the enameling of the dogwoods.
There was the day's snowfall graciously yielding to moon and star.

In Poor Richard's almanack for 1733
February counts as the twelfth month.
In Poor Flora's almanack for 1985
February counts as the sixth month.
You see what I have collected.
You ask what I have comprehended.
I have comprehended nothing. And am I about to say
What no one has said in two thousand years?

There was the whitening of the elms.
There was the darkening of the cave.
There was the darkening of the dark despite the unlikely white of the
    night sky.

February is the third month.

Anne's book was green.

Many of its pages were dark,
Too many of its pages were dark,
But even now the brightness of its golden letters is being deciphered.

Mine was the black one
That closed before it opened,
That was foxed before it was printed,
That was old before it was folded.

So wrote Flora in the middle of a February night.

Then came a tuning, like a blue
Hyacinth in an earthen pot.
Then came a turning, a heard verdancy.

There is spring's incense.
There is Anne's green music.
There is Anne's music. Shall I laugh or weep?

In the Copernican system
The center was
The mean sun not the sun.

If you are moving
The unmoved center like a shore
Will seem to move.

In the modern revolution
The center was
Not without a grand role.

Sunday, February seventeenth.
A respite from gray.
You can see the sun moving across the sky.
You can see the river moving across the ice, slightly, here and there, slightly, above the still ice, if you look closely, from close on the bank, if the wind blows strong.
You can see the pale, shocked shoots moving up into the spots where the sun reposes.
No flowers are open.
What are those tiny triangular tips?
Crocus, daffodil, hyacinth, coming, still hidden, still closed?
It's a bit chilly for spring's warm frenzy to begin.
Thalia sits in her hillside cave.
There are no crocuses open in that sun-trap on Craigie Street.
There are no snowdrops open by that fence on Sparks Street. The fence has been mended. The sun is shut out.
There are no snowdrops open where they bloom on Brewster Street.
Amazing! This is Highland Street. On a southern slope some six or eight botanical snowdrops, white and fresh in the dull grass, clump.
On Fayerweather Street four witchhazel flowers look out, their curling lashes golden.

On a

On a Brattle Street terrace one small saffron crocus blinks in the sun.
On Hubbard Park Street five crocuses, all pale purple, gaily laugh above
   the dead leaves.
There are three crocuses giggling in that sun-trap on Craigie Street?
   How? Have they opened during this hour and a half, or do I see
   them, gleaming pale purple, almost lavender, only now that my eyes
   have opened?
The snow is mostly a few gray rags.
In this book, Petrarch said, a gray rag is sewn with cloth of scarlet.

Giovanni Dondi dall' Orologio,
Petrarch's admirer and friend,
Maker of the astrarium, that amazing astronomical clock
(It had to be geocentric; Copernicus was not yet born),
Wrote to Fra Guglielmo di Cremona
That when Petrarch had bound his own *Bucolic Song*

Together with Virgil's *Bucolics* in one volume
And a gentleman, holding out the book, asked what it was, Petrarch said,
In this book a gray rag is sewn with cloth of scarlet,
Showing clearly by his reply that modern works are surpassed by
   ancient.

Monday, February eighteenth.
It is not the twenty-second.
It is not the eleventh.
It is not the dreaded
Monday. The extended
Sunday, worshipped Sunday, sunny blue-skied Sunday smiles to greet
Our eyes as they relinquish sleep,
Lighting, delighting, as they open not
On Monday, on Sunday, adored Sunday.

In 1776,
February eighteenth was a Sunday.
In Cambridge, Massachusetts,
From his headquarters on Brattle Street, at the Vassall house (later
   Craigie house, later Longfellow house, the house itself elongating
   history even here where all history is short, is modern, archaeology
   and ancient tale having ill supplied the incommensurably longer
                                                                story

story of the great and glorious forest of which does not the soil still
  dream?),
George Washington, forty-four,
Or to be forty-four in four days,
General and Commander in Chief of the Army of the United Colonies,
Wrote to the President of Congress, Sir:

The late freezing Weather having formed some pretty strong Ice from
  Dorchester point to Boston neck, and from Roxbury to the Common,
  thereby affording a more expanded and consequently a less dangerous
  Approach to the Town, I could not help thinking, notwithstanding the
  Militia were not all come In, and we had little or no Powder to begin
  our Operation by a regular Cannonade and Bombardment, that a bold
  and resolute assault upon the Troops in Boston with such Men as we
  had (for it could not take many Men to guard our own Lines, at a time
  when the Enemy were attacked in all Quarters) might be crowned
  with success. . . .

Thalia, who had looked out of her cavern,
Tapped me very gently on the shoulder.
In order to succeed, she suggested,
Regard the ancient linden that is standing
Commandingly beside the clapboard house
Waiting for June, when dull reds will splash gold.

To sing of presidents and revolutions,
Apollo chided, tapping the other shoulder,
Crouch in your cave another twenty years,
Piling the volumes high above your head,
Tunneling through big books until you see
The culmination of your drawn-out song.

What can I do, I said. I am a slave —
A slave of many masters: First is Time;
Employment next, which chains me up all day;
Then Laziness, which drugs me after five;
Distractedness, which drags me through the streets
All weekend; and the strangest master, Space.

Do I want him not to be so far away?

Will is close. He might as well be far.
His absence rescues me.
Joe is far. He might as well be close.
His presence captures me.

The rescue was slow.
The captivity will be long.
Meanwhile, I'll read on freedom.
Meanwhile, I myself must capture
Proteus, Silenus, Socrates —
Someone who knows.

                Thalia called,
Come back into the cave. It is February still.
Do you want to be nipped in the bud?

                    Inside I found
A fire that became a fountain that became a bee that became a bird that
   became a dog that became a deer that became a lion that became a
   light that became a thug that became a tree
That stood beside the river Eurotas while Apollo sang to a hyacinth on
   the bank.
I was hot, I was wet, I was stung, I was pecked, I was bitten, I was
   shaken, I was deafened, I was blinded, I was beaten, and I found
Myself with my arms around a tree
That seemed to have a melody of its own.

Apollo sang: My love is fair,
My love is sweet, my love is rare,
My love is fresh, my love is pure,
My love is strong, my love is sure,
My love is blossoming, is nigh,
But first had to sink and die.

The laurel sang: I saw him coming,
Beautiful and strong.
I ran because I knew he wanted
Me to be his song
And I was mine and I was humming
How I would be free

                                            And now

And now my soul and his have haunted
What is called his tree.

The fragrance of the bay leaves
Drifted before my eyes
Up to the embrace of the sun.

The sweetness of the hyacinth
Lifted before my eyes
And mingled with the warm sun.

The blueness of the hyacinth
Flew up before my eyes
And flowed around the hot sun.

The evergreen of the laurel
Grew up before my eyes
Freshening the ancient flame.

I, a gray patch of snow,
Just caught the scarlet glow
That rose to the gold I hoped to know.

That wasn't the end. Before I melted
The tree turned into a philosopher,
Who did not have a song. He had a question.
But it wasn't Socrates. It was a woman.
I knew it was Diotima. She had a question:
What do we think would happen if it happened
To one to see the beautiful itself,
Unmixed and pure and simple, not defiled
With human flesh and colors and much other
Mortal silliness but one could see
The beautiful itself, unique, divine?

It was Socrates again, it was Plato, it seemed for a moment like Jove, I almost let go, it was a bull, bold and resolute,
Huge, horned, garlanded, white, wide-eyed but not innocent, foxy, flighty, mighty, muscular, determined, that seemed to have run up from the fens
And was carrying me, back across the Charles, through Roxbury, into
                                                                     Dorchester

Dorchester Bay, across the ocean, to Europe, to old Europe, where
    Jove was at home,
It was Jove again, it was Joe, it was Will, it was Anthe, I was Thomas,
I was Flora, it was surely Thalia, I was Flora, I was only that Flora, Flora
    Baum, sitting there still in the rocking chair, wanting to know.

I saw a woman wandering by Permessus.
My view was not too clear. Another woman,
Taller, with a radiance all about her,
Approached, conducted her along the stream,
Over the stones, up to the pleasant spot
Where other shining women sat. They rose
To greet the shy, exhausted parvenue.

This is new, although
I have come before, new
Like every purple petal every
February, new
Although it is my purple self
Unseen among dead leaves, gray rejects
Of last year, my true gray self
Yet with a purple gleam, the gray
Gleam of purple. Must this not
Be old and very new?
I sense I should keep silence, but
In this light, far from usual eyes,
Nothing long hides.

That is, I think, what, very softly, she mumbled.
The brilliant women did not seem to mind.
She sat with them, unbrilliant though she was,
And played the purple flute she had been given.

From nothing
Or from something
There was something,
There is something,
Something will be
Or nothing.

Hyla, Hyla, we called from the pool,
Enter the hyacinthine waters.

From lovely bodies
To lovely minds
To beautiful ideas.
In the saffron of the crocus
I apprehended summer.

Purple distances shimmer within.
Hyla, don't dread suffocation.

The lines of gold connect the gold of sun,
The gray of raindrops and the sky of gray,
The violet bridge, the indigo stair,
The blue balloon, green rocket, yellow
Welcome, lengthened orange adieux, with room
For silver maples on the red brink of bloom.

An infrared telescope on a volcano in Hawaii
Has spotted Halley's comet, icy still but closer to us
Than Jupiter. The comings and goings throughout the universe
Are multifarious. Halley's poem honors Newton in Latin,
Summoning those who banquet on nectar to celebrate with him
Newton unlocking the library in which truth was imprisoned,
Newton dear to the Muses, Newton within whose pure breast
Apollo dwells, whose mind he has entered with all his godly power,
Nor is a mortal allowed to come closer to the divine.

The recent eclipse of Pluto
Indicates a moon.
The sun may have a twin,
Or possibly a tenth planet, like a tenth muse
Or like a tenth symphony, accounts
For certain earthly extinctions every twenty-six million years.
The remnants inhabit our museums.

Museums cost a lot.
Schools cost a lot.
My ma can't read to me.
His father's in jail, too.
Jails cost a lot.

How many million Americans never
Will banquet on books?
How many of us will always find
A black and white
Labyrinth lacking both thread and Daedalus in
This morning's paper?
How many of the illiterate will win
As room and board
A local habitation in our prisons
Without the risk
Of coming too close to the sun? There are other ways
Of getting burned.

Ranting is never a poem.
The sentimental and general never
Dwell in twentieth-century belles lettres.
Writing about what you know next to nothing about
Effects not even the didactic genre.
Pastoral has no prisons, epic
No doggerel. Lyric is trampled
By galloping horses, whether of the sun or of the soul.

Phaethon, I understand, it's wonderful, the tugging reins,
The surging gales, the thinning air, the dwindling fields, the shrinking
    seas,
The mountains gleaming into dots, the lunging sun, the waning earth.
Sisters of Phaethon, I understand,
His crash, your weeping trees.

The earth's ellipse has two focuses:
The empty focus and the sun.
Then can we elect
To which foyer we will turn?

Sunday, February twenty-fourth.
The late snow's gray relict waits over here.
Over there with the most bridal snowdrops,
There with the most kingly purple —
There with the most queenly saffron —
Crocuses,
                              Bees

Bees are banqueting on nectar.
Heralds trump clarion.
The cardinal's call is of clearest scarlet.
The dove's gray wings have a violet tune.
One half wishes finch into robin.

It is a Bermuda high. The climate of the world is changing.
The day is very warm. This is kerygmatic of spring.
The air is thick with airplanes.
A helicopter like a skyey motorcycle keeps circling and circling and
    circling Cambridge.
The streets are thick with the scent of automobiles.
Nor is a mortal allowed to walk or hear or breathe.

Nothing counts except ideas.
And where are they? At the end of what ascent?
What thesis was it that I had proposed,
Even as a question? I must have had a question
Even for the telescope trained upon Parnassus.
How would I analyze Apollo's songs?
How observe them? How experiment?
How labor toward what kind of synthesis?
How explicate the summer in the saffron?
How demonstrate the purple in the tune?
How question everything and yet conclude?

Will I forge hypotheses?
Figure dough for paradise?

Newton has not been born.
Kepler has not been born.
I am back with the circle.
The telescope has not been invented.
The sun is spotless.
Copernicus has not been born.
I have sat on the static earth
Surrounding myself with crystalline spheres.
The earth will soon be flattening.

Silenus from the cavern's door
Sang the songs Apollo sang.
The valleys, struck, referred them to the stars.

Flora, I'm perplexed. Are these jottings
For a thesis or scraps of a song?
For my thesis, she responded, of your song.

A knowing, a dancer, a dance.
A reading by Paul de Man.
A wind on the first of March.
The clarity of the blue
Totality of the sky.
The sway of the amber ailanthus.
The ambagiousness of the amber paths.
The fates of the children of the sun.
A saffron star skied among brown clouds at our feet.

Is the greater desire
From the greater power
Or the greater lack?

Is the bluer sky
From the tenement's pane
Or from Everest?

Later the sky was gray and upon it
Was silver maples' sudden dusky bloom.

And here comes Meliboeus, remembering
An oak, a singing match, and how he put
The singers' play before his work. Our work
Is poetology, our play the poem.
If Petrarch in the fourteenth century
Allegorized Virgil's *Bucolics,* we
May structuralize or deconstruct the same.
And yet how well they deconstruct themselves.

The loser loses and the winner wins.
The winner loses and the loser wins.

The victor and the vanquished suffer loss.
Do not both singers triumph in the match?

How does a Wagner write a losing song?
How does a Virgil win against himself?

O Corydon, O Corydon, you've won.
O Corydon, who are you, Corydon?

Corydon is a piece of paper. Flora
Writes a paper on the paper. Fair,
She holds. A stone
Exists. We breathe the known
As necessarily as air,
Exhale through mouth and pipe and pen,
Begin again.

Make music, Socrates, I heard. I thought
The greatest music was philosophy.

In prison, facing death, just to be sure,
I wrote a hymn and, knowing that a poet

Is mythological not logical,
I put some myths of Aesop into verse.

The greatest music was philosophy.
Make music, Socrates, I heard. I thought.

Think, I heard. I sang,
Music, most resonant thought.

Virgil planned, when he finished his poem,
To give his life to philosophy.

Music and thought may win.
Thought and music may lose.

The lessons of the very great
Are lessons to the very small.

A woman need not slay
The fathers. She can play.

Yet each, whatever his/her song may be,
Must hope the swan song is philosophy.

Philosophy is not my subject.
I'm just listening to old songs
And writing what I hear.

I hear songs of songs.
I hear songs of song.

I hear Virgil
Hearing Meliboeus
Hearing Corydon and Thyrsis
Fight it out in song.

Our work is that for which someone will pay,
Sang Thyrsis, and the rest is play.

Our work is that which lives beyond our breath,
Sang Corydon; the rest is death.

Sunday, March third. I've gone and polled
Blossoms. Each crocus not too old
Has closed itself against the cold.
The silver maples, tough and bold,
Are threaded red or tufted gold.

Shall I mention the delicacy of the thread,
The callistemon redness of the red,
The fine-spun goldenness the branches ted
And bundle, tinily, for March instead
Of harvest, the beginning not the end,
The premature sun-honeyed dividend?

And here in most unlenten yellow
The witchhazel with its bright fellow
The cornel cherry, inch by inch
As cheery as the bubbling finch.

No sign of a bee.
It's thirty-three.

But why is it just thirty-three today
When seventy-three is a mere week away?
One learns this by remembering the past:
It cannot last.

Eternal spring of Rome,
Living in the lines of a language called dead,
The resonant oak
Argues very clearly
That your melodious bees
Above the green Italian banks of a river
Offer the honey of Arcady.

Monday, March fourth. It's nineteen degrees,
It's nineteen degrees, the radio says
Over and over. That's for Boston.
In Cambridge it's colder. This afternoon, snow.
Tomorrow, rain. It's not Dakota.

Slim crocuses
Wrapped
In pale purple cape
Or strong saffron cloak
Stood unfallen
In a white glaze.

And evenings continued to arrive.
The library lights,
The angles from which the elm is whole,
The blackest balconies of the oaks,
The pasted paper of the moon —
All these I left behind.

With wings of purple and blue —
But it was not
Love —
The visitor came.

Arrows of lead and gold —
But they were not
Love's —
The visitor held,

And a fearsome silver bow.
But this was not
Diana's.
This was not

The amorous or the chaste
But did arouse
A fever,
Did demand

A chilly purity,
The crystal swan,
The swan
Beating the ice

To streams of red, to brownest
Mississippis,
To seas
Of liquidity.

To what end
Envisioned wings
Over your head

If the crowning wreath
Is withheld
By the shepherds?

Why on earth
These secret wings
Upon your shoulders

If the gleaming flight
Is denied
From the ground?

The shepherds see
The songs that crash,
The songs that stride

Among them, bodied,
Rivals, models,
Hale companions.

The wings of purple and blue
Draw one up to crimson treetops,
Sweep one down to golden pistils,
Balance one on reds, divert one

Deep in yellows, lead one
Into azure and vermilion
Heartbeats, let one glide along
Silver breathstreams, slide beyond

Ultraviolet, hold one
Skimming emerald, lapped with lapis,
Tattered. At the fall, fold one's
Rags beneath a gray virgilia.

Fold them, Thalia, but if chrome remains
Send it orbiting, readable from earth
And reading the infinity of heaven
Where blackest black and whitest white are one.

Those wings — whose were they?
If they were blue and purple were they not —
But no — not mine. I watched them very high
Above me, very low above me, yet
Above, great singing pinions whipping the wind,
Smooth volants hovering and shimmering
And darkening, absorbing my whole stare,
Blue, purple, purple, blue, absorbing me
Through my fixed eyes until I maybe flew
Under their might, not violence. And why?
It was a find. I found them. They found me.

Those wings — whose were they?
They were those
Of the self beyond,

Those that the utter
Other rests
Above the eyes

Drawing the self
Concretely through
To the abstract,

Essence that must
Exist, it feels
So true, that beauty.

The fragrance of the witchhazel on air
In March, when it is warm enough for fragrance,
Even in a gray wind, when silver maples'

Bloom is blotches on the uneasy sky,
Resembles this essential selfless self,
This selfless essence recognized at once,

Fresh, ever fresh, again, again, surprise.
Thus great things are compared with very small.
The great, though, are the reckless meditation,

Rocketing ever yet into amaze,
Extending restfulness unendingly,
Pulsating agelessly, glimmering now,

Shimmering in the twisting of the elm,
Incarnate in the pallid purple droplet,
Infinite in whispered limitation.

Knowing what you feel,
Feeling what you know,
Knowing what you know,
Knowing nothing . . . Minerva,

I will set up your image on the Quinquatrus
In oils of Delacroix, in bronze, in marble
With crimson boots, in ivory and gold.
Pray, guard and garden in my wretched yard.

Here I hope to plant
Facts, behold ideas
In brilliant flower, cull
Rich, juicy paragraphs.

Sunset, Saturday, March ninth.
Why those sudden half-unbelieving smiles?
A sweetness from the resonant sugar maple.
Sunset on the breast.
Sunrise in the voice.
Loud, confident creation in the song.
The creation of the world.
The entry into the lost garden.
Why our stance unmoving in the road?
Nothing but the first robin.
Mingled forgetfulness and remembering.

Minerva, I must remember, I must not forget.

What should be studied the most?

The things that are most beautiful
And worthiest of being known,
Copernicus wrote. And these include
The divine revolutions of the world. . . .

What should I study the most?

The things that are most beautiful . . .
The revolutions of the word.
I sit here, and before my eyes
They pull the stars across the skies.

Not only I, Petrarch wrote
To Cicero, but all of us
Who are decked with Latin's flowers thank you,
Supreme parent of Roman speech.
From your springs we water our fields.
With your light we have seen our way.
And there is another; necessity required
That one astound with speech and one with song.
You know the man. Virgil is this other.

It all happened when I caught sight of Daphnis
Sitting under the oak and he saw me
And called out, Meliboeus, if you come
And rest in the shade your work will take care of itself.

Your ludicrous may be my serious.
There were great issues: poetry at stake.

Can this be my proper study
When I'm seeking truth, not beauty?
O Minerva, wisdom-weaving,
Am I caught in texts, in reading?

There is a river in Arcadia,
The Mincius — it flows by Mantua —
A river of green banks and fringing reeds.
Beside it schoolboy Virgil surely played.
Beside it Daphnis sat beneath an oak
While shepherds gathered with their tuneful reeds
And alternating song. Beside it rose,
Later, a dazzling temple built of song.
Was it Arcadia then? Then it was Rome.

There is a river in Arcadia.
Something is happening. Something is happening there.
There's quite a crowd: sheep, goats, and cows; there's quite a concert:
    waters, grasses, bees, reed pipes, and human voices, and the leaves
Of the oak. The leaves
Are what I hear,
Not the last brown lamentation,
Not red reveries, not pink
Cooing of infants, not the embryonic
Proto-sound of pulse or push, those promises.
I hear reality, the green
Mode, and see the glints,
And feel the shadows.

There is a river in Arcadia.
Beside it students dawdle along the path.
Shut out the joggers and the bicycles,
Radios, automobiles, and cigarettes.
Keep, though, the strollers, whisperers, and seers,
Leave in the softening shimmer between the banks,
Leave in the shimmering ripple of sleek sycamores,
Solidity, liquidity conjoined,

                                                    Leave

Leave in the eerie leafless wintry sheen.
And then restore the ducks and softening leaves.

Did the tremendous arch
Open on a vacant lot?
Was the tune a musical joke?
What really happened?

I was about to understand.
A theory trembled on the tongues of the oak,
Globed in the mouths of the competing shepherds.
The theory undulated along the air.
My ears throbbed subtly.

I don't want to write it down.
It began like a clarification,
And before I could run out into the sub-carved morning
Clouds were everywhere, were above all
Between my eyes and the great knife of the light.

I think it was
That understanding
Is undermined.

Hurrah! Each robin-
Throated dawn
Is first and only.

Horror! Each brick-
Walled sunset is
The last. The arch

Is filled. You're blocked
In the avenue
Or the weedy field.

Ob- or subjectively?

I came up against it.
I lay flat beneath it.
How can I say?

In the beginning
It was the exhilaration
Of a truth. That was flight.

I could have flown over
The arch, arch
Upon arch. In the end

I tried to call
The closing in
An endlessly open.

The poem did not close. What closed was cloud.
The cloud was concrete, bricks that build the dark.

Our play is poetology, our work
Endless elaboration of the poem.

But it has an end.
A few pages back
You passed the middle.
There's a beginning, too,
Not the believed but the seen.

Something was seen —
Daphnis sitting
Beside the river,
Calling out: Hurry and Here
And Rest under the shade.

Something was seen —
Lycidas met
On the road at noon.
Something was heard — some songs
Sounding through two thousand years,

Songs of songs,
Songs of song.
Here is an opening,
Here through the dark the stars
Tremble, the planets globe.

Morning. Friday, March fifteenth.
A sparrow in the swaying Norway maple
Outside the window. He seems to sway the maple
With his preening, but it is the wind
Preening and swaying.

A wind of swords
Preened Julius Caesar
Swaying the world.

He pulled his wings about him
And fell. Came Caesar's comet:
His soul, they say,
Blown to the sky,
Flown into apotheosis.

If Daphnis is Julius Caesar,
There is a break, an opening —
Trumpets, the tramp of troops
Across continents, the triumphs
Trebled, quadrupled. There is a closing,
A city wall around the garden,
A thicket about and within the city.

If he is not, the sparrow
Sits in the wind, the singer sits
In the wind, in the singing wind,
In the wind that he sings.

If he is and is not — Minerva,
Quinquatrus is the fifth day after the Ides,
Quinquatrus is a festival of five days,
The Quinquatrus is the festival of Mars,
The Quinquatrus is your festival — Minerva,
I've got to weave, unweave, and weave again.

If Daphnis is David or Orpheus,
If Daphnis is Tammuz, is Attis, Adonis, Apollo,
I know my good shepherds, great poets, and famous lovers,
I know my big volumes of comparative mythology,
They're lying open on my horizontals,
They're piled like hills upon my horizons.

I knew a shepherd
That smiled upon me
Like the triangle of light that first shines through my window in March.
Each day, little by little, the triangle enlarges, it lasts longer, it shines brighter, its warmth comes closer and closer to my chair.
And in the maturity of the year — fall, fruitfulness, and harvest — it slips away,
It is gone.
That sun is gone.

I heard a poem
That was breathed upon me
With the sweetness of virgilias in June.
I walked through the grove, inspirited, as the gleams glanced about me, upon me, and from me,
Candid, silvery, verdant, the foaming blossoms flowing like milk and honey,
While the foam bespoke its oceanic origin, a depth, a vastness, a titanic song.
I felt the breakers. The flowers fell.
The ocean slipped away. I stand at the edge
Of a crater on a cold moon.

There was a love
That burned within me
Like a star that also burned in the sky.
Tortured by the one I toiled on toward the other,
Dragging along my photographs, my telescopes, my mathematics, stowing away on spaceships, hitchhiking on comets, hoboing on light, dilating time, straightening space, approaching.
The one star keeps slipping away with its warmth and its light,
The other fuels futility.

Saturday, March sixteenth.
The aspen on Massachusetts Avenue,
Near the laundromat, opening,
Up near the sky. The orbits,
Circular, closed, of the clothes.

Head Quarters, Cambridge, March 16, 1776.
Parole Pensacola. Countersign Havanah.
As the weather is so bad, and the roads so mirey, the Regiments and Companies of Artillery, ordered to march this morning, are to halt until to morrow morning.

I believe in rhyme:
March is the arch,
April the way till
May, when play
Has its proper time.
June is the tune.

Daphnis sat under the oak.
He seemed very like a god.
As soon as I saw him he called,
Hurry and come and hear.
He listened. He did not judge.
He listened. He comprehended.

Head Quarters, Cambridge, March 17, 1776.
Parole Boston. Countersign St. Patrick.
The Regiments under marching orders, to march to morrow morning at sun-rise.

Head Quarters, Cambridge, March 17, 1985.
From the garden, the distant bugling of the robin.
Not long before, the blue jay's bell.
Out here in front, the dark twinkling of the elms.
Not far away, the dark constellations of the squills.

To sing of presidents and revolutions . . .
The linden seems unmoved,
Ancient, waiting.
Warfare seems disproved
Among new changes and old institutions.

March eighteenth.
Both snow and Monday.

Pressed

Pressed
Milky
Ways
Along the elms.
Bad traffic jams.

Head Quarters, Cambridge, March 19, 1776.
[To the President of Congress.] Sir:
It is with the greatest pleasure I inform you that on Sunday last the 17th. Instant, about 9th O'Clock in the forenoon the Ministerial Army evacuated the Town of Boston, and that the Forces of the United Colonies are now in actual Possession thereof. I beg leave to congratulate you Sir, and the Honorable Congress on this happy event, and particularly as it was effected without endangering the Lives and property of the remaining unhappy Inhabitants.

Do I attend to incident and date?
Do I advert to person, place, and thing?

The Enemy had left on Sunday.
The General was writing on Tuesday.
On Monday he had toured the Town.
His letter to the President of Congress gives details:
I have a particular pleasure in being able to inform you Sir, that your House has received no damage worth mentioning, your furniture is in tolerable Order and the family pictures are all left entire and untouched.
That George Washington was the General all well know.
John Hancock was the President of Congress.

It was an American robin that warmed my soul
On Sunday. What did he think of Monday's snow?
It was American elms that lifted my heart
On Sunday. How did they feel under Monday's weight?

Tuesday again. Again March nineteenth.
Mardi in March: keep up the fight.
Ovid's calendar for today makes no mention of Mars.
It is Minerva's birthday, he affirms.
It is the fifth day after the Ides — the Quinquatrus.

High above the ermined fire escape,
High above the gold epaulettes of the ailanthus,
Spreads the blue tincture of the morning.
I dip my ribbon in that cerulean dye.

Goddess of a thousand works,
Goddess, she, of song.
Will she be my studies' friend?
Can it be a wrong
To hope for more than my deserts,
Or will I offend
By offering with a flourish as of frills
From the trumpets of today's new daffodils
My skyey scrap to one so bright and tall and strong?

What would she say to something made by great-grandmother?
On the one side a new expanse of blue,
On the other a constellation of old patches —
Shall I call it bricolage?
I'll call it patchwork, I'll call it
An heirloom, an inheritance.

I'll call it gathering, a plan, the interplay
Of plan and chance, the skill of stitching,
Utilization and utility
And desperate imagination of
Shapes, colors, samenesses, differences, juxtapositions,
Outrageousness and balance, maybe art.

Minerva's statue shines
Like a star. Did I put it there?
Did I weave its dress? Did I paint
Its oceanic eyes?
I gaze into that gaze
Ready to plunge, to find
What I have gathered, if only
It will wait.

Behind me do
I hear green spring
Descend? It is
March twentieth
Already and
Eleven fourteen.

And what if it was not till 35
That Virgil called Octavian a god?
How many gray-green-gold-gray revolutions
Of earth (or sun) can claim reality
Once the hot track has faded out of space?

That temporal has turned
Eternal. Vernal veiling mazes here
And now as coppery.
The realms of elms endure, do persevere.

The *Annals* of Volusius,
That poem countrified and drear,
Those verses of Hortensius,
Five hundred thousand in one year,
Will be recycled to wrap fish.

Tied with my blue ribbon?
Signifying a sky
That hovers lovingly over impetuous
March, the constant sometimes seen,
Sometimes believed, above inconstant
Spring, persuasive appearance
Of sweet-through everlastingness,
Outlasting disappearances
Below and who knows what
Above, eternal morning in the eyes

Of morning, lasting in a mind
Of morning, ready to begin
To see in this blue atmosphere
The exquisite, sought, sought out blue,
The clarities that it protects,

      The umbratile

The umbratile that it provides
With bright perspective. On this fourth
Morning of Minerva's feast
My ribbon floats incipient.

To grave beginnings and great professions
A purple patch is often sewn,
Bright against gray truth. The gray
Beeches and virgilias now
Show life subtly. Arcadian woods,
If living, live in subtlety.
But how that loud unsubtle flute
Squeaks upon the quiet gray of the morning,
Squawks between the shepherd's lips,
Shrieks into the shepherd's heart,
Whitens, gleams a purple-rose.
Soon, and surely by April first,
Or even now, to the south, in gray Manhattan,
On Madison Avenue pear trees will be white,
Magnolias lavender-rose in Gramercy Park
And in front of the New York Public Library. Breathe
The unbreathable hyacinths of Manhattan. See
The sun come out at five p.m. and light
The Crown Building's golden crown, appearances saved.
The sun has come out, I think happily,
When it is I who have flown up into the sun.
I recognize as mine the blue of the sky,
And as for the tops of the clouds, I recognize them
As below me, as below my wings, my gray wings,
My cloudy wings, the gray cloud that I am
Up in this blue, one of the clouds of gray,
One of those cloudy clouds, those fogs, dank, gray,
Stranger to mazarine or cochineal
Or any thought to which my words might blaze.
Then what are these red dots on the gray canvas,
And what bright blood bejewels blue
Tents of Lent, what garish garnishes
Liturgicize the grayish floors?
Choice wines, rich chalices luxuriate

Far

Far underneath the azure canopy,
The azure parody that clouds and clears.
The tiny vivid red aceric flowers,
The gleaming purple, glittering golden,
Crocuses are brave beginnings.

Begin, my flute, with me
This tune of Arcady.

It was long ago.
I saw him springing up the steps.
He turned and addressed the crowd.
But it is not of Will
Nor of the hyacinths bloom by bloom released
To April,

When a sun and a daffodil
Were kin, when a flaring sun
And forsythia were companions,
Like with like,
In their golden blaze,

When the hyacinths blazed darkly,
Blazed up with the dulcet
Smoke of their blue aroma,
Were whirlpools,
Were pulsing pools,
Were stillnesses,
Were blue abysses,

It is not of Will as he leapt through April,
Not of his spring, his sprite, his solid words,
Not of his language leaping into the ear,
Not of magnolias easing into the air
Of April, stellate white preceding,
Sailing, purple-pink succeeding,
Sealing spring, unsealing April's
Fragrances again, the fragrances
That sail uncertain seas of sun
And float along spring's sunny certainties,

It is not of Will as he walked through April,
Nor of April as I walked on the shores of the seas of squill,

But of the goddess Apru arising in the mind,
But of divine Cupido upswelling in the soul,
But of a heart like a million magnolias about to blossom

To light in the Arcadia of April,
The particular Arcadia of intellectual April,

I must sing.

One morning the magnolias' brilliant bloom
Was found in rags.
Shall I describe the chill of the night? That dawn
The heart, the soul was found
Condemned to lesser pleasure than the mind's.

Now cease, my flute, with me
This tune of Arcady.

We cannot all do all.

Turn, O spheres of fire,
Ringing my desire.

It is far away.
I see him strolling up the path.
He puts his argument.
But it is not of Joe
Nor of the sun that entered by the Golden Gate,
Releasing every hue,

Nor of the golden hair my hand caressed
Occultly, without touching it,
Nor of a lust called love

But of a love called lust,
Receiving every hue,
Revealing every tint,
Not of the earliest azaleas of April
Suspended purpling through the afternoon

           Or Joe's

Or Joe's soft gold arriving out of the sunset
Among the golds of April: the cornel cherry
Continuing, forsythia begun,
Narcissus generous, not self-regarding,

But of the gold for which the purest lust
Blazes like noon ascending
In cloudlessness, like dawn
Ascending delicate clouds of April
Azalea, like sunset amazing
The gray of the antecedent rain,

A lust ascending above
The passing monstrous April moon,
Above the barbarous planets in their travels,
Along the dangerous courses of the stars,
Running in the hot sidereal courses,
Wrestling with the heavy densities
Of incomprehension, schooled in the moving hues
And harmonies of the stars of intellection,

You must sing.

I turn to abstraction.
              I allegorize. I touch
The stars occultly by my gravity,
Caress azaleas without touching them.
April's azaleas hover subtly, subtly
Blaze like visitant purple stars. Among
Their tints I turn to them and to the stars
And to the many-hued bright objects of
My far from subtle gold-crazed stellar love.

Turn, O spheres of fire,
Bringing my desire.

Did one fail and one succeed?
Did one lose, the other win?
Did one sink in spuming seas,
The other clasp the love brought home?

The hues are red and yellow, green and blue.
There is a gold that is red, a yellow gold,
A gold that is green. And blue
Is gold's most golden longing.

Here are a few red tulips,
A flock of daffodils,
Little green leaves on the hedges,
Unnumbered herds of squills,

Lights in the purple azalea,
Whites in its purple dye,
Whites in the pink magnolia bud,
Gold sun in the sky.

The only gold is the idea.
The fire is thought.
The stars are understanding.
The star magnolias represent the stars
As high and white; azaleas, as purple,
Near; the squills, as blue, below.
She never picks the flowers.
She picks at the ideas.
The golden fragrance of the stars
Suffuses her with bluest longing as
She bobs below, most starry-eyed.
The stars are tears.

Muses, tell her song.

Songs draw down the moon,
Songs can stop the sun,
By singing we can reach the stars,
One by one.

I sing to the big round moon,
I sing to the nearing sun,
I raise my song to the utmost stars
That barely run,

Or barely seem to move
From here, they are so far.
I will catch them with my song,
Star by star.

My song will make them move
Toward me or take me far
Toward them. Where is my song?
O song, where are

The English words, the French,
The Latin and the Greek,
The Sanskrit, the Chinese,
Squeak by squeak?

Where are the words to wrench
The meanings from, to seek
The meanings of, to squeeze
Tunes by the cheek?

If I could sing the song that Virgil sang,
Which was the very song the Muses sang,
Which was the song Alphesiboeus sang,
Which was the song that Amaryllis sang,
Which was the song that brought back Daphnis.

But Damon sang before Alphesiboeus.
How did that song end?

It ended with cruelty.
                        Do
Hyacinths bloom in concrete —
Hyacinths, those blue ideas
Not to be scented in gutters under
The buses' fumes?
                        Why did you show
The hyacinths' idea when
Dandelions fit the crack?
The gray hairs split from their small heads scatter.
Far off, the heady hyacinths awe
In the garden.
                        Why did you show

Yourself, not give? Open,
Not reveal? I give
(Aware of the ridiculous) up.

Let house sparrows
Be wood thrushes.
It is Easter Week.
In this well
Beside stiff, smoky bricks
Far below the sheerest blue
Enlightenment of sheerest sky
From the skinny maple that held
On tight all winter,
Blossoms, fresh and green against
The sterile weathering of walls
To blackish redness, are about
To spill.

Let owls be swans, let tamarisks yield amber.

Is the adynaton a prayer?
Let the dandelion
Be a daffodil
Blooming on the aspen
Beside the laundromat.

Let my song be a gift
Honoring you although you pulled
The clouds about you.
Is my gift the plunge
That pulls the waters over my song?

A horsechestnut ungloves its hands,
But white magnolia stars bear the brown tips of cold.

A second song, a second chance.

Words are chances, charms between
The concrete and the idea.

Words are suns that pull
Up the bulbs, not muddy
Rot but spreading skies,
Dawns and blue-gold noons,
Sunsets blossoming with glory,
Nights that blossom stars,
Spilling over with stars.

If I spill
Forth words, so green
And fresh, they will
(I say it) mean.

Hello,
Yellow
Words; be stead-
Fast, red;
And blue,
Of course, be true.

Words are like those violets,
Lowly, precious coronets.

What were the three colors
Of the triple threads
That drew back Daphnis?

What of the thread
That entered and left
The labyrinth? These

Were the word-colored threads,
The spinnings of words.
Words thread the brain,

Words ascend and bind
The sky to draw it down
Or pull us up.

If I could live on words alone.
The hyacinths have turned to stone.

The words are pebbles dropped
To show the way.

Let way be sky;
Pebbles, petals, stellar

Blooms upon the hyacinthine
Suasion of the minded sky.

Call it sky or call it bloom,
Call it Daphnis, call it Rome,
The desired, the paradigm,
It is diadem and dream.

The secret name is Amor, or Desire,
Binding all by divine desire for the city,

On account of which the poet in the *Bucolics*
Darkly calls the city Amaryllis;

The sacred name is Flora, or Flowering,
Accounting for the festival of Floralia;

The civic name is Roma, Lydus says
In "April," for the city has three names,

As Amaryllis has three threads, the threads,
Three binding colors, bringing Daphnis home.

Flora, my patroness, I live
In the civic scrub, outside the city
Of desire, of vision, of the free.
Powerless, one does not live.

Flora, my patroness, I live
In desert sand. I live on a rock
Assaulted by the salty sea.
Flowerless, one does not live.

Flora, my patroness, I live
In a cave that never opens, an ocean
Unpenetrated by solar key.
Without a sun one does not live.

The mean sun is an idea.
The circular is a beauty.
The elliptical is a truth.
And of his study of the harmony of the world

Kepler wrote: If you are annoyed
I will bear it. Behold, I cast the die,
I write the book, whether to be read
By contemporaries or posterity

Makes no difference. Let it wait
A hundred years for its reader,
If God himself could wait
Six thousand years for a contemplator.

Sing a song of mathematics.
Sing a song of stars, of years,
Of distances. Numbers are words;
The songs, the harmonies of words.

The harmonies of Virgil's words
Can still be studied. Your mathematics
Is Latin. You will hear the pips
Of desperation, the boom of doing,

The bloom of the song planted in paper,
In coverings, the flowerings
Through centuries, beginnings, resumings,
The songs arising from the page into the air.

You look into the air.
You carry no laundry, no groceries, no books.
The aspen on Massachusetts Avenue
Sounds good, but is it an aspen?
It is a poplar, of course. Why not just call it that?
It has form, likeness. Were the leaves
Trembling or triangular?
Vaguely you remember both.
These wormlike flowerings, whose are they?
Populus, of course, produced them, but you tremble
From tremuloides to deltoides to some third angle.
You look into your books.

You know, if you cannot remember,
The Muse has left and Minerva
Never come. The flowerings,
Once fallen, turn to litterings,

Litterings of the quaking aspen
Or of the eastern cottonwood
Or of the unpopular poplar
Rising brightly colorful into the sky
Above drab Massachusetts Avenue
Populous with litterers less tall, less bright.

Must one leave home,
Must one leave behind
The city's litter, flee
To, no, from
Forgetfulness?

Dizzily I passed at dusk
Through a purple forest of hyacinths,
Spent the night beneath the magnolia —
Huge opened glinting globes of magnolia —
Beside the blue waters of the squills,
Wandered at dawn into the delicacy and the delight
Of pink and yellow, the weeping cherry
Dangling over the forsythia, the pale pink
Dallying with clear yellow with no shock
Or smear or confusion, spray
Just grazing spray, roseate, aureate spray.
All morning I discovered the leaf green
Of elms and maples, as though the fruits and flowers
Were leaves, like the hedges' leaves. At noon
I found the blue forget-me-nots.

                                          I must not
Forget. I must remember. I saw
Forget-me-nots, remembered skies; I saw
Blue blaze above harsh bricks, did not forget
A blaze of azure, gentle at my feet
In the soft garden.

I remember
One cherry mingling with forsythia,
Many forsythias separate, distinct,
Gold focuses, and many flowing cherries
Springing, pouring pink from their own centers,
Sources, surges, streams, fonts, fountains, fluxes,
Alone, rose-colored universes, forms
Of total satisfaction, bright ideas
Of pink as joy, as knowing, and as end,
Flowing along its endless curving flow.

With memory I could ascend
From April to the idea
Of April, from the idea
Of April to the beautiful.
Without ascent or memory — it was there.
The cherry flowered, dripped
With beauty. The idea? I forget.

This is an idea: Paint
Is far superior to words,
Unburdened by the pettiness
Of pink, the ugliness of orange,
The indeterminacy of purple,
Gold's crassness, yellow's silliness.

This is an idea: If
Critics may write literature
On poetry, the poets may
Write literature on criticism.
But how does copyright affect
Intertextuality?

This is an idea: Rome
Flowers by the weeds, the stones,
Along the Charles, upon the shores
Of Massachusetts Avenue,
Rome flowers under eyes that find
The words of Rome in flowing bloom.

Ducite ab urbe domum, mea carmina, ducite Daphnin.

From the city bring him home,
My songs, bring Daphnis home.

                                            But how?

Incipe Maenalios mecum, mea tibia, versus.

Begin Maenalian things with me,
My flute, Maenalian verses.

                                            How?

The color and the texture of that juncture,
That bit of air that was filled by the kiss
Of cherry tree and forsythia,
Of perfect pink and perfect yellow,
Of soft profusion and bright profusion,
Of subtle flagrance and gleaming restraint —
So like the goldfinch of Vivaldi's flute.

Sunday, April twenty-first. The birthday of Rome.
It's just after midnight. Shall I celebrate?
Shall I discover, delineate, devise
The Midnight Mass, the Easter Vigil,
Inaugural of this great day
When they began to build the walls of Rome?
Can Rome compare with Christ? Or, to ask better,
Romanity with Christianity?
When Romulus began to build the walls,
Taking up the trumpet he proclaimed the city's name,
As Lydus says. The city has three names,
As Lydus says. He says that Rome is Flora.

Day seeps in, first gray, then blue.
The green of April, that distillation
Of green, begins its instillation
Throughout the varied streets of Cambridge,
Subtly, slowly begins to flow
About the yellows, pinks, and blues of April,

                                                   On toward

On toward the green-leaved garlanding of May.
This is the eleventh before the Kalends of May.

Here, among the Cambridge backs —
Not the greens that float to the Cam,
Lawns and trees, green, green by the Cam,
But backs of Massachusetts Avenue,
Squeezed and dreary backs
Between unaltered bricks —
On the little Norway maple,
Spread the flowers, flowery bunches,
Soft and bright and live, of green,
The verity of the city's green.

In Rome the virid, flowery, or green
Color flew in honor of the city,
In honor of Rome itself, for Romans called
Rome Flora (Lydus says), the Flowering.

Not yet Floralia —
Friday, April twenty-sixth.
No festival this day, a day
Added by Julius Caesar to the calendar
Here and not at April's end, not interrupting
Floralia's flow from April into May.
Here it is, beginning, this April day,
Burgeoning, warming, fey.

Hark, the flute of the morning,
To the player morning star,
Morning prayer, lauds rising,
Praise ascending, lofted Te
Deum, bud and blossom and rosy day,
To the other, the inevitable,
Intent upon some alien stellate
Point, a Lucifer,
A weed to overshadow her weak,
Tentative, and tempted bloom.

What is this sour filling
Sandwiched between the good bread?
                                    How

How can you deplore
Moments, when what you dread
Is that she above and she below,
The quietest people in your building,
Might go,
That they, the quietest residents of Cambridge,
Will move away, exposing you
Through thin ceiling and through frail floor
To what you eschew,
To noise, loud, constant, unendurable?
Surely Allecto has hurled the infuriating
Snake that has glided into your heart,
That will drive you raving crazed through Cambridge,
That will drive her below and her above
Away and cruelly substitute in their stead
When they depart
A sound loud, endless, and unbearable.
Juno's to blame.
Amata loved and was given love,
But a Fury's snake compelled her raging through the city
As she sped
Wanting war, resisting fated Rome,
Shunning compromise and pity,
Driven, led,
Embraced, pervaded by the intolerable.

Sweet singing sounds from above.
Attend, the struggle of the song,
For I must sing my soundless song,
Sweet, bitter, sour.
Our songs have crossed, hers sweet,
Attend, mine sour.

Attend, the struggle of the flute.
It's only fifteen or twenty minutes
Two or three times a day.
And a little time to recover.
That goes over; this may, too.
Attend, the struggle of the mind.

What is this weedy madness? Rock
Is your enemy, thrown, rock after rock,
Through floors, doors, windows, walls, and ceilings,
Airy distances, solid bars,
Into your tremulous, wounded garden.
Solid, stereophonic sound
Is your foe, not a lilting song, not a breathing flute,
Alive, aspiring, fay, and friend.

Dulciana has answered when I called
Needing a neighbor's reply.
Letitia has listened to my songs
And understood. Shall I
Find that I am she who wrongs
Her neighbor and, appalled,
Hear my own nightmarish, hellish cry?

Letitia understands
My songs. I understand
Nothing. But do I know
That I must sing, that she

Must play? Is my song play
(Where is the play of mind,
Where is the play of heart?),
Her playing hymnody?

The song of Letitia's flute,
The song of Letitia's mind,
The song of Letitia's heart.
My destitute
Science or art.
What could I learn if I could find
A way to learn, if I could start
To substitute
A soul's audition more refined
For a body's hearing too acute?

Against all my tenets —
Even for a few minutes —
Can her scaling of the better
Grade

Grade me down to the bitter,
Her joy
Annoy,
My flower
Prove sour,
Her pure tibiciny
Rouse this cacophony?

If, hour after hour,
I compare
Tunes of this tower
That beat on my bower,
Am I fair?

Pound, pound,
Across the hall —
A musical sound
To my neighbor Paul.

A chain saw screams
Through his fastened door —
Or so it seems
To me. A roar,

And airplanes come.
That is my gaffe.
All this is from
His phonograph.

My song makes no noise,
Exerts no compulsion,
Invades no one's space,
Plunders no one's time.
How excellent my song!
Even my ancient typewriter
Proclaims itself as noiseless.
Everything is relative.
Silently my pen doth glide.

Is a dissertation a song?
Will my notes be a dissertation?

Is silence writing? Is writing speech?
Is unnumbered speech a song?
Are the speechless numbers song?
Hissings a goose's or a swan's?

She understood — enjoyed — my song.

Letitia's sorrow understands.
Its buds will flower in new song.
Letitia's joy — it understands.
Letitia's joy — its blossoms dance.

I will see the dance and laugh joy's laugh.
I will hear the song and understand.
I will listen to another's song.
I will hear joy's hymn, hear and rejoice.

I saw Letitia and the bloated giant
Standing on the immensurable plain.
He roared. He expanded. I was afraid.
She breathed into her flute, and he was silent.
She stood small, slender, shining, and her light
Irradiated his emptiness. She danced away.

There is a concentration in silence,
A blissful meditation after midnight,
Consideration in the ageless dark,
A sweep close, closer to the inmost star.

There is a concentration in noise,
A weaving where two strands are self and other.
This is no villa, this is a city, this,
This is location in this space, this time.

This is a city, governed by the giants.
Its buildings disappear. It is a plain.
The giants, like its buildings, loom in cloud,
Shout down the many little Jacks and Jills.

There is no urban pastoral. There are
Gigantic contests, screams, and trumpetings,
Shaking the rocks from which the great Timavus
Emerges as the wellspring of the sea.

The city spreads, dilutes, refocuses,
Dissolves, is gathered, sounds with the sheeplike cries
Scattered about the darkness as lost lambs
Rally and fall. A quiet. Then a siren.

Is there a concentration with no center?
Since when has noise been most authentic song,
Nausea the sense of music of the spheres,
Absurdity the highest seriousness?

Puckish, the sparrows play.
Friendly, reedy, the sparrows sing.
Up in the feeble, weedy maple
The sparrows sing and feast among the green flowers.

Sunday, April twenty-eighth.
The festival of Floralia.
From Linnaean Street as you look up the slant
Of Washington Avenue's hill, you see
A queen, majestic, supple, standing
In her soft pink cloak, Dido perhaps,
The beautiful, the magnificent,
Perhaps (the red rose meddled together
With white) Elisa of princely grace,
Perhaps (you look more sharply) fair Flora herself.
The robin intones fair Flora, Flora the fair.
On Washington slope   the weeping cherry,
Spring-warm, still   softly blossoms,
Weeps not for woes   as Weland might,
Weeps not for wars   as well it might,
Weeps for joy,   joy that brings tears

To the gazer grasped   by the gushing pink's
Bonds of beauty   binding the eyes,
Freeing the mind   as the flowering light
Of the tree touches   the troubled soul
That arches and floats   to its form and release.
That has flowered;   this may, too.

Monday, April twenty-ninth.
The second day of Floralia.

The feast

The feast and heavenly birthday
Of St. Catherine of Siena,
Who died in Rome, for Rome, in 1380
(On Sunday, April twenty-ninth,
The Sunday before the Ascension,
Easter and her thirty-third earthly birthday
Having occurred on March twenty-fifth, the Annunciation),
Fragrant with the sweetness of the saints,
White-hot with their fire.
Beaduhild went   to Weland, the smith,
Her husband, the clever,   his hands a maker's,
Raised the warrior,   Widia, son
Of them both, planted   a pear tree there
By the fortress, setting   flowers about it.
From among the hyacinths, white, pink, purple, blue,
And daffodils, and multicolored tulips two
Mourning doves fly up into green, their wings singing,
Not mourning, ringing
Ascent, elation,
Elevation.
White the pear tree rises,
Its stair of clouds of white
Rising through shine of green,
Its lush white clouds,
Its luscious clumps
Of pure white rising,
Its ladders of cloud,
Its clusters of candor,
Pure puffs of white
Ascending through the new green.
Beaduhild might laugh, and Catherine
Find figured here the soul's elation,
Each seeing with her spirit   as her self's thing
Her mind's matter   mirrored in the tree,
For Beaduhild at last   beatitude at home,
For Catherine still the call   to climb still farther.
To a sky that is scrubbed,   scoured pure blue,
The tree here rooted   rises white.
That has flowered;   this may, too.

Tuesday, April thirtieth.
The third day of Floralia.
She thinks of this as the feast
Of St. Catherine of Siena.
She is out of date.
It was moved for history's sake.
And was Caterina Benincasa
Born in 1347,
The year when Francesco Petrarca
First drafted his *Religious Leisure*
(Shall we call it *Religious Stillness*?)?
She never knows enough.
She never knows.
On Maethhild's moans   she muses a little.
She knows too little.   She knows they have passed.
She is witness. Winter's   world has passed,
Supplanted by green's   gradual, sudden
Subtle sylvan   splendor, she knows.
The woodpecker whittles   the wintry catalpa.
The cardinal exclaims   as the chlorophyll of the maple
Edges his ruby   with emerald silk.
Sleep's deepest   dream is pale.
Her open eyes   are attempered to the year.
She sees the crabapple's   starry heaven.
That has flowered;   this may, too.

Wednesday, the first of May.
The fourth day of Floralia.
From Jove let the work arise, cries Ovid,
For on this day around the infant
The horn of plenty was poured by the naiad
Amalthea. The horn is filled with flowers.
May, the month   of Maia, the Latin,
May, the month   of Mary, the virgin,
Is announced by a moon like a chaste Amazon's shield
Behind the voluptuous bloom of the rosebud cherry.
But the Kalends of May, though a call, are far from a call to war.
They are the proclamation of peace—
The labor and leisure,
                                        The business

The business and stillness,
The seriousness and joyousness of peace.
Can the labor and the leisure both
Be both solemnity and joy,
Be effort, effortlessness, and exhilaration?
Is the rosebud cherry's a frivolous delectation?
The maiden tree announces May,
Declares its nature,
As Claudia the virgin, who alone
Pulled the Great Goddess in her great ship through the mud,
Dedicated on the Aventine,
To another goddess, the Good,
On a slope of the rocky ridge, on the first of May,
The temple to be entered by women alone.

The maiden tree is an éclaircissement
Of May, the hardy month of delicate bloom,
The month of lovely, tough, uncommon, common,
Decorative, useful, ornamental,
Exquisite, vigorous, and fastidious lists,
Incipits, explicits, ends, initiations,
And flowery fulfilments.
The tree acclaims this May.
The velvet trunk is sturdy, strong, and staunch,
The satin branches capably perform,
The blossoms are Catullan kisses, hundreds, more hundreds,
    unnumbered thousands, more thousands unnumbered,
Pleasure fresh and soft and pink
On a clean spread of blue
Or equally perhaps on a layer of gray.
No effusion is equal to this profusion.
The pleasure has not always been present. The robin's
Sweetest notes were dropped, and he flew toward the south.
Theodoric passed   thirty winters
In northern exile.   That was known to many.
We have passed   winters unnumbered
In non-existence.   Now the blue
And pink and green   push them away,
Not violently but filling   the void of the enormous past,
                                                                    Exile,

Exile, emptiness   ending in countless
Bursts of blossom   bussing from the tree,
Blessing from the bounty   of the beauty of the tree.
That has flowered;   this may, too.

Thursday, May second.
The fifth day of Floralia.
The redbud's bits   of rose of purple
Glint and glow   and gleam on the tree
More ethereal, more austere than the rosebud cherry,
More lustrous, more seductive perhaps,
Perhaps more elusive, more alluring.
My words are too heavy
For this fragility that clings to the boughs,
This dainty, this productive power.
My words are too light.
Not more seductive; why compare?
Both draw; neither betrays —
Neither the cherry tree with its osculations,
Nor the Judas tree with its name.
Name it in Greek, the weaver's shuttle,
Name it in English. Now no leaves
Are flashing as the shuttle flashes,
No bud is red like a drop of blood.
This is the flowering time, beyond the names,

Beyond the Latin, Greek, or English names,
Beyond the genus or the species names,
Beyond the adjectives, beyond the nouns,
Eluding all the woven words,
Eliciting the shuttle yet again.
Many have sat   mourning injustice,
Warriors waiting   the withering of a rule.
Some have sat   staring at a tree.
Some have walked there   to wonder. Is it true —
The precious, palpable   purple luster?
That has flowered;   this may, too.

Friday, May third.
The last day of Floralia.
I will not say what gleams in the May rain,
I will not ask what luminosity
The lilacs and the dogwoods offer, whether
Maroon tulips are glinting edged with gold,
Whether the silverbell is ready to ring,
How gold tassels hang and sway on the birches,
Try to speak of the pour and the swerve of their tassels,
The shimmer of bows and tassels of gold on the oaks.
I will not ask if, thanks to Flora's
Flower from the Olenian fields,
Mars was Juno's child without
Aid of Jove or any god or man,
Or if Mars, mindful of his birth
Through Flora's flower, promised her
A place in his own children's city,
Honor amidst the flourishing of Rome.
No, I will ask, I will learn, for good Flora will readily answer.
You are entitled to learn — if you will ask, she will say.
Teach me the flowers and colors, the meanings of flowers and colors,
Teach me the meanings of Rome. This I will say of myself:
That I have been for a while   a Harvard student,
Flora's fosterling;   Flora is my name.
I have spent many springs   spell-bound by bloom.
Blossoms appear below,   above, around,
From the soil, on the trees,   from the sky, in the mind.
May-skied is my mind;   I'm making notes.
That has flowered;   this may, too.

Sunday, May fifth.
When Flora left
Her fragrance remained.

May remained, the month of Maia —
Φρόνησις, as Lydus says.
May remained, the month of Mary —
Virgo prudentissima.
May remained, the month of Mary —
Sedes sapientiae,

May, the month of Maia bringing
The in the invisible
Hidden to the visible,
Lydus says that Proclus says —
Not perhaps epiphany
But aphany to emphany.

Why did we always hate the Virgin Mary —
We Catholic American virgins exhorted to love her?
She was the ivory Maiden Mother
As Washington was the wooden Father,
Two goody-goodies, he with his cherry tree,
She with her May processions, her crowns of flowers,
Her downcast eyes, her celibate priests
Urging us virgins to nurture her virtues
In girlish souls: silence, passivity,
Obedience, humility, belief.

May remains, unbelievably blooming in silence,
May, its blossoming accompanied
By the audible flowering of the flautist robin,
May, the month of silence and of song
And Maia, the wise mother of eloquence,
The mythological, the logocentric,
But not the logostatic, for allegory,
Enigma, and the wings of words remain.

If the populus was deltoides,
If the myosotis was brunnera,
If the hyacinths and violets are not
Hyacinths and violets, and if
The flute is more like an oboe,
My words are not winged, they are
Wayward, wayworn. Why
Did Stevens find his myosotis
On a bush? On their green mounds
Rise violets that are white,
More violets that are violet.

Monday, May sixth. No error. As you wander
This luminescence — lilac, dogwood — is light
And more light in the rain, luxes unnumbered
As kisses were, as winters were. If light

Can grow so, can the mind not truly bloom
In May's illumination? Let us stray,
Though we are garbed in blunket liveries,
Among the lights and take account of May.

Let's tell the tale of blossoms as of sheep,
Noting the newest as one notes the lambs,
Putting a meter to each lilac's fragrance,
And measuring each dogwood's incandescence.

The redbuds are not painted; they are drawn —
Drawn into lavender, drawn into light.

Tuesday, May seventh. Longfellow's linden
Is just greening. Longfellow's lilacs
Are just purpling. I dare not call them
Washington's. On Brattle Street
The traffic rattles by at five.
The ranks and formations, the squadrons
Of lilacs stand there sweetly.
The rugged, aged, awesome
Linden waits there tenderly.

From the American Revolution
Grew Longfellow, sprang Whitman.
Out of the Roman Revolution
(Was it a true revolution?)
Virgil steps.

          Did Virgil lose
His peaceful farm in the confiscations
That followed battle? Was Mantua
Too close to Cremona? Did poetry
And patronage regain the place
For him — the poetry the cause
Of patronage — or songs prevail
With Mars as doves when the eagle comes?

The unconditional surrender
Of Germany — a dissipation
Of the titanic Hitlerian cloud —
Was forty years ago today.
There were other clouds. One hundred one
Years ago tomorrow Harry
Truman breathed his first. Can war
Be cloudless, power blameless? Gaze
At Washington the uncorrupted,
Awesome, pure. Gaze tenderly
As at the ancient giant linden
With its soft young leaves. The Roman peace
Was wrought by one they called august,
For whom they named an age, who, young,
Was cold and cruel and calculating,
Who, old, wielded peace as power.
For him they named an age of gold —
Of golden speech and golden song.

Who received the farm? A soldier,
Worthier of the land than Virgil,
One of Philippi's veterans,
Worthier than the rural singer
Of purple spring, of green shadow,
Of varied flowers, of the white poplar
Imminent over the cave, of peace?

Arms he will one day sing. What meaning inheres in the singing?

May eighth. Wednesday. Western
V-E Day. Like Easter,
This victory is dated
One way in the East,
Another in the West.
      The soft
Rosebud cherry blossoms are softly,
Sharply pink between the soft
Blue of the river and sharp
Blue of the sky. The cardinal is sharply,
Softly red on the green pine,
           The pink

The pink dogwood, the white dogwood,
The sharp white of the garden chair
On the green of the soft lawn.
By the stolid harshness of the brick
Backs of the apartment houses
Ailanthuses now doff their rags
And are shaking out their soft red handkerchiefs.

Shall I now hang the wistaria
From fences, porches, gables?
Shall I set the swifts clicking
Crazily about the sky?
Shall I set the comet columbine
In the sun and in nocturnal
Purity set Daphnis watching
Not the ancient risings of the stars
But an apparition? This is the new
Comet carrying Julius Caesar's
Soul among the very gods.
What weather will that comet bring?

A song placed Daphnis there.
I remember the numbers. Can I remember the words?

Six measures to a line,
Four counts to a measure,
Half notes and quarter notes.
Dione and the doves of Dodona.
What can they do against the eagle,
Jove's predator, the Roman sign,
Large and startling on the American
Embassy in lovely Mayfair?
Jove and Dione both possess
Dodona, both are ancestors
Of Caesar, both are guarantors
Of the glory of Rome.

                        The golden age
(I must be accurate) was half
Augustan and half Cicero's.

They might have called the first half Caesar's,
The second half Augustus Caesar's,
The first half Ciceronian,
The second half Virgilian.

A golden bough
Showed them the road.

Where are you going? Where the road goes, to Rome?

There are other cities.
There is the city.

But Latin has
No article.

Where are you going? To town?
Where are you going? To the city?
Where are you going? To a city?

I go evicted by a Roman
Foreigner who said: These are mine.
You old colonials can move.
His was victory.

   I had heard
That the countryside, from where the hills
Begin to slope, to the stream and the old
Broken beeches, was saved by song.

That's what you heard. But songs are doves.

I've left the mourning doves among the trees.
They seemed far off, but they were very near.

I've left the horsechestnuts
With all their extravagant lamps on,
I've left the laburnums
With gigantic golden earrings on,
I've left the virgilias
Almost gleaming with what are almost
Little elongated pearls.

Everything is relative.
Cambridge virgilias bloom for the Ides of June, the Lesser
    Quinquatrus, the feast of St. Anthony (losers' finder).
Cambridge virgilias bloom for Harvard Commencement (end,
    beginning).
Harvard Commencement will be a week early.
The wistarias were two weeks early.
I've left the virgilias on the (Gregorian) twenty-first day of May,
The twelfth before the Kalends of June (Julian and pre-Julian) —
May having been a long month always in Rome —
About (I fear, I doubt) to flower.

How will I write my literary thesis?
How will I analyze and synthesize?
How will I deconstruct and how construct?

Flora, where are you going? Where the road leads, to the south?
Flora, where are you going? Where the road says, to the west?
Are you traveling with or toward the sun?

I'm trying to drive the sun's chariot.
I'm traveling from Harvard via Yale to Princeton.
And there is nothing that I know.

May twenty-first. The sun
Is entering Gemini now —
In the time of Hipparchus.

My thesis will be paraliterature
But not saprophagous. No saprophyte,
No mushroom, it will be an aerophyte,
An airy orchid up in the living oak.
Altera, it will dwell in your song.
Geminissima, your song will dwell in it.
I do not speak of the Mantuan, whom if
I do not understand do I not love,
Upon the scraps of whose linguistic banquet
Do I not batten with no need to battle,
So rich it is, and if my intellect
Is not replenished, have I not eaten paper

                                                And drunk

And drunk deep of the pure Pierian ink?
I do not speak of those who have gone before.
I speak of you, my fellow traveler.

Where, Flora, are your feet taking you?
My feet are not taking me. The road is taking me.
My feet are stretched out before me. I recline. I recline at
  table. There is a legrest. There is a footrest. There is a
  recline button. There is a tray table.
It is not an airplane. I expect to see white clouds below me.
  There are no white clouds. There are gray clouds above
  me. There are green clouds speeding by me. This road is
  slow. It is obsolescent. There are no wings.
A low flute sounds through Rhode Island, through
  Connecticut. A swan song? There are no wings.
There are the swans. There, like white clouds floating, there
  floating on the water are the swans, swans and swans, not
  innumerable, numerable, numerous swans.
Along Long Island Sound sound
The long lines, the innumerable lines, the rumbling notes,
  the tumbling syllables, the aging epic, the long song of the
  train, the long train of the song.

May twenty-first. Flora
Is entering Princeton now—
In the age of relativity.

Flora, why do you look up
The antique risings of the signs?
Einstein has become a drive.

If a twin should voyage to a star . . .
Paul Langevin restated
The paradox of the clock.

If he had known that Germany
Would not perfect the bomb
Einstein would not have advised . . .

Everything is relative
The pacifists abandon peace.
The wars are never won.

The ignorant can play
With words, be played upon.
If the only weapons were words . . .

He was in essence a question
Of thought and not of doing
And not of being done to.

She is in essence a question
Of words. If words are desire,
If desire draws down the stars . . .

If she were even a question . . .
If she were more than a constant
Protasis . . . If that constant

Were a good hypothesis . . .
If only the weapons were words . . .
The hypothesis became a desire.

Einstein has become a drive.
Where are you driven to, where the street leads?
Tree Street has become her beat.

Although of Princeton virgilias she found
Just one, quite broken down, though flowering
Bravely on its few sound limbs, the Princeton
Trees are princely, regal, royal, kings,
Benign giants, living divinities,
Awaiting with their patient patent stance
Advanced study, advancing adoration.
From tree to tree she advanced in adulation.

And there, alone, on the battlefield
(So green the field) there stands the oak
(So green, so old), the Mercer oak.

The people have become names.
The names are words. And words
Will never, names will never
(According to the version) hurt.

            If only

If only the weapons were words.
Was Mercer hurt beneath the oak
That lives, robust, on the great green field
Of Washington's quick victory? Do, here,
The slain of both sides lie in a common grave?

The people have become places.
Einstein has become a drive.
Mercer has become a street.
Einstein lived on Mercer Street.
Flora drives on Mercer Street.
Flora walks on Einstein Drive.
She walks among the pagoda trees, the Norway spruces, the wood
    thrushes.
She walks out by the grazing deer, the feeding geese, the guarding oak.
The geese are in the midst of their great move.
The oak leaves move. The oak is motionless.
A lightning rod protects the oak, which stands
Bearing the name of Mercer. The bayonets
Pierced him on that peaceful green. Did he think
Of names, of titles: Brigadier General, Doctor?
Did he think of Culloden, Kittanning, Fort Duquesne?
Was he a medical student in Aberdeen?
Was he assistant surgeon to the troops
Of Prince Charles Edward? Was he alone in the woods
Of Pennsylvania, wounded, living for days
On a few berries, on two crabs, and on
One rattlesnake? Was he captain, colonel?
Was he, provisionless in the wilderness,
In danger from the French or the Delawares
Or from the Six Nations, or they in danger from him,
First commandant at Fort Pitt? Was he physician
And citizen and vestryman and mason,
With partnership and apothecary shop,
In Fredericksburg, with practice, land, and wife,
The father of five children, the last of whom
He had never seen? Revolution, the call
From Washington came before the baby's birth.

She drives beyond the oak on Mercer Road.
She drives beyond on Quaker Road. At Trenton
She waits for the train that comes from Washington.

Has it crossed the Delaware? Deeds
Have become paintings, paintings
Names. The phrases are titles.

The colonies. The united
Colonies. The united
States. The names
Were weaponry, not only names.
Not only names were weaponry.

Varus, your name, if only Mantua
Survives to us, woe, Mantua, too close
To neighboring Cremona's wretchedness,
Singing the swans will bear aloft to the stars.

The stars gleamed over the darkened trees of Princeton.
But were they princely trees? They were august.
But were they tyrants, despots? So celestial
An article is freedom (see Tom Paine),
The price is high, and tyranny like hell
Is hard to conquer. The trees were not monarchic
But citizens. The trees were presidential,
Presiding over lawns.

              Washington wrote
From Trenton, January first, 1777,
To Robert Morris, George Clymer, and George Walton: Gentlemen:
Yours of the 31st of last Month, incloses me sundry Resolves of
   Congress, by which I find they have done me the honor to intrust me
   with powers, in my Military Capacity, of the highest nature and almost
   unlimited in extent. Instead of thinking myself free'd from all *civil*
   Obligations, by this mark of their Confidence, I shall constantly bear
   in mind, that as the Sword was the last Resort for the preservation of
   our Liberties, so it ought to be the first thing laid aside, when those
   Liberties are firmly established.

A small train ran from Princeton Junction to Princeton.
She emerged into the breeze of the afternoon.
The tulip trees were blooming along the track.
The cedar of Lebanon spread out over the garden.
The empress tree presided in the park.
On the institute grounds the Norway spruces stood
Tall and grand and gracious in their robes.
That greenest field, that greenest May-green field,
After the battle (see Doctor Rush) was red.
From the greenness rose the oak.

                       Washington wrote
From Pluckamin, January fifth, 1777,
To the President of Congress: Sir:

We found Princeton about Sunrise with only three Regiments of
   Infantry and three Troops of Light Horse in it, two of which were
   upon their March for Trenton; these three Regiments (especially
   the two first) made a gallant resistance and in killed, wounded and
   Prisoners must have lost near 500 Men upwards of one hundred of
   them were left dead in the Field, and with what I have with me, and
   what was taken in the pursuit, and carried across the Delaware, there
   are near 300 Prisoners, 14 of wch. are Officers, all British.
      This piece of good fortune, is counterbalanced by the loss of the
   brave and worthy Genl. Mercer. . . .

General Mercer was still alive.
His horse had been shot. A musket butt
Had battered his head. The bayonets
Had penetrated seven times.
Stabbed on Friday, January third,
He died on Sunday, January twelfth.
In the paintings he is forever newly fallen in the field.
The oak, if not there then, stands as in a painting now.

The names passed: Cambridge, Boston,
Providence, New Haven,
New York, Princeton Junction, Princeton.
The signs passed: Princeton, Trenton,
                                                          Newark,

Newark, New York, New Haven,
New London, Kingston, Providence, Boston.

Harvard was a subway station,
Massachusetts an avenue.

Friday, May thirty-first.
Alas, the battle of the flute.
Ready, the contest of the song.
Why is she unsoldierly?
Why can't she endure it?
Why is she unpastoral?
Why can't she enjoy it?
Alas, the battle of the mind.
Ready, the concert of the mind.
Can't she conquer sound?
Can't she pasture sound?
Is her mind no general?
Is her mind no shepherd?

Move, the soldier said
To the shepherds and farmers. Alas,
What if the singer above
And the flautist below should move
Out and lengthened loudness enter?

What if loveliness should leave,
Float away like petals crushed,
The concert of minds crushed?

How can the mind corral itself?
If only she did not mind.
The question becomes desire,
The positive negative,
The noun a part of the verb.
Desire for peace or victory?
Who beats a piano across the way?
Enemy, why must you break her peace?

A mind that can even flourish upon care:
George Washington's (see Thomas Paine).

Clump, clump.
Clump a clump a clump.
Bump, bump,
Bump a bump a bump.
Thump, thump,
Thump a thump a thump.
Music from next door
Making her a bore.
Hasn't she said it before?

Down near the river,
Up on the hill,
The virgilias are blossoming
Or are on the brink of blossoming.
The virgilias are on the verge of June.

And must she lose or win?
She seems defeated. Still
Virgilias begin
The tenth eclogue, the last.
The mountain laurel almost
Shines, the roses glow.
Virgilias begin
To light the Arcadian way,
To illumine future and past.
Gracefully interlaced
With neighbor in the chaste
Love that never can twist
Either one's tune or tone —
Each one can grow alone,
Everyone play and win,
All give and have their fill —
She will write on Virgil. She will.

The last labor of the flute.

Arethusa, virgin fountain, spring
From Arcadia, dive beneath the sea,
Flow through the ocean and arise
Unbriny in an American mind.

Verbiage, wrote Pound
To Williams, is American.
Verbum sap. Let us be quick.

Let us tell their solicitous amours.

What groves or what glades
Kept you, Naids, when they were dying?

Gaius Cornelius Gallus,
Known as a general and poet,
Lay beneath a rock in Arcadia,
Dying of love.

Flora Urania Baum,
Known as a graduate student,
Rocked upon a chair in Cambridge,
Thus dying, too.

Apollo came to the soldier: What
Insanity, Gallus. Lycoris
Has followed another man through snow, across
The Alps, across the Rhine.

Apollo came to the student: What
Absurdity, Flora. Cognition
Is seeking another sort of mind, beyond
Sounds and appearances.

Silvanus came. He was garlanded
With white and gold and purple
And orange and brown and mackerel
And blackest irises.

And then Pan came. He is the god
Of Arcadia. He was painted
As red as the roses on the trellis.
He said: But Love is cruel.

Groves of virgilia, glades of mountain laurel,
Held the Naids. June had begun.

I myself saw Pan.

You saw the god Pan?
And you heard him say
Something? Be quick.

Love is never satisfied,
He said. There never is an end.
Desire has never reached and touched
The final star. Amor must send

Arrows past the universe.

Saturday, June first. The feast
Of Juno Moneta. Remember the geese
Of Juno on the Capitoline?
They saved Rome. Up through the night
The Gauls climbed. The geese cried.
The hill was saved. Later,
In battle, the temple was vowed. Later,
Sitting in the church of St. Mary
That stood where the temple of Juno had fallen,
Gibbon remembered Rome. Later,
Sitting there, Henry Adams remembered.

Now I remember the aspens along the stream.
Even on Saturday, even
On Saturday on Massachusetts Avenue,
One sees things clearly in June.
It is an eastern cottonwood.
The green triangles move in the wind.

One June Galileo abjured
In the Church of St. Mary over Minerva.
St. Catherine of Siena was buried there.

Risen, glistening purple churches
Of purple beeches. The grand expanses.
Lifted, golden chalices glinting
On tulip trees. Innumerables.

From the first until the eighth of June
I celebrated Virgilia,
A new feast, movable, conceptive,
And every day I made a lustration
From gleaming station to gleaming station.

Most like pearls and lace,
Like constellations, galactic snatches
In great green space,
The blossoms hung, like latches

Opening,

As the blossoms opened and opened along the grand triune down-dangling of their panicles,
Here along the virgilia walk, the avenue through the enclosure, through to the open gate, the iron gate open, the college gate that is open upon the highway and the river and the green field,
Two lines of virgilias lining the path, rising over the path and the glimmer of grass with the grit of trunks, the glint of boughs, the green glow of leaves, the glisten of flowers in sun, the gleam of flowers in shade, the white shine in the shade, the rays of fragrance spirited by the wind,
The lifting boughs, the dripping blossoms, descending without descent, with lunar light without light's glare, white clouds without clouds' obfuscation, the clouds of swans and milky ways and honeyed emanation,
Papilionaceous clouds, their droplets resolving into the millions of white butterflies, sweet psyches gathering and still distinct as they lift little wings,
Alae papilionum, ailes des papillons pressed from piano keys, papillons danced on piano keys, rising alive and alate and significant from the keys,
Keys, clefs, signatures, scriptures, documentations, denotations, connotations, notations, notes,
Phonemes, morphemes, semantemes, graphemes, grams, calligrams, easy beauties, difficult beauties, pedantic beauties, poetic beauties, callemes, poetemes,

> Here,

Here, in the Yard, above the chairs, presiding over the
   commencement chairs, though the trunk of Child's virgilia,
   as I must call it, is much more pockmarked than President
   Washington's face, that was only very slightly scarred by the strong
   attack that freed him in 1751, and so almost twenty-five years in
   advance, from one great danger of the Revolution,
While the long white clusters, pendants, pennants, glisten in the
   midst of things, hang, fly, solemn, celebratory, luxurious, and most
   frivolous, above the mayors, presidents, celebrities, seriousnesses,
   gently petaling the heads, the chairs, the grass, ever glistening over
   the grass, unnoticed but most noticeable,
Here, in the virgilia grove, where, if I notice, I want, I have, to say
   what the giants forbid,
That the grove is magical, its satisfactions multiple, its loveliness
   existing (shall I say that it does not exist, that it does not exist again,
   shall I not say it exists, not say again?), existing, rich, mysterious,
   gray, green, white,
The blossoms affluent, effluent, defluent, fluent beyond my fluency to
   match, in candid tongues, in multilingual cadences, in incantatory
   arrangements, in chants, charms, riddles, mysteries, proofs
Of the truth of what I say,
In reiteration of precious edges, edge upon edge, of luminaries
   throughout the vault, of clouds about the verdurous dome, of the
   first warm sweetly odorous snowfall begun as they open, open,

The way to a conception.

The yellowwood has a silver bough,
But to me it was gold.
I saw through it. It led me on
To the very old

New blossoming, the very newest
Opening, new numerousness,
New pluralism, the polyseme,
Sheen shadowy redundancy of candor
Of which I would be scholar, would be cantor.

Geminissima, how can you be
So heavily pedestrian, so flightily poetic,
So witlessly visionary, so preposterously pedantic?
Oh, you're so hopelessly phonocentric.

Simply
The smooth gray trunks with their smooth gray glint,
The soft green leaves with their soft green glow,
The abundant long white clusters of flowers,
The whole umbrageous and agleam —
These are or seem . . .

Φαίνεται, videtur, it seems to me so
Like to godhead here to be sitting staring
Long at beauty. Only if mind could stare, too . . .

Saturday, June eighth. The feast of Mind.
Mens quoque numen habet.
The Mind has divinity, too.
See Ovid, who could see
The gods because he wrote
Of them and of their feasts throughout the year.

I saw Apollo, Silvanus, and Pan.
I did not panic. I did not move.

Don't be crazy. Accept what is.
What is includes this flowering.
What is includes the limitlessness

Of love, for endless is desire
And Amor knows no moderation.

Those who should know know
That one can never know.
I who can never know
Know that I must so

Aim as I have been aimed at by
Desire and penetrated by
Those stochastic strategies
Employed upon the flowering trees

That never reach conception. Graft
Me, then, and let me flower, I laughed.
Or let me bloom on air, I laughed.
I blossom past the margins graphed

For me by what I can
Do, since what I must
Try will cross that ban,
Abandoning to trust

The mind that finds it trusts the trees,
That flourishes among the flowers,
Desires the stars, and ever sees
The guides that step from ivory towers

And witness to ideas. It knows
It cannot know, but on it goes,
In upon etymology,
Out along logodaedaly,

Round and round upon each word,
Round on the rhythms that have stirred,
On on the flapping, frantic wings
Of love of what and how it sings.

Then they were love's wings after all?
If love does conquer all
They were that after all;

Before that petals of a great
Flowering; before that great

Flowings down from being,
Up from grounds of being.
Then before all there is being?

There is a mind that cannot know
Writing what it has to know.

Thursday, June thirteenth.
I awoke to the sound of a flute,
A long, low lamentation
Of long gray trains, an undulation
Of purple ocean, the respiration
Of being, of a being breathing
Being, or of breathing being,
Contracted and expanded through
Bamboo, through human flesh, through one
Heart and mind, without constraint,
Strain, or diminution,
Happy in a delicacy,
Without dilution,

Exploring and transforming sad
And happy, here and there,
Won and lost, received and given,
Essence and existence, yes
And no, is not and is.

He painted her portrait.
He expected her to be ecstatic.
Don't you understand? You will be immortal.
He did not understand. She did not explain.
She wanted to immortalize herself.

The give and the take, the now and the then.
The ocean rose and the ocean fell.
Letitia entered silence. Flora
Or Altera began to sing
Of a purple sheep, once shepherded,
Now leaping free, once laid upon
The altar, now roaming the grove.
The fall and the rise, the one and the more
Than one, the others, the other.

If Gallus is Daphnis,
If the infinite has no center,
If I have no share
In the roses from Pieria,

> If the

If the grove wants an altar,
If I am embattled
Among the flowers of Arcadia,
If a Muse is Memory's daughter,
If Gallus was the friend of Augustus and Virgil,
If Gallus saved Virgil's farm in 41,
If Virgil wrote about Gallus in the 30's,
If Gallus helped to capture Cleopatra,
If Augustus made him the first prefect of Egypt,
If later Augustus recalled him and renounced him,
If Gallus killed himself in 26,
If rosemary is memory
Dewy like Venus from the sea,
If a pansy is a thought, inviolate,
Viable, like Proserpine out of the earth,
If there are many flutes
Of many materials and constructions,
If one may play more than one,
Now one eastern, now one western,
Now one ancient, now one modern,
Now one softer, now one louder,
Now one lower, now one higher,
Now one mastered, now one untried,
Now one that eludes binarity,
A star flying free,

If I'm planning to be a classical scholar,
If I'm training to be a literary critic,
If everything is relative,
If there are no classics but only canonizations,
If there are no values but only evaluations,
If they were love's wings after all,
If even a word can hurt,
If even a word not meant to hurt can hurt,
If the word-hurt can be word-healed,
If Mercury, Maia's son,
Can come with his wand, on sandals with wings,
If Augustine chided Cicero,
An important man and philosophaster,
        For shouting

For shouting in the city's ears
That he must placate Flora by celebrating
Games which are the more devout
The more they are shameful, or if
Augustine wept that he had wept
For Dido when she died for love
And had not wept for his own death
Caused by not loving thee, the light
Marrying mind and the heart of thought,
If all closure is premature,
If you got used to the robin
Throbbing on every block,
If the Latin language is masculine,
If shepherdesses recenter songs,
If Western culture belongs to men,
If males created civilization
And citizenship and urbanity
And idylls and bucolics, too,
If shepherdesses sing strident songs,
If George loved Flora, Flora Will, Will Barbara,
Gallus Lycoris, Virgil Gallus, and Flora Virgil,
If Publius Vergilius Maro
Is seventeen papyrus rolls,
If Flora Urania Baum is a piece of paper,
If Altera Geminissima is, too,
If Flora Urania Baum is a thousand pieces,
If I, you, she, and we, you, they
Are impersonations, if their songs
Are recantations, if their hyperuranian
Escapades are escapist out-of-date evasions
(How do I love thee? On paper, in protases, with protestations),
If certain abstract rhymes are imitations,
If collages are imitations
Of modern scholarship without the notes,
Or with the notes, and if an ancient stream
Protects its flow from muddying citations,
If music must be played,

If it has been play,
If I have played with Thalia
And she with me and in me and upon me,
And now it must be labor, and Arethusa
Gushes but gushes pure, chaste, classical,
If density brings implosion,
Expansiveness explosion,
The fragments flinging through the vast,
The fullness crushed in on itself,
If the center wants infinity,
If the scent is of infinity,
If the fragrance lasted past the moment,
If the pipe that was played two thousand years before
Was heard today, if I hear a Virgilian
Note, I will write it down.

Surgamus. Solet esse gravis cantantibus umbra.
Then let us rise. There is a shadow that is bad.

Thursday, June thirteenth. The day
Is dark, the building still. In the distance
Those are trucks that bump and boom.
In the distance that is a robin fluting.
This is the Ides of June. I find—
When I wander like a tibicinist through the city—
Surviving white on Child's virgilia,
Brightening yellow on Longfellow's linden.
Just for a moment the sun is shown.

If opacity is good,
If obfuscation is bad,
If the divine is light of light,
If the song is dark of dark,
How shall we sing?

The Ides of June are called the Lesser Quinquatrus
Because that day is the festival of the flautists,
Who worship Minerva, whose own feast day
Is the Quinquatrus in March.
                                                  Thus

Thus Festus, in his epitome
(In twenty books) of Verrius Flaccus.
The people in the forum turn and stare
When, masked, in varied robes, the flautists play
In the midst of serious business, public and private.
They wander through the city making music
And gather in the temple of Minerva.
See Varro, Livy, and Valerius
Maximus for details. The festival
Continues for three days. When Ovid asked
Minerva for the meaning of the feast
He wished that he could reproduce the words
The learned goddess used when she explained,
Well, I am the inventor of the flute.

Did she throw the flute away
Because it puffed her cheeks out? No.
I've said or I've at least implied
That those who tell that tale are wide
Of the mark. To this we must assent:
The flute is wisdom's instrument.

It was a tunnel rather than a cave.
Through it blew a wind, one wind, one breath,
One spirit, issuing
In different notes. Perhaps
The breath was white, the notes
Of many colors. Was
Letitia's a fine gold perhaps, perhaps
Letitia's subtlest rose, Flora's a purple,
A fuzzy purple but a purple still?

Anne's book was green.

On Child's virgilia, to mention only that one, some flowers are
   open. Others have been.
On Longfellow's linden, to mention only that one, some
   flowers are open. Others will be.
Others are opening, small and multitudinous,

                                                                                      Now

Now they are opening, bright and dulcitudinous,
On the huge tree.

Sing out my song, sing it out, it is meant
To be sung, it intends
To be heard, it is burdened with the heavy
Necessity of its performance,
It must be sung, be shouted aloud,
Be loud, not overpowering, not
Denying, not
Negating, only
Equal to ears if opened, to mouths
If mobile, to responsive woods,
To towers that tower.
In New York I was born, among the towers
That cried impentametric to the sky.
Nevertheless, intention is not mine.
It is the cry's.
The notes are jotted.
The paper crackles.
The song wants singing.
It may be sung in silence, may
Be shouted silently, be loud
Only in muscles, blood, and brain,
Be sung unvoiced along the breath.
It must be sung.

        Will that do?

                No.

It must be read. And written.

              Must?

It is already half covered with dust.

Nought weigh I, who my song doth prayse or blame.
Colin, in June.
There are cases which cannot be overdone by language.
Tom Paine, in December.

Will I analyze,
Will I synthesize,
Will I thesize by inditing
A song of a song of a song,
Song of song of song? Is this
The miss in the abyss,
The missive in the abyss of
Song? Throughout the immensity of the linden
Scents begin to glimmer on
And on and on. Flourishes glistened,
Flourish on flourish on flourish, on the virgilias.

Part Three

Umbrageous Vision

Umbrageous Vision

Chapter 1: VMBRA
Chapter 2: ARDOR
Chapter 3: VIA
Chapter 4: ARBOR
Chapter 5: VISIO

Nos patriam fugimus; tu, Tityre, lentus in umbra
formosam resonare doces Amaryllida silvas.

Virgil, First Eclogue.

Par le mot *par* commence donc ce texte
Dont la première ligne dit la vérité....

Ponge, "Fable."

The circular arrangement of the axes of the Difference Engine round large central wheels led to the most extended prospects. The whole of arithmetic now appeared within the grasp of mechanism. A vague glimpse even of an Analytical Engine at length opened out, and I pursued with enthusiasm the shadowy vision.

Babbage, *Passages from the Life of a Philosopher*.

Le pré gisant ici comme le participe passé par excellence
S'y révère aussi bien comme notre préfixe des préfixes....

Ponge, "Le pré."

Pan deus Arcadiae venit, quem vidimus ipsi
sanguineis ebuli bacis minioque rubentem.

Virgil, Last Eclogue.

CHAPTER ONE
UMBRA

Shade the word shade beneath the rusting beech
Whose shade is gold. Shadow the silver word,
Shadow, not mirror. And silver the word
Silver, not the page, not gray living skin,
Chryselephantasize in fall, in spring
Read the bronze promises of rustling truth,
Troth of reality's expansiveness.

Imagine Darwin striding across the pampas,
Paradise Lost in his pocket. In Darwin's garden
Grew worms and flowers. Plants moved. These adumbrations
Move across our rest. Motion and rest,
Said Newton, are the same; at least he said
They differ only in the way you look
At them. Across the grass the shadows show
The sun moving. At noon, at night, you rest,
Virgilian flocks, if you eschew, escape,
Ignore the Roman Revolution. Shade
The shade. Or face the music. Music plays
Under the broody summer of the beech.

The virgilias this year have lambed but lightly
Above the silver staves; below, however,
An emerald rest in emerald shade is still
June's, noon's, prerogative. A shadowy
Confusion is the negative assessment
Of undeniable dappling undenied,
A mediator of the sun's perfection,
That rare perfection of Lowellian June
Sifting through Cambridge, Massachusetts, rippling
Above green Elmwood, into its green grounds,
About the yellow clapboard mansion, through

The tree

The tree that stands on the green lawn before
The house, one of the trees, virgilia
Or yellowwood, the tree, silver or gold
In the vocabulary of rarity
And either/or. But the virgilias
(Or yellowwoods) are rarer, living, swept
Into white frenzies one year or the next,
Pure frenzies, sweet and calm, just luxury.
James Russell Lowell, when Charles Darwin died,
Was pallbearer in Westminster Abbey.
When Lowell died Henry James took a walk
To gaze at Elmwood. Flora took a walk
To gaze at Elmwood on a day in June.

In some respects shadow first falls in autumn,
Our best season, the clear, the sharp, the brilliant.
In some respects shade commences in April
When, as you walk, the first few raindrops halt
In maples' green bouquets. You walk in love
With mere Aprility. Dappling is sweet.
The shadowy, the shady — what are they?
The question is too pointed, much too clear.
Do not take umbrage at my clarity.
This measure forces this sententiousness.

Dark, dark, descends upon mine eyes. Despair
Debouches sloshing into the wide sea,
The empty ocean of my mind. Despair
Spews darkly from my sagging mouth. Lightning
Cracks the green tree. The images are wrong.
Our sea, our central sea, lies to the south.
Heat, not the dark, threatens our blessed shade.

That is, the opposite of shade is heat.
That is, an enemy smiles from the sky
And slips the shirt of Nessus on our shoulders,
Making our walk a Herculean labor
In which we zig to shade and zag to shadow,
In which we zip to bushes, zap to buildings,

Hope

Hope for alleviation from each pole
Between us and the unturned tropical
Torridity in heaven, whose repercussion
Assails us from the concrete hell below.

Then know, before catalpas' major shades,
The mountain laurels' white umbrellulas.
And greater fall from the high mountains shadows.
I sat at table, eating and talking.
The mountain rose before me. It was time.
The mountain has already been traversed —
If it will be. Kismet. There is no God
But the eternal. Shadows of abstraction
Fall from highmindedness. The dancing shadows
Dance through the dazzling days of June, the days
Of timelessness. These are the days of sweet
William, Japanese lilac, honeysuckle,
Lindens, tiger lilies, and bittersweet
Nightshade. So there is night. Beyond the lengths
Of sunlight lying like columns across the grass,
Beyond the perfect yellow rose, beyond
The subtle sunsets sung by the subtle thrush —
Snapdragon sunsets which the woodthrush sang —
I cannot match heartbreaking subtlety
In silence, song — beyond all these night fell.
In other days I could have said fell night.

Yet, if the center is meridional,
How is it that one has a northern mind,
How is it that one finds oneself among
The long, long shadows of the long, long days,
Swifts screeching after supper in the skies
Of afternoon, of afternoons that merge
With midnights and the merle's finales, where,
Above stone walls, the roses dream? Blackbirds
Are thrushes here. My subject is not black
Or white or red or rose or colorcast
Or colorfast or chromatology
Or Merope, who hid her face because

She

She blushed at humanness. Meropia
Is human. There is too much shade for shadow
Only sometimes, only sometimes sun
Itself is shadowy, roses of shadow
As good a subject as the roses' shade.

Isn't it best without a subject, with,
Alternatively, only itself as subject,
With, in fact, no only, no without,
No (shall I declare it?) with, no fact,
No declaration, no alternative?
Isn't it best without its questioning,
Its questions, its red question? Will the swans,
White, smite the atmosphere of green and blue,
Strike, white and purposeful, the mellow green,
The hazy, lazy blue, or, smooth and slow,
Guard their white shadows?

High up, on the plane,
The shadow of my writing cast itself
Upon my writing. Shadows fly like love.

The bright-red-beaked black swans are not the shadows
Of white swans flying or of white swans floating
Along the ripples and beyond the islands
Where willows lift and fall and float and ripple
As windlets lift and fall and feathers ripple
Green on the willows, white on the swans, or black
As black swans arch, nor are the white swans shades,
Antipodean, analogical,
Of their black cousins out there past the huge
Dapplings of the green-great London planetrees
Shadowing our observations.

All
My observations are in shadow. All
My green-great thoughts are shadowy. I have
No thoughts that are not shadows. Do I have,
At least, these shadows? No, I have no thoughts.

Plop. The bait descended like a stone
And no fish soared. The ripples may have gone
From green to gold. Gold was irrelevant.

The golden shadows of Grynean groves . . .
No, the gold shadows were irrelevant.

The golden letters of the vellum leaf,
Mingling with green and red and blue and purple . . .

Is this an unintelligible script,

She wondered. Will the nymphs give lilies, plain
If purplest in their glinting plenitude,

Or will the golden characters be locked —
As though spring's, summer's, all fall's gleams were mocked —

Within some sempiternal glaciation?

On a pale day a gorgeous glittering
Of paling green and brightening deepening gold
Pulsates through gray panes and a flittering
As wind dips swishing through this radiance
Uniting movement with the lumining
Moving already with the message of
Salutatory moribund November
Communicates unchanging changeables.

If, covered by the baleful woolly sky,
Skirting the earth's bright vegetable flames,
She walks the slick gray street, gold leaf and bronze,
Crimson and scarlet, painting the way before
The uncertainty of her step, she may yet hail
Night's shade, which, hastening along the rain,
Night's shimmer, rubrous night's great goldish glare,
Still heralds with a bronzy trumpeting.

Thoughts of the heroes, of their heroisms,
Rise from the fires, descend the downpours, skim
The misty meadows of her brain. One night
May be the prize. Their reddest battlefields

                                                                            Are green

Are green now and their golden altars sweet
With frankincense, with frankincensial flowers
From all the meadows. Daisies in the sky
Or snowflakes glimmer. Are the stars that white,
And do they shine on, white, red, green, and gold?

Whiteness of snow on boughs, on leaves of gold,
Snow cold on roses, slow snow's premature
Descent upon November's gilded paths
Do contradict the reconciliation,
And purple swans fly like desires, like shades
Of black or white evading gray, escaping
The way ordained, as though the golden tree
Were evergreen, the snow its complement,
The vision in the white night day's.

                              As though
A hemlock shouldered candor now, the beech,
Grand in its goldenness, was shadowed now
By white.

        But shade the word.

                                  To you,
Tityrus, under umbrous beech, I think
I must get down; of you, resting, at rest,
Under the umbrous summer beech I think;
With you, singing at ease, I — do I? — sing.

Remember and remember how and how —
In study how we whirled the year around,
Around, and singing set the sun.

                                And how,
Forget, we fell in dim streets, stiff with hours
Of listlessnesses, mindlessnesses, blinded
By unenlightened days, sickening, sick
To death of weeks whipped out of tune, of months
Drummed down, of all the unmelodious years.

Forget the decades of forgetfulness.
Forget today. The night has come, when light's
Dark orphans work, whose labor is their play,
Shade their illumination, shadow rest
Beside Permessus, eddying with excitement.

With the paternal Jove shall I begin,
Wondrous, thundrous, thumping, bumping, dumping,
Heightening, brightening, lightening, frightening, rightening,
Grounding, hounding, pounding, pondering, pensive,
Serene, the bluest blue, the whitest white
Behind the blue, the white fire of the sky,
Jupiter through and through, true blue, tried white,
Who carried Europe on his wide, white back,
Tracing a culture's track, who also spake,
Nature's Homer, or with the civic prince,
The youth and sister's daughter's son and son
And father of the fatherland and name
August and patronage imperial,
Or with the famous daughters, Julias,
Or with the daughters that give fame?

                              O Muse,
Late is my beginning, late is the year,
Late the month, cold this November, dark
This Thursday night, silent witchy midnight,
Its rumbling distant, although the building quivers.
I quiver, Muse.
                Thalia, how you came
I will not explicate, nor how I went
Into your ruddy cave. How, now, you come,
How, now, authoritative, you slip in,
How you are here . . . Crass, cruel sleep enfolds . . .
Enfolds . . . A shade . . . I cannot go on with . . .

With the word with commences then this text
Of which the first line tells the verity.
And truly truth is what this text desires
                                              In secret

In secret and its texture what it works
Its words to wind. Its window secretly
Opens, the curtains blow, their texture thin
Enough for wind and thick enough for shade —
Shadow or mirror of the encompassing cave.

And when a shade is raised, a window shut,
A light left on, a curtain twitched away,

One stands out there, clasping a grayish book.
The brightest lamp obscures a whitish lamb.

The only sun that enters is reflection,
And even that, under a cloak of black

Or gray or white, whatever positive
Covers this negative, must exit if

The bending and rebounding binding in
And out are not become irrelevant,

Just as the risk of glass is not alone
The stone thrown but the seeing being seen.

What silversmith hath made the silver bowl
Turned over us in an old-fashioned way,

Filled with the milk of sixty million ewes?
Out there the lambs, untarnished, dream, in the black.

One sees out there, beneath a roof of white,
White bridal clusters, late gold, but nées green,

Out there one sees, beneath a vault of gray,
The juniper's grave shade beside the lamp,

Out there one glimpses, twitching a cloak of blue,
Milton risen at evening from the lawn,

Darwin reading Milton in Argentina,
Darwin in London reading Adam Smith,

And one has sat beneath a sky of blue
That curves beneath a sky of gray that rolls

Beneath a sky of blue; there one has perched
With Marx and claimed the famous azured room

And, gazing from the blotter to the dome
Of blue, seemed to have worked, seemed to have thought.

Return, Thalia. Silent is my night.
The white that glittered gracefully all day
Subdues the evening. Let the arboreal snow
Curl up in sleep. Let the ice be content
To dwell outside, where it is right at home.
Why, if the door is locked, is ice within?
The door is locked. Return, soon, with a key
And pines and gushing brooks. All day the pines
Were gleaming whiter than their names. Return
With fire. Shadows will ripple from the core.

The radiator hisses. There is ice
Within. How do I know this? If I stand
Without how do I know? If I just lay
A hand over my heart I know all day
I felt the pines' stiff gloved and mittened fingers.

The silver eddies of the river slowed,
Froze. Oh, so far the Alps stand from, ah, sweet
Aonia. So far the Rhine, so far
The Charles runs, lumbers cumbrous, numbs from, ah,
The argent source. One was undone here, stunned,
Stunted, and stumped. Yet one had seen, had sung,
Sun and spun shadow whence the song had sprung.

The edgy, tense land of the pluperfect.
All the exuberant leaves had blown away.
Their blown shadows also had departed.
I stood beside the bronze tree on the bank.
I saw myself like Cyclops in the ice.
I was the shadow. That was my wide eye.
The blown blossoms, pink puffs on blue, had been.

And then the great shade almost supervened:
December. Only Thanksgiving prevents
Surrender to that apparition creeping

Over

Over our horizon even when the
Noon moon is puffs of shades of white and gray
Adrift in azure. Only adventitious
Bits of glisten outlive the near-fictitious
Witchhazels' bits of gilding living on
Into the ultimatum of the sun
That stonewalls most reporters' questions, if
It can be called the sun's, given the distance,
Given the intimation of a will
To pathos.

    I, Tityra, am a slave,
But we don't mention that. It's not a part
Or parcel of the genre. Nor do we speak
About a gendered subalternity.
That's not a part. For Thestylis must cook
At noon, when each and every one except
The madman and the lover and the cicada
Rests in the rustling shade by rivers' merry
Mirroring tuneful waters. Thestylis
Stands at the stove.

      The Muse sits in the shade.

Primus ego, he said, in patriam . . .
Prima — it does not scan — into a land —
My land — of fathers I will dance among
The daughters dancing from Aonia —
If I can live . . . I have already lived
Longer than he who first to Mantua
Led the indomitable Muses.

       Rome,
How many have you dominated?

        War
Is not a way. Fathers, into your land
I bring your children — will, if I can live
A lifetime, will, if they can live a life,
Bring them.

          See the many daughters dancing
Through the dappled gardens, over the hills,
Into the mountains, high above the trees,
The snows, into illimitable skies.

Shade the skies gold. The sun gleams. Golden fruits
Glow from the boughs of the Hesperides.

Only fruits may be grown, the bill declared.
Who legislated flowers from the world?

The golden apples of Hesperides
Grow from white blossoms flecked with hints of gold.

Fleck the boughs gold. The boughs are silver, gray.
Make their shade gold. Shadow the silver word,

Shadow, or mirror. Or silver the word
Silver, or the page, or gray living skin.

Blue Proteus at noon in shaded sleep
Nestled his sea-blue body deep in a nook
Of the gray cave. Slinking among the seals
I sought to shake his sky-blue mind, I thought
To grasp his thought. This was not violence.
This was but metaphor carrying me
Beyond intangibilities of sight.

Descend to blue. Arise to blue. The west
Holds the gold sun. Hesperia is yet
The land of Saturn, happy Sabbath land,
Though the Carpathian Sea is purpled black.

The sky was gray when Flora took a walk
To gaze at yellow Elmwood in December.
The spruce was green, the grass was green, the wreath
On the gray door was green, the yellowwood
Was the dark silver of virgilias
After a night of rain. Another night
Silvered the purple layers of the sky.

This is my thesis, Julia. Why must you
Keep interrupting with incention?
Playing pentameter may be a game
For you, but this is serious for me.
Can you not be content with your assigned
Role as third reader, after Mr. Lane
And Mr. Stevens? Why must your shadow lie
Across my page, where mine alone should fly
Before my pen's pursuit? The light is where
It ought to be. Why is your shadow there?

It is a matter of language, she replied.
Umbriferous authority has waned,
Authorship vanished. Contexts last, texts last,
Letters advance, and writing waxes great.
There are no authors.

                      Then what language is it?
American? or Ada? or a Latin
Branchlet of English? spindly ramification?
Or a sere silken English, nitid, slick,
Liquescent and lentescent? dull or grave
With dulcet mellifluities? or heavy
With the molasses of the Latinate?
Long slack weighty words? verbs turning nounward?
Verbalizations now denominated?
Cucumber- or most-porcine-sausage-words?
Legends as leguminous as lentils,
Plain as potatoes, various as soup?
Thick chewy or thick tender steaks of speech?
Or reruminated ruminations?
The streetcar storming up the empty street?
The earthquake shaking us out of a sleep?
Fat maximal packed within paragraphs?
A bit of minimal slipped in between?

Since Hesperus came later in the west
I sailed into the blackness of the sky,
Evading the great shade of waste December,
                                       The terrors

The terrors of untaxied afternoons,
Arthrosclerosis in the city's limbs,
The blue-and-gold-starred farewells of the ground,
The golden constellations of far earth,
My gaze from space beside the sky's one star.
The golden liquid in the plastic cup
Danced, as streams dance like fire upon the banks
Of rock, upon the seat back. Then I met
The gold and silver stellules of near earth.

Doves cooed and roses bloomed. Oranges adorned
Their trees like Christmas trees although the day,
Like the October hours of August in
Midlothian among sweet bees and sheep
And lime trees sweet as lindens sweet with June,
Was an October day of breeze and sun
And blue above and green below and red
Leaves on the sweet-gum boughs. And could this be
December? Palms and pines and pepper trees,
A creamy plane tree, an extravagant
Live oak, aged, alive, enormous, strong,
Vigorous, balanced, bonny, host to a host
Of bees, shading at noon the walker drained
By the solstitial sun, grateful to see
Green baubles rise and fall under the blue
Burning ocean of sky beyond the birch,
Cactus, cedar, cypress, oleander,
And bottlebrush — all stood about, all hale
And heartening.

                Once the Hesperides
Dwelt in Arcadia, and now they live
Beside the golden gate, where Heracles
Posits extremities of west and peace.
The seals slip from their rocks into the vast
Lunging Pacific. Rising above the tides,
A bright, a painted land cheers the depressed
Visitor from the east. It was a visit.

If you sit to the south, high over snow,
You must adjust the shade against the sun,
But shadows give the definitions, brown
Cuneiform from Colorado spreads
The message, puffs of white with blue depressions
Signal South Bend, Indiana, golden
Sacklets of honey-roasted peanuts pass
Along the cabin. By the portholes passed
The sugar-coated pills, white atoms, massed,
And rushing in their horizontal flow.
This was reentry. Why did we return
From rushing for Arcadia's umbration?

How will we reach the shade beneath the beech?
Hear pipes at noon? sing to the noontide flute?
Listen to Pan? How will we ever see
The god at midday under the central tree
That makes the shade that plays about the root
Of song, of sight, of silent thought, of speech?
Where is that vision? Why do I repeat
My sheepish tale, my overshaded bleat?

The trees, those lovely brides of long ago,
Wear blossoms that are white as — that are — snow.

I am a bride, snow-gowned and veiled in ice.
The shadow of my bridegroom keeps me cold.
That is a lie. This white is whitest fire.
The shadow is a mirror of my flame.
This is a fiction. Light pours from the sun
And trickles through the foliated shade.
Here is the tree under whose shadowy
Leafage I garner things sung and things seen.
Twirled in the turmoil, I return to clasp
The bole, the pole, the pipe, the telescope,
Earnestly playing, suddenly played upon,
Earnestly looking, suddenly looked upon
By my own eyes, suddenly looked into
By the spouse, other, player, mirror, shade,
Shadowy sun, dark double, bright delight,
Mild January, blue-breeze-cool July.

Confusion is the negative assessment.

Who is the one that rests beneath the tree?
Who is the one that plays beside the stream?
Who is the one for whom the lawns grow green,
For whom the hills turn blue, for whom the leaves
Lap the hovering skies, for whom the breeze
Carries responses to soliloquies?

We go most wrong in that which we deny.
Shall I deny that Virgil is my theme
As he induces blossoms from the dew
And sprinkles shade about the sleep-soft grass,
As he seats Tityrus beneath the beech,
As he sits shadowed by millennia,
Inflections, botanies, philosophies,
Shadowed by latitudes, by lexica,
By empires, imitators, breezes, jests,
Colors, theologizing, spices, notes,
Under Lycaeus, by the Mincius?

He stands, twitches his toga, climbs the steps
Of Widener, finds me waiting by the door.

Speech they call silver, but his words are gold,
As gold as silences, as melodies,
As gods in marble temples, as the first
Small crocuses, the last chrysanthemums,
The golden letters of the manuscript,
The golden ginkgo's growing golden shade,
The gray beech shadowy in gray November.
His words are shadowy.

                You, Tityrus . . .

What made his golden words, in my heart gold,
Silver on my gray lips, on my page gray?
His platanine, robust, fagutal shade
Extends for centuries, magnificent
And gentle. What penumbra covers me?

You, Tityrus, at rest where the beech spreads
Its tegument protectively above,
Ponder, compose, practice aloud the song
Whose subtleties the wild, wood-haunting Muse,
The mild, mood-haunted Muse, first formulates.
Inklings of barbarism, hints of war,
Mingle with inkhorn otiosity.
But the half-shadow falls here, not the shade.

And Sunday morning's study summoned not
Pan's playing, as I waited, not the long
Roll of Virgilian drums, the mountainous
Virgilian sweep, ascent, declivity
As, funneled to my over-opened ears,
His fluting, fraught with grand geographies
In tenuous enreedments, filtered through
My gaping cave, not these, but, physical,
Material, shocking to my intense
Vacuity, an actual sound, too loud
For the attunement of my magnified
Reception. Dread. A duo that would fill
My quiet cavernous abeyancy
For hours. The instant held the hours of loss.
I jumped up, jerked back my chair with a bang.
Silence. Remorse. A friendship banged. The flute
Played by my friend for moments probably,
Not by the two who would rehearse through noon.
Pan vanished long before his apparition,
Virgil unheard. The radiator sizzled.
A chill breeze filtered in from sills of snow.

Urbanity, how will you countervail,
Facing shady pastoral blandishment?
Civility, how will you sit at peace?
Neighborly noise again. Desist and cease,
Intrusions, musacs, rantings, harassment.
Peace be to all, the doughty and the frail.

Babbage's battles with the fluted scale
Of pavement organists: embarrassment.

The heroism of the poetic life —
A critic's phrase, praise of a hero — stirred
An unheroic heart to restiveness,
Dim listings, definite endeavors, quick
Impassioned strict envisionings, the smart
The critic would consider quite quixotic,
The valor of the dauntless scholar's art
In one the critic would dub idiotic.

The snows shone cold. The shadows took their part.
The mirror smashed. And ice stuck in that heart.

It was a fetish, harsher critics cried.
But what idea, what ideal, is not
A fetish if it burns brilliant and hot
Along the shining filaments of mind
And feeling, and, if scrutinized and tried
And innocent, is not a golden find?

This measure forces forth a measured thought.

The Japanese sheen — truth — upon the wall,
Shone bold, black, balanced, brave, and beautiful,
The character, shod, hatted, multiple,
Composed, contained, content, collected, sole.

This measure measures out a silver rule.

The sun was silver in the silver sky.
The silver stream was silver with its ice.
The silver was not gray; it was the white
Of January's shade of argentine,
Foiling and mirroring white unto white,
Light that seems shadow, shadow that seems like
Reflection, like the moon, the idle light
Of waning, with a shade of an excite-
Ment, an incredible élan, a bright-
Ening, the post-solstitial solar height.

The snow stuck to the northern verticals
For days. One was a northerner. To one
A whiteness stuck, a blankness, a veneer
Of innocence, of purity, which cold
Causes to cling to coldness, to inert
Surd surfaces unseen by southern shade,
To the huge superficiality
Unwed by depth, unnurtured by a third
Dimension. That blanched flat abstraction shadowed
A whole exposure, one's entire direction.

Yet, though immobile, one rose through the snow
Towards a white sky and tended towards a root
Whose food minute flakes could be or assist.
Assisted by the parable one laughed
Shadowily, abstractedly, and fast.

The flakes fell fast. The maple was awhirl
With still, round, revolutionary beauty.

She was returning from the seminar:
Feminist, Deconstructionist, new Marx-
Ist views, reviews, revisionings of art.

Virgil, that maple, plane tree, beech, bold oak,
Shaded her squinting, dripping, blistered gaze
From the cold glare, the snow, the page.
         The poem
Groped its way toward the tree. The essay slid
Across the ice. The thesis skated off,
Revolved, resolved, leapt, landed, tramped, tracked, slipped.
The grandeur and the freshness of the tree
Mingled. The leaves were hoary, bronze, gold, green,
Pink, as the breezes, rendered zephyrous
On contact, apochromatic though they were
Themselves, created coloring and shade
For a too anxious and too scrupulous
Attention. How her sentences, that meant
Caresses given by her mind, could blow
With such gruff bluster, how could her mind know?
            Her mind

Her mind was summer's, but her wintry gush
Of speech was snow, its lying, grayish slush.

Virgil, the shadowy, is never gray.
The overwhelming blizzard of his lines,
Piled up at dawn, he, like a sun, all day
Heats, shades, shapes, shifts, reduces, lights, refines.

Cicero wrote to Atticus in June
Of 44 B.C.—June twenty-eighth—
That he had settled to the treatises,
Which, though, he wrote, I fear will need the mark
Of your red wax in many places. Times
Were bad, distracting, hampering. He wrote
November fifth, now gratified and glad
That Atticus had liked his work, had quoted
The gems, brightening them by his approval
In their creator's eyes. I was, he wrote,
Terribly afraid of those red wax marks.

Criticism, she admits at lunch
With five writers, is, I find, no use
To me at all. This makes her blush. Perhaps
The consequences are embarrassing.
Yet if the Muse speaks what can one . . .

                                        But if
Pan or Silenus speaks to us or sings
To us, his countenance is smeared
With elderberry or with cinnabar.

How necessary miniation is
For manuscripts and gods, most foul, most fair,
Most red-faced, most red-penciled, most red-gold.

Tityrus, you . . .

                    Shadow the shadow, Muse.

What can the Muse do?

Lie or tell the truth,
Silver the gray word, gild the silver, show
The gold as golden, ice as icy, glass
As silvered into mirroring, a word
As shadow, as reflection, as relief,
As cool opaqueness, shade, not luminous,
Not hot, not vision, dim frigidity,
A silver chilled and tarnished, sloughing off
Of sunbeams' squamous summer chains, rebuff
To sunlight's long oppressive tyranny,
Rebuttal of the tough meridian
That kills with sunshine, wars on us with warmth.

O Muse, cool the word cool.

                    You in the shade . . .

Virgil, a mortal man, became a shade.
A mortal man — let me not be obscure —
Can never be the spouse undying, skied,
Divine, not so much skied — let me be clear —
As sky, light's light, heat's heat, cold's cold, obscure
Obscurity's profoundest obscuration,
High clarity's most highest altitude,
The god, the grand idea, the ideal,
The heroism, not the hero's gest,
Singing itself and not the singer's song
And not the singer singing in the shade
And not the easy shade. Shade difficult,
Simple, and infinitely implicated
May be divinity, and implication
With and within the umbral depth without
End or commencing, if the nuptials must
Be consummated, such a consummation.

My subject is a spacious ancient shade,
Ageless, new, cooling, with delimitation.

Must that theme's negative be the rebuffed
Tyrannical oppression of the sun?

The Grynean grove is Apollo's. Its beeches, oaks,
And laurels shade an oracle. Its full
Or flimsy shadows seem the messages
Of a god of scholarship, a divinity
Of erudition. It seems like a museum,
A library, an academy, a school
Where leisure is life's work. Its marble trees
Gleam. The glint of ivory and gold
Signifies the god. The greens are fresh
With the fresh breaths that circulate among
The living leaves and leaflets. Shadowy
Peace spreads, rustles above the rivulets
That rush, arisen, sprung from depths, toward breadths
Of sea.

   I, Judith the obscure, observed,
I, pious Flora, from the edge observed
The evidence: foil, flowering, and fruit,
And the fall's aureation of the shade.

I saw that poets walked there. Virgil walked
Among the shadows, sat among the shades.
The shades were living there, the shadows green,
The umbratile red-blooded. Virgil was
Alive there.

   I was ghostly, marginal.

Virgil was alive in Arcady.
Was that a lost paradise for me,
Or a walled garden of which I could share
Only the wall? And yet who met me there,
Opened the gate, and took me by the hand?
If I admit it, who will understand?

Who will, though understanding, not avow:
We've heard all that before?

      Before, not now.

Now Tityrus is sitting in the shade.
Now the book spreads its words like a repast
Shadowed, like a picnic beside a stream,
Beside a patulous sea, beside an ocean
Awaiting fathoming as letters patent
Expect perusal, as more belletristic
Texts expect a plunge, as the Permessus
Expects a sip. With the Permessus, then —
By the Permessus, then — must I begin
My climb to song — by the word by begin?

Among the Eildon Hills, where the thorn tree stood
By the spring, a beech tree spreads its silver roots
Over a hollow. There Thomas took his plunge
Into the earth. But beech trees do not grow
By water. But a beech tree grows there now.

Now Tityrus is sitting by a beech,
As the book says. The beech is patulous,
Tityrus recumbent, or recubant.
I see him, but I want to see the shade.

Do I see? Will I ever see? Will the
Day spread branches and leaves of light across
These skies, across these eyes, across this mind's
Waste wilds, across the feverish unseen
Unseeing emptiness, incredible
Desert in heat, in a fever of cold
Unseeing dolor, dim chill, dark data
Undated, unrooted? Can these shallow
Heated, cooled sands — are they January's,
Can they be? — uphold, hold, boles, boughs, and the
Lusty unfolding of the leaves' luster?
Heat, not the light, wars upon our good shade.
Heat, and not light, is the foe of the shade.

The shade cools him at noon, and I am glad,
Not envious. I am amazed, not sad.

I sit at least a minute in his school.
This is the metric of the silver rule:

To write what shadows show you must be read,
To say what shades assure you must be said.

With the benign assistance of the shade
Tityrus sings.

                Divine must be this aid.

Oh, how my elbow hurt, and then my back
Hurt, then suddenly I comprehended
The heaviness was my umbrella's, silvered
With ice. Then I slid home again to study
Summer.

         But the bronze buds of the beech
Were silvered, silver catkins hung along
The glassy boughs, from the brown leaves had sprung
Long silver galls. Doves' wings dropped silver sounds.
The brown leaves of the beech were petrified.

Tityrus was a rather passive person.
Virgil calls him inert, meaning, I think,
Not lazy but weak, ineffectual.
He must have worked quite hard to send to town
All those fat animals, all that rich cheese.
The job was done without hope and without
Profit as long as Galatea held him.
He fed fine animals, pressed dreamy cheese,
Never went home with money in his pocket.
This is the negative side of human relations.
He did his best. Then Galatea left him.

There is a positive, and Amaryllis
For him was only positive, possessed him
So selflessly, so helpfully, with such
Soft tenderness, such rich exuberance,
Such subtleties of intellect, such shrewd
Devices of the practical that he
Could hope and save — and buy his liberty.

That is a shock. Tityrus was a slave.
The women, though, we may regard as wives,
Successive wives, friends and not mistresses.

Tityrus was a slave, and he was old.
Under the barber's blade his beard fell white.
But freedom looked on him, though late, it looked
On him, it looked . . .

                Why did he go to Rome?

Tityrus was a dreamer, a good fellow,
Lacking in practical imagination
But full of poetry and of good will
And good intentions. He stuck out his job,
Plodded his dutiful way through his daily tasks,
Was loyal to his friends even if they
Drained him, was blessed, finally blessed, with one
Friend who could save him: bring out the best in him,
Enable, make that possible which was
Essential — preparation for the one
Bold move, going to Rome. For there alone
Could he shake off his slavery and there
Alone know his present god. There he saw . . .

It's hard to make it sound right, now, in English,
In 1987, in the third
Millennium since our tale was invented
And Roman emperors first seemed divine.

He saw what saved him, saved his livelihood
And gave him leisure lying in the shade.

The great things were compounded with the small,
The small things placed together with the great.

What did he see? A youth. What did he see?
Caesar (Octavian), strong man at Rome
(His colleague Antony being out east).
What did he see? One whom he would be pleased
To call a god. One whom he would be moved
                                  To worship

To worship as a god. An Eastern god-
Ruler, although a son of Rome. Rome's power.
The might of and the might within. Relief.
Alleviation after civil strife.
Peace, if for just a moment, during war.
Rome's slow pacification. Rome the grand.
(Was it not Roman grandeur that he saw?)
The grant bestowed. The artist's trust fund founded.
Philanthropy. A national endowment.
If not benevolence then benefaction.
Not an enslavement but a liberation.
A social order in its ordering.
A revolution in its settlement.
Political arrangement. Patronage.
Poetry paid for and the poet paid.
(Is there a market just for beef and cheese?)
A writer's job, not quite a sinecure
But something useful, something nurturing.
Charity joined with justice. Something good.
Ability permitted to reach need.
(Even Utopia has need of beauty.)
What did he see? Luck or society
Allowing thought the leisure to be thought
And art the shady leisure to be made.

Then he came home, where his resources lay,
His sources, his cool springs, the holy springs
And the known rivers running under cool
Shadows at noon exuding music. Here
He played and nature harmonized. Here he
Created and the world was taught to sing.

This is the idyll, this the pastoral,
This the desiderable shade of Rome.

I will go, I will go to Rome, I will
Find this freedom, gain this liberation,
Though late, though I am old, I will, must, see
This god, this nature and this nature's god,
This luck, this fortune, this transcendent gift,
This social

This social good, this good society,
This life, this liberty, this leisure, crown
And aureole and shade desired for all
And for myself, this sacred shade, this right
Desired for all, for us, who must not feel
That by society or fortune we
Are exiled as poor Meliboeus was.

Latin, the language of a man, a land
Of liberal pursuit, of leisurely
Literature, of study and of art,
Of history, of empire, of the west,
Of humanism, heroism, high
Culture, tradition, class, the classical,
The classic, and a masculine salvation,
Save me, this drudging Meliboeus, save
Me trudging on forever into wastes,
To waste, to barbarism, to the shores
Of inhumanity, the silent shore
Of incommunication, the dead sea
Where learning, art, and humanness are drowned
And good is useless, looking on a void.
Save me, O past. Be here, O present god.
Grant even Tityra, O future, leisure.

Here, I want to stay here, this is Rome, here,
This is home, here, I see Virgil himself
In the doorway, Virgil under the beech.

Here I am, at home, in Rome, in Naples,
In Cambridge, Massachusetts, flourishing
In noble study, in most Roman leisure
(The empire and the emperor but serving,
The love of letters spurring), here I am,
Ignoble Flora flourishing in Rome,
Sitting and living in that vivid shade,
Shadowed so foliaceously by Latin,
Beech- and book-shadowed, pupil, student, scholar,

Or I

Or I am Servia, the scholiast,
Allegorist and allegorical.
Thus the audacious sphragis fades and fails.

Yes, I am Servia or Meliboea
The exile or that Thestylis who stands
Cooking for all the masters as they sit —
The poets and the scholars — in the shade
Of noon, the beautiful creative shade.

Tomorrow will the groundhog see his shadow?
Today is Sunday. Golden was this day,
Golden the glimpses of Grynean peace,
Golden the leafiness and gold the leaves,
Golden the lettering and gold the words,
Golden the waving edge of every page,
Golden the wavering edge of the afternoon snow.
White was the snow and silver and the blue
Of evening but a gold this afternoon,
New February's ivory and gold,
Long my titanic shadow on the glow.

The terror of the error. Am I then
That which I fear, am I then Meliboeus
En face de la Blanchotian truth: not truth
But exile?

        I have begun, I will begin,
With a Virgilian sip, a Pongian plunge.

Am I then Meliboeus realizing?
Am I then Meliboeus realized?

Must I revolve to the beginning, to
The shade (another's if not mine) beneath
The tree, protected by the document,
By the word by, with the word with, beneath
The beech to teach the sylvan syllables
Of Amaryllis to the willing wood,
Or am I whirled, hurled back before beginnings
And by the bye to shadowless withouts?

What shady places wait, what arid vasts,
What gentle springs or what relentless falls,
What drynesses or what docilities,
What Amaryllis or what Galatea,
What Tityran repose, what Meliboean
Migration, or what Tityran request
Or quest or visit, what great trip to Rome,
Or what Promethean, Derridean,
Cartesian, Heideggerian, Platonic,
Hegelian, Aristotelian,
Parmenidean, or Thomistic thought
Waits in the wings, waits in the shadows, for
I do not think and therefore not I am,
Not therefore, not not can be cogitated
By me but I am not, the knot uncut,
Unchopped by logic, nonsense or negation.
Non sum, I think, ergo non cogito.

Videte (Paul) vocationem vestram.
See your vocation. What has God elected?
Et ea quae non sunt: that which is not.

Philosophy is not my discipline,
Nor is theology though I must write
Much about gods, for did not Tityrus
See, when in Rome, a god — see, when in Rome . . .

In Roman Sicily a noblewoman
(Self-proclaimed slave) was chosen. She became
A saint (virgin and martyr) in the reign
Of Decius (emperor) when Quintianus
Was praetor (at Catania). Her name
Was Agatha. It was revered in Rome.
Her festival was February fifth.

Saint Agatha of Sicily was chosen.

On February fifth a satin sky
Satisfied us at five — a pale blue satin
Bannering us as we poured forth ourselves
From all our varied martyrdoms. The shadows
                                                          Were

Were all one on the whiteness as it lay
In plains and mountains. On the avenue
A shoveling and leveling, with shrieks
From tractors, was in progress, into trucks.
It was a day that was too cold for slush.

The sixth of February. Anne would be
Fifty today if only she could be
Sitting in the kitchen. Shady Hill Square
Stays there. And I remember a December
First, a seminar in Sophocles,
Cedric the professor, fire and shade,
And a depression after class, explained
By the professor passing the bare beech:
I am fifty today. And I remember
Cedric, Promethean, the hero and
The scholar, Anne, the scholar and the saint,
The martyr, the good Agatha, the good,
With all these words, with many shadowy
Abstractions, with foreshadowings and aft.

His last book, *The Heroic Paradox,*
Was published after Cedric's death. It stands,
A monument among his monumental
Pillars, as they all stand along our walls
And rest upon our shelves and are held, read,
And living in our living hands. Anne's book
Was green. Its leaves, gleaming above the snow,
Rustle. Their notes are music. Shadowy
With abstract words, my book, like the gray beech
No longer scanned by Anne's or Cedric's gaze,
Aspires to stand in their sweet shadows like
A gray stone pillar, in their bitter shadows
To sigh with the distress of brownish leaves,
In their gold memories to search the blue
Vibrating over gilded branches. Buds
Hint summer, buds with pointed utterance
Insist: Summer will come and summer's shade.
Shady Hill Square refrains from vanishing.

Was it the groundhog's shadow that I saw
The other day, the woodchuck's, marmot's, mus
Montanus's, that of the mountainous
Mouse? But that was a squirrel perched upon
The twig, that must have been the shadow of
A squirrel on the unbent slender end
Of the enormous elm's last lengthening.
The finch was singing Februarily
That effervescent cheer, quick, quickening,
The sun recovering. Was what I saw
The elm's grand shadow down upon the church,
The elm's gaunt shadow up against the wall?

Rome, which gave shade to Tityrus, denied
The same to Meliboeus.

                      That sweet god
Who showered leisure over Tityrus
Snatched it from Meliboeus, to bestow
It not upon the old slave but upon
The warrior, the foreign barbarous
Soldier who fought in the discordant wars
Of distant Rome, of Rome whose shadow fell
Such sun-long distances.

                          The distance grows.
What shadow can that pole, that post, display
In a postludial, postliberal,
Posthumanist, posttheological,
And — shall we hope it — postimperial,
And — shall we post it — postmilitable
Now?

       Does, with one tree felled, the forest fall?

Post hoc, I posit, ergo propter hoc.
I am revolved into beginnings or
Subsumed within a newer revolution
Or made a byword for the passerby
                                    Bypassed,

Bypassed, the never-with-it, and withal
The ever-withershins, postiche, postdated,
Postfixed, postscriptive, postpostpositive.

Therefore, I will postpone to chapter three
The exposition of novanticism
And the proposed exposure of novantics,
And I defer to chapter four the charge
Of posing every postwoman's difference,
Wondering only adumbratively
Whether the post will be a prefix here.

This is a mere first chapter, Flora thought,
Like a hyacinth tip before a wall,
Green among purplish elderly attendants,
Attended by the dead, wooed by the south.
This is a kind of preface, Flora wrote
Posthaste before the heavy gray became
White and then whiteout, polar and shadowless.

Her brother saw her spirit penetrate
The sky like a bright dove. Her festival
Fell on the tenth of February. Day
Blew blue and white and cold. The northwest wind
Whisked through the Widener windows. Every gust
Like a brusque spirit whipped out a report
That tortured Flora, chained as she was, enslaved
To day's pale azureless faint spiritless
Gray uncreation: Saint Scholastica
Will never be a patron or a name
For such as you, unskied, unearthed, wind-chilled
Yet uninvigorated. Witchhazel rays
May stretch their gold on white, their golden bright
On blue. Their sweetness cannot reach your cold,
Their breath your pallor, their first fine unfurled
Bright shade your infinite unsubtlety.
Such dullness cannot bear a benediction.

Flora remembered, though, and said it well:
This is a metered thesis, not a poem.

This is

This is a dissertation, not a work
Of art. This lusts for truth, not beauty. This
Studies the truth of beauty. This must know,
Not be; shadow, and not reflect.

         The slave,
However, never, even if in Rome,
However deep in Rome, never will see,
From that unfreedom, truth, let alone tell
The truth seen, not to mention say it well.

Don't worry, for the words shade one another.

Then Flora saw the *Georgics* spread their fields
And skies . . . But her discourse on method flows
Through chapter three. This lies before and after.

Rome the great unknown became the great known . . .
But Rome will be disclosed in chapter five.
This chapter is the shadow of a shadow.

But if a leisured shade waits at the end
As it bends over the beginning, what
Can be the point of all this lusiveness?

The Chronicle of Higher Education
Has advertised the ultimate position
Exactly, adding no greater or lesser
Irrelevancy to the job description:
Department: Leisure Studies. Rank: Professor.
Requirement: Doctorate in Recreation.

He whom I called a god permitted me
To play. Virgil was standing by the door
Of Widener. I had gone to meet him there.

Widener is nothing but a library.
Widener my spouse, how can you be my master?
Widener my love, how can I have become
Your slave? If I, so deeply implicated
Within your inmost gray and multicolored
Shadowed labyrinthine fact-full fantastic
Recesses, never cease to find that first
            Bursting

Bursting fiery excitement and never fail
In love's eternal steadfast loyalty
Lasting enlarging multiplying filling
The world with wordy offspring as though I were
Nature herself and you that cultivation
Which first changed chaos into cosmos, how
Can you, dear, chain me to the stove while all
The schoolmen and their pupils sit around
Beneath the green beech leaves in beech-green leisure?
I know that I know nothing. And I know
I was not made to be a Martha. How
Can she whom knowing wooed and who communed
With him in somber forest, stupefying
Oceanic depth, awake to hew
Wood, fetch water, serve as a ferry boat?

And Flora wept. But Julia said: If you
Are a student you have no right to tears.

Yet Flora floated like a lily on
The sylvan pool of her own outpouring.

Let there be no misunderstanding, said
Flora. If I pour forth a shadow of
Myself I cannot help it. If there is light,
If one stands in the light, one must endure
That dark companion. But my purpose is
To stand in shadow, understand the shadow,
Cast only the shadow of a poem,
A group of poems, first select collection,
Poem by poem, poem with poem, choice
Fruits from choice bough. Look at the *Eclogues* then.

I wondered why the fruits hung on their trees,
Continued Meliboeus. Amaryllis
Just left them there. I was amazed. And why
She called so mournfully upon the gods
I could not understand. But now I know,
For Tityrus had gone. The very pines,
The very springs, these very vineyards called
For Tityrus.

                    I had to go to Rome
So that the woods might call out Amaryllis.
That which a yearning love could work through her
Only a leisured art achieved through me.
The trees which shouted Tityrus now sing
Beautiful Amaryllis.

                    Seeing Rome
Accomplished both. Then must the artist's friend
Let the friend go?

                    The loss is short, the art
Longer than life.

            Is it that easy?

                            No.

Was it a song that Amaryllis whimpered?
Was it a prayer? Was it a magic spell?
Did the trees listen? Did one see in pools
The presence of an absence, hear from the hills
The pining of the pines or pine-veiled Pan
Shaking his veils or the sheer sound of sound
Or the blood's brooding — luminous behind
The eyes, tuned in the temples, loosed
Upon the auricles' oraculation,
Stuck in a stannic and stanniferous ear?

Was the tain tin or silver? Was the mirror
Miraculous or was it a mirage?
Was that a smile? a smirk? or admiration?
Was the noise tinny? silvery? or white?
Was it all done with mirrors? Or upon
Reflection did it prove a stagnant sea?
The marvel was a looking glass creating
A silver laugh on trumpets argentine
Out of the sol-fa, out of the do-re-mi,
Out of the crinkled tinfoil of her song.

For Tityrus was singing Amaryllis
(Playing not playing with her in the shade).

Letitia played a drum. Letitia's hands
Were playing on her drum. Study held me.
Apartments must be decelestializing.
It is not ennui that embraces us
Within their walls. It is their walls and floors
And ceilings that betray us. Isolation —
Their Roman name, their promise — is a lie.
Where is my hermitage, where my celestial
Cell, and where oh where an uninterrupted
Study, sunny or shady, as the occasion
Asks? Where is the musing meditation
That lasts, outlasts tenuous penetration
Through shadowed woods of matter, up the high
Great-shadow-casting mountains of idea?

The drum had penetrated to the stream
Of my own blood, pounding against the current
Of my own heart, wasting away my mind.
Letitia's mind I loved, her heart I held
In reverence, her hands I saw as held
Themselves in meditation, as themselves
A meditation. How those hands could pad
Across the drum, be paws, be claws, be squirrels'
Feet rattling in attics, be the feet
Of rats scratching and scrambling through the walls
Between apartments — this I could not see.
I did not see them. Squirrels pawed my eyes,
Rats gnawed my mind, mures montani bit
Mountainous chunks of wood out of my heart.

Why couldn't Babbage give us a computer?
You are the rodent, whispered Baudelaire.
Yes, Iris Murdoch said, the mousy one.
Poor Flora, Amaryllis sympathized,
You're silliest in your self-pity, but
You're craziest on paper. And you're most
Immoral, Flora, in your sentences,
Basest in phrases and in images,
Worst in your words. Can words be bad, I asked
The beautiful and brilliant Amaryllis.

The artist and the scholar and the saint
Are three yet can be one, was her reply.

If I have framed and written evil words
Have I not sinned in thought and word and deed?

My question, my confession, went unheard.
We heard the woodland learning Amaryllis.

It is Book Four in which the good is sought,
Thought Flora as she stumbled through the forest.

And then she saw it. It was what she heard,
What she had heard, not silver trumpets, not
The drum, the pipe, the flute, though it was noon,
Cool — cold — , smooth, blue noon. Circling in the air,
The thing appeared that she had heard for hours,
The thing she had been hearing, not a song,
Not Amaryllis, not Scholastica,
No, not a soul, though bright, not Agatha,
Not good, not blessed, not giving benediction
(Nor was the watcher Benedict). It was
A silver winged thing like a seagull breaking
The unbroken blue of the sky. It was a stiff
Seagull, no seagull. It was a machine
Relentlessly revolving in the heavens
Around around loud loud loud loud loud loud,
Mercilessly circling through the azur,
Meaninglessly gleaming through the céleste,
Without a message, with no bannered phrase,
Without a trail of words. It was brute noise,
The purely noisome, absolute annoyance.

He heard the woodland answer Amaryllis
When it was Amaryllis that he sang.

You would be heard if you played by the rules.
Hurt and alarmed, I asked, The rules for what?
Decasyllabics and pentameters?
The brick walls guessed it did not matter which

                                                            Rules.

Rules. The brick walls were fairly regular.
The sidewalks hazarded stress and the times.
The sidewalks glinted, dry here, icy there,
Here snow-piled, there deep-puddled in depressions.
Late shade came later. Snowdrops opened. Three
Closed crocuses yet hinted purple, gold.

Darkly within the purple bud we played
Lest February open into March
Before we had concluded winter's game.
I was afraid the shadow would be peeled
From the deep chamber when I had not sunk
Enough, or, if you will, before I plunged
To play's profundity, before I plumbed
The lusory, before I could perfect
The study of repose. Summer will come,
Thalia said consolingly. We then
Again will rest steeped in the depths of shade.
Deeply within the golden bud we played.

And Tityrus was playing Amaryllis
To the deep grove. Enclosed, I listened in.

On February twenty-eighth, however,
When the first crocus actually bloomed
(The sole gold crocus opened that gray morning),
There was a momentary opening
Of one's own self right there on Shepard Street,
Of one's own solitary spirit right
There on the sidewalk, one's pedestrian
Soul in a smile, almost a sole gold laugh.

And Tityrus sat happy in the shade
While bees buzzed happily from bloom and blade.

Gold laughs are hard, feel forced, seem cynical,
Whereas the golden laughter of the gods
Is of the gods, divine. And silvery
Laughter belongs to Tityrus, to song,
To art. The silver laugh is never tarnished.
                                        The golden

The golden laugh may be ironic but
Softly ironic, far from sarcastic. Still,
Pure golden laughter has a purity
That thrills along its ripples from its depths.

These are the rules for laughter and for laughs.

And there are other regulations — made
To break? or to observe, conserve, subserve?
Does it depend on how you conjugate?

Never, never yoke two trochees together.

Never endure the inconcinnity
Of matching sennet, tucket, trumpet stern
With oat, the instrument so tenuous
It begs in whispers otic nicety.

Twice in oral examinations Ponge
Found himself unable to say a word.
The nicety of writing triumphs, though
Speech like a dumb drum beats the barbarous ear.

Some writings must be drummed, be trumpeted.
They must be shadowed on a silver reed.
They must be photocopied invitations
Posted at nightfall, slipped along the morning.
They are not overheard. They use no force.
You need not play them, need not listen in.
They whisper: We are marvelous. They chirp
Admirability. They whimper some.
They weep a lot. They laugh: Play your own tune.
They supplicate: Don't force your tune on me.

They are sung safely in a soundproof room.
Is it quite safe for phonophobes to sing?

Not only photophobes desire the shade.

Reflect that light is not at issue here,
The proet added. And on our great goal:
To demonstrate that shadow flows with song.

Who can it be from whom that music flew?

Lear's shadow, said the fool. Who is whose shadow?
This was what Julia asked. Flora proposed
A question, too: Who is it in the shade?

On Saturday, March seventh, clothes were swishing
And swashing in the querulous machines.
On Shepard Street — only on Shepard Street —
The crocuses had warmed to the caresses
Bestowed by master sun. No longer bold
And brazen but relaxed and happy, they
Were opening, were amorously open.
But it was old white winter in the shade.

How did the bees discover what I found?

Lucky old man, said Meliboeus, bees
As they have always always will for you
Flit fed upon the willow flowers from
The neighbor hedge that suasively will edge
You with soft buzzes into slumberdom.
Song soft and sumptuous will sound among
Blossoms from under rocks up on the hill
And scud each rill of air. Song will be sung
And air upon air blending fall from the elm.

And shadow upon shadow from the mountains,
Dear Meliboeus. If you cannot stay
Long here in song's perpetual blessed shade
Rest here as long as this night's shadows are long.

March was martial. Long before the Ides
Those crocuses had time to smile and die.

In the First Eclogue there are two kinds of shade,
Noon's and night's, day's shade and evening's shadows,
Umbra and umbrae.

                      Um, there goes the drum.
There goes a savage animal: the drum.
There goes the rude flute. There goes the brutish drum.
There goes the beastly drum. Did I pretend

                                  Appreciation

Appreciation of Letitia's flute?
Did I pretend to understand the growl,
The howling of the vina? There goes the flute
Piercing through like assassins' swords. There goes
The drum like pots and pans: Bump bump, bump bump,
Bump bumpity bump, bang bangity bang, bang bang.
And on comes the machine gun of the drum.

Only the faun's ears show his forest nature,
Said Hawthorne.

          Hawthorne said, How difficult
It is to write about America,
A country where there is no shadow. Rome
Is different. You can write a romance
Or poetry when ruin lets them grow.

Some monuments survive intact. Within
Their shadow we reflect upon their gleam.

Poets read history, John Adams thought,
For flowers, not for fruits.

          He did not add,
Flowers are what we see, fruits what we eat.

Fruits hung on trees. Flowers are what the bees
Sang to the shade of noon. At night ripe fruits
And cheese and chestnuts lay before the guest.

The Ides of March. Fortune be with us now.
We'll study all day and determine how
The one was put to flight, the other stayed
Relaxed and undisturbed (lentus) in shade,
And whether what we have affirmed is true —
That the distinguishable shades are two.
A quiet sunny Sunday morning looms.
Surely in this cool peace sweet music blooms:
Shadows of silver wings upon our eyes,
Jove's constant thunder in the azure skies,
Glass, bricks, cement resounding silver dread,
The airy flight path routed overhead.

Varro in *Country Things* has Atticus
State that from when the Vergiliae rise until
The autumn equinox, in the midday heat
The sheep are driven under shade-giving rocks
And spreading trees. And in his farming poem
Virgil advises: When noon's heat seethes seek
(What shall I say? a shady vale? a shadowy
Valley? a shady valley? a shaded vale?)
A shadowed valley where one gigantesque
Oak from its strength — its ancient trunk — immensely
Stretches branches or where the black and thick
Grove rests in sacred shade (in holy shadow).

In newspapers and on the radio
And doubtless also over television
The instant of the equinox was preached.
It was quite easy for us to believe.
We found the augmentation of the days
Self-evident. Hued crocuses grew common.
Cried beech buds brightened. Therefore, it was spring
That we pursued. Therefore, it was spring.

When the Vergiliae are Pleiades
They all have names and faces — Sterope;
Maia, the mother of fleet Mercury
And May's sweet nurturer; Taygete;
Celaeno; Electra; bright Alcyone;
And one whose face was hidden: Merope.

It was the verge of April, not of May.
Sun and not shade was nature's annunciation.
What was that old culture's annunciation
To May's new nurturer, March's new mother?
Breath overshadowing the one who breathed
In answer: I am a slave. And she conceived
The truth that preached the truth would make you free.

It was announced: A Holy Breath will come
Upon you and a Power overshadow —
Et virtus obumbrabit tibi.

> Bellow,
My soul, the umbra, umbra.

> Oom, the boom,
The brutal boom, the doom, my doom, the drum.

The oak was Jove's oak, not a giant's tree.
In Descartes' letters God and Galileo
Mix with physics. Can moral criticism
Mix with aesthetic? Merope is the name
Of a brighter Pleiad now, the astronomer said.
Virgil said the oak was Jove's, implied
The grove of holm oaks was Diana's. I
Thought I could posit holiness without
Naming the gods. My topic there was not
God or the gods but shade — the shade of noon.
The shade of noon provides both place and time
For gods or for the music of the gods
Or for a human music. Is a Muse
Anything but Jove's daughter and divine?
Or which divinity will mingle with
Emily Dickinson's dactylic name?
Emily said the shadows held their breath.

A god gave Tityrus the shade of noon.

The Bible says the truth shall make you free,
My mother said, and said, You must be free
To find the truth.

> How could her daughter find
Herself a slave?

> Philosophy is not
My subject.

> Seeking freedom, Tityrus
Journeyed to Rome. Freed, he gained the shade.

Shade is a leisure for the beautiful
And for the true.

> Is that philosophy?

Can there be an aesthetic in an age
That spews the name of beauty, for which art
Is pathological, aesthetic means
Estheticism, beauty spells oppression?

You must be free to find the beautiful.

She found the truth of beauty in a gloss
Provided to a cloudy afternoon
By purple crocuses closed and agleam
In the massed shadow.

                            Art is a disease,
A garden a cheap Eden, excellence
A chauvinism, grandeur rot, they found.

Flowers the others found effeminate.

There was a purple grandeur in that gleam.

Oh, did I lie asleep in Italy?

Shelley called science, poetry, and thought
Lamps of serenity. He called free words
Of freedom sharp swords and wide shields that shade.

To find the truth, she said, you must be free.

The free, the good are ethical — must be.

The good, the true, the beautiful are three.

Three is the Book on truth, Two is the Book
On the aesthetic, and the ethical
Is treated in Book Four. Philosophy
Will constitute the subject of Book Five.
Three is the tract on academic truth,
On the pedantic, on the classical,
On poetry as studied not as felt,
Literature as read not written, life
Lived in the cave, the grove, the beech's shadow,
Among the books' shades' ageless reverberation.

Thus each Book treats its subject. Thus Book One
Describes the holy, Two the beautiful.
Thus Three describes the true and Four the good.
What is reserved for Five? As shadows fall
Is there imagination of a whole?
Book One is the lost paradise, Book Two
The paradise regained, Book Three a pole,
A post, a proem, a meridian
(Oh, silly woman, silly, silly girl),
A shadow of the grand quotidian.

They wonder which age spewed out beautiful.
They are to come. They wonder, they will ask
In which time art was abnormality,
By which norm too poetic was too bad.

They ask if they exist. The ethical
Is what is known as the political.
If they exist they ask. If poetry
Exists it asks if it is luxury.

Each crocus seemed a mirror of sweet sun.
What was it doing in the universe?
Each crocus holds the shadow of cold star.
Are little things the limits of the big?

Oh, to throw Jove's own thunders down the skies.
Whew, if she threw her blue across the heavens.

Luckily greatness remains to explicate.

Emily, self-astounding bolts now throw.

Luckily, words stay on to be explained.

Umbra occurs in the *Eclogues* fifteen times,
Umbrosus and umbraculum each once.

March left us with the witchhazels' sweet farewell,
Their faded flowers fragrant in the sun,
And with the up-and-coming cardinal's hail,
His sharp shrill red heart pulsant in the sun,
                                            His brilliant

His brilliant color and his brilliant call
Significant conjointly in the sun,
And, through the gray of evening, hyacinths
First purpled nightfall with their rising light,
And day raised the umbrella-shredder storm.

April came in with snow, taxilessness,
And two disabled Red Line subway trains.
My train backed up like the New England spring.
Still it was April. And I caught the bus.
This was a pilgrimage, not taken, though,
To Canterbury, to unvanished Rome,
To Mantua, to Andes, but to Amherst.
Our emblem with the five gold shadowed stars,
Green Peter Pan seemed fleet as Mercury.
We slogged west wingless through snow-feathered pines,
Wondering how we could invest our snow,
To eye a dry and purple-wooded west
And rusted pines and the reluctant sun.
Cold Springfield's yield: bloated magnolia blooms;
Holyoke's: mountains; and Northampton's: floods —
For her perfection my redundancy?

I stumbled from the bus, found Pleasant Street,
Found Main Street, took it, passed the Evergreens,
And saw the solid bricks, the real red bricks,
The real red house, the awesome newfound place,
Replacing lost time irreplaceable.
No trespassing. I would not trespass there,
Content to rest my step before clear signs,
Moved to be outside where she had been in.

This was a dual pilgrimage: to see
The breathing poet, who most dazzlingly
Gathers the shades (Amata is her name
Who to South Pleasant Street will add her fame);

To see Aemilia's imposing home
On Main Street and, just up the hill (its chrome
Alabaster), that small resting place.
Clouds moved. Sun burst. Sky was a bigger space.

I could respect, deeply I could revere
The pewter beech bole silver in the clear
Post-equinoctial ambience, the few
Squills birthed beneath in their unearthly blue.

The pine had gone. The marvelous barred owl,
Back, big in Harvard Yard, boxed with the squirrel.

Motion and rest are different in respect
Only. Shade is rest. April is restless.
In April, in respects, our shade begins.
In the beginning, beech buds only point —
Though they have fattened — as they did all winter.

Under the beech the squills were sky's blue shadow.
Shadow not mirror were they of the sky.

Common now seemed the silver maples' hints,
Among the glints of brass, of dints of gold,
And the red maples' unambiguous red.
Here pushed the daphne and the daffodils.
Here strove a tiny tulip with the sod.

One moves through April filled with the intense
Inertia of emotion, filled with the force
Implanted of the spring.

                        Coppery shades
Hover about the elm boughs.

                               Under a branch
Unshadowed, lifeless, on the dead elm, a small
Woodpecker largely drums, unconscious of
(As we must judge) the gravity of earth.

Are we in judging earth a bit too grave?
And can we judge the gravity of shade?

For Virgil there are both good shade and bad
And day's and night's shade; hence, twice two. I have

Been oversimplifying. Day's a cave
Cordoned by green or a great tree has made,

With night's the mountains have the valleys clad,
To night's the hearth called home. Need I more halve?

Does this not the appearances all save?
Is this not clear enough about the shade?

For days and days there was no clarity.

It rained. It rained. It rained. The April rain,
The more-than-April rain, painted the grass
As green as the green grass of Aberdeen
Nearly; nothing on God's green earth can be
As green as green in Aberdeen the gray
City, its stone the setting, as it can
Be, for unearthly verdurous surcease . . .

Magnolia blossoms were about to be.

The grass sat softly on the nebulous
Earth, in session on the cloudy ground
Like a green constellation easily
Gleaming in cloudlessness, a galaxy
Of green gleaming serenely in a pure dark.

In the First Eclogue, though, is not the shade
Good, in the Last first hurtful and first grave?

Sniffing sweet hyacinths and sweet magnolias,
As the forsythia shed its greenish tinge
And shone in yellow clarity among
Sweet robins and sweet mockingbirds, and sun
Began its long concoction of sweet pears,
Apples, plums, and cherries, she observed
Sweet nature is adept in every art
Save one, for nature's painting, sculpture, music,
Perfume, cuisine are famous. Literature,
However, is a strictly human gift,
And if the human and the natural
Are two the literary art is one
Subsumed within the human and removed
From the hand fashioning the first azaleas
As sculptured

As sculptured purple luminosities
And decorating yellow tulips red.

In literary study one must shave
Each plane with care, with care plot every grade.

Emily's brother's lover's daughter said
The bricks were painted yellow in those days.

Saturday, April eleventh. The birch at ease
Decked in the ancient dressmaker's fresh supplies
Of yellow fringe; erect, the cottonwood
New-furnished with old-fashioned tassels — red.

Saturday, April eleventh. A wedding day
Eliciting the maple's first bouquet
For the green bridal — green initiation
Of the green season which the maple blossom
Tosses into existence every April.

Nature, indulging in photography,
Posed white magnolias on the azure sky.
Nature had sewn the blue-spread quilts of squill.
To nature connoisseurs attributed
The petrine architecture of the beech,
Great and grave and gleaming in its reach,
Its grandeur perfectly distributed.

Perfectly elm-backed, the creeper ascended the elm
In Harvard Yard, grove, wood, his shade-tree realm.

Saturday, April eleventh. Gleaming and grave.
Hot sun at last. Alas, sun without shade.

It all depends on how you look at it,
And I was always looking at the sun —
Not like Orion, to whose blinded orbs
That orb was brilliant doctor; I was one
Who walked in circles at meridian
And wandered westward all the afternoon
Until at last the sweet cool shadows came
Down from the heights and breezes up from the sea.

So many places still are inundated
I will not name them. Nature gives no name.

The twelfth of April. Sunday. Hot. Hot sun.
The purple-sunned azaleas shadowing
Themselves, their suns and shades within themselves,
Themselves their shadows and their suns. Monday.
The Ides of April. Snow on the magnolias.

Roll on, roll, cinematic weathering.
The toll time takes shall be retold, the reel
Slowed, reversed, ingrafted, graphed, engraved,
Published as edited, auctioned, and read.
Nature herself is quite illiterate.

April fourteenth. Tuesday. After toil.
Longfellow's lilacs leafing in the sun.
Longfellow's linden looming in the sun.
Lowell's lilacs leafing, Lowell's magnolias
Holding on snow-whitely, launfally.
The lawn is ever setting for the robin.
Azaleas are a dawn in the dusk.

                    I know
Little about the dawn.

                    I know much dusk.

What happens if you send snow through the mail?
The envelope is postmarked the fifteenth.
Let us assume this as the letter's date.

On April fifteenth, 1862,
She wrote to Thomas Wentworth Higginson,
Enclosing snowy samples, to inquire
If her life breathed.

                Higginson's happy home
In Cambridge, built in 1880 for
The man of letters and his second wife,
Was home, too, for the abolitionist,
Naturalist, reformer, militant,
                                  Soldier

Soldier of free and beautiful and true.
She wanted him to tell her what was true.
Was she yet free, he asked after she died.

The colonel's gray house has as cordoning
Glorious gold forsythia, as sentry
The robin uniformed upon the lawn,
As bugle of moaned youth the cardinal's cheer

In April, when forsythia and white
Magnolias at Elmwood, a robin in Longfellow's elm,
Picture and compose the time of year.

Again, still leafless, purple distillation,
Azaleas, ecstasy objectified,
Pend in the air, intense, fresh, and mere.

No man, no woman, can now be alive
Who witnessed William Dawes, heard Paul Revere,
On April eighteenth, 1775,
Launched like two thunderbolts not far from here.

Rose there a supernova in the west?
The robins ever ornament the evening.
I know April's azaleas very well.

Here, not deprived of supernovelties,
Higginson's privets, semi-evergreen,
Show thirty old leaves, thousands rosebud-new.

Back here, among unyielding brick red wall,
April is the Norway maple, is its yellow
Yield of green, its blossoms, its green blossom.

Virgil wrote barleys, Emily a hay.
Higginson edited to make the a
A the. O grammar. O stern Bavius.
Flora, a critic strict as Maevius,
Relished Vergilius and Dickinson.
What of her taste for 1987?
Finding now's new insipid is a feature
Of those without a present or a future.
Higginson,

Higginson, though, was much more than a critic.
Flora must stand or fall like an enclitic
Leaning upon a word. Flora was and:
Arma virumque. Retrospect. A sand
Deep in a lettuce, not deep in an oyster.
A mind refected in a whited cloister.

Longfellow never heard of Dickinson.
Longfellow's life was done by Higginson.
Merope was the wife of Sisyphus.
Emily was the wife of Mythicus.
Emily was the star invisible.

What was that song I heard upon the night:
Daphnis, why do you watch the ancient stars?
Lo, a new sign advances through the skies.
So, singing can continue in the dark.

How does it walk along, clumsy upon
Monosyllabic feet, most terrible,
Clop . . . , clump . . . , the elephant, the drum,
The interruption ineluctable?

The month may then walk on beyond description.
Are its ideas indescribable?

To dangle words of joy from the weeping cherry,
Untangle every pure pink syllable,
Must be, if nature cannot write or read,
That for which I am held responsible.

Maioresque cadunt. And greater fall.

Higginson said the Dickinsons' brick was brown.

Back in the shabby dim apartment house
Should one describe without illumination
The shadowed splendor of an Easter evening,
The yellow blossoms of the weedy maple
Before these brown-red bricks, magnificent
As the magnolia's purpled pearly bloom
At noon before the elegant gray mansion?

We close the shades and open up the books
That swing their shadows like the night's high mountains.

Will the books blossom in a mind, the blooms
Breathe upon an intellect a thought?

Night may or may not be a time for song.

On April twenty-third Anne's ample beech,
The bulky, bulging beech, comedian
And tragic hero, operatic queen
Battening guiltlessly, the orotund
Orator with his rostrum, the gray stage
With its suspense, its burgeoning excitement,
Its pleated leaflets and flounced flowerlings,
Summons the audience of underlings,
Of groundlings who look up and gape and smile.
But not by nature is the beech inscribed.

The real is merely metaphorical.
Did nature's god say: Now let Einstein be?
Did nature say that goodness, beauty, truth,
Denatured and denaturalized, must go
Unsaid? Does nature wait for vocal cords?
The chords that swell from the accordions
Upon the beech fan themselves into shadow,
Said Flora, flouncing, floundering, and foundered
Among such thingmade words and wordmade things.

Floruit first century B.C.

The ultrasound showed her a perfect flower
And spoke of something pulsing that would speak
Some day, say something, show itself a someone.

Someone has spoken. Someone yet may speak.

In the white weeping cherry one alleged
The silver sun along the utmost arch.
By the bright bricks one mentioned emerald,
The gems of sun among the verdurous jewels,
The flowers and the shadows of the flowers.

If one admits the human had a hand
In painting tulips, may one still deny
Nature the palm of literary skill?

The twenty-eighth of April and the first
Day of Floralia. Snow on the magnolias,
Snow on the snowy cherry trees, and snow
On thoughts of gods that had not up and gone.
The maple on the twenty-seventh filled
Fancy with verdicts of perfection, filled
Circle on circle orbed eternal green.
Nature herself dragged down that loveliness
And placed there a new empty space of sky.

The great things are collated with the small.
The silly things are uttered as the true.

Magnolia blossoms petaling the snow
Combined the toga-white and toga-purple.

He said that beech trees do not grow by rivers.
He was the teacher. He was the professor.

May's madness will pass unreiterated,
She said among the purple palaces.
Once more the golden oaks, once more oaks' gold,
She said among the golden cornices.
Without ideas, nothingness, she said
Once more, among incipient fullnesses.
Since there is winter, let there be no spring,
She thought she heard among the trellises.

Our Georgia beech trees rise right by the water,
She heard them say. She saw their photographs.
When the lake rises they yet rise, she heard.

But surely what I heard was that from where
The hills begin to lift themselves and let
The ridge down in a gentle inclination
To the water and the old now cracked-topped beech trees
Menalcas had saved everything by song.

The teacher said that beech trees do not grow
By rivers, and she wrote down in her book
That beech trees do not grow by rivers. When
She walked at Cramond by the River Almond
Beech trees had grown along the sloping bank
And she had seen them growing. And she wrote,
Beech trees do not . . . The commentator spoke.
Caesar said beech trees do not grow in Britain.

You heard it. It is what was said. But song . . .
We used to sing the sun to sleep. We used
To waken night with singing. Song, as strong
As doves against the eagle, cannot save
Anything in war's night. Even Menalcas
Was barely saved and that only through silence.

Menalcas nearly lost? Whose song would raise
May's violets and draw down soft May's shade
Of beech-bright green, soft shade of beech-light red?
Who would sing the nymphs? And where were they
When from the beech's silvers copper shone
Gentle at noon and shade leafed lovely? Shade
Was leafy on the soil, copper was
Gently, softly leafy on the tree.

These were the beech's shadows from the sun.
Menalcas, can you find them? Muses, can
You find them? Nymphs, can you? Both Muses and
Nymphs are awkward in electric light.
Muses, can you find us? Tityrus, can
Such shade serve song?

                If you have gone to Rome
And found the god there, shade may serve and save.

Who is that god?

                I thought that Rome was like
Any old city. Rome's shaft shed a shade
Of redwood length and deep as depth of the beech.

Tityrus, can such shade save studied song,
Study of song, song's study of song's self?

Listen, the hissing of the syllables
Witnesses as the geese of Juno did
Once to the creeping, groping foe, the threat
From the back door. If faced, the danger may
Be obviated, as in chapter three.
In the fifth chapter you the god may see.

Already on the beech I see bronze shadows.

Bronze shadows are expanding in May's sun.

Is the god awkward in electric light?

The nymphs, however, took to television,
The Muses to computers, and Apollo
To rocketry.

                Rome rises like a cypress.
What can resemble scents from this viburnum
That functions from afar like gravity?
Rome is the subject, Rome the study, Rome
The tough conundrum. This arrest, refreshment,
This flexibility, far-floating-flowing
Fragrance must be the song.

                      Oh, sweet, sweet, sweet:

O fresh-air sweet, O spicy sweet, O sweet
Obvious, far or near. This is the song.
Sweet and right it is to die for Rome.
Sweet is the shade when sweet and hot the sun.
To conquer the taboo repeat the crime.

If I could just remember. That red rhyme
Was not so utterly forgettable.

Be hither, Galatea. It's no fun
Out there. The waves are not the place to play.
Here is the green, white, pink, and purple May.
Here, switched on by the amber-fingered sun,
                              The fluorescent

The fluorescent lilacs have begun
Purpling the breeze. Here, where the violets lay
Their dark still on the green below, a ray
From the wistaria peacefully has won
Space in the light above as spacious light
Breaking through dear air over kindly earth.
The breakers are as hostile as frore tundras
Forever foreign to the ludic rite
In the geographies of vernal birth.
The beeches' texts were umbracules, are umbras.

Oh, don't you wish that you were me? These fields,
Though treeless, seethe with leaves and breathe forth flowers.

Then you can read the month that has been written
In water, while to me the tract is blank
Without the tulips, crabapples, and dogwoods,
Without the rosebud cherries and the redbuds,
Without the dawning irises of May
Here, on this calendar, for time is space,
As writing is time stamped on space and space
Captured by time. But nature is no scribe
Or scribbler. The inscriptions and the legends,
The beech-bark lectures and the beech-leaf texts,
Reader, are yours or mine, said Flora, though
I would not scrape my name upon these silver
Slates or quench the lilacs, gathering
Those lamps for any anagnostic ends.

The candid dogwoods have no messages,
Then, and the burnishing of the beech at evening
If the beech is copper or the beech is purple,
Or the verdancy of the beech at dawn
If the beech is green, secret no lessons: See
The glint of the trunk, the gleam of the leaves, the shadow.

If you can read the seasons of the seas,
Springs of the oceans, summers on the tundras,
Mays at the poles, had I not read myself
In ice? Myself, not May. Me, not the year.

                                                   Not foci,

Not foci, though perhaps elliptical.
You can decipher May itself inscribed
In ice, you can translate it from a page
Of water, while to me the silver tract
Is blank, shadow not mirror, mirroring
A shadow if it mirrors anything,
A shade of gray regarded as the sky's,
In which the seven Pleiads may arise
In May, invisible, not lassoed by
The solitary circle of my eye.

In wild Epirus loud Dodona's oak
(Or speaking beech) was not the thing that spoke
To me. The sounding of the soundless rock
Glanced back with self's own self-reflecting shock.
High in the Highlands every barren blank
Rising before me shadowed me and sank
Deep into my reflecting self, as bleak
And superficial as each mirrored peak.

Brushing the screen, the maple whispered May:
Shadows of leaves and on leaves in a play
Of sun and wind, the drama of this day,
This almost-summer-sleepy matinée.
Nature gives no scripture, I inveigh
When not inveigled by her roundelay.

Repeat, sweet, sweet. Repeat without demur.
Who knows the shadow from the shadower?

Sinking along the beech's ancient spine,
Reclining as the boughs themselves recline,

Tityrus, sing. Trees, ring, reechoing.

It was not narcissistic to be awed
At the spectacular and specular
Glory of grand, drab landscapes, much as if
At expositions of wide emptiness,
At the exposure of long denegations,
At one's celestial self, or at one's shade.

At Franklin Park in Boston beeches border
Scarboro Pond. These are the European
Beeches, at Boston in America.

Are there no beeches growing by the river
Below? That Tiber flowing through the green
Is the Ohio, over which one hard
Bird begins to raise gray feathers on
Its stiff pinions. Our way is hard. The clouds
Do it so easily. Whole pueblos float.

Shade the thought shade beneath the argute oak.
Spring here is summer. Look at the catalpas
Reconstellating the hot noons of May.
The swifts are swift above. My thought comes slow.

Then the lakes flame in turn and all the bodies
Of water fire up, struck by the sun's late match.
And later there is lightning from our wings
And thunder from our heart. We redescend.

It is too dark to read the beech tonight.
The leaves are shadowings upon the sky,
Which is an antique blackboard faintly chalked.
It is too light down here to read the sky.
It is too dark to read my penmanship.
It is too light to think without my pen.

Still I can see the beech's arms and hands,
The beech's paws, the beech's claws, the fins,
The feathers of the beech. The arms are wings.

Shade the word shade beneath the rusty beech
Whose rust must be immaculate of all
Its connotations save one: coloring.
But is its color rusty deep in June?
That red suffused — red subtly fused — with green
Is much too deep. The shade is deeper still.

Shadow the shade beneath the ruddy beech
Whose shade shades you. For it is noon. The sun
Acts in its aestival capacity:
                                        Assassin,

Assassin, executioner, avenger
Of sins of thought and word against wan winter
And sins of deed at winter's funeral.

Fade in the shade beneath the russet beech
Whose shade you shadow. It is June. The sun
Is summer's murderous accompanist:
While summer sings peace, leisure, laziness,
And Sunday noon, the sun plays heat too hot
And light too light. Your shadow vanishes.

Your shadow vanishes into the shade.
Or do they merge there on the ground, as green
And red merge in the beech leaves, as the green
And blue of the blue spruces coalesce,
As the pink melts into the white of white
Roses, or are they pink, as whiffs of linden
Slip into the air, or as the nighthawk,
Swimming in its whirlpool in the sky,
Shades loudly into the oncoming night?

The beech is black as night. Its swarthy globe,
Seen from the street, where sun deals strictly, looms
Black, a black marooned, maroon, a blackness
Silvered as black swifts silver-note the sky,
A black of purple, bronze, red. Is that green?
Beneath the beech the beech's leaves are green.
This is the otherworld, green, dark, and cool.
This is the shady heaven where the sun
Is still a quivering, a brightening.

Beneath the beech the beech's leaves are green.
Out at the edge they redden. Out from under,
You know that they are black, that they are bronze,
That they are silver. Shall I call that gold?
Angle is all. And one tree made her country.
And there are many different kinds of shade:
The beech's shade, the oak's, the honeylocust's,
Shade on the sidewalk, shade on the grass, the soil,
The fuscous fashioning of beech's shadow.

The beech is far from black. The beech is purple.
The beech is green. The noon is hot. The noon
Is June intensified and concentrated.
Beneath the beech, noon, June, the summer's sun
Are all diffused. Even the red brick sidewalks
Of Cambridge are beech-blossomy, beech-blessed.

The beech's blossoms bulge now towards the beechnut
As easily as words bulge on the page,
As slowly as thoughts grow along the lines.
The lines must be the branches and the thoughts
The purplish egglets or the rusting hanging
Handlets. The shady words must be the leaves.

The words shade into night as nighthawks do,
Shaking out the air in which they are.
She stalked the nighthawk by the nighthawk's cry
As it shook out the droplets of the sky
And voiced its cousinhood to the nightjar.
A dome is half a globe, my speech half true.

Am I a teacher? Think this out with me.
The poem is on the verge of making sense,
Must be just on the verge of intellection.
Am I a thinker? You must cross the line.
The thought is yours. The words for thought are mine.

If I thought I should cross the Rubicon,
How could I step twice into the selfsame stream,
How share the oceanic undulation?
How could I think about Vergilius?
How could I teach about umbrageousness?

Am I a teacher? We must teach ourselves.
Am I a thinker? We must think our thoughts.
Am I a writer? I must write my words.
Echo was voice, Narcissus mirroring,
Caesar was deed, the Rubicon a thing

Given a name that gave an act a name,
Named action. Must we choose our acts and name
Our choices? To recline beneath a tree
May be to dream. To lie beneath the beech
May be to sleep, to speak, to teach, to preach.

Will the trees listen? Can you hear the trees?
Longfellow's linden lumbers into June
With brick intestines and an iron spine.
Under the hot meridional sun
The sundial says this day will not return.

The linden's ancient hulking rugged trunk
Speaks of an ancient day. Fresh fragrance sings
The newborn reborn small sweet yellow flowers.
Do the trees listen? Do you hear the trees?
In tiny blossoms those big buzzing bees?

Gone then virgilian snowstorms, late so loud,
And linden wind and bright catalpa cloud.

July. Do try what Julian luck achieves.
I rose up with the nighthawk in the sky.
The silver light of morning on the leaves
Silvered the leaves, turned nighthawk into sparrow.
Cicero, Julius Caesar, Virgil, Varro
All soared before me. Sparrows also fly.

Dream on the goldenness in fall, in spring
Dream on the dream in the stream of promises,
In winter realize the elephant,
The ivory, the elephantine cold,
In summer realize the dream. The shade,
As if a promise were reduced from binding,
As if a Midas were released from nightmare,
Releases you from the too golden gold.

Above the water's gilded glint the bridgehead,
The beachhead, is the beech trees fingering,
Forming their ridge.

                    Danger. Keep off the ice.
The sign stayed there all summer, while one saw
Oneself green-shadowed, silver-rippled, gold-
Bannered. The painted words escaped all change
Unless it was change when solidity
Was liquidated, when the danger seemed
Above belief, below imagination.
Ice! Hot hands hold the clinking goblets high.

Piper, sit thee down and write thy book.
And so I stained fresh water with my song
As the sun stains the ocean with its dawn
And the eye stains the mirror with its look.
Green are the hemlocks, green, green are the pines,
I murmured, verdant is the Norway spruce,
And verdurous the beech tree. More abstruse
Is the green glitter of my emerald lines
When they recover from the clearest pond,
Where the fish flicker green and flutter gold
And feathers flash from heavens never old,
The verd antique of rusticated sound.
Then to the university I turn
Back to make ancient every new I learn.

Stand at the Elmwood gate. The elms are dead.
The river has been moved. The herns have fled
Who can say where. The poets do not stir.
Like herns their words blur in nocturnal air.
The nighthawk loudly calls upon the night.
The poets called upon a day. Some blight
Falls now upon their words. Upon the page
They still ring loud but not upon the age.
An angel made them ring, and so they rang.
The angel said to sing; the poets sang.
The angel said to write, and they complied.
The herns' words, uninterpreted, yet hide.
Longfellow, Lowell — lost. They have a name,
But it grows dim. Can the wild song grow tame?

Longfellow did interpret Virgil, though.
Longfellow called that coolness shadowy.
In the cool shade of Virgil we sat down
When an age glared upon us like a sun.
We sat and heard him. Virgil's words swung, swirled
Among the pines and hemlocks of a world
Called new. The trees seemed old. The words seemed new,
Seemed fresh green, seemed fresh red and white and blue.
Primeval forests and disconsolate
Oceans have learned how Tityrus could sit
Safely beneath his beech and sing his song
While Meliboeus had to bear his wrong
Songless through alien and hostile lands.
We sat and heard him crying on our strands.

Are we in exile? What place or what time
Suffices for our story? What is Rome
Or where? And when are we back on the farm
And free and happy? And what is our norm
Or metaphor for liberty and truth
And union with the everlasting? Ruth
Left her land and went to Bethlehem
Of Juda. Is the past or future home?
Another woman came from Galilee.
She went to David's city by decree
Of Rome's Augustus Caesar. What has Rome
To do with Athens or Jerusalem?
When Virgil went to Greece to finish work
On his great song Augustus called him back.

I am called back from somewhere to somewhere.
If I leave Mantua I go to Rome.
If I leave Naples I am coming home.
If I reach Carthage, see a city there,
And find a temple sparkling with my story
Forming upon its portals, I can guess
That I must stay a while under duress
Until I edge with unexpected hurry
Along time's waves to small Lavinium,

           My spousal

My spousal town, and on to Alba, long
The city of my fathers, and, among
Stern omens, on to everlasting Rome,
There to erect an everlasting temple.
The gratifying parable is simple.

And what has Rome to do with Massachusetts,
Connecticut, New York, or Delaware?
And what has Rome to do with California,
With Kansas, Idaho, Utah, Wyoming,
With Michigan, Missouri, Mississippi,
Father of Waters, Texas, Iowa,
Latin Virginia, Florida, Montana,
Romance-imperial green-hilled Vermont,
Snowy Nevada, ruddy Colorado,
Or with Kentucky's dark and bloody ground?

Washington could have crossed the Delaware
Dreaming of Cato and of Cincinnatus.
Virgil was born across the Rubicon,
On the other side of the tracks, not the Roman side.

I know I am a Roman, Flora cried;
I know my Virgil.

            Look at the *Eclogues* then.

Thalia, blossoming in Rome, decrees
It is all right to play amid the trees.

Thalia plays with Flora. How they play
Is it for sober scholarship to say?

They play as white clouds play across blue skies,
As between trees the green plays on the green,
As among leaves the light plays with the light,
As past the leaves a bird plays at his singing,
As in a pool the plash plays from the fountain,
As through the pool reflection plays to shadow.

They play like bluejays shouting to their shadow.
They play as blue hills play beneath blue skies.
They lie as blue pools lie beneath a fountain.
They rise as blue hues rise in blue-spruce green.
They open their blue eyes. The woodthrush singing
Blue sapphire star songs closes day's blue light.

That azure song, that lapidary light —
Cutting a passage through the avid shadow
That would bruise sooner were the light not singing
Blues of white clouds like blues of mountains, skies
Ever forget-me-not above the green
Blues of the spruces silvered like a fountain,

And silvers in the tree that is a fountain
Whose leafy chips of water, light as light,
Rustle before the fountains of the green
Dark trees that from behind the fountain shadow
And, shadowing, sharpen acute blues in bright skies —
Plays as they play, because their play is singing.

Hence, evidently, this their endless singing
Continues endlessly just as the fountain
Makes endless revolutions into skies
And into skyey mirrors, gyring light
Into accepting air and casting shadow
Upon the grassily receptive green.

And will the future judge their play was green
If an end ever ends their endless singing?
Will it allege their play was played in shadow?
Their shadow in the pool beneath the fountain,
Though gray, was straight and stable, while their light
Haloed reflection wobbled through the skies.

They played, and skies revolved about their singing,
And snows turned green, and ice turned into fountain,
And light lit light, and shadow shadowed shadow.

The robin on the lawn is like a lawyer,
A banker, a stout businessman, not like
                                        That angel

That angel heavenly among the leaves.
Flora the scholar read about Thalia
While two white naiads, naked or nearly naked
Above the waters, stretched and unstretched the limbs
Of marble bodies mirroring soft moon
As under sun's incessant battering
The fountain with its glassy shattering
Gushed icily against blue blaze of noon.

Must there be patronage and place for play,
As the First Eclogue surely seems to say?
Can study build far from the stones of Oxford,
Boulders of Göttingen, or bricks of Harvard?
This Tunis, sir, was Carthage. Can a lyre
Ever erect a city in the mire?
What else but a Djerassi Ranch or Yaddo
Can offer space to paint play's dance of shadow?
Though the doves' voices mourn, their wings are singing.
Can there be work or play without some jingling?

If one perused Thalia she could play
Prettily, greatly, choosing to display
Enormous courtesy, to stand and grace
The grand huge curtsy of the Norway spruce
Or to amuse by doodling on white lines
Along green hemlocks and among green pines.
This dainty lineation was abstruse.
Lines are the muse's measurement of verse.
If they are blank the versifier earns
The right to stock them with her dearest runes.

Thalia, Arethusa, shoot or fountain,
Abstrude from play the laboredness, from work
Any too ludic synergy. Apollo
Once touched one's ear. I hear, deep in the cavern,
The song that opens as aubade and closes
As vesper. Caves are chambers or cathedrals.
Deep in that space feel the reverberation,
I shouted, sensing choirs reechoing
The god that opens a barred door and closes
           The night

The night around his sweetness. Through that night
The hymn continued, and the incense filled
The shadows, and the god moved, came to rest,
And moved. And soothed. His great work was but play,
And that was but the vigil of great day.

Was it a huge mosquito or a pigeon?
Was it the beauty of the ink-blue swallow,
A dim-starred blue attacking in huge dudgeon?
Thalia, Arethusa, or Apollo
Entered my ear or beat with huge blue wings
Above my head or swooped before my eyes
In purple glitters or, slow, with a king's
Or queen's solemnity of gait, the wise
Measuring look of critics, or the cool
Green gaze of meditation, paced the sands
That stretched before my door, did not say, Fool,
Why are you waiting here, but took my hands.
The fixed stars turned as we were thus embowered.
One will have planted, one poured, one empowered.

Was there a power then in a ballet
So revolutionary? It was play
She watched as panting statues were unfurled.
Is it sooth or assuagement if the world
Itself is play? In play you can get hurt.
Many a player lies there in the dirt
Though he once proudly pranced in the parade,
Hard at work, hard at play. She was afraid
Since her work panted for eternity.
She recognized that first infirmity
And that last ludicropathetic dream,
Last playful, potent, perilous sunbeam.
At noon it is much safer in the shade.
At nightfall danger rises in the glade.

The beech trees rose above the stagnant lakes.
Must the game end soon? Was it for our sakes?
You do assist the storm. This blue-eyed hag
Imprisoned you inside a pine to drag

         Your

Your life out in pine-pain. Those other crooks
Reft you of realm but left you your loved books.
The Roman Revolution whirled your home
From you. You regained all, gained more, from Rome.
The dancers moved until their movement spent
All of the music and all those light things
That were the particles of music went
Down to the crevices from which bright springs
Issued and lifted, lifted themselves and bent
Into the rifted air their long white wings.

Where should this music be? The nameless city,
The city of the secret name, one loves
Just as one loves one's books. One hates its name
As one hates power. What, by power, may
People the universe, and what one's books
May plant or water or breathe into blossom
Could be the questions that one poses when
One sits beneath a beech tree of a noon
In summer and the traffic thunders less
Loud than the waterfall and cares rise less
High than the fountain and the music plays
Out from the earth and up bright in the air
And shadowily among the leaves. The book
Shadows you with dark leaves, shades you with light.

In the First Eclogue umbra is encountered
Twice: in the fourth line in the singular
As umbra, shade, and in the eighty-third,
The last line, in the plural, umbrae, shadows.
Umbrae, moreover, is the poem's last word.

The shade at the beginning is noon's shade —
Or day's at least, and very likely noon's
(Compare the passages from Virgil's *Farming*
And Varro's *Country Things* cited above).
The shadows at the end bring on the night.

Tityrus sang in shade under his beech,
But Meliboeus had to hope to reach

Alien wastes beneath some foreign prince
Who knew no music. Tityrus had once

Made the long trip to Rome. Thus he could best
Return to noon's shade's song and night's shade's rest.

The pines, the fountains, and the fragrant arbor
Where tiny fluffy pinks of roses play
Among white columns and white trellises
And white slats twined with pinks and spaced to let
The blues of skies ooze in above the fragrant
Stroll which is sweetest-scented meditation
On subtlest puffs and delicatest ruffs
And pinks of heartiest of fragile stuffs
And watchets undelimited by spaces
Left in the laddered roof like those blue rests
Left by the woodthrush sweetening the wood
With the rose-petal ruffles of his song —
Or were the roses not the rustlings, were
The rests between the movements of the tune
Deep purple silences between deep blues
Of sound? — the sounds, the silences, the scents,
The swallow bearing bread to swallowers,
The squirrel bringing pine cones to the pine,
The ugly groundhog whom you saw beneath
The shadow of the beauty of the spruce
And who saw you so shadowed that you thought
He thought you were his shadow as you thought
Him yours, the musing shadows of the spruce,
The hemlock's shadows gently gesturing,
The sipping shadows of the swifts that rim
Their dishes on the tables of the sky,
Shades in the sky and shadows on the earth
Will all be calling you. Why must you go?
The libraries, the bookstores, the books dug
From dust, the newest books, pine-stiff, pine-slick,
Pine-crisp, and fresh-pine-scented, the old pine's
Old place where it once entertained the owl
Until owl flew on up and pine fell down,

The crossings

The crossings crossed, the red bricks contemplated
Or walked on, bricks grown rosy over dawn
And rusty under dusk, the beech that rusted
Among the soughing summers, autumns sweet
With opulence, the elm that held the moon
In its grand shadows, its grand shadows all
Will call you. Why then must you go to Rome?

For freedom. Furthermore, being once free,
To see the god whom seeing I will see.

Ariel gained his freedom. Prospero
Studied in exile and returned home. So

Tityrus is my shadow, I am his.
Far from me fall the shade of Meliboeus.

The woodthrush hummed a silver melody.
The woodthrush strummed a tune that was pure gold.
If the enchanted silences between
The measures were as golden as they were
What are the measures that can spell the spell
Set in those treasures? Turn the golden ring,
Flourish the golden wand, let Virgil sing.

O lucky Tityrus, said Meliboeus,
Here, by known rivers and by holy fountains,
Although the white-hot horror of the sun
Burns in the parching pastures of the south,
You will touch dark cold, feel the shadowy
Coolness at noon as ever, ever hear
The soft sweet singing whisper from the bees,
The resting farmhand sing out to the breeze,
The turtle dove sing high up in the trees.
That's it without the song. Let Virgil sing.
That's what he says a trip to Rome can bring.

Why must I go to Rome? It is always
Difficult to say. Let me try again.
Let me say it in decasyllabics

                                          Constructed

Constructed to sound very much like prose.
I must go to see Rome and its grandeur.
I must go to obtain my liberty.
I must go to see the resident god.
I must go to obtain leisure for work.

Work is of earth, leisure is of the gods,
Leisure for work is like an incarnation,
Leisure for work is what shade is at noon
When work is play, song's play, the work of art,
Leisure is what becomes incarnate as
The woodthrush works divinely in shade's woods,
The woodthrush plays divinely in wood's shadows.

And listen: Amaryllis, Amaryllis.
And limning Amaryllis through the green
Dimensions, singer, listen. From the leaves
The Amaryllis, Amaryllis, Amor,
Amor, Aryllis, Amaryllis rings.
The brilliancy sinks deep into the shadows.
Aryllis, Amor, Roma, Amaryllis.

The amorist was not a trifling gallant,
The brilliance not a petty amourette.
Grand amaranthine love was what was sung.
It was enabling freedom that was won.
Love, Amaryllis, Rome, sight, liberty,
Light, leisure, shadow, art, love, Amaryllis
Become the burden that unburdens me.

I must go where I never more shall sing,
Said Meliboeus. Never more shall I
Lie in a green cave watching, on the sky,
My goats play through the thornbushes and cling
Suspensefully, as safely as in meadows,
Ever on points, poised, to the rockiness.
Yet rest with me one night, said Tityrus
To Meliboeus, under longer shadows.

Thus the First Eclogue ends with night's great shadows.
The Second opens on a burning noon
Where, though the beech trees rest dense, shadowy,
The hopelessness of singing in the sun
Is the despondent theme, the wretchedness
Of unloved loving is the unrecked tune.

Here, in line three, the beech tops are umbrosa,
Shady, to roof noon's song, and in line eight
The sheep seek umbras, which I'll call the shade
(Though Pope has shades and Virgil has two plurals
Here — shades and colds — in a hendiadys),
But by the sixty-seventh line, the seventh
From the poem's end, departing, too, the sun
Doubles the growing shadows, umbras.

        Corin

Burned for beauty.

      And that madness sang
Not in the shade but in the noontide's fire.
How can I explicate this incandescence?

What blue and white were strewn across the sky,
Sky's blue, clouds' white, sky's blue's blue, clouds' white's white,
Clouds' white's blue, sky's blue's white, white's blues, blue's whites,
White's whites, what whites moved, what blues burned unmoved
Above blue mountains, mountains' blues, above
Mountains' blues' whites, above blue spruces' blues'
White's moon's blue's white, most ungray gray's white's blue,
Unfrosty hoarfrost's frostiness, moon-blue
Like the moon blue at twilight, when blue spruces
Are moon-white if the moon's white is a blue
And not the noon moon's white cloud in the blue,
In the coruscant clarity of blue,
The white-in-azure clarity, when white
Nebulousness is splendor, blue is flash,
And the meniscus but a bit of cloud,
A brightish bit of white in blue's vibration,
A pure but dullish white in the effulgence
            Of a huge

Of a huge and cerulian shimmering
Transparency through which no stellar light
Glitters with fifty million scintillations,
That clear blue where once stars shone in the murk,
That blue where lunar laving brightened the ink,
The inky blue like the blue backs of swallows
Suddenly starlit as they curve and curl,
While space achieves its leisured curvature
Out and around the workaholic whirl,
The workaday, the hurly-burly whir
Of wings of birds that twitter as they twirl,
Of swallows lovely in their purposeful
Centered frenzy, as they swing and swirl,
Circling about our poles, turning the mill,
Turning their swallow tails, not in retreat,
Turning their columbine spurs, turning the white
Clouds of their breasts eccentrically until
The clouds float by once more, float by and soar
And splinter like bright fireworks in the sky
Because the nursery turned into a school
Where all the little swallows learn to fly
(Could I learn?), how they fly in white and blue,
How their white circles, their blue revolutions,
Their blue-as-ink or white-as-paper shadows
Circle my shadow (if I, too, could learn!),
Why it grows dark when there is so much light,
Why when we gaze through space out into time
The stars do not perpetually dazzle,
The unknown beauty does not shine forever
Dense in the shadeless forests of the skies,
What is the sweet concordance of the spheres,
What are the universe's bright harmonics
Of starlight sizzling through the temporal drift,
How the moon rises, beauty's whitest moon,
Beauty's blue moon (if I could learn), what moon
Has been the whitest, when the blue moon shines,
What is the whitest white and what will be
Blue's bluest and what was the whitest blue,
                                        What

What was the bluest white, what was white's blue,
What was blue's white, what was clouds' white, sky's blue,
What white and blue were spewed across the sky,
What blue, what white, fumed, flumed, bloomed through the sky,
What white loomed luminous, was light, what cool
Blue was a fire, tell me, O skyey muse,
O blue muse, O blue flame, O cool blue fire,
O cloudy muse, naiad of bright white cloud.

That blue, that blank, blazed in the azure soul,
The sapphire spirit, and the white-hot heart
Of Corydon as he lurched into noon,

In love, like any lover, with one beauty,
Not of the dilettante but of the master,
Delicacy, deliciousness, delight,
Somber, solemn, and delectable,

Seen and not seen enough and seen too well,
Loved and too well since here is too well seen
The cruelty of beauty unattained
And unattainable.

                The crudity
Of slavish pantings matches, by the chasm,
The rude, rough rumble of the half-hewn rocks
That tumble down the abysm they meant to bridge.

Vast-shadowed forests, distant-glistening
Mountains, mazed dignity and daintiest lace,
Ensnare you, lover of the beautiful,
Doomed, fated, damned amator of the sheen,
Arrested, then condemned, and then suspended
Encroaching, poaching on umbrageousness,
Flagrant in dark delight and in bright pain,
Dim delicacy and rich outrageousness.

What white and green glint from the green white pines:
Hint of this, too. Or do they glisten there,
Or glitter? Is it glistering though mere

                                          Green

Green and white — yet emerald and diamond
Sometimes in sun, or was it in the rain,
And was that not the rainbow where the shadow
Drooped heavily about the dreamy white
Of the erect and never-drooping tree,
The ever-bristling tree hugged by the cloud
Cognizant of the bristles' softness, of
Their tenderness, their flexibility,
Their brisk ability to be, if stiff
And sticky, still of supplest mollitude,
Not rigid and not brittle and not limp
But limber, pliant, pliable, and lithe,
Yet not too ductile, lenient, or easy
But crisp though wispy, misty, milky, silky,
Fine-fibered, fingerable, and strokable,
Not lax but lentous, lent, mellow, and mild,
Yet sturdy, tough, rough, their configuration
Unchanging, their banked bristling unabated,
Lush bunches, luscious puffs, still trumpeting
Their chaste, slick, sleek green-white concelebrations
Phrased in their fit Sicilian quintets:

In fives we feel the air, finger the breeze,
And fiddle with the wintriness that whines
Among us till we whiten whiter, freeze,
And glove each gust that joustingly combines
With winds we mitten until winter flees

And our freed fingers, like small solar keys,
Reflect the sunlight from the fine white lines
That are the slivered mirrorings which seize,
Sense, and surrender what the dawn divines
For us and what is dulcet dusk's reprise

But lock and unlock power that decrees
Within our citadel, from which it shines
Green and alive and vivid and at ease,
The breath each breathes, the food on which each dines,
The execution of the mysteries

Performed in Quintile, say, when human pleas
Are like an exercise that undermines
Its sweaty end, for they can merely tease
The sun that, most like Latin heterodynes,
Beats out its rhythms and its melodies

Against the words despite the harmonies,
Yet when from purple signposts we hang signs
Along our horizontal beams, green glees
Greeting the sun above us, as we pines
Know how to do, and shading you, we trees.

Thus they went on. And was it really they
Or Pan piping among the pines? He lay

Beneath needles that do not needle, needles
Soft as thread along shelves, levels, layers,
The pines' bright parallels, their pleasant green
Latitudes intersecting longitudes
Of mauve, those staunch, strong longitudes, those straight
Mercator-mapped meridians, at noon.

The pines were shadowy at noon, the hemlocks
Shadowier.

        If pines have fingers yet
Hemlocks have hands which they will spread in blessing
And tongues with which they have said benedictions.
Amid the incense and the incantations
They bless and do not curse with the aspersions
Filtered from intricacy and delicacy,
The delicate green spray, whose somber sparkle
Lightens and darkens on the columns, dark-
Barked along nave, ridge, hillock, and hill
Locked in the hemlocks' grip. They hold the rock.

Thus hemlocks are more somber than are pines,
More shadowy, more shadowed, more serene,
Their white more hidden in the two white lines
Beneath each little dark bright leaf of green.

Pines fence the field, wall the lawn, edge the meadow,
Pines line the meadow, hemlocks hem the hill,
The Norway spruce stands like a monarch, rules
Regally, robed in raiment of a queen
Whose garments, suited to the grandeur that
They represent, do also beautify
With superfluity the beauty which
They borrow and which bears their borrowings
With all the royal ease of beauty clad
In beauty, vesture of which to divest
It would mean neither lessening nor lack,
Dress like a habit neither making nor
Masking the monk.

     And yet to be a hermit
Is not required of every Norway spruce,
For two or more may make community.
They stand together and they dance together.
The abbess may process among her nuns,
The queen step out among her princesses.

And still the spruce's clothing is herself,
She wears herself and wears it very well,
And it wears well and wears the centuries
Well, very well, wearing the shadows well.

Massed, ranked pines guard the field but do no battle
There, at last shadowing the meadow, hemlocks
Are shadowier and spruces shadowiest,
Shadowing most themselves.

       They shade themselves
In their own beauty.

     Can one use some some words
Too much? Beauty! I overuse that word.

But of the quality itself there is
No diminution, if not in my versions
Yet in my visions when I turn again
To the repository where it is,
          Where

Where it reposes, where it wakes, and where
It gives repose, offers awakening,
Where it is, where it lives, and which is it.

And so I live it there.

                Let it live here.

But here are sparrows, chickadees, swifts, chatter,
Spurrings, sparrings, sparrows, padding, patter,
Cicadas, sweat, mosquitos, deer flies, clatter
Of inspiration, respiration, splatter
Of suspiration, perspiration, harrows
Of expiration underneath the arrows
Of noon, the silences of noon, the sparrows,
The empty nests of swallows, sparrows, shadows.

The shadows of the Norway spruce are beauty.

O Phoebe, Phoebe, Phoebe. Chickadees
Outgleam each other, gleam out to each other.

Gleams in the blackness of the Norway spruce
Reveal a darker green, disclose a white
More highly fantasized, than those described
Upon the pines and hemlocks. I prefer
Not to imagine but to describe. The whites
That ray the spruce are astral, are fantastic
Facts that are images and imitations,
Glinting and gleaming on the spruce-green cave,
Great, of greater, on galactic caverns,
Glances, glints, gleams, and glares.

                      Nothing glares here
Except, above the spruce, the hellish sun,
Satanic sun, high hovering, damned dazzle.
The deep tree, shadowed, shadow-embraced, light-loved,
Light-lined, light-limned, light-limbed, light-coated, faced
With light and lined with dark and lined in light,
Light-quested and light-questioned and perpending
Light and plumbed by shadow, stands and holds

                              That slow

That slow sweet rising slowly to descend,
That slow sweet raising sweetly to suspend
The suavity that is green gravity,
The dulcitude that is dark pulchritude,
The sweetness of the brightness of the sheen
And of sheen's shade.

     The whites tipping the blacks,
The lapping blacks, the overlapping blacks,
The whites in a suspense of green, a slide
Of music that descends the green, the wave,
The many waves of fringes on the huge
Unwavering bole, the green waves in the breeze,
Long lentamental waves, green, deep in the wind,
Deep in the protean caverns of the sea,
Green seaweed, light vibrations of green strings,
Dark repercussions, draw into the nest,
Into the circle, under the great green wings,
Great harmonies, great rhythms, and great rest.

These are then fledged and fly forth like small sparks
Or rise out as great emanating shades.

Can one abuse some words? Do not take umbrage.

The penalty of pedantry fell hard.
I was in love. My love was very deep.
I loved the deep high object of my songs.
Why did I, with such empty studiousness,
Cast them upon the mountains and the woods,
Cast them before the ranges and the leaves?

The leaves were evergreen, and so my love
Was everlasting. But the leaves were white.
And so my love was blank or candid. Fire
Was closer. And yet there were many tears.
Why did I shed my tears into the fountain's?
Mine like the deer's bestowed upon too much
Still more. Did I build city walls, not songs?
Did I see beauty mirrored and not made?

There were white blossoms on green stems and white
Butterflies like white blossoms on green stems
And white light blowing like green breeze, and green
Breezes combing like light through the green tresses
Of black-eyed birches shining white as light,
A portico, white preface to green texts
Titled gardens, white roses illustrating
The greenery, a hollyhock with green
In its white pages, white in its green leaves,
A white fountain down a green length of lawn,
A white city above green strips of plain.

I listen to the beauty of my song.
Amphion's was not more desirable
When it called forth the stones from out the sod,
Summoned the boulders, built them on the soil
As seven-gated walls for fountained Thebes.
The fountain sinks in beauty to the pool.

I gaze upon the beauty of my face.
Daphnis's was not more desirable
Than mine is as the double of its shadow,
Than mine is in the bubble of this cool
Mirror. But my unmoving countenance
Moves. And there must be trouble in the roil.

Did, then, the wild boar wallow in my fountain?
It was the cat. It was the cat in the grass.
It was the groundhog wallowing in the grass.

The white, the glistening naiad stepped to the grass
From the fountain, touched the rust-colored marigold
Or the rubiginous chrysanthemum.

The rusty chipmunk runs among the mums
Subtly and subtly sprints into the rust
Resting like shadow underneath the pines,
Hemlocks, and spruces, while up in the breeze
The spring's rust of the beech about to be,
The autumn's of the beech that has been, green
All summer,

All summer, are not dull or lustrous but
Non-existent, and what airily,
Aerially, glares, flares, fluffs, flutters is
The rust of summer on the butterfly's
Wings, the robin's breast, the swallow's throat,
The tanned face of the moon. Beyond the fountain
The roses rust. The marigolds turn gold.
All the chrysanthemums become chrysanthous.
The rusty moon is changing into gold.
At noon those rags, those curls, upon the birch
Some think are rusty I see all are gold.
The rust is being whitewashed from the arbor.
The chipmunk is rust, gray, white, washed in gold.
Along the rusty shoulders of the ridge
Draped in the fabrics fibulated by
The bronze brooches and buckles of the hemlock
Roots, loose-swathed in scarves of fine, rich shade,
The sun's awarding fingers have just pinned
Gold stripes and medals, gold bars and medallions.
The moon turns silver in the silver fountain.
The fountain turns gold in the golden noon.
The roses glint gold in the golden garden.
Here everything that gleams is sterling, here
All that glisters must be gold, at noon,
At midnight. Naiad, shade the golden shade.
And when, with the cessation of July's
Arising towards the Ides, the argyry
Deep-tinkling in a woodthrush heart has ceased
To glitter and those sylvan argentines
And aureoles have ended their sweet beaming,
A silver mirror flashes in the woods.
Straying along the rusty rustic paths
Playing my hemlock pipe I mirror Pan.
The pines extend their silver salvers. In
Majestic music rooms or in gigantic
Dining rooms or lofty drawing rooms
Or dim-resplendent-raftered reading rooms,
Libraries light- and shadow-paneled, -paned,
           Beech-lined,

Beech-lined, pine-shelved, spruce-cased, and hemlock-ended,
One reads more bibliothecarily,
Bibliosophical-, bibliophagically,
One dines on, drinks in, draws, sings, studies more
Studiously blue spruces and white pines.
Blue's whites turn silver and white's greens turn gold.

Chrysopoetics or chrysography
Alone can render this chrysology.

When sheen and sparkle are called Amaryllis,
When Amaryllis sparks with beauty's name,
The woodland starts with a's, with amorous ah's.
Is it the same when beauty is Alexis?
What are those answerers? Are they cicadas?
It ends with bugs' interminable z's.

Cruel beauty, will you have no pity on me?
O beauty, do you care nothing for my songs?
Must I be uselessly consumed in fire
To which nothing of me ever belongs?

Here is the shade of noon. Here sit and sing
Bright beauty in the shadow of the beech.

Here Corydon comes stumbling through the sun,
Burning for beauty, green, elusive shadow,
Burning for beauty, white, rust butterfly,
Burning for bosky beauty, blue, gold shade.

Here comes the shade of evening. Will it quench
Hot beauty's rapid and rapacious fire?

Substitute for your fetish something real,
Substantial, useful, practical, and solid,
Said the psychologist to Corydon.
Substitute something geared towards mankind's good,
Counseled the citizen and social critic.
Your doomed pursuit of beauty must be deemed
The substitute, added the analyst.

Psychology and sociology
Themselves are fetishes, the artist said.
Marxism is a fetish, shining still,
Still gilded with our guilt, still rubied red,
Still warm. Worn are some others, old, faint, cold.
Beauty is ancient, new, cool, shadowy,
Opaque, transparent, luminous, on fire.

Capitalism seems to be ignored
In your hot approbations and detractions.
Capitalism never shone and soared
Before admiring eyes as my ideal.
Why cry against what one has never poured
One's heart out into? Do you really feel
You have served something other than distractions?

Served? Is there service in democracy?
Has my religion not been liberty
For all, has it not been equality
Of all, not been, for all humanity,
That nameless noun which Friend Latinity
Will father on Friend Anglo-Saxon, re-
Placing the fallen heir, fraternity?

Brotherhood, comradeship, the poetess
Called Men against the Women. Yet the fetish
Is feminism, finishing the race,
The prize that consolation offers when
All has been lost, the poet countered. Then
The silver bells rang out. This is the danger.
It is denial. Speak for, not against.

That not against is negative, one said
Simply and frankly, ending at the end.
Undo, no, loosen, that hard not, replied
The futurist, and when you have untied,
No, freed the phrase, against becomes again.
Speak for, again speak for, again, again.
This is a thesis, drawing a finer line:

That pro and contra, that for and against,
Stem from another field, less strictly fenced.
This is about the true, not for the good.
This chatters of what is, not for what should
Be. This looks, mutters, on both trees and wood.
This speaks about, of, on. This is a shadow.
See chapter three if it seems hollow, shallow.

The good, of course, is treated in Book Four,
As I have said. This book is on the true,
And merely on one aspect of the true,
About the study of the beautiful,
One aspect of the beautiful that looks
Leafily out upon us through the nooks
Hidden among the verses of some books.

Against you, whilst you speak, amidst tangential
Remarks, it will be said: Please be prudential.
Your explanations do prove excrescential.
Let us return, then, to our true, essential
Sheep, goats, and cows. We come to Eclogue Three.
Here we find beechen bowls and bitter banter
And songs matched on soft grass, without a shadow.
Umbra is not explicit here, we see,
Although it may be noon, there may be laughter
In every frond and form and field and fallow.

Why did the woodthrush, on the eve of August,
Beyond the white blue spruces, white white pines,
Under the white gold crescent in the sky
Utter the white gold crescents of the song?
That half and half, half silver and half gold,
Not milk and cream, not cheese up in the sky,
Half gold, half silver, had wholly eluded
The study of the last half of July.
She bent in study over rust and over
The pine brooms rusting on the rusting floor
And brushed off deer flies but, fearing mosquitos,
Swept away too easily what seemed
A total silence as a total silence,
                                                    Not

Not pouring skim milk down the drain because
It was not cream but dropping song from song
Because it was no longer song, because
It was no longer.

              Will such sciolism
Answer the questions that it has itself
Created? Be found adequate to strict
Verification, to vague verity?
To the scioptics that may be required?
What will the said be to the seen or half
Seen, to the heard or quarter heard? How will
The sung be mirror of the heard or eighth
Heard or the said be shadow of the seen
Or be a shadow of the shadow seen?

How did the woodthrush on an August morning
Pure gold, august, imperial, mere blue,
As one moved through the sun and through the morning,
Under the pure gold sun's, the mere blue morning's,
Incandescence, through the incandescence,
To where blue spruces' standing shadows pointed
To absolute and shadowless flat blue
Curving without a wrinkle, thin as air,
Thick as shadowlessness, dense as age,
Etherial as everlastingness,
Deliver from the shadows a cool blue
Breeze like a boon blue fever like a keen
Green flicker like sweet silver odors like
Fleet golden measures of the measureless
And evermore unmeasurable blue?

The darkness sometimes plays in beds of light.

The sun was a fire in the pine, was blinding through
The pines, came pounding through the pines, was plain
In the air, beam in the eye, crown on the head,
Infernal in supernal inanition,
Devilish in celestial emptiness,
Hell in the heavens, glory of the world,
Ornament of the universe, bright source.

What shadow would there be without the sun?
With what shade would noon soothe the never febrile?

A rusty fox went rushing through the field.
It was the foxy fox that sat in the grass.

But noon is coming on. Go find a shadow.
Bury your short and restless shade in shade.

Sicilian muses, gods of sylvan worth,
Forgive me if I skip the famous Fourth.
As in the Third I found no umbra, so
I find none either in this golden glow.

Leaving our sweet fields . . . No, that's the First.
My tenuous meditation . . . That is, too.
The sylvan repetition, Amaryllis . . .
That, too. And also the reverberate bricks
That listen and reply like the ailanthus.
The trees repeat my teaching or they speak
Sentences of their own much like the walls
Rusty beyond the rusty samaras
Or sidewalks rusty underneath the beech,
King of shadows. The beech argument,
Die Buchenfrage . . . But here are the elms.

Why do we not sit here among the elms
Mixed with hazels since we both are good
At music — you at playing, I at singing?
This is the Fifth Eclogue. The zephyrous
Shadows are moving in uncertainty
Beneath the trees, or, look, here is a cave . . .

Eluding August's open windows' trumpets,
Televisions, telephones, tall talk,
I walk through August's stifling night's great cavern.
The nighthawk squawking — hawking — through the night,
A figure skating through the ice-gray sky,
An arrow swerving on the silver screen,
Directs me past Frost's house. The pagoda tree
Expands into the evening's heat, its blossoms
Silvery,

Silvery, frosty, icy. The elm is gone.
On the hot sod its chips lie icily,
Unmelted, fallen where they might, cast dice
Undotted, numberless, uncountable.
We counted every nuthatch on that elm's
Sun-golden nut-brown trunk's long loveliness.
I must describe. This is the tough compulsion
To truth where you want beauty, where I want
Beauty, imagination, language, laughs
Of startled delectation, not your eyes
Glazed and your features frozen. Dull, dull, dull.
The samaras are rusty on the ailanthus,
The leaves are rusty on the beech. The beech
Is bronze, not rust. The samaras are rosy,
Not rusty. And the samaras are orange,
The beech is green with coppery touches, and
Longfellow's linden suddenly seems old,
Aged not ancient. The abolitionist
Higginson's forsythia is green.

Why must I go to Rome? I am obsessed
With the First Eclogue's question and its quest.
The book keeps opening at that first rest
Although my fingers and my bookmarks move
Slowly forward, creep through the shadows, prove
The force of shade. Why am I in this groove?

Daphnis of Virgil, of Theocritus,
Daphnis remembered in Miltonic Latin,
Daphnis as Daphne in *Daphnaida*
(Spenser), in *Winter* (Alexander Pope) . . .

The house was noisy and the world was not
More than a noise and all the opened books
Closed with a bang, kept closing with big bangs.
At least the reader was the whimperer,
And not the books and not the noisy world.
Out there, beyond the gold, the blue grew loud.
She stared at the Pacific, and all the books,
Open

Open again, got louder than the house.
She was the reader. When she found a space
Between two lines, a quiet spot along
An edge, a fire escape on which unwinged
Birds could be perched, she took wing from the books,
She sang, she sang aloud above the house,
She sang beyond the sea, above the world.

Could Meliboea sing here? Here there were
No fire escapes, no caves, no elms, no beeches
Until she felt fall's finding of the trees,
Until, under Kentucky skies, beneath
That blue, fires bloomed along the hills and trooped
Along the valleys like redcoats: the oaks
Soaked red, the maples painted red, the dogwoods
Lit red. Its gold fell from the elm. A beech
In bronze and gold emerged upon October.

The beech leaned over the scholar as she lay
Reading. The book leaned over her. The leaves
Gleamed winter-white although they had been brown.
She could remember that: They had been brown.
And she could think they had been green, or was
It red? Remembering was difficult;
Thinking, to rise through snow, shoving the cold
Out of her hair, shoveling pathways through
A brain in which the storm had long since ceased,
Leaving the leaves, the leaning book, the lying
White nevada, blue-valed, peaked with gold,
Blue-shadowed by the golden-shaded tree.
She thought the tree was true, that it might be
The tree, that she might be true to the tree.

What is truth, the Roman governor
Says to the king. He is the friend of Caesar.
He does not wait to hear the king's reply.

What is the tree? What is the shade? And what
Is freedom? Am I not as free as Caesar?
What is Rome, and is there room for me?

What me? What mirror backs upon the sun
That I might see my shadow? From behind
The looking glass is that not Tityrus?

It is Aeneas. I must go to Rome.

I stand a moment in the happy grove
Most rich in shade. Lucus a non lucendo.
It is a tunnel, and there is a light.

There is a temple, and it is a light,
A mirror, a reflection, and my shadow
Inscribed before I came. I came, I saw,

I understood that Carthage was a shadow
Of Rome. I would see Rome. I will see Rome.
The black cow glitters in the whitest cold.

The white cow glistens in the blackest heat.
Rest is unnecessary. Stars fly down
Through thick night to the slim flame of desire.

Was this Rome? Was it home? Was this my home?
Mere mirroring is plainer than confusion,
That negative. Flora is never Julia

Nor Tityrus nor Meliboeus nor
Tityra. Poetry is subtlety.
This is a thesis, a plain mirroring

Of subtlety so shady and shadowy
It has been mirrored for two thousand years
And never plainly. This is Flora's thesis.

Was this then home, my new Kentucky one?

Pasture of pastures resting on Peach Bloom Hill,
Pasture, planet, patria, mother earth,
Bosom, toga fold, and breast and breast
And tunic of the goddess and a rest,
A place of rest from which a throb of song
Arises to the sky, the shadowless.

Earth shades earth here. The blue Kentucky sky
Is of the shadeless shade of endless blue
While the green pastures curve into green shadows
Drawn by unmoving motion down green meadows.
Quiet is motion here, motion is rest,
Shadow the planet pacified. This peace

Is not clamped down upon it, stuffed in its mouth,
Bound about its breast. It is its force,
Endurance, and solidity revealed
In softest non-aggression, in a shield
Of shade that is the thinnest veil, that is
No obscuration but earth being earth,

Curved as earth curves and stirring as earth stirs
And resting as within each instant time
Rests in noon shade or in late afternoon
Layers of shadow, light and not heavy, strewn
And not strewn, laid and not laid, lying and not
Lying but true as flesh and spiritus.

I flew in the blue sky and flying peered
Down at the jagged golden peaks, more gold
Than gold is gold, and stared at valleys, wide
And deep and blue, blue shadows, while the skied
Blue was still shadowless, the infinite shade
Unshaded. In the blue valleys shade lay cold.

Here the familiar infinite, down there
Immensities unknown and unattempted.
Here the Italian blue, the Attic blue,
Blue of Manhattan, blue of Massachusetts,
There the incredible white heights gone gold,
Vast valleys blooded blue but blooded cold.

Is this Nevada? Never has there been
Such blue, blue snow. This then must be Nevada.
Is this Montana? Never have I seen
Such golden mountains. See, snow-gold Nevada.
Up in the sky my space is very small.
Down there enormous spaces rise and fall.

We long for spaciousness. Could this be home?
Home in Kentucky sun rose in the sky
And shattered all across the lawn of snow.
The fragments glitter, but the trees are shadows.
The shattered mirror and the shadowed trees
Share day. At evening golden footprints freeze.

The golden footfalls of the evening steal
Late across the lawn. The western edge
Of the east's time falls here, and you can rise
At eight and see the sun rise after you,
And the long-shadowed afternoon will end
His welcome visit late, like a good friend.

Is winter friendly here? This is the south.
You must feel right at home, opined a neighbor
Who met me puffing, huffing, through the snow.
Gruffly I answered her: I have come south.
The slender girl from Alabama told
Me how she feared Kentucky's northern cold.

But it was summer when I came — late August.
I came as Cicero came back to Rome.
From exile late in Sextile, 57
(Augustus then was not yet six years old,
Was only little Gaius, not Augustus).
Cicero came from exile late in Sextile,
Reentering the city September fourth.
There is no letter of September fourth
Extant, but there is one to Atticus
Written about the tenth and telling him
(For he had stayed in Greece) how Cicero
Returned to Rome: Ad urbem ita veni . . .
To Rome I thus came: There was simply no one
Known to my nomenclator who did not come
To meet me save those enemies by whom
It could not be disguised or be denied
That they were enemies. When I had come
Up to the Capene Gate, the steps of the temples
Were

Were filled with crowds of people, all applauding
In loud congratulation. Such applause,
Such throngs, went with me to the Capitol.
In the Forum, on the Capitol itself,
There was a crowd that was incredible.
The next day, in the Senate, September fifth,
I gave a speech in which I thanked the Senate.

The August-warmed Atlantic was as blue
As the Mediterranean is beyond the white
Village, and great parades of cheery clouds
Feted us over Pennsylvania, and
The grand and gracious oaks gathered together
To greet us when we gained the soil of Kentucky.

I say we, for I was accompanied
By three as by a rare bouquet: by Porcius,
The tall blue larkspur, and by Claudia,
Red rose, and by the little bud, unbudded
As yet but beautiful, Porciola.
How sweet they are, how noble, and how strong:
Strong as Catones, noble as Marcelli,
And sweet as the virgilias in June.

These blossoms, wafted back to Massachusetts,
Flourished there, but I found virgilias
Here, too (and would they bloom in May, not June?),
And I found redbuds, dogwoods, tulip trees,
Locusts, catalpas, promising spring, spring
(And would catalpas be spring here, not summer?),
And I found big magnolias, promising,
Beyond a northerner's imagination,
Spring, spring, although it was only September,

Although we labored on on Labor Day,
Receiving Cicero's condolences:
Si quis . . . adsit . . . If one . . . should be here . . .
Vos laboriosos existimet . . .
He would regard you as laborious,
As toilful, overworked, and overburdened . . .

Quibus

Quibus otiosis . . . to whom at leisure . . .
Ne in communi quidem otio . . .
Not even in the nation's leisure time . . .
Liceat esse . . . it is allowed to be.

You look down from the sky upon the clouds.
You move through realms that rest above the shadows.
Forget that from those dazzling clouds fall shadows.

The brighter it is here, the solider
The white light lying snow-thick far below
In this unshadowed land, this shadeless space

Far above land, the darker is the land.
The denser brilliance is the denser shade.
She brought the dust of Cambridge on her books.

Yet there were few clouds here. The brilliant fall
To her was Maine or Massachusetts, to
The woman from Kentucky was Kentucky.

Yet there were few clouds here. What should I say
For "praeter eos inimicos"? "Save"
Perhaps is obsolescent in this sense

But fits the meter better than "except."
For "similis" I should say "similar"
In "similis . . . frequentia" and "plausus,"

Or I should say "the same" or "this" and "these,"
But "such" or "like" sounds better in my lines.
Why could I not say "like"? Or should I say

"Except those enemies," not "save them," and
"Similar throngs and similar applause"?
What should I say about the brilliant fall?

It was September twenty-third, a blue
And golden day of warm sun and cool breeze.
A sudden sweetness in the air said fall.

The fragrance of the maple leaves said fall.
This is Kentucky, said the woman, this
Makes you feel glad that you are in Kentucky.

This is a real Kentucky autumn day.
It was the birthday of Augustus. Flora
Had almost said, This makes you feel nostalgic.

This is a real New England autumn day.
This is a day for rest. This is a Sabbath.
I feel I have moved back home to New England.

What is it like to move? The papers go,
The books go from the shelves, the shelves, too, go,
The shelves are gone. The rectangles of dust

Upon the floor must go, the refrigerator
Gape dry and warm and dark. The lights must go,
The gas man come, the gas go. When the phone

Goes off we must be off. That number is
No longer ours. We lug the phone along
To numbers new in places different.

We rest. We do not rest. We must keep moving
In noon beyond shade and above shadow.
There is our shadow moving as we rest.

We have moved out and soon we will move in.
Our ship is moving in. Our ship comes in.
We moved above cloud. Now we come to rest.

Kentucky was unclouded that September.
She found no beech trees by the waterways.
She found no beech trees. And she found no water

In Brushy Fork. No, she could see a pool,
A few pools, here and there, by the dry rock.
It was a hard bed and a rocky road

Where those pools lay and running was forgotten.
The hard oaks, though, arose in grandeur, green
And shady. And the tupelos were blue-

Fruited, blue-berried, with blue drops of blood,
Their deep-green leaves — first specimens or segments
As yet — as deeply, brilliantly, ensanguined

In a red resurrection. Was it fall?
Was it not summer? Underneath the oaks,
Whose strength and verdure and umbrageousness

Endured, a summerer could rest in peace.
The grass was blue. The horse with the white star shining
Upon his forehead sauntered up to stare.

The stars stare here. Each night she takes out the garbage
And she takes in the stars. She takes them on —
Takes on Orion and the Pleiades
And . . . who is out there? Owls and stars. In two
Registers voices ask: Who, who, who, who?

Caesar rested like the northern star.
He did not move. When he, no beggar, went
The comet had to come. A bird of night
Hooted at noon.

     Did his eyes blink or stare?

The steady stare of stars is a pulsation.
Blood pulses in my head. The sound is loud.
How can that dull thud be so very loud
Under the sharp silences of the stars?

Stars are to night as shadows are to day.

But, Caesar, every like is not the same.

By day she saw the horses, corn, cows, chickens,
Hedgerows, gray barns, those black tobacco barns,
Those lengths of shadow across the pasture.

         Rest.

The star of evening, over the yet-red west,
Glazes, shines, smiles, laughs silently, and speaks
So softly through that silence that the spark,
The silver bit of ice, is mine, is not.

After the final word there is a further.
After the final vow there is a new
Dispensation. Who had the final say?
When she said yes had he at last said nay?
When she responded had the question changed?
She answered that her no was no negation,
Was a new yes, was the old yes remade
In a new moment, when the light had shifted,
The dark had deepened. Deep, oh very deep,
Years afterward, she found him. It was he.
Had the red shifted from infinity?

Over the silver sliver of the moon,
Over the yet-red west, the silver star
Laughed her bright silver laugh. Bright Venus stared
Steadily from her loveliness. And Mars —
No, Mars was not below, beyond the moon —
Mercury, tickled pink, twinkled, blinked, winked.
The beautiful slim moon embraced herself.
Deep, deep, I found him, found him beautiful.

It was October when she found the beech.

It was October when he found his theme.
Gibbon sat on the Roman Capitol.
Must ruin be the shadow of the dream?
Must rising find its echo in the fall?
She found the beech in February hacked
And chopped and, on the next day, gone. Destruction
Succeeded no decline. The choppers lacked
All reason, all excuse, beyond construction.
Sooner will stags find pastures in the air
And fish begin to breathe upon the shore
Than, if I go to Rome and find him there,
I will forget that countenance. Before
I find him must I find a road, one lucky
Road to Rome? My road led to Kentucky.

But we must cross the chalk-snatching Oaxes
Muddily rushing up toward the Aral Sea.
                                        Smooth

Smooth white rock paves the road of Brushy Fork.
The Louisville and Nashville has one track
Straight northward, curving southward lusciously.
The trees dip toward the dry stream as toward water,
The curves call for a current, for a surge,
Call for a torrent tearing through the boulders,
Call for a slow sweep, call for a glassy flow,
For ripples, for moist mirroring where only
On the white slabs shadows lie dry and low.
No heart of darkness and no heart of light
Pulse here. The gray shadowy heart lies so
Silent that stillness is its undertow.

Beauty I sing, I sing Rome to the woods,
Knowledge I teach, love to the woods impart.
The woods recite love, beauty, knowledge, Rome
To the professor. Is the recitation
Theirs? Do the trees, my teachers, docilely
Answer, my class? I am not Doctor Baum.
I cannot cure the bushes, teach the trees,
Heal flowers, lecture leaflets, or profess
My meditations as the mouthed, mulled Muse,
Call my work play, or call my play my work,
Call this my place, or call my place my home.
Now go, goats, go, the golden willows glow,
Come back, for you. Tree medick is your feed,
The rusting beech our golden shadower.

Widener, my love, I will return and sing
Of you among the books, between the shelves
Heaped high with books, beneath the bookish beech,
The elms extending foliaceously.
The folios are open to my song.
Widener, my spouse, my song opens to you.
It is, of course, an academic marriage.
I will return, I will return and sing
Widener, the incarnation of the spouse.
If the betrothal happened in Book One,
The wedding in Book Two, what of Book Three?
                                    Remember,

Remember, said Thalia, that Apollo
Insists the meditation is the shade,
The composition is the consummation.

Why (miring Meliboeus will inquire)
Did I hie into exile, you to Rome?
October, oh, October in Kentucky!
Who thinks of February in October?
Two cows are moving now across the pasture.
Two cows have moved. They slip behind the ridge.
The animals have vanished from the painting.
The hills halloo Hellenic clarity
Which azure (famed Mediterranean)
Grants in the middle of the continent,
But this awakening of red and gold
Is called New England's closer to the ocean.
So bright and bloody is Kentucky now
It could be north, be autumn-red Japan.

It could be any of the realms of gold.
The sugar maples lord it in the land.
Gold they are. Gold, they know gold's purple, too.
Purple is hinted in the chickory's blue,
Hinted in the euonymus's red.
Without asyndeton let it be said.
Nevertheless, the chickory is blue.
Moreover, the euonymus is red.
The standards of the dogwood are red, true
Red standards. Heaven is the standard blue,
Blue's standard, the blue standard. What conjunction
Links it with chickory's wild-aster function?
Eight cows appear. They are of varied hue.
The slopes are those we city children drew.

Skyscrapers, for us, did not mar the sky.
In our apartments we drew those gray barns
Upon those slopes. Our crayons colored cows
Like those along those lines whose points we plotted
Surely, implanted with geometry,
Whose curves our eyes and fingers calculated
Without

Without instruction, with no calculation.
Beethoven's Seventh is much like those slopes,
Cicero's sentences resemble them.
This is urbane delight: delight in pastures,
Joy of the trees, pleasures among the hills,
Loves of the earth. That bale of hay is gold,
Is golden-brown, is brown. That pale brown barn
Belongs to earth. Is straw, is gold, in the pines?

Gold on the mountains, gold in the valleys, gold
Of trees, the trees of gold, the golden cow,
Fire on the mountains, fire in the valleys, fire
Of trees, the trees of fire, all flame, all glow,
All are aglow, agleam, aflame, a gold
Afire in the sun, yet in the shade a cold
Comes, a little chill crossing the meadows
Slowly swings along mountainous shadows.
The stream's bright leafy loveliness is real,
Not a reflection. Red and yellow leaves
Fill the dry bed instead of water, heal
The barrenness that lay there and conceives
Or makes our sympathy conceive and feel
The still, waterless beauty it achieves.

The fifteenth of October is the earthly
Birthday of Virgil, Virgin-Poet, and
Celestial birthday of the Virgin-Doctor
Teresa, now reborn four hundred five
Earth years, now just that long at home in heaven.
Virgil is now two thousand fifty-six.
Sweet purple plays upon the sweet gum now.
Now amber laves the liquidambar bough.
The summum bonum is not this high blue
Above our heads, this sky-of-heaven sky,
This blue-of-heaven blue, this lapidary
Blueness, not stone, not gem, but, through and through,
Summum blueness, summit of blue, blue high,
Celestial phrase not in earth's dictionary.

We drew those barns, but all our barns were red.
Our barns were scarlet, fresh in their red glow.
We drew that stream, but it was full of flow
Silver and wet and rippling as it sped
On towards the ocean. When did the rain beat down,
When did the water hustle Van Gogh green
Between the brushy banks? November's scene
That must have been, green in November's brown,
Among more stringy shadows, bristling hills.
The falling leaf became a butterfly.
The fallen gold that had been glistening high
Among the now fresh spring green winter quills
Became straw underneath the pines. White rice,
Pearls, finally gleamed in Brushy Fork's green ice.

Was it December? Was it January?
Or was it February? Was it the seventh
Of January, one day past the sixth,
Or was it February, the eleventh?
The letter came in winter, and it said:
Graze your cows as before, girls, mate your bulls.
It said: Do something old, make something new.
All in together, girls, how do you like
The weather: January, February . . . ?
Boys and girls together: London Bridge . . . ,
The sidewalks of New York, the walks of Cambridge,
Massachusetts, weathering together.
The letter went to many, all together.
It came to me uniquely and alone.

Epiphany? Appearance? Miracle?
Message? Epistle? Missive? Revelation?
Go into exile. You will find him there.
Go, go to Rome. There you will surely see him.
Go, go, go home. Dare to embrace the vision.
Revise. Review. Open your eyes anew.
In February who thinks of October?
How in October could she have imagined
The January crocuses revived

In February

In February and reresurrected
In March, the February daffodils
(How Mother Nature kills the daffodils,
She marveled) reincarnate in sweet March.
Could she foresee in fall Kentucky's spring?

Christmas is coming, Advent is second coming.
But it is still the fifteenth of October.
Yet it is almost Christmas in the holly.
Yet, seeing sun in the red-breasted trees,
A robin thinks, sings spring. The Norway spruce,
As spruce as spring, has known no touch of autumn
And poses young and lovely as a princess
Among the maples' golden crowns, the dogwoods'
And oaks' red heraldry. Its partial changes
Leave the euonymus full, perfect, green,
Green-purple, purple-red, and red. The dogwood
Is luminous in utter self-possession,
Standing there all aglitter, all alight,
An idol, an ideal construct of light.

Why must I tell the truth? This is a thesis.
This is a dissertation, not a poem.
Upon the fairly frosty morning lawn
The sun fingers its way into the shadows.
These are the shadows of the morning, these
Webs, these snares, these bulks assaulted, these
Shadows rebutted and retreating, not
The meditative shade of noon, and not
Evening's shades unfolding and enfolding.
The folding and unfolding of the pastures
At evening feels the late sun lay its gold
Along its lines and surfaces, upon
Its grassiness, upon its gleaming leaves,
Along the flanks and backs of the sleek cows.

Such gilding, the belonging of the barn,
The satisfactions of earth's undulations,
The undulations of earth's satisfactions —
None of these is my theme. This is the birthday
                                          Of Virgil.

Of Virgil. Birthdays are irrelevant.
This blue celestiality, this eyed
Sky, this untoward strained straining toward unstrained
Unstraining elegance and excellence
(Excelsior! Elegantissime!),
Toward color and toward cause, toward causal color
And color's cause, toward the ineffable
From the unspeakable, and toward the said
Blue, the aforesaid gold — these, to the skied
Eye, reek of strain, stuffing the elephant.

The elephant is elegant. He climbs
Higher and higher. Chips fall where they may.
They are not cheap excelsior. The Alps
Receive the snowfall not as emptied cloud
But as transfiguration. Hannibal
Seeks Rome. Even among transfigured hills,
Golden and rubicund, under a sky
Unnebulous, made of the piercing blue
Which is a spear that does not hurt the eye,
Which is a sword that does not harm the heart,
Flora must find the Roman road, must take it,
Take or be taken, climb on through the shade
Cast by the hills, the shadows thrown from the mountains.
The golden leaves fall like excelsior.

Flora the pacifist must conquer Rome,
Capture and captivate and be the captive,
Take and be taken and not be mistaken,
Not err. The shadows wander with the planets.
The accents wander through the poem. Here
They reinforce, here they resist. My cows —
For Rome allows this — wander, as you see,
Says Flora as her eyes go grazing down
The pastures and go straying up the slopes.
We leave the sweetest fields in homodyne,
Relax in shadow which diaeresis
Renders bucolic. Tityrus fills a foot,
And Meliboeus sets a feminine
Caesura right before the unnamed god.

Was it November when the god returned
To Brushy Fork, the nymphs to Silver Creek?
Why had the nymphs departed, what dread voice
Shrank the past streams? March sees the daffodils
Bloom on the bank above the green and silver
Waters. November saw the green and silver
Waters, the mirrors where the green god glimpsed
His brushy hair and where the silver nymphs
Regarded long combed tresses. Sweet creek, run.
Forked god, remain. Water remains in ice.
The bottles, cans, and plastic cups endure.
The daffodils will fill their cups with tears
Of joy regardless, whether snow or rain
Serves the advance of March. The tears remain.

How can one's tears upon the Ides of March
Resemble those upon the Ides of October?
The weeping willows showed the selfsame gold
In fall and spring, at dawn and as the sun
Sank like a golden cow behind the pasture.
The willows wept the selfsame golden tears
After the fall and long before the spring.
Spring, Arethusa, sing. Those tears are past.
These tears do not resemble or remember
Laments upon the streams of Babylon,
Long lamentations by the Black Sea, loud
Outcries beside the white, crashing Oaxes.
Soft! The reflecting stream of March displays
The daffodils' unnarcissistic gaze.

The dogs of March splash in the stream. October's
Hounds reechoed from the flaming hills,
Reverberated from the flaming mountains.
She heard the hounds, and then she heard the sirens.
The hounds keep waiting. Flora is the one
Lapping up the leaves laved by the sun.
The sirens sound of fire and not of water.
The leaves are fireless flames, no interruption
And no deterrent, pause as pleasure, peace
             And no

And no encroachment, arias, ariettas,
Airs in the air, rhythms on the hills,
Upon the trees metrical syllables.
She measures all, for Flora is the one
Pursuing leaf, sky, and the scent of the sun.

She deemed the leaves gold, called the branches silver.
If the sun glisters is it not this gold?
If you kiss silver do you kiss a shadow?
You find, if you unlock a leaden sky,
The drops of silver on the golden foils
All in the universal shadowing
Where shadows vanish. Let the leaden heavens
Unlock their secrets. They are silver high
Beneath the blue made by the golden sun
Over the rainbow, under the veil, behind
The looking glass. Is lead the heaviness
Of sacrifice without the penetration
Of vision, pedantry without the art,
The arc, celestial, sans the unlocked heart?

The lead may be the cloud that promises
The rain, may be the smoke where there is fire.
The meter and the meaning of the poem
May be the shadow and the substance or
The substance and the shadow, be the matter
And the substantial form or be the form
And the high matter, or may be the light
And the great conflagration. If the shade
Is the last foot it will be homodyne.
The same thing must be said about the shadows.
Diaeresis made one relaxed in shade,
As I have mentioned. In the final line
Diaeresis sent from the peaks the shadows.
But the true role only the pauses played.

A pause accompanied diaeresis
When all geography became confused.
Parthians breathed the north, Germans the east.
After the third foot there was a pause.
                                    There

There was a pause that tore the line in two.
I cannot show it. I can only tell.
These fives can rarely illustrate those sixes.
These threes can hardly represent those fours.
How can iambics be dactylic? Why,
Spondees are said to be impossible
In English. What? Not possible? How now,
Brown cow? Pasture your cows in dactyls, yoke
Those bulls so that a spondee ends that line.
But three lines showed five spondees each. Define.

In sixty-two there was diaeresis
With pause right in the middle of the verse.
In sixty-three five spondees culminate
The five-line passage in which Tityrus
Pours forth his feeling for the gracious god.
Ante, et, ante, aut, aut, and then quam
Mark the long lines, lead to the great conclusion
That Tityrus will not forget that face
Forever gleaming golden in his heart.
The first four lines begin with dactyls. Through
The fifth five solemn spondees march. At length
The figural becomes the actual.
What is for one man an adynaton
Is for the other one the wide wild world.

The opposite occurs in those four lines
In which a realistic happening
Becomes a figure, called the sympathy
Figure by those who are in sympathy
With pastoral, but called a fallacy
By others — the pathetic fallacy.
Lines thirty-six to thirty-nine present
A sudden understanding: Amaryllis
(Now Meliboeus comprehends) was sad
And called upon the gods and left the plums
Neglected on their trees, for Tityrus
Was gone. Anaphora with polyptoton
Shows how the trees all called for Tityrus.
There are five spondees in line thirty-nine.

There are five spondees in line fifty-two
Which reinforce the theme of shade at noon
Within the eight-line scene of rest and peace.
Within bucolic song bucolic song
Can happen at such noon and in such shade.
Many viburnums tolerate light shade
But flourish best in full sun, snowy, green.
Many viburnums burn in fall. Do Virgil's
Lenta viburna mean the ones we term
Viburnum opulus, the guelder rose,
Cranberry bush — the European kind?
Viburnum trilobum — American
Cranberry bush — is very similar.
Those maple leaves will flame red in the fall.

Viburnum opulus can stand wind, dust,
Grime, smoke. It is resistant to our cities'
War upon life. Limit its pruning. Leave
The loveliness that is its nature's grace,
Is nature's grace, alone. Like cooling snow,
The blossoms gleam in summer's sun. All winter,
Too bitter for our taste, the fruits delight
Our eyes as if they bore the nature of
Blooms of red blood, unwarlike, painless, sweet,
Peaceful, unpreyed upon, persistent, bright.
What are those leaves that flame upon the fall?
The flames die down. The leaves that flame must fall.
Burning viburnums are our cities. Rome
Is like the sempervirent cypresses.

Is Ruskin just another? Can the great,
The truly great, do anything and wait
And watch and see it grow both great and true?
Virgil, in my opinion, cannot do
Anything false or paltry even though
Apollo bids him cultivate the low,
The lowly, stoutly plowing through the glade,
Driving his goats, and lying in the shade.
My eyes like kittens' paws play with the bright
                                        And moving

And moving baubles tempting from the trees.
My eyes like children's tongues lick at the sweet
Lollipop red of sourwoods. Like a bite
My eyes sink into reds that by degrees
Sink into greens of oaks. The eyes must eat.

The eye devours yet never will destroy.
Reds on the hills and scarlets on the mountains,
Stirrings of light in leaves, blurrings of shadow
Across the grass, gold trees by lead-gray barns,
All of orange autumn in the sugar maple
Fed the eye, undiminished by its stare.
The progress of October slowly gave
Hints of the greater spaces of November.
Then came the day of equilibrium
That balances the old leaves on the trees
Exactly with the new leaves on the ground.
Still trilling leaves upon the boughs were flames.
Flaming October opened on November.
Flaming October then became November.

The metaphor became reality.
The dry sounds sound of more than dryness, speak
Of the aridity torridity
Turns into torrents which, allwaterless,
Lick as they rise, swallow as they ascend,
Gulp as they grow, gobble, consume, destroy.
Those clouds are signs of fire, not promises
Of the desired desiderable rain,
Omens of present agony, not pledges
Of benefits descendible from heaven
When for that blue is substituted lead:
Plumbeus portal pouring, silvering.
We breathed black air, gazed on black boughs, afraid
Of summer's sun bereft of summer's shade.

November ninth it rained and then it snowed.
From the lead caskets silver cascades flowed.
Later the white turned gold across the meadows.
If you are one who kisses only shadows
Will you

Will you have only shadows' happiness?
Daphnis has died and Daphnis lives to bless
The golden dawn, the silvery noon's shade,
The leaden dark of night. She hoped. She prayed.
It rained. It snowed. Then the chill water came
Through roof, through wall, and pooled upon her floor.
Shall we protect ourselves within the cold
Cave or beneath the elms whose well-sung fame
Mingles with their shadows evermore?
She found the elm when foliage turned gold.

If trees turn into truths, if figures turn
Into the literal, if letters turn
Into great spirits, authors into ghosts,
Ghosts into writers, writers into plays,
Plays into works, and beeches into books,
If Flora is the writer or the written,
Is in the beech's shade or is its shadow,
Virgil is the beech tree even if
The beech tree is belated, is an oak.
Dodona's oak may well have been a beech.
Did its leaves prophesy the less for that?
She found among the great oaks of Kentucky
Three little beech trees planted on the lawns.
The little beech trees rustled through the winter.

I, Flora, am not Fagus. That is certain.
Uncertain shadows flickered from the elm
And subtly played croquet across the lawn.
The gold leaves flickered from the elm and fell
And somersaulted on the autumn lawn.
The shadows were diminished by November.
In March the flickers send their telegrams
From boles and punch their messages along
The lawns with equal zeal or bend like swans
Into the iceless lake of softened soil,
Engaging with the creatures of the deep
Like Beowulfs with black mustachios
And bloodied pates. No, they are but red-polled.
They fly towards me. Their wings are lined with gold.

Daphnis has risen with the daffodils.
Was it then February? Is it March?
Upon the pink and white of flowering trees
We meditate, assisted to ascend
By incense that arrests us on the air,
Lifting our airy breathing spirits higher
Above the purpling cercis. Is it March?
Daffodils, dandelions, hyacinths,
Tulips, magnolias, winter honeysuckle,
The fragrantest, the fragrantissima,
Well named in Latin if not quite in English
(This fragrance is not winter. It is spring.),
Uncertain umbras fluttering from Ulmus
Americana summon: Sit and sing.

Was it November when he left us? Is
It March? How can the violets be sweet
And soft and fresh and dusky-lustrous then?
If flames are gold, forsythias are flames.
If violets are violets, they spring
Here by the road. However low, they spring.
Low, these white starlets rise across the grass.
Those star magnolias rise above the field.
A summer's sun without a summer's shade
Directs our rash research into the season.
Is this then March? Is this Kentucky's spring?
If all the ranks of daffodils must fade,
Is this uncontrovertibly the reason
Why quinces listen as azaleas sing?

Pathetic. Synesthetic. And synthetic.
The critics criticized fallaciously.
Flora must tell it all veraciously.
Flora goes stumbling on through the magnetic
Field, through the large penumbra, of the poem,
Hearing the hollow hoot and hobbled howl
Of the eternal question of the owl.
Who can resist the pull? The pretty proem,
The ugly catalogue, the tedious
Reiteration,

Reiteration, and the slow processions
Through endless heavens, through the latest fashions
Of earth, must not be judged egregious
Errors but ordered strayings through strong hours,
Wanderings through the poem's wanded powers.

In the Fifth Eclogue umbra occurs three times,
Twice in the plural, once in the singular,
Once in a speech by Mopsus, in line five,
Once in the song by Mopsus, in line forty,
Once, in line seventy, in Menalcas' song.
A plural form (accusative) appears
In verses five and forty, which both end
With umbras, and the singular is found
(An ablative, after a preposition)
In seventy, where umbra ends the line.
Line forty, in the song that Mopsus sings,
Is twenty-first of twenty-five lines, while
Line seventy, within Menalcas' song
Of twenty-five, is fifteenth. Am I wrong?

O those uncertain shadows of line five!
I think they are the shadows sought at noon
For rest and song; note Varro and the *Georgics*.
But maybe they are not, for Tityrus
Must watch the grazing goats while Mopsus sings.
If the goats graze, it is perhaps not noon;
Note Varro and the *Georgics*. But the shadows
Resemble noon's. Therefore, I am uncertain.
These are the shadows that the zephyrs move.
Of this there can be no uncertainty.
When do the zephyrs move? How has the vine
Sprinkled its scattered clusters? I can prove
The use of a, r, s repeatedly
And of five spondees in a golden line.

Is this a different Tityrus, not the one
Who sang beneath the tree while Meliboeus
Listened amazed, faced, found, felt, could not fight
Songless eviction, saw the songlessness
                                    Of exile?

Of exile? Yes or no, see on the cave
The wild rare sprinkling of the vine's racemes.
This is line seven, golden and spondaic.
This is the Fifth Bucolic, not the First.
This is the Fifth Selection. This is the vine
Select, sylvestrian, sparse and not spare
Over the cave. This is the cave selected
To be the shade in which to sing the song
They could have sung under the elms. They chose
Cavernous shade, pale olive, punic rose.

The pallid olive and the cavern's shadow
Are choice, the cave's shade and the paling olive
Select, the punic purples of the rose
Election, and the purple shadows of
The cave shades of sad happy hymning of
Mortality and immortality.
The hymns have shadows. Daphnis, purple grape
Upon the vine, has vanished. For the soft
Violets, for the purple daffodils
Purpling in a true spondaic line
In which the fifth foot is a spondee, thorns
Spring. Fling petals, bring on shadows: sow
Flowers, plant great trees around a tomb.
Drink in the shade and dance. Daphnis is home.

The blossoms drooped when Daphnis drooped and fell.
Daphnis has bloomed again among the gods.
For Daphnis there is neither death nor hell.
Daphnis has triumphed over all our odds.
Daphnis is home again among the heavens.
March is at home with subtle violets
And blatant daffodils, which prove it evens
The contest on which we had placed our bets:
Midwestern winter versus southern spring.
The other contest came out even, too.
Each singer, when they both had ceased to sing,
Bestowed a gift upon the other you,
Not envying the other's gift but praising
Gift with gift, phrasing with gracious phrasing.

I am not envious, I am amazed,
Said Meliboeus. He saw Tityrus
Sitting beneath the beech while all the other
Shepherds and farmers had to rise, stand, crazed
Flee fields in turmoil and in conturbation.
Let us sit where the elms' wind-shifted shade
Lists unpredictably and yet protects
Those who despite fear without perturbation
Entrust themselves to its uncertainties,
Or let us sit in the grape-dappled cave,
Said Mopsus. He had heard his greater friend,
Menalcas, on the higher frequencies.
Tityrus sang, Meliboe faced eviction.
Mopsus sang death, Menalcas resurrection.

Rejected by one's time, one wants to win
The war with time. There is another war,
Not figurative, the consequence of sin
Not mythical, which will bang shut the door
Not of a paradise but of a world.
The sin, untimely, is of one's own time
And ticks the time until time will be whirled
Into eternities beyond one's rhyme
Or reason, hell or heaven. Purgatory,
Abbreviated, lengthened, is the wait,
Limbo, the art that cannot know the story
Of pyramids and capitols, the fate
Of fame. The Muse hums. If you want to climb
The temporal be literal. Save time.

Is it a pitiable love of fame
That makes you a well-wisher to the earth?
Is it a love that flames with purer flame
For a great mother that gave you your birth?
Is it the love of the great human mass
That has been and that is and that could be
As seconds and millennia yet pass?
Is it the love of that great looming tree
Shadowed in green through August, a grand pyre
                          In rubicund

In rubicund October, old, not old,
Crowned by Phoenician crimson phoenix fire,
New hoary locks, May-crowned in green and gold?
Is it the love of little Porcia, long
Lulled in your arms by your tree-topping song?

When April's redbuds in their Tyrian purple
And oaks in purest Mycenaean gold
(Kentucky's oaks are aureate in April,
In May both emerald and aureoled),
And silken gleams of green on maples, puffs
Green on the tiny European beech
(It is not May), upon the lilacs snuffs
(It is not May) of lilac, on the birch
Tinsel not tinsel but rich golden fringe,
Dogwoods as candid (but it is not May),
As strange, as wonderful, while they impinge
Upon the azure of an April day,
As Daphnis, are perceived and do not fade,
Daphnis I love in April's shining shade.

The dogwood was as radiant as Daphnis,
But Daphnis was not strange. It was the place.
I was the stranger underneath the lapis
Lazuli of April's skyey space.
The dogwood on the threshold of that sky
Was white and shining up against the blue.
Candidus, as it could well modify
Daphnis, could modify the dogwood, too.
Insuetum, next, is strange upon the tongue
Of one to whom the way the words progress
In space or time will make them right or wrong.
In the eternal language words process.
Inflection gives bright light to this parade,
The order of the words a subtler shade.

I must not say this in my thesis, though
Books that forget it issue from the press
Of a great university. The glow
Of Rome will fade if teachers do not stress

(I turn

(I turn prosaic and pedestrian)
Latin's immutable eternal law:
To read one must be a grammarian.
Rome will have fallen if one fatal flaw
Enters and penetrates and undermines
Its adamantine everlastingness,
The Latin language. When no one declines
And conjugates the rubble is a mess.
Build up the stones again as they must be
Constructed and construed eternally.

But read. Read as the Romans read, aloud,
Word after word. This is not really rubble.
The Roman stones already are inscribed
In order. This is not a game of scrabble.
The Latin that one loves was once hard work.
The Latin that one loves is subtlest play.
Happy are they who somehow did not shirk
The one. They see the other's blessed day.
Like Daphnis they will marvel as they stand
Upon the threshold of Olympus, where
They look down on the clouds and planets and
The traffic of the stars and, breathing air
Azure, celestial, pass through the facades
And learn they are conversant with the gods.

Daphnis is standing in the court of heaven,
Contemplates beauty, contemplates the truth,
Needing no more the shadow of the seven
Veils, not demanding any shade of proof.
On earth the proof is May. The tale, so old,
Is new. The lofty locust blossoms gleam.
Virgilias silver and laburnums gold
Accept the torch and carry on the flame.
On earth, if May should pale, should fade and fail,
The song, beyond the shadow of the moan,
Is both the revelation and the veil.
Grammar and ars poetica alone
Are in my court. Philosophy may moot
A beauty infinite, truth absolute.

Infinite beauty cannot be my goal.
Absolute truth is not my destination.
My study is a part and not a whole.
My teaching will not be indoctrination.
My page will not affirm and not deny.
My lecture will not be infallible.
My text will not seek to demystify.
My tutelage will not be mystical.
I will not play among the esthetes, will
Prize the aesthetic. I will never rot
Among the cynics and the skeptics, still
Will choose agnosticism. I will not
Deride truth with the ridiculing sect
Or detest beauty with the mob elect.

A spoon drifts down the stream. It is not silver.
If Silver Creek drifts through a tarnished wood,
Silver the word silver, silver the word
Silva, silver the wood. The sylvan scene
Dons silver winter weeds prelusively,
Assumes armorial vernal argentines,
Expands into the full obscurity
Of aestivation. If the sylvan scene
Is aestivating, will the silver speech
Be hibernating? Will the cloud be lined
With silver and the fall coated with gold,
The selvage be obscure, the spring be clear?
The spoon is plastic, and the stream, the river,
Fills with liquidity plastic with silver.

Daphnis departed in November when
The metaphorical became the real,
The flaming trees became the flaming trees.
Daphnis returned in February with
The daffodils. Anne, born in February,
Left one November like a leaf of gold
Illumining a beech's golden shadow.
Autumnal copper, bronze, and gold revealed
The big Berea beech on Center Street.

Berea,

Berea, Greece, received the word. Berea,
Kentucky, heard the truth. In February
The beech was killed by human engineers
And engines. While the men, indifferent,
Said little, all the mechanisms wailed.

I know the blossoms in their times and seasons.
Mays claim the redbuds and the dogwoods. Mays
Are wafted into Junes on locust fragrance.
Virgilias suffuse Junes with their incense.
Tulip trees cup the sunsets of long days.
Catalpas have their overwhelming reasons
For choosing waning Junes or new Julys.
July fourths often crackle with catalpas.
The record blazes up before my eyes.
May claimed virgilias, tulip trees, catalpas.
The redbuds, dogwoods, locusts all were April's.
The first of April saw redbud's pink purples.
First, fourteenth, thirtieth were April's days,
Ninth, tenth, and eighteenth (nota bene), May's.

Is it to be pedantic to note well
The date of every vision that Kentucky
Offered the visionary visitor,
Settler, homesteader, colonist, husbandwoman?
Here is the record: redbud, April first;
Dogwood, April fourteenth; the thirtieth
Of April (April!), locust. Not on record
Are early April's lilacs and gold oaks,
Nor do I count laburnum on May seventh.
Here is the count: virgilia, May ninth;
Tulip tree, May tenth; the seventeenth
Of May, a huge high white magnolia flare;
And May eighteenth, catalpa. May was June
There then. Then there was spring with summer's tune.

Green leaves appeared upon a beech tree, not
The beech tree. That was gone. When had she found
The others, three, all tiny? She forgot.
They were not beechy yet, not tall, not round,
                                  Not full,

Not full, not grand in shadow, great with shade.
Two were American, one European,
Two fagi grandifoliae, arrayed
In brown all winter, one, familiar, foreign,
Fagus sylvatica, from its own north.
She found the big beech on October second,
Two little ones October twenty-fourth.
The little ones would never have been mentioned,
Although declared by silver, bronze, and gold,
Unless the greater's story had been foiled.

Menalcas, you are greater, Mopsus said.
Greater, says Servius, may be in age
Or merit. Yet a death not merited
By age came to the greater beech. A rage
For something called construction or expansion
Brought it its death when it was in its prime.
What syntax or what subtleties of scansion
Can justify that slaughter in my rhyme?
I had not found the fourth beech by November.
I found it at the end of January.
It was a little one. And I remember
The greater died the third of February.
Like nestlings, in November, orange burs each
Opened an empty beak from the big beech.

If silver, bronze, and gold are names for merit,
Structure is more, and energy is all.
If later time from greater can inherit
The precious, structures may not have to fall.
Energy may not have to be diminished
If age adds more than aging takes away.
Centuries may not find that they have finished
Their roll if May may ever follow May.
Two little beeches clapped, giving me pause,
In February, knowing no defeat,
Continuing their plausible applause,
Not guessing what befell on Center Street.
That bronze-tipped silver energy was spoiled
Which in October had been domed in gold.

The old leaves vanished as the promises
Of new truths verged upon veracity.
Before the new truths, fuzzy, verdant, grew
To grandifoliation, when the buds
Were merely big, a modest nest appeared
And the big beaks, those implements and signs
Of such desire as, big even among
The small, exfoliates the fuzzy young,
Scizzored the empty air. The empty nest
Revealed desire for air as satisfied,
Volition for volation as fulfilled,
Wings' airiness transcendent over rest.
The airy leaves became less rarified.
With the full foliage the nest was veiled.

Sun, stop. Time, stop. Day, wait. Night, never come.
Blue, be. Gold, do not dim. White blossom, stay.
Green leaf, keep. In the honeysuckle hum,
Bee, honily. Gleam, gleaming buds of May.
Shade, shade. Tree, do not die. Apostrophe,
Endure as incantation. Song, remain
Enfranchised ever in the air. Sweet tree,
Welcome the woodthrush and imprison pain
Forever, ever in your shadows keep
The singer. Shade frees song. Tree, do not die.
Play, thrush, forever liberated. Sleep,
Honey, bud, babe, for now. Sweet, do not cry.
Fair infant, in this instant we are free.
Porciola, we have been, you will be.

A letter reached her one day in Kentucky.
It said, Seize freedom on a fellowship.
This ship can take you to gray Massachusetts
Or set you high upon the continental
Meadows, black Ararat, or let you cross,
Criss-cross, white Alps, for you have gone to Rome.
The snow turned silver, bronze, and gold. The air
Turned azure. Verdure ruffed both sun and shade.
This simple letter was a watershed.
                                        Roaring

Roaring and pouring, black and white, it said,
Your ship is coming in. It has come in.
This was the only ship that she had seen.
The letter said, Yours is this white, this bold
Black, this polished silver, bronze, and gold.

Before he knew Suzanne Curchod, he told her,
Writing a letter from Lausanne the ninth
Of February 1758,
L'amour de l'Etude faisoit ma seule passion.
And in the manuscript called Memoir E,
Composed, no doubt, in 1791,
Gibbon speaks still about the love of study,
A passion which, he says, derives fresh vigour
From what he terms enjoyment and supplies
Each day, each hour, with a perpetual source
Of independent pleasure. On May third
In 1786 he does admit
A woman might add something to his life.
He was contented with his other wife.

I think on thee, truth-beauty, mistress-master,
Oak-violet, Grand Canyon-Everest,
River and lake, fresh waterfall and ocean,
Avenue-trail, sequoia-skyscraper,
Labyrinth-prairie, crocus-chrysanthemum,
Cosmos, chaos, crystal, catalyst,
Chasm of coal and precipice of snow,
Green-red, pagoda and pagoda tree
Shimmering through an occidental August,
Dawn rose and gold, star argent on azure eve,
Venustas-veritas, wellspring and font,
Window and mirror, oasis and mirage,
Serenity and storm, a lord, a love,
A sun, a shade, nameless, unnameable.

Fair well, farewell, addio. Every fair
Is unfair now. Accept my valediction,
Dame verity, dear veriverbiage,
Darling verbigeration. Now adieu,
Monsieur

Monsieur Le Beau, et mes adieux à vous,
Mesdames Belles Lettres. Par un mot commence
Mon texte, ma thèse, ma dissertation,
My proem, my non-poem, my old fare
Mixed in a new farrago, a new fashion
And fashery. Now pay your dues, your fare
To Charon. Now farewell. Tyrannical,
Totalitarian truth, tremble. By
Fair well begun, by shade, by tree, by by,
Lullaby, end. Bye bye, now, beauty, bye.

The shadows of the shadows of the shadows
Fell on my face. I felt the taste of shade.
Was it disputable? I savored April
Redbuds (finest raspberry ice), March (peach)
Tulips on Peach Bloom Hill, and February
(Yolks of) daffodil and crocus, though
January brought the crocuses
Together with the robins. January
Brought the Arctic air. Audaciously
The crazy crocuses came anyway,
As did the raving robins. Soon the bees
Buzzed in their crocus cups. Soon robins sang
Their Anacreontic song: spring. If I heard
The first song January thirty-first
And saw the first thirst-quenching bee the third
Of February, on which day accurst
The beech was executed, it was spring.
A diary is not a dissertation.
A calendar is not a work of art.
Ovid and Spenser play in a tradition.
History and myth each takes its part
Around the great symposiastic ring.
Sitting alone, one sits with all the sages
If one can hear the medleys of the ages.

It was at Rome, the fifteenth of October,
That Gibbon, sitting on the Capitol,
Heard his great call and saw his great idea.

An early

An early version of the famous lines
Says that the place and moment are recorded
In a contemporaneous account,
His journal. They are not recorded there.

Under the beech I lay still wondering
Whether to watch my image in the pool
Or rise and follow where no shadow waits
My coming but I am myself the shadow,
Where I embrace no unsubstantial shade
But am the very shade that is embraced,
Whether to be the image and reflection,
However beautiful, of more than beauty
And multiply the image of myself
Which is the image of another or
Plunge like Arethusa through the pool
And rise a fountain, break into the glass
And live with Alice on the other side.
A shade may be no shadow but a tree,
The tree itself, branching in Vallombrosa
Like Daphne in the Vale of Tempe, neither
She nor he but it at last, like Virgil,
Uncertain omo or uncertain ombra
But certain well-leaved book, whether or not
The bookish age is ending or has ended,
Whether or not the forests echo still
With spirits that are neither he nor she
But angels, each sole member of its species
If matter is, as sapients have taught,
The principle of individuation.
The earthly paradise, whether the center
Of universal matter or a speck
Of green upon a cog in the computer
So huge and ruthless even Newton used
It awkwardly, is the well-authorized,
Self-authorized, as sapients have thought,
Deme, doom, dominion of one species and
One gender, still erect if fallen, man.

Gibbon himself, no longer merely man,
Became a book, became the fall of Rome.
Milton himself became the fall of man.
Is paradise refound within, in here,
The garden of the existential self,
The structured subject, the positioned agent,
Or is it there, way out there on the page
Or what will be the sequel to the page?

April is paradise here in Kentucky.
Purples glint everywhere, from redbuds budding
To one transfixing full-fleshed spiritual
Magnolia blossom, while across the gulch
The golden glory of forsythia
Gleams and azaleas glisten in the rain
And weeping cherries smile through purple tears
(I am no fool; it is the first of April)
And the viburnums are the ultimate
In sweetness. In the learned journals, in
The gatherings of scholars and professors,
Penultimate is more than ultimate.
Perhaps viburnums are penultimate
In sweetness if, past April, there is May.
The first of May is white with locust blossoms.
Here in Kentucky May is paradise.

Was Milton's vision paradise or fall,
Milton's blind vision, myth-historical?

Is Gibbon's vision myth or history?
It is today the anniversary
Of the last preface, which he dates May first.
Twelve years of leisure, health, and perseverance
Wished and required in 1776
Brought him to May first, 1788,
And to the choice of new work or new leisure,
The freedom and variety of study,
Or writing, which confines but animates
The daily application of the Author.
Flora, on May first, 1988,
                              Can contemplate

Can contemplate this preface to the final
Three volumes of his magnum opus. Did
Gibbon sit contemplating Rome's great fall
October fifteenth, 1764?
Was his great vision history or myth?
The year the famous *Wealth* of Adam Smith
Was published, the first volume of his own
Famous *Decline and Fall* was published, bone
Of his bone, flesh of his flesh. The famous year
Was 1776. The revolution —
A revolution which will ever be
Remembered, Gibbon said, and is still felt —
To Gibbon was a Roman turn, presented
In the first paragraph of chapter one.
His history was quickly called a classic.
His history was later called an epic.

The labored revolution of the days,
The leisured revolution of the week
Seem speedy. It is Sunday now again.
Now it is May eighth, 1988.
And it was May eighth, 1788,
When the last volumes were officially
Published. May eighth was also Gibbon's birthday,
His fifty-first, in 1788,
Although he had been born the twenty-seventh
Of April, anno 1737.
At fifteen, while a student, undirected
By tutor or professor, though at Oxford,
Already well-versed in chronologies,
Sir John Marsham's or Sir Isaac Newton's,
He planned to write a book during the long
Summer vacation, dating the life and reign
Of great Sesostris. To his great surprise,
He later wrote, the summer, the vacation,
The months of August and September were
Curtailed, eleven days of recess dropped,
Days chopped away, the season lopped, time stopped.
This was the alteration of the style.
                                                            He turned

He turned fifteen on April twenty-seventh
In 1752, turned fifty-one
The eighth of May in 1788
And was confirmed in his identity.
He was historian, was history,
He was the Roman Empire, was its book.
Gaze at the pages, gaze in the glass, look, look
Upon the image true in the glassy brook.

The brook is watery and green and clear.
The trees gaze down and see their greens appear
Where once their dry reds lay on that dry bier.
It is the eighth of May. That was October.
It is the eighth of May. The honeysuckles
In the fleet eastern and sweet southern sun
By the back windows bloom big buzzing bees
And blossom beaming ivory and gold
Sweetness succeeding sweetness of viburnums
Yielding the season as all rule together
There, white or green, as little birds, all song,
Keep issuing big song from little bodies
And cardinals keep conversing in big clicks
There as the irises bloom by the paths
And clematises on the trellises
And locusts by the sidewalks and laburnums
Across the lawns. On one green lawn the leaves
Of little beeches, light, young, fresh, light green,
Keep leafing, and beside the old gray barn
Where once the maple glinted gold the dogwood
Gleams Parian across the pastures where
The white cow glistens and the bobwhite greets
Flora, who listens from beside the fence
And underneath the hedge of juniper.
And there the rooster crows and crows once more,
And over here and here shade trees give shade,
And here virgilias stand on the verge,
Echoing distant places, different days,
Of lavishly, of recklessly revealing
All of their clustered pearls. Venus pearls bright.
                                            Venus

Venus and the nighthawk draw the night.
Flora keeps walking. Locusts sweetly sigh.
Orion has walked clear across the sky.

They had a chearful litterary dinner
To celebrate the double festival,
His birthday and the publication of
The last three volumes of *Decline and Fall*
On May eighth, 1788. He seemed
To blush while they read, following the meal,
The compliment in verse from Mr. Hayley
In honor of his talent and his toil.
O Genii of England and of Rome,
You have now raised on high this English name,
For like a star above his English home
History's Newton shines with Roman fame.

Thirty-two years before, from Switzerland,
Exiled by his own father to Lausanne,
The nineteen-year-old student sent a letter,
Written, no doubt, in French, to Crevier,
The editor of Livy and professor
Of rhetoric in Paris at the College
Then called Beauvais, suggesting a correction
Which, by the simple change of d to t,
Would make sense of the speech of Hannibal,
Emending odio to otio,
Hatred to leisure, peace, tranquility.
Gibbon's letter is lost, but Crevier's
Of August seventh, 1756,
Praises the conjecture and accepts it.
Do not believe, said Livy's Hannibal,
The Romans cared about your peace and comfort.
Do not believe the Romans had in mind,
Said Livy's Hannibal, your otium.

P. S., wrote Gibbon for his preface, dating
The postscript March first, 1781,
When Rome's fall was accomplished in the West,
Perhaps

Perhaps [the Public's] favourable opinion
May encourage me to prosecute a work,
Which, however laborious it may seem, is the most
Agreeable occupation of my leisure hours.
P. S., wrote Gibbon for the final preface,
Dated May first, 1788,
As often as I use the definitions . . .
Beyond the Alps, the Rhine, . . . &c.,
I generally suppose myself at Rome. . . .

In 1760, some time, it may be,
Between two styles of anniversary,
As Gibbon seems to indicate when he
Says he is twenty-two or twenty-three,
He wrote to ask his father to agree
(They lived together, but he felt more free
To use a letter to express his plea)
To let him make the trip to Italy,
A country which every Scholar must long to see.

Milton longed to go to Italy.
In 1638 he crossed the sea.

Three hundred fifty years have crossed the skies.
We must endure our fears when old time flies.
We must endure our tears when time goes slow.
How can we study history when we know
It is impossible, we ask ourselves
In 1988, if we have selves.

First loved as books, the books turned into men.
And then one knew that men turned into books.
One wanted shades then, wanted Elysiums,
Wanted to stride across the asphodel.
And yet one had the better part. The books
Were better and their beauties better far
Than manly grace. Was this not wisdom? If
The books were shadows, if the beautiful
Was shadowy, if beauty's books were dim
Images, if the beauty of the books
          Shifted

Shifted as the wind whipped through the leaves,
The leaves still glittered, glittered the more, were still
Read when autumnal, more to be read, as gold.
One turned to vitae and biographies,
But these were not the beauty or the books.
One turned to letters and to photographs.
Those lacked the substance of the shadows made
By the perfection of the struggling tree
That rises consubstantial with the tree
At ease expanding, spreading facilely
In easiest descents of dangling held
By eldest strengths and ever tipped with new
Beauties. Such were the shadows' substances,
The ultimates stuffed in those images
Before dim endings to outshine dim ends.
Yes, it makes sense, the book almost makes sense,
It is the penintelligible poem,
Not the penumbra, not penultimate,
But the last shadow and the final shade,
Ancient each morning, new each breathless noon,
Golden each evening, stellar every night.
I have pulled out the plum, eaten the peach,
Wrapped the trash, and carted out the garbage.
The first star, birds' last silver songs, soft bats,
The soft gray cat's gray silvered by the moon
Receive me and the searching cat's gold eyes.
Ave atque vale, for I never knew
Beauty or truth. Yet I have read the books.
The books are day's shades and night's brazen stars.

Besides, if margins wide enough and pages
Blank enough and interumbral spaces
Bright enough and interstellar shadows
Black enough beckoned as being empty,
I stuffed the silence with excelsior.

Excelsior exists no longer. Now
Plastic exists. Now there is styrofoam.
Now there are dry white snowflakes, crumbs of hail,
           That gloam

That gloam within our packages, escaping,
A trail not leading home yet not devoured
By birds or dogs, not leading higher, out,
Away, nor yet reentering the cycle,
But stuffing all our turkeys evermore.
Yet I design to dance upon the moon.
Yet I desire to sing among the stars.
Yet I must get to Rome. If I forget
What I will find in Rome, then Parthia
Will find herself at home in Germany.

Akkadia has roamed to Germany,
For silver is an Asiatic word
Expressing ancient industry and leisure,
Smelting, refinement, and urbanity.
Akkad's silver seems so civilized.
The sylvan silvers roam nomadically.
The silver maple is American,
The silver linden from Eurasia, and
The silver beech a native of New Zealand
And therefore not a beech at all. The word
Silver bestows a name on Argentina.
The argentometer, effective though
It may be as a tool, is surely less
Elegant as a term, confusing as
It does the Greek and Latin languages.
Would you not rather be convicted of
Argyrophilia than rudely called
Argentophile? German may be confused
With Babylonian, Germanic with
Babble, the English in America
With babelism, or the Anglo-Saxon
Of Roman Britain with barbarian
Enunciation and vocabulary.
The forked tongue may not be satanic. May
A triple tongue not be an epic one?
Ennius said he had three hearts because
He spoke three languages. My heart is true
To my three tongues and thus my triple tongue
                                    Is faithful

Is faithful to my heart. The triple fork
Found in the mouth may be as precious as
The silver spoon with which others are born.
The dragon with the silver tongue may free
The golden apples from the silver tree
Not as the fruit of sin and death and woe
But as maturity, in which we know
What brassy yes may antidote negations,
What brazen mess bloom with illuminations,
What golden guess may sow verifications,
What silverness branch into constellations.

What knowledge burst, in 1945,
Upon us from the heavens and showed us hell
Descending to the earth on those alive
Below those constellations as they fell?

The serpent said to Eve, Look up and see
How good this is, for you will know and be
A god or like a god. If you were she
What would you think as you stood by that tree?

All by herself and still beside herself,
Flora was gazing down into the stream
Of consciousness. Flora was cogitating.
Three sentences were heard. I cannot think.
I am not. If I am I am not I.
Therefore she crept into another hell,
Reptant like Proserpine from realm to realm,
And hence she leapt into another self.
In Latin I am ego, I am nos,
Even without a pronoun I can be,
Even without a pronoun cogito
Or cogitamus, ergo possumus.
And therefore, while I write in English, I
Will think and be and be myself in Latin.
Echo then reexpressed herself in Greek:
Ἠχώ, ἐγώ, χώ, γώ, ώ, ώ, oh, oh.
And soon the Muse chimed in. You must remember
That you are merely passing through Book Three

Hoping

Hoping for shade and for a Roman vision.
Book Five will be the place for theory,
Epistemology and metaphysics.
Now you must merely read, must only know.
Then you will reason whether you can do so.

Eve cared for knowledge, Adam cared for Eve,
Said Milton, and the snake cared for himself.
My care is threefold, Flora said: to rest
Under the tree, sing in the shade, and make
My pilgrimage to Rome.

      Milton in Rome
Called on a cardinal, dined with Jesuits,
Visited the Vatican to see
A scholar, was received there by the scholar
With, as he said, the greatest kindness. Then,
Admitted graciously without delay
Into the library, he was permitted
To look at the incredible collection
Of books and, in addition to the books,
At the large number of Greek authors there
In manuscript, equipped with lucubrations
By the same scholar who had welcomed him.
Of the Greek authors there in manuscript,
Some, not yet seen in our age, so he put it,
As if in readiness for action, seemed,
Much like those souls in Virgil deep enclosed
In a green valley and about to go
Up to the world above, to need only
The unimpeded hands of printers and
Delivery, while others, even now
Brought into the world by publication
Through his host's efforts, were being snatched up
Eagerly by scholars everywhere.

Thus Milton wrote from Florence to the scholar,
Lucas Holstenius, at home in Rome,
In 1639, dating the letter
The twenty-ninth of March, as it was there
           In Rome

In Rome and Florence, though at home in England
It was the nineteenth still. Milton went on
To mention that Holstenius sent him forth
Enriched by the twofold gift of one of the books
Edited and published by the scholar
From among the manuscripts in the library.

The manuscript of Milton's letter to
Holstenius was found in the library
In 1952 by Joseph Bottkol.
The letter had been seen in our age, though,
Published by Milton in 1674,
Dated March thirtieth, 1639.
Arripiuntur in the printed version
Is given as accipiuntur, snatched
Read as received. The lines from Virgil still,
In the text discovered in 1952,
Have limen, and not lumen, which we read
In Virgil, threshold, and not light, above.

The commentators quote from Virgil's lines.
Milton has threshold here for Virgil's light.
This is the way the commentators cite
Poets in conflict, seeking anodynes.

The souls enclosed deep in a green valley,
About to go up to the world above,
As I translate evasively above —
And inattentively for Virgil, too,
Since his souls are not quite about to go,
For some will not go for a thousand years
And thus the future active participle
For them is better rendered going to go
Or, with a relative, who were to go —
Those souls enclosed deep in a green valley
For Milton go ad limen, not ad lumen,
Go to the threshold, not the light, above.

What lines, pray, lie from pedantry to vision,
Go to the threshold, to the light, above?

When Milton writes of meeting Galileo
He does not say the scientist was blind.

The editors of Milton's letters for
The Yale edition of the prose works note:
It is impossible to say (I quote)
Whether Milton's "limen" is a misprint
Or a misquotation. Volume One
Appeared in 1953, before
The editors had time to scrutinize
The holograph, to which they do refer
But which they do not use, for on its page
Limen is very clear in Milton's hand.
Must Milton's memory thus be mistaken?
Are there not other possibilities?

The recent texts of Virgil do not print
Limen as a variant for lumen,
But looking at much earlier editions
One learns that limen had appeared already
In manuscripts consulted for those texts.
Can one with ease assume deficiency
In Milton's muse-protected memory?

Do I know all the bibliography
Come to the light since 1953?
Have I refound what someone else has found?
Have I resaid what has been better said?
What is the poem? What is the dissertation?
What is the image? What is the great idea?
What does the artist, what does the scholar, do?
To Milton Galileo was an artist.
Scientist was not yet an English word.
Milton is not my field — not that fair field.
Not there is my research. And still I search
Out everywhere that τοῦ καλοῦ ἰδέαν,
That image of the beautiful.

                    That field
On Peach Bloom Hill was green and beautiful.

                                  Whispers

Whispers of shades existed, as shades did,
At intervals. I heard but did not listen,
Listened but did not hear, though it was May,
The sky was blue. I saw but did not look,
Looked and could see the green, the blue, yet not
The beautiful, though it was everywhere,
It oozed from blue and grew in green and slanted
Across the backs of cows and smoothed the rough
Slats of the barn. It pattered from the sun,
Patting the hand that grasped the fence beyond
The junipers. It rested in the shadows.
It blued the bluish buds on tulip trees.
It dripped from the virgilias, distilling
Itself in silvers similar to whites,
The whites of silver similes. It dropped,
Not falling, from laburnums in their golds,
Their golden metaphors. It was no likeness.
It was the image that was the idea.

The woodthrush said its name, said, τὸ καλόν.
The bobwhite asked, καλόν; καλόν; I, asking
The robin for elucidation, heard
Καλὸν καλὸν καλὸν καλὸν καλόν.
The mockingbird was more insistent. Then
The woodthrush spoke, explaining, Beautiful,
And paused and said, O beautiful, and waited,
And said decisively, The beautiful.
I listened, did not hear, heard, did not listen.

It was blue May, blue, white, green, silver, gold.
Blooms in the grass, the robins on the lawn,
Cows in the meadows, sunlight on the fields,
Leaves on the trees, shadows in the pastures,
Were beauty on my mind and in my heart
If I could understand. The irises
Smiled standing in the garden, understood.
It was blue May. It had been brown November.
Leaves on the lawn lay in the sunset. Who
Can think of May in November? The gardener
On Peach

On Peach Bloom Hill. I listened and I looked.
I heard May promised, saw May as it came.
Soon I will comprehend May come. The leaves
Of little beeches light green on the trees
And leaves of light lie on the shadowed grass.

This is a Friday, this is the thirteenth day
Of May. It is not June. It is not summer.
It is not summer. It is just Kentucky.
To Ovid it is summer, and to me
A real June day, a real Massachusetts
Day in a Massachusetts June. To Ovid
Undoubted authors and authorities
Affirm that this date is the vernal end,
End of the tepid, and the aestival
Beginning. You will see the Pleiades,
He says, together, all the sisters there.
And on small beeches all the leaves are green,
The promised leaves expanded, explicated,
Summoned into light and unto shade.
The locusts, slowly leafing, slowly leaving,
Relinquish their white scents to yellowwoods,
Lending their pendent pensiveness, their lambent
Lusters to yellowwoods and to laburnums.
The yellowwoods (virgilias) are white,
Are silver, the laburnums yellow, gold,
All rich and rare and plenteous and perfect
In the luxuriance, the lavishness,
In the extravagance of magic May.
The branches are the wands of this magician.

Virgil I only saw. I heard Propertius,
Macer and Horace, Ponticus and Bassus.
Vergilium vidi tantum, Ovid said.
Virgil I only saw.

        Milton I heard
High in those pastures, musing among those shades.
Ovid he knew, Spenser he meditated,
He listened to Theocritus and Virgil

                                          At dawn.

At dawn. He sang at noon. All, all I heard
Enchanting as the sun, sunk in the west,
Set on the occident. What is the best,
To strive, to love, to question, or to rest?

Listen. An answer dawns. Listen to me.
The student loves the known. This is Book Three.
The good, around the world, will find the door
Of home. This will be clearer in Book Four.
The wise are never exiles. They will thrive
Throughout the universe. Consult Book Five.

What students know, wherever they may roam,
Is their own room, will be their only home.
What students see depends on Argus eyes
Surveying earth and shades and blazing skies.
And what a student hears depends on years
Through which, despite sharp fears, gods touch dull ears.

Green beech leaves trembled in the golden breeze.
Soft were the leaves upon the little boughs.
Soft were the shadows on the lawn and soft
The lawn and on the lawn the leaves of light.

Beauty is light, is thought, is joy alone.
The locust blossoms are just joy, joy, joy,
Just joy, just joyous joy, the first of May
Thoughtless and unreflective, justest joy
Unjustified, unjustifiable,
Justification, joy, just joy, joy, joy.

I have referred, though, to a pensiveness.
Locusts are pensive when virgilias,
Joy, too, but stranger, more solemnity
Than celebration, take our gaze, take on
The praise, take up the hymn. The locusts are
The nuptials, the virgilias coronation.

Beauty is light. Beauty lies in the shade.

The shadows shortened as the shade increased.

I have not overused or overstated
Or overshadowed any word or thing.
All has been true, all balanced, all related,
All known, all part of beauty's Roman ring.

Beauty is, has been, is about to be,
Is going to be, if bronze buds, little lights,
Long little lights, all winter, are the green
Lampshades of summer, if the twenty-seventh
Of April is the eighth of May, the eighth
The thirteenth or the twenty-third, if May
Is, as Urania in Ovid feels,
The month of the maiores, of the elders,
And June that of the youths, the iuvenes,
Or whether, as Calliope affirms,
May is the month of the most beautiful
Of all the Pleiades, whom Jupiter
Loved, and a son was born to him and her,
And when the exile from Arcadia,
Evander, came and saw the grass, the tree,
The sheep, where Rome, capital of the world,
Is now, the son of Maia came along
With him, was worshipped there, and gave the name
Of his mother to the month and seven strings,
The number of the sisters, to the lyre.

Evander went by ship to what would be
The city and took with him Mercury,
A god of thieves and lies and poetry.
Milton by ship went on his way to Rome,
Carried off volumes, carried away hell's dome.
He crossed the Alps only on his way home.

Now no more, icy jingles, and no more,
Prosings of snow. My power lines are iced,
My tracks are slippery, obliterated,
Or obviated by the Saint Bernards.
No more now, shadeless sun. My vestiges
Are obvious. Be grateful, travelers.
Express your gratitude. Now I plant shades.

The shades grow green. And then the shades grow gold.
The gold turns bronze. And did the gold turn silver?
When did the gold turn gray? The golden hair
Was gray quickly. The face was gray. The gray
Skin was not silver. And the shock of hair,
Gray and not silver, shocked. What of the eyes?

Gray city windows, silvered mirrors, bronze
Blanks for jewels glowing in the temple,
Golden apples growing in the desert.

Perhaps the robins never left. They often
Winter in northern states, though unobserved
By most observers, being more remote,
More unobservable. If they are not
Observed, it is still winter. If they are
Seen on a January afternoon
Or in a burst of March, that January
Moment, however cold, is spring, that March
Onrush the flush most delicate, the flash
Most sweet, the hush most promising of spring.

The thrush is designated, specified,
As migratory. Will the honored names
Of robin, migrant, spring all be deceptive,
Deceiving even these observers, whom
The thrush misleads no longer, not deceiving?

I tell the truth but cannot tell the whole.

On what Holstenius told Heinsius,
On Heinsius re Milton's Latin poems,
On Heinsius re limen in the passage
From Virgil, or on Henry James's Rome,
On Freud and Rome, on Freud and Hannibal,
I will not shed a light or cast a shadow.

I must not stray in Latin pastures late.

In Milton's Latin epitaph for Damon
Daphnis is praised, Damon must reach the shades,
Under the elm Thyrsis must sit and mourn,

Among

Among the branchy shadows in the valleys
And, led by error, over airy Alps
And down to see — for what great cause to see? —
A Rome once visited by Tityrus
And now in sepulture, near violets
And myrtles, near Italian streams, among
Italian beeches that have learned his name
From men renowned for scholarship and song,
Thyrsis must pass. Damon must pass to shadows
Of palms, a gleaming diadem, the splendors
Of virgins, to the wildness of the lyre,
Ecstatic dances, hymeneal hymns
Bacchic of everlasting sanctity.

From Daphnis I must pass to Eclogue Six.
No umbra hovers there explicitly,
And yet because the song the laurels learned
Carried from pulsing valleys to struck stars
Vesper processed against Olympian will,
Evening proceeded while Olympus wished
It would not call the sheep and stop the song.

The student hears. Despite some trembling tears
Olympus clears before the face that peers.

Daphnis, shade, and shadows all return
In Eclogue Seven. Umbra comes three times,
Once in the speech of Daphnis in line ten,
Once in a song by Corydon in line
Forty-six, and once when Thyrsis sings,
In fifty-eight, the arid lack of shadows.
Umbra is ablative and singular
In ten and forty-six. In fifty-eight
Umbras is plural and accusative.
In all three lines shadows and shade are good.

Quickly come here, Daphnis urged Meliboeus.
If you can stop a while, rest under the shade
Beside the green-fringed stream and bee-voiced oak.

Mossy fountains, lawn softer than dream,
Strawberry tree's spaced (later checkered) shade,
Corydon sang, protect the flock from summer.

Dry are the fields, dying the thirsty grass,
Diseased the air, begrudged vines' shadows (shade)
By Bacchus to the hills, lamented Thyrsis.

The sunlight sears. Each burning stallion rears
Before the charioteers. Hope disappears.

The chilly shade of night had barely left
The sky when Damon, heavy on his staff,
Began the song of desperation. This
Is Eclogue Eight and this its only shade,
This umbra of the fourteenth line, the subject,
Nominative and singular, but shadows
Less literal play over the whole poem,
And there is Hesperus, the evening star,
In Damon's song, and there is nocti, night,
A dative, in a simile about
The love the woman longs to have from Daphnis
As sung by answering Alphesïboeus.

The icy leers, the jeers, the snowy sneers
Will turn to cheers if the whole poem coheres.

The thesis reaches the penultimate
Eclogue, the ninth. The poem, marvelous,
Inducts the springs with umbra, ablative
And singular, appearing in line twenty,
With umbra viridi (What can one say,
Belated and belated?), with a green shade.
The implication made by Lycidas
Is that Menalcas, through his saving song,
Can, with green shadow, canopy the fountains.
Trees by suggestion or by implication
Or by deduction or by inference
Shade springs. A tree, a poplar, overhangs
The cave. This tree is white. And this tree shines.
The cave

The cave is shaded by the pliant vines.
Explicitness is shifting in such lines
As twenty, forty-one, and forty-two.
Line forty-two opens umbracula,
Plural, accusative, diminutive,
Shadelets which slow vines weave and Moeris sings
Slowly, remembering nobility
Of song. Who is the you who sang alone
In the pure night, pura solum sub nocte?
Who speaks line forty-four? Who is addressed?
Who sang of Caesar's star? Who sang of pears
Grafted by Daphnis? Why are the songs forgotten?
The boy could sing long suns until they set,
Mourned Moeris. Let us quickly sit and sing,
Lycidas suggested, for this is
The middle of our road. There is the tomb.
We'll reach the city. Here the foliage
Is dense. Or if we fear the drizzling night
Let us go on and sing on as we go.

The farmers strip the thick leaves from the elms.

The hated shears must not lop off our years
Before, through spheres and spheres, the vision nears.

The last labor is at hand. Now, Arethusa,
Grant it to me. Umbra occurs three times
In Eclogue Ten, once in line seventy-five,
The antepenultimate line, twice in the next
Line, line seventy-six. And in both lines
Umbra is nominative and is the subject,
But it is umbra, singular, the first
Two times, once at the end of seventy-five
And once again in the middle of seventy-six,
And it is umbrae, plural, at the end
Of seventy-six, the line before the end.
Moreover, in the next line, seventy-seven,
This Eclogue's last, the last of all the *Eclogues*,
Hesperus, the evening star, is coming.

The shade and shadows, then, must be of evening.
The shadow of the juniper is bad
For singers and for singing. One must rise
From underneath the juniper and go,
As the goats, too, must go, must all go home.

Shadow is bad for singers, Virgil says,
The shadow of the juniper is bad,
Shadows cause harm. Or shall I say he claims
That shade is dangerous or that the shade
Is dangerous and that the shadows harm?
The use of solet in line seventy-five
Suggests that I should generalize the shade
Or shadow in the English way, omitting
The article, against the evidence,
Perhaps, of all the good shade in the poems.
Is good shade day's, bad shadow night's, the shade
Of every tree except the juniper
Good for farm and pasture, good for song?

I have collected shadows from *Selections,*
From *Pastorals,* not from the books on farming,
Not from the epic deaths. Selected shades
And shadows are examined in this chapter.
The singer's shade is chiefly studied here.

I sang in shadow.

    And what of Elias?
The shadow of the juniper is his.
The juniper is his as well as Virgil's.

But Virgil is my subject, and the shadow
Of Virgil's juniper is my concern.
The shadow, bad or good, of Virgil's tree,
His beech, his elm, his oak, his strawberry tree,
His overhanging poplar, or his grave
Juniper is my study. Two small beeches
Were round but not round, domed and yet not domed
Because small though American and full.
           My subject

My subject is a bigger, better beech,
That paramour so sparkling in the heart.
The true meaning of Rome is what I teach,
Of freedom, grandeur, godhead, leisure, art.
There is a hero in all that I preach.
I do not preach at all. I guess at part.

To know Rome is my subject, to know knowing.
A subject can be an infinitive.

Isn't it really best without a subject?
In the curriculum an incoherence
Is not so bad. I wish that everyone
Could study Virgil. Unpolitical
Though it may be, my class is democratic.
My affirmation is democracy,
If I have not denied all affirmation
And all denial. Or have I distinguished
The classroom and the thesis and the poem?
Is there not something which I have affirmed?
Yes, in denial we most go astray.
The parts of beauty are the beautiful.
The whole of truth is not my subject, but
Novanticistic tendencies as well
As neopositivistic inclinations
May be detected in my thought and work.
My work is brazen play. My thought is silver,
If tarnished, yet forever polishable.
My speech is lifted from the golden rivers
And sifted from beech-shadowed streams of gold.
If Gold be foliated, Newton said,
And held between your Eye and the Light, the Light
Looks blue. If eyes be stars, one sees both art
And knowledge there. I go on through the night,
Tripping between the bronze or silver stars
And golden eyes that shine out of the shadow
That is the cat. Next door the eight-year-old
Lucius is playing on his violin.
The little Lucius plays, and Flora smiles.
                                    Hearing,

Hearing, she sees the sparkle of big dark
Eyes in a little face, sees little fingers
Press with delicacy the chosen strings
(They slipped into the mitt this afternoon),
And sees the little arm crook to the bow
(This afternoon it wound up for the pitch).
She listens. Eyes are twinkling. Little Lucius
Is playing Twinkle, twinkle, little star.
The little Lucius plays, and Flora laughs.
She hears the shadow of Letitia's drum
And laughs. Shadows are bad. Shadows are good.
There comes in darkness, just as shadows come,
Light on, from the light of, Letitia's drum.
Once we sang Mica, mica, parva stella.
We laughed and sang above the world so high.
The star that twinkles is the light above.
The light above in Ennius, Lucretius,
And Cicero's translation of Aratus
Gives an example of what Virgil knew
Of light above in Latin poetry
Or could have known and thus knew, one assumes,
Since for the learned Virgil one assumes
The knowledge of all that he could have known.
The poem of Aratus was a version,
Still extant and once very popular,
Of scientific prose by an important
Scientist, Eudoxus. Virgil could,
Of course, have known the Greek originals.
The scientist Hipparchus wrote an extant
Commentary on the books of both
Eudoxus and Aratus. This work, too,
Virgil could have known. What do I know?
What of a shadow universe? What dark,
Far more than light, exists, is what exists?
Is shadow lack of light or light the absence
Of shadow? Thus was freedom understood
Where there were slaves? Tityrus was a slave
And had to go to Rome to gain his freedom.

Fee

Fee came to teach freedom in Kentucky.
Must someone, something, free us from the evil
Thing or one? The people of Berea
Received the word. The pastures here were free.
The university is pastoral.
The university must be a pasture.
One must be loath to take the literal
And to disfigure it into a figure,
To mingle subtleties with obvious
And blatant evil, good, truth, error, beauty,
And ugliness, to mingle work with play,
Confuse the beneficial and the noxious
Umbrageousnesses and umbrosities.
The university is far away,
Among fruits everlastingly delicious,
Far from one's bovine mooed monstrosities,
Off in the shadows. Motion must be rest.
Knowledge must wait for one among shades blessed.

Does not Thalia in the cave preside
Over a knowing, as, in the grove, Apollo?

There had been Corydon and Thyrsis. Now
There is just Corydon and Corydon.

Song is of noon's shade. Damon sings at dawn
To the departure of the shade of night.

Someone can sing at night or under night
As some could sing all day and down the sun.

Do, Arethusa, when at last the sun
Goes down, shadows and junipers preside?

Such are the questions asked, such the conclusions
Glimpsed as I contemplate those shady pages,
The last half of the book. Shall I arise?
Shall I declare an end to questioning?
Shall I imagine ends to shadowing?
Is shadow good for pastoral and bad
For epic, good in pastoral and bad
                                      In epic?

In epic? In didactic poetry
What place is there for sun and what for shade?
I sat in shadow working on my thesis.
I think I will see light by chapter five
In an old grove or in an ancient glade
Or in an unimagined space, a time
Utterly new, unknown to prose or rhyme
And inaccessible to both, a Rome
Never to look like or to sound like home,
A university or universe
Which neither words nor music can rehearse.

She heard first hounds, then sirens, and then silence.

The virgilias were invigilating still.
The Latin teacher handed in her grades.
The catalpas were passing all their examinations,
Going slowly, gradually, not too fast,
From O's to A's, from openings to all
That one could ask of nestled plenitude,
Of elegant particular perfection,
Of total excellence. Commencement saw
Catalpas' caps of candid verity,
Gowns lined with gold and purple pulchritude.
May is at length ending. The cows are gleaming.
The cows are leaving their gleam. They feel for shade
Beneath the catalpas. Catalpas are still gleaming.
The cattle and the catalpas have doubled the dappled
Shadows. Catalpas bubbled, then bloomed, then shadowed
Cows with sweet gleaming clouds, clouds of albed incense.
Such white clouds can lay such black shades along
The mountains and such mountainous cows can gleam
White, gleam black, shade pastures underneath
The mountains, for such difference is such
Sameness, white's gleam so accurately black's,
Fire's shadow so like water's light. Catalpas
Differ from dogwoods, locusts, and virgilias,
From opening magnolias isolating
White islands over evergreen green seas,

Differ

Differ from clouds, differ from stars, from suns,
Gleam like all. All gleam. Many are sweet.
They all are sweet. Sweet gleam yields to sweet shade.
The cattle have sat in the catalpas' shade.
Leaning luxuriously against the tree,
The shaded singer sweetly sings sweet shade.
Sweetnesses differ, sweetness is the same.
The song will live, the singer never lie.
The beautiful is truer than the true.
Catalpas bloomed in spring and not in summer
Unless we call it summer, June, July,
When May observes catalpas following
Close on virgilias and tulip trees.
The buds of May are summer's in our tongue,
Upon our tongues, but not upon our soil,
Not in our country, not upon our land,
Not in our land. Catalpas gleam like alps.
Bubbles become bunches of bloom, bouquets
Of blossom, bubbles become clusters and clouds,
Catalpas in majestic cloud, their own,
Catalpas dearer than a summer's day,
Elegant in expansiveness, frank, free,
Fearless in frivolity and frill,
Catalpas grand, unguarded, guarding gold.
These are the abc's inscribed in purple
And gold within catalpan chalices,
Imprinted on ascending, branching, circling
Catalpan altitudes and architectures
And attitudes. Unstinting is the wine
Poured in those palaces from that largess.
Such alpine atmospheres, such palatine
Graciousness and imperiousness poured forth
A heady message to harsh Hannibal,
Wilfrid considering the calendar,
Gibbon continuing from Switzerland,
Tityrus, if cisalpine, distant still,
Me, distant still, that we must go to Rome.
The woodthrush sang. We had gone. We would go.

                                            Who are

Who are we, the woodthrush wondered. Then,
Think who we are, he said. Then, Sing who we are,
Was the exemplified injunction. Yet,
Sweet, oh sweet, the woodthrush added. And,
Bitterly sweet, he clarified. And then,
Better than sweet, became the closure. Still,
From the green wood the green song, ever fresh,
Never did end. We have gone. We will go.
The woodthrush measures restlessness and rest.
The woodthrush sings the sweetness and the ache.
Windows and doors open upon the south,
The lawn, the little wood, the woodthrush singing.
I wake to the song, I breakfast to the song,
Lunch, dine, walk, wander to those melodies.
I con the words as some have done before
And comprehend them as none yet has done.
Truth has more beauty than the beautiful.
The suite was beauty pouring from the tree
Continually and shedding everywhere
Movements of music, rests of meditation,
Golden speeches, silver silences,
Green palpability, elusive blue.
Nature does nothing, so they say, in vain.
Nature herself asserts that more is more.
The rabbit danced on the lawn in the shade of the morning.
The bounds of the rabbit leap to the bounds of the hills,
The boundaries of the mountains. I climbed one hill
Beyond the silver maple, muscular,
Elegant, and sublime, passed poppies, passed
Snapdragons and catalpas, trudged to where
The sole shade was a hedge of trees, the only
Shadows the juniper trees edging the pastures.
I stood in the shade of a juniper at noon.
May was as rare, as beautiful, as June,
As perfect. This is a real Kentucky May,
The woman from Tennessee had said from her garden
As I climbed up by the catalpas. Now I could rest
Under the juniper hedge and meditate

                                                            Green

Green meadowlands, green hills, the green-blue mountains,
The blue-blue sky. The junipers were green,
Their berries blue as mountains, blue like sky.
Into those greens and blues the bobwhite's bright
Fire sizzled white much as the orange flames
Zigzag across the blue-green of the petals
Upon the tulips of the tulip tree.
The bird's fire was a bell as bright as day.
The day's hawk hovered silently like night
Through the blue noon. The meadow's yellow flowers
Were constellations to sharp scrutiny.
To contemplation bits of shade must hover
Under each ray. Shade is sharp on grass,
Soft on a lawn, subtle and tenuous
Across a pasture at meridian.
But I stood in the pastureland's penumbra.
To be a mockingbird became my call.
Heat, roses, honeysuckle, peonies,
Swifts, whizzes, twitter, glitter, clarities,
Bees, buzzes, butterflies, cries, distances,
Heat, breezes, breaths, scents, songs, and silences
Commingled with sun's touch and shade's embrace.
Now all was silent. All is still. Now only
The sun king and the umbra queen exist
Beyond the sun-stroked, shade-soaked consciousness.
As burning is majestic, dreaded, red,
And photosynthesis green, gracious, power,
So solar potency is not unknown
To Flora when she must deliberate
The saving grace of staying in the shade,
The dangers of remaining in the shade.

A breeze blew over the pastures. O the sea!
O sweet sea breeze that seeps, that sweeps, from the ocean.
There was no saltiness. There was no ocean.
She called it Rome, but it was Cyzicus.

A red sun disappears. A cloudless blue
Assumes a rose. A rising moon appears.

              Tonight

Tonight the moon is orange, and tomorrow
It will be blue. We leave sweet moony gleams
On the magnolias, we leave the little beech
With its grand foils, long leaves each ruled for script.
Figuratively, orange will be blue.
Literally, the little will be big.
We pass the silver maple's energetic
Ascent, exalted silveriness, and mighty
Strenuous delicacy. We climb the hill.
Beyond the catalpas, where the junipers
Show dark, the moon shines bright upon the pastures,
Not waters, Wabash or Atlantic, for
The landswell is not oceanic, is
Moonscape of mound, a foreground to gray mountains.
The fireflies echo the stars. The moon says, Oh.
Transformations happen in the sky.
Orange is gold, gold cream, cream silver. While
Natures are altered, kingdoms overthrown,
Peace perdures. The moon is a gazing moon,
And peace gleams in that eye, beams from that brow,
To illustrate my ultimate lustration
Out from the junipers' long lunar shadows.

It was an evening when he found his theme.
He found his theme and finished in the evening.

Imagine Gibbon carried across the Alps,
Well armed as Hannibal. In Gibbon's garden
The last fruit fell. It rolled across the lawn,
Skittered along the lake, and skimmed the mountains,
Revolved the revolutions of the orb
Called Roman, spun in London, brightened Britain
With the great glowing of the luminous
Page. With the flowing of voluminous
Pages it floated on across the ocean
To revolutionized America,
Not revolted by those English colors,
So truly Latin were the banners flown.
Well armed by study, Gibbon crossed the Alps
                                    At twenty-six,

At twenty-six, saw Rome at twenty-seven,
Finished at fifty that last page, that final
Line, of the work conceived that autumn evening,
He said, upon the Capitol. The most
Beautiful sun, he said, gilded the Alps
And gave the scene a somber coloring.
Now it was almost midnight. He arose,
Walked through the garden under the acacias,
Watched the reflection of the silver orb
Gleam from the lake. He had transcended mountains,
Had sat beside the waters of Leman,
Sat in the temple as the shadows fell.

Can one reliteralize the figural,
Replant the overplanted littoral?

Can I explain shade, explicate the shadows?
I must still find the fire of chapter two.
I must still run the road of chapter three.
I must still try the tree of chapter four.
I must gaze on the god of chapter five.
Now I must leave the shadows in the shadows.

A small beech tree arises in Kentucky.
I did not place a jar beneath that tree.
But did I jar that tree? Or could I sing
Beneath it? Could that beech tree sing to me?

One night, twitching your skirt, you will arise,
One day you will escape the easy shade,
Though it is hard to read the beech's shade
And greater falls from the great Virgil shadow.

CHAPTER TWO
ARDOR

I wake up burning. Corydon at noon
Could not have felt the fire that I at dawn
Fight through my corse though all the shades are drawn.
June is July. August arrives in June.

If only all the shades could be opaque.
If only I had chosen not to look
East. But you cannot say I chose my nook
When it selected me. I chose which ache

To ease. The sun is hot, is cold and mean.
Buses and trucks cant for the woodthrush, thrust
Their airs down shafts of ears, their air (if dust
Is air) down mines of lungs. Their gasoline

Censes for fragrances hummed by the bees,
Scents of viburnum and of honeysuckle.
Their pollens are the grains of grime that bruckle
The shelves just wiped, each volume as one frees

Books from their cells. And through the shades all night
The streetlamps glare. The nuisance caller calls
Almost before the telephone installs
Itself in one's own home in its own right.

Night hears the street musician croon and play
As sweetly as the emulated trucks.
Night hears the upstairs fan, clavating crux.
Somehow night hears the nighthawk in his day.

Day is infernal. I awake and burn.
If only I had opted not to face
East. But you cannot claim I chose my place
If it chose me, if I chose to return.

Not far from here, a very little way,
Just a short walk, ten minutes from this hell,
Past the great elm, past where the gray tree fell,
Or must have fallen, towards the end of May,

Where the lawn's tonsure baldly reprimands
(Here the virgilia would blossom, bless
Commencement, chant in white how joy — not less
But more — begins), past the great elm (which stands),

In the great temple, past the colonnade,
Wait the cool tomes, heat, light, fire, silence, shade.

CHAPTER THREE
VIA

Is this pedestrian? I work my way
Inscribing Georgics in Bucolic play.

Is mine the old road or the newest route?
I choose both. Do I script an absolute?

CHAPTER FOUR
ARBOR

Article One
Again Bright, Gray

If you move north the thirty-first of May
May will repeat itself in June. The tape,
Simply wound back a bit, will partly ape
And partly with complexity replay

What it played simply. Locusts are in bloom,
Have sweetened all those last examinations,
Withdraw before virgilias. Vacations
Commence with this strange candor and perfume.

Visiting the virgilias, I greet
Longfellow's, Lowell's, Holmes's, Asa Gray's,
One on Observatory Hill. I praise
Those on Sparks, Appleton, or Craigie Street.

The scholar Child's virgilia was razed
Before Commencement. Tityrus stands amazed.

Article Two
A Brief Grammar

Point One

Nouns in -or are masculine in Latin
(So labor, amor, ardor, and the rest)
Except for arbor, which is feminine.
Arbor, tree, is feminine in Latin.
Its gender, then, is hers, not his or its.

Point Two

Arbor does not occur in Virgil as
Nominative and singular, since when
It does appear in such case and such number
(In Eclogue Three, line fifty-six, for instance)
It is not arbor but the ancient arbos.

Article Three
Anne, Bronze, Gold

Early November 1988.
Anne has been gone four years. The beeches glint
Silver and bronze and emerald and gold.
The oaks glow ruby, amber, gold, and oak.
Barberries burn. Euonymus is fire
With light. The air is savory. The dark
Comes on soon. How long have I not known
What I was born to know? Dying to see
What waits for me behind the bough, beyond
The bole, I contemplate the lying leaves.
The leaves are beautiful. The leaves are dead.
The elm, the maple, the virgilia
Leaves are deceiving though the trees are true
And understand the sky. The dark comes on.
I must go grumbling through the lying leaves.

I stand here in the grandeur of the great
Golden oracular Grynean Grove.
Where is Apollo?
     This is Arcady,
Resonant with the singing of the gods.
Why do I not hear Pan?
       This is a glade
Upon the holy hill of Helicon.
Why, when nine sisters dance here, do I see
Not even one?
      Since there is so much shade
           Why am

Why am I songless?
                    Rome laughs all around.
Why am I sad?
              When I have meditated
Four years upon my Maro's ten short poems,
How can I know so little, understand
So much less than I know, and write so much,
Though much, less than I understand?
                                     I now
Am freed. Why am I wretchedly afraid
Of an invincible enslavement?
                             Virgil,
Why has your awesome wand not touched my closed
Eyelids and filled with vision the blank pupils?

Are these your questions? Who will sympathize
With these? Silvanus said. It was Silvanus
From the tenth poem, speechless there although
He looks at Gallus.

             That was the beginning.

I am in love, I said. What can I say?
What can I ask? What can I hope for when
I love on hopelessly? What can I say?

Through luck and labor and the gracious god
Of patronage and through the primal cause
That moves the universe and all its parts
I came here. But the end is not the end.
I came here weary from the road, worn out,
Worn down, debilitated by desire,
Too weak to touch that which I yearned to hold,
Too tired to see that which I meant to touch,
Too deep in dream to think what I came to see,
Dreading too much the end to find dream sweet.

The end is not the end. One must begin.
I lay on bronze leaves, dreaming in the shade,
Rehearsing dreamy questions. Where is he?
                                        Where

Where are the sisters? Why am I motionless
With the exception of a point within
My wilderness that buds there and within
My night that twinkles deep there like a star?
Witchhazels flower gold as gold leaves fall.

Silvanus, rough with golden leafiness
And green with needles and the pointed holly,
Saw the bud in the wood and let a ray
Of gold awaken it and lit horizons
As when the gold sun gilds the golden trees
If the clouds go before the western sun
Goes, when the light is high, the sun so low
One's feet are dark although one's eyes are gleaming.

In summer rest in shade, Silvanus said.
In winter find a place beside the fire.

My love is in the Alps, high in the mountains,
Crossing cold heights, which way I do not know.
If he were here we could sit by the tree
Gazing and conversing and creating
Brilliance of gold and purple conflagration
Like autumn's cherry leaves and sunset's sky.

I stumbled through the darkness, through the leaves,
Over the roots, and came before the temple.
A fire burned on the altar to the god.
My posy was a particle of flame.

Apollo saw the golden rose of the fire.

The rose of Rome, he said, once opened wide
And fresh upon the world. You are in Rome.
Act like a Roman. This great rose is focused,
This grandeur has a center and expands
Laughing throughout the golden universe.

I tried to breathe. A sweetness and a heat
Swirled on the chilly hearthstone of my heart.

I burned with longing. Then I saw red. Pan
Stepped jauntily from dogwood, barberry,
Euonymus. With Virgil I saw Pan.
And when he spoke to me I heard Pan speaking.

There is no limit to desire. Endure.
Endure the pangs. And, while enduring, search
Out the desired, not for the pain's surcease
But for the mere embrace of flame with fire.

Anne came the fourth, the woman, and the whole,
Fair as the moon, beautiful as the night,
Lovely with our earth's own loveliness,
Bright as the virgin, dark as her nocturnal
Sister, soft and strong as the mother's clasp,
Her face white as Diana's argentine,
Her hair the bronzy jet of tall still Nox,
Her great eyes deep with Terra's gleaming gold.
Her speech came flickering its golden wings.

His name is not Noman but Knowable
And Knowing. Hold him. If the look, the word,
The touch is momentary, it is yet
The star, he is the star, that validates
The overarching shadow of the dark.

Anne spoke. It was November. She had gone
Four years before, Teresa in October
Four hundred six, and in September Virgil
Two thousand six. They left us not unheard.

Listen to Sibyl. Now the sound is spume.
It is blue Proteus. I'm holding on.
Let the invisible be Proserpine.

Thus Flora. Some November afternoon,
In Indian-summer-sunned short autumntide,
Rush to the beech, sit in the golden shade,
If you should wish to see what I have seen.

CHAPTER FIVE
VISIO

Et quae tanta fuit Romam tibi causa videndi?
Libertas, quae sera tamen respexit inertem. . . .

                                    Virgil, First Eclogue.

ille deum vitam accipiet divisque videbit
permixtos heroas et ipse videbitur illis. . . .

                                   Virgil, Fourth Eclogue.

Vergilium vidi tantum. . . .

                                              Ovid, *Tristia*.

SECTION ONE
QUESTION AND ADDRESS

DIVISION ONE
GATE

His Vision

Rome was a place he would have liked to see.
He fainted when he tried to buy his ticket.
Rome was a name, a dream, eternity.
Why did each eye grow dark in each dark socket?

Benediction

O well-said word, betray, do not betray,
The benefaction. First the golden tree
Surges. It urges one stunned gaze to try
To scent among the spangles of vitraux
What well-eyed webs approach, reach, touch the true.

Unnamed

It must be fall. Yearning for words the wordless
Eyes eye the elm. Fine bright gold elm things fall
Airily gravitating to the sun
As to the earth. Eyes rise into October.
It has to be October if the elm
Is yellowing into the afternoon and since
The elm is glittering out of the afternoon.
It is October if the sugar maple

Has tapped the last, non-saccharine extreme
Of sugar-maple red, has reached, of red,
Beyond extreme, extremest gaud without
Gaud's gaudiness. Eyes gape and wordless lips
Gape at the maple. If they were able to name
Each part, each cluster of totality,
What sweet name would they give each sugared shade,
With what clear call call out each designation
Of each design austerely clarified
Like a Greek pediment by reds against
Blue heavens? No kenosis yet occurs.
Emptiness fills with elm. Replenishment
Flushes the luscious roses of October
And gilds the marigolds. Yet nature is
Refined. The gold of honeylocusts is
Not garish and their honey cannot cloy
The wordless eyes although the words can cloy
Unhearing ears that hear their sweetnesses.
The sweetnesses are subtle in the sun.
This is a scent of sugar maple; this,
Scent of red rose; that, by the iron fence
Wrought black and definite and delicate,
Perfection of sheer white, the purest; gold,
The finest; or the lightest — or the lightest —
The lightest lavender, the violet,
The pink, the rose as pink, the roseation,
The lightest roseation, lightest touch
Of rose among the whites, among white yellows;
Or all, full-blown, evolved into the full
Of white here, pale gold here, the palest pink
There, three and one, vision and fragrances
Rounded by clarity and azure, clear,
Dulcet, utter, musk, unutterable.

How sweet this momentary evolution.
How sweet this moment in the evolution
Of petal, leaf, air, as the earth evolves.
How sweet this subtlety of honeyed air
Unto the voiceless bitterness. The earth
                                                              Revolves,

Revolves, and, if the music of the spheres
Plays on, it plays on noiselessly. This surd
Nonverbal version of the revolution
Goes slow. The green goes yellow or turns red
Unheard, unhonked, untrumpeted, if not
Unspied. Among the maples of New England
The trumpeting is silent like the march
Of redcoats moving though immovable,
The music is like nothing known as martial,
The likenesses are like unlikenesses,
The marching redcoats are not colonizers,
Nor are the redcoats turncoats. Treachery
Is not a name in Cambridge or a term
In Lexington or Concord. Revolution
Is red yet bloodless while the tupelo,
Red maple, sassafras, are sanguine, not
Sanguinary. Fall, then, is not fell.
Autumn is not autumnal. And it must
Be autumn. Must I leave anonymous
Rosying leaves well-named euonymus?

Blessing

First for the world is something; first for us, blood,
The blessing literal and natural
(With Harvey see the book of nature, whole
And holy, with old and new masters see
The documents of etymology);
The sacral water, first grace for the soul;
First for the mind, conjoint, elliptical,
The circulated world and searching word.

Halley's Poem

Surgite, mortales, terrenas mittite curas. . . .
(From the ode by Edmond Halley in honor of Newton's *Principia*)

Apostrophes: Mortals, arise,
Put earthly cares aside,
And learn the vigor of a heaven-born mind.

The comets terrified
Us. Now we are so wise
The bearded star we feared we comprehend.

Apostrophes: Muses, rejoice
With me and with my voice
Sing Newton the sky-seer and the enskied.

Halley, I found last night
A bit of fluffy white,
A fuzz among the stars. Your name was said.

O far-flung fuzz, O ice
Afire, and, O, precise
Numbers discovered, visions still to find.

LOCUS LOCANDUS

Will I see Caesar's comet? Will I know
The route of Holy Road if I reach Rome?
Will Varro show the way to my own home,
And will I find the house of Cicero?

Will I be met outside the wall with Quo —
White question — or response in polychrome?
Will Peter welcome me beneath his dome?
Will Catherine from her cell tell where to go?

Will my Great Mother graciously attend?
Will Jove, the Best, the Greatest, be the Mild?
Will Father Tiber guide my azure raft

Through blackest thunder? Then will I ascend?
Will there be nuptials? Will there be a child?
Will Grandpa Janus look both fore and aft?

October Twelfth

O Italy and Portugal and Spain,
New gold, new golden trees, new golden grain
Answered your ancient visions. Was the pain
New? Does a minor anguish mock the main?
Am I not headed towards old Saturn's reign?

October Fifteenth

Are the virgilias gold? This is the day
When first the genuine Vergilian child
Seen by his mother, seeing his mother, smiled
Across the River Mincius, far away.

Throw down those arms, my blood.

                                      The line remains
Forever endless.

                O my blood, what grace
Superinfused allows you entrance twice
Within the gate of heaven?

                           This is then
An end or is the premise of an end
That is an endlessness, the promise of
An ending that will end all termination,

The boundless fountain sembled in the elm
That fills with grace ascending, condescending
In no ungraciousness of condescension.

The elm is gold, the golden buckeye gold,
The honeylocust gold and gold and gold.
Spontaneous in change, the maples flood
The grass, the paths, with mingled gold and blood

Which I . . .

    But I . . .

        Shall I, beneath the froth,
Rise up among the jewels of the sea,
Whom the unsounded smashed, the loud winds shattered,
The vast spume spewed?

        Shall I caress the waves,
Collect the gems, compose both fond and foam?

If I begin to listen, catch the line,
Cast off my armor with a clatter, can
That clang craft graceful consanguinity?

How may the bobbing infant be cajoled?
Does the Atlantic laugh? And do you mark?
The Mississippi deepens into dark.
Are the virgilias gold, or almost gold?

PORTA

    And at an arch

Here may I pause   Peer in to peace

DIVISION TWO
CONVERSATIONS WITH THE ITALIAN

Comedy

Dark walk, dark wood, missed path, and life half done:
That was the way I felt about the passage,
Obscure and indirect, open before me.
Was it a tunnel? Was it the breakdown lane?
Catalpas, is it cloud or light enskied
In your green heavens? Perfect pointed folds
On yellow rose, the rondure of the red,
The lindens' golden fragrance on the wind
Or in a windlet equally enchant
With no necessity for confrontation.
The honeysuckle's cry beside the aisle
At night is like the nighthawk's from the spire.
Obscurity, while the authentic sylvan,
May be the intermezzo in our play.
What is the track to the authentic trove?
The straight lane had been lost. I found myself,
In consequence, not on an unmarked road,
Not on a marred one, but on one that was strange
Because I was a stranger in the forest.
I found myself taking that foreign way.
Obscure and indirect it was yet vital
And viable. It had a happy ending.

STUDI LEOPARDIANI

1. PER POCO IL COR NON SI SPAURA

Deep in its visions of infinities
Of silences far from this sighing breeze
That slips across the hill and through the hedge
Of hawthorns whispering along the ledge,

One's

One's heart but by a little missed distress,
One's for a little knew a happiness,
One's in those spaces almost felt afraid,
One's for that moment felt its fear allayed.
O moment of eternity, what motion
Plunges one from you into time's small ocean?

2. INTERMINATI SPAZI DI LÀ DA QUELLA

Past that I found unending distances,
Interminable spaces, blue beyond
Blue, celestes, ceruleans of azure,
And blacks surpassing altitudes of black.
That was this hedge, this mentioned hedge, which hedged
Part of the ultimate horizon. Or
Was it that part, that farthest part, regarded
And yet excluded from regard? I saw,
Through all the green exclusions and the blue
Negations and the blackest negatives,
The positives of possibility,
Which, partial, hedging, pointing, I might find
To be, as I remembered or discerned,
Purples of that, then reddest reds of this,
This much or little, nothing or everything.

3. S'ANNEGA IL PENSIER MIO E IL NAUFRAGAR M'È DOLCE

It is not sweet to drown. The dearest dear
Is the far more than oceanic you
Seen on an evening gleaming still beyond
That utmost star. I stand upon the shore
Of that unbordered uncontainable
Sea. I am burning in this distant sun.
I rest upon the edge of that white sky
Without horizon. So peripheral
Am I, I can lie cold beside the star
There posed, this huge, hot, sharp centrality.

I am

I am so overwhelmingly submerged
That when I limp along in endless desert,
Immersed in countless sea-deep leagues I swim,
My wreckage reassembled here by you,
The uncreated: great creation of
The star-struck mind's sidereal desire,
The vast dry ocean's crater in the heart.
Poet, you are the third. I fall apart.

EPPUR SI MUOVE

Whether or not he said it moves, it moves
If it moves.

Whether or not he says he sees, he sees
What he sees.

That which he said he said. If we hear we hear.
Will we say

What we see?

Heartwood

> Lo ferm voler qu'el cor m'intra
>
> Arnaut Daniel

> lo mio fermo desir vien da le stelle
>
> Francesco Petrarca

I must endure the pruning of the trees.
The trees endure. Between their boughs that star
Appears unconscious of the chastened form
Of its enjewelment. The oaks had grown.
Who with the power felt a sharp desire
To simplify, to oversimplify?

I do not wish to oversimplify
Because I walked for decades through the trees
And drew down score on score from keen desire
Looking through centuries upon that star
To snatch illumination not yet grown
From point into the pointedness of form.

The elms, the oaks, the beeches have their form,
In part that which we oversimplify
Perhaps regarding it as wholly grown
From the deep essences within the trees,
In part what we consider of that star,
Our sun, existence, hope, and strong desire.

I had to hope, for, lo, my firm desire
To find, force, a center inside a form
Found centerless descended from that star
Which did not, could not, oversimplify
The sky's exactitude of blue through trees
Branched black before the dusk had fully grown.

However the duramen may have grown
It must hide like the core of sheer desire.
The dark does not obliterate the trees.
It does obscure the losses of their form
Which office dared to oversimplify.
Hidden or visible beams seek that star.

The oak boughs still are pointing to that star,
Miniature, illumination, grown
Beyond the texts that oversimplify.
The elm boughs weave a tale of wild desire.
The beech boughs pencil in the book of form.
Thus do the topmost branches graph the trees.

The trees will hardly oversimplify
Themselves the form that is our mad desire
Shared, grown this dark night under that huge star.

ROMOLO PROFUMATISSIMO

Lindens and lilies, listen to him. He prays
That fragrance be as true as truth is sweet
To studiousness. He studies dulcitude.
Tigli e gigli, dite la verità.
Digli, ciascun fiore, grand or small,
Secrets of breeze, dawn, noon, and evening's ease
Chanted by robins. Languages of rose
And honeysuckle are their tongues. Be his,
Linger, give him your lasting syllables,
Grant him the sweet, avert the dolciaster.

UNA COSA VERA, BUONA, BELLA

What touched my ear?
Was it the kiss of the heather
Purple with August, honey-
Sweet to the bee?
I lay in the heather.

Who touched my ear?
What was that fluttering? Did
Homer's lilied sirens,
Like loves, fly?
I flew through the waters.

Who gave that touch?
If the Virgilian quiver,
Gift of Apollo, Apolline,
Could come to me!
I wished as I listened.

What was that touch?
Was it Italian words, their wings
Brushing, their rushing
Wings doves'
Wings' song?

Sonnets to the Italian

SONETTI PETRARCHESCHI

CCCII

Levommi il mio penser in parte ov'era
quella ch'io cerco, et non ritrovo in terra:
ivi, fra lor che 'l terzo cerchio serra,
la rividi piú bella et meno altera.

Per man mi prese, et disse: « In questa spera
sarai anchor meco, se 'l desir non erra:
i' so' colei che ti die' tanta guerra,
et compie' mia giornata inanzi sera.

Mio ben non cape in intelletto humano:
te solo aspetto, et quel che tanto amasti
e là giuso è rimaso, il mio bel velo ».

Deh perché tacque, et allargò la mano?
Ch'al suon de' detti sí pietosi et casti
poco mancò ch'io non rimasi in cielo.

Francesco Petrarca,
Rerum Vulgarium Fragmenta

1. POCO MANCÒ CH'IO NON RIMASI IN CIELO

But it is literature. It is not love.
You smile. You nod. And then you take my hand.
Like demigod or angel I can stand
Above what just now towered far above.

Clouds are those towers, dazzling temples of
Divinities on paper in a land
For ivory and ice, not built-on sand
But air for airy castles. Why the glove?

You smile and grasp my frosty fingers. I
Am warm, you say, and draw me toward the sun.
What if my wings are wax? I take your arm.

You are the gentleman. This is the sky.
We climb sedately up the stars. We run
Suddenly through the phrases of the charm.

2. LAURO

Latin made tree and laurel feminine.
Italian makes them masculine for me,
Belated female lover of a tree,
A prize desired, high, Apollonian,

Desirable, and difficult to win.
Was it a dream, or did I really see
Grand-branching or sweet-wreathing form? Was he
(Was she) a firm gold good, a breezy sin?

My father is a river, and I pray,
Straining, panting, as I row up-stream,
To reach the land and climb the foliate hill.

Virtue is feminine, a man's bouquet,
Aureole, aura. I will seek the beam
Breathing resplendent on the Capitol.

3. ET ALLARGÒ LA MANO

Why did his grasping hand release its hold,
Opening when I wished it tight? For my
Weak hand was what was held, and it was I
Whose fall that sudden loosening foretold

As if a document had been unrolled
And read: She is unworthy of the sky.
Her wings are false and yet she hopes to fly.
She missteps and her fingers are so cold.

He did not push me down. That widened hand,
That slackened grasp, sufficed. I could not stay
With no support. I dropped into the foam.

He kept on smiling. If you cannot stand,
He said, swim. For a goddess points the way.
Venus, his mother, showed Aeneas Rome.

4. SE 'L DESIR NON ERRA

Heaven and Rome and liquid lilies lending
Enchantment to the breeze and one strong voice
That in a crowd of sounds I can rejoice
To listen to alone; I hear it sending

Its messages, its delicacies, blending
Only with mine: Have I perfected choice
With my selection or do I devoice
Joys of whatever source, thus merely bending

My language to my longing, to my lust,
My greed, my gluttony, my pride, my error,
The ancient list? I list long robin's song;

Long lindens' respiration; azure's dust;
The city's grandeur sans the city's terror;
Beauty; and truth. Could my desire go wrong?

5. LEVOMMI IL MIO PENSER

What rose before me was the Capitol,
If only in the vision of desire.
Then I was raised by thought and by the lyre
Of one who sang the ancient citadel.

Between two groves, two summits of the hill,
Lies the asylum founded by our sire
Quirinus, divinized in blinding fire.
I was not blind. I saw the principle.

But is abstraction good for poetry?
Beyond the smoke a god loomed in blue air,
Thunder was heard, and brilliant suns were seen.

Rome is renown, renown is liberty,
And freedom is the tree whose branches bear
The golden inflorescence of the sheen.

6. ARBOR VICTORIOSA

Arbor victoriosa triumphale
Might be in Latin till the final e.
The only neuter names I know for tree
Are tree itself and dendron. Ideale

Neither, O deep, sweet, lofty, immortale
Pneuma, do all your adjectives agree
That yours is triumph, yours the victory,
Or shall I slowly, fondly bid you vale?

O animus or anima or both
Or two by two or two and one or one
In three or three as four or single file

Of five, of nine, of all — for I am loath
Even to posit that dread pronoun none —
I breathe parole: I am the dendrophile.

7. VEDEVA A LA SUA OMBRA

That laurel that she loved or golden elm
Or oak of gold or autumn's aureate beech
Was a true tree perhaps, just beyond reach,
Or was perhaps a man but in a realm

Beyond her borders. She stood at the helm
And piloted the ship beyond the screech
Of greediest gulls and out toward shores where speech
Governs and rules but does not overwhelm.

It must have been the almost understood
And almost understandable thing made
Of sense and sound and making. Must she add, oh,

Oh, must she guess the nature of the wood?
The thrush sang on, ungreedy, unafraid.
She was the tree and sat within its shadow.

8. A PARLAR DE' SUOI SEMPRE VERDI RAMI

If I am she and she is I and you
Are he or she or it and they are we,
I will have explanations for my tree,
But will my explanations all be true?

Pronouns in prose deliver up their cue
Or are convicted of a mystery
Unjustly perpetrated since the key
To each gate is inevitably due.

Green are the leaves, green in the silver rain,
Green in noon's gold, green in the rose of dawn,
Green in post-purple splendors of a moon

Agaze with countenance so clear of pain,
So radiant though furrowed, that I, drawn,
Reach greens of gold, rose, silver, and maroon.

9. DISSI 'L VER

Ovid saw Virgil, Petrarch Dante. I
Never stared rapt at Yeats or Frost or Pound
Or Eliot or Stevens. Does the sound
Of the great fathers, with their vision, die?

The widows and the daughters do not lie,
For they divine that as the world spins round
Their men may all precede them underground
Yet go before them up into the sky.

Nine are ye Muses. Come from Helicon,
Dance from Parnassus, shimmer in the blue
Like nine moons, sweet celestial spheres all ringing.

Cassandra's words, unheeded, yet live on.
Sibylla's leaves, though scattered, still sift through.
Daphne, immortal sung, must triumph singing.

10. FACENDOMI D'UOM VIVO UN LAURO VERDE

The man, the poet, turned into the laurel
Itself, which he had thought would be his crown.
With all of his regret or his renown
Comes my relief because this simple moral

Serves to alleviate my unwilled quarrel
And smooth away my undesired frown
And take my flaming rage and let it drown
In sunset seas of ruby, sapphire, coral.

Must I regret my love? Each verdurous bough
Issues the fragrant sempiternal breeze
Mingling in spring with vernal fragrant gold.

Thus that which lived then is that which lives now,
He whom she meets as, straying through the trees,
She finds young, vigorous, what is grand, old.

11. ULMUS-OLMO

O tall, triumphant tree, victorious
In the long combat, be to me the sage
Reaching to burdened from unburdened age.
Those summers, autumns, winters, onerous

To me, to others — I might say to us
If you and I were we in fear or rage
Or a more labored turning of the page
In our big book — to you do not seem thus.

Your arms rise, wind, weave in their dance of green.
Your arms rose, wound, wove in a play of gold.
You changed your white sleeves for those soft bronze things.

Now it is summer. You are king or queen.
In autumn you were glorious and old.
It had been winter. We must reach spring, springs.

12. A FERRAGOSTO LA ROBINIA DEL GIAPPONE A
    CAMBRIDGE NEL MASSACHUSETTS

One must read spring in August when each bough
Whitens with blossom. This is not Japan.
This is not Rome, not Florence, not Milan.
Is to assume assumption to kowtow

To possibilities that would endow
Our matter, like this bright etherial fan,
With bright celestial change, surpassing man
Or woman? No pagoda stands here now.

This is mere middle August. A pagoda
Tree is now blooming here, and that is all.
Well, there is speech. This is the Scholars' Tree.

This is not Padua. There is a coda.
If this is not Bologna one may call
This garden still a university.

13. LAURORA SCRIPSIT

She writ no language. That was what they said.
Non scrisse nessuna lingua. Lo dissero.
But she could read. Did she not have to show
The influence of everything she read?

To Galileo nature, more than bread,
Was a great book, and to her it was so
Likewise. She heard the trees and flowers grow.
But most of all she listened to the dead.

How loud the leaves become before the fall.
Night's choirs sing arbored Compline, chant branched Matin.
By day the sugar maple's greenest choral

Is sweeter with initial notes from all
Of autumn's rubrics. Sempervirent Latin,
So vespertine, may also be auroral.

14. LAUREOLA

Did he not say then: You are barbarous,
Or if he did not say did he not think
There was some problem with the kitchen sink
To mention which might not be courteous?

Every experiment is perilous.
The brinksman loves the pleasure of the brink
So well he laughs with joy at every link
Which critics laugh at as incongruous.

Sunflower, August's image of the sun,
Or image of an image which we knew
To be of that which was beyond compare,

Be a comparison, not ever un-
Thinkable even crayoned as we drew
That bright face and those golden rays of hair.

15. LA DISIATA VOSTRA FORMA VERA

Who was the aureoled, the auricome,
Seen of a summer on a golden hill?
Whose was the springal step that reached the dome
In springtime, when I hardly knew my will

But followed on the stairway through the gloam
That heralds light and love and joy until
The follower finds that the stars fulfil
The promises? I promised Rome and tome.

One was aureolate, one argentine.
The gleaming godlike foot, the burning hair
Are now one vision in which I can hold

One great desideration. How can I hold the line
Between external steep and inner stair
If there were two, one silver and one gold?

16. PRESSO A L'EXTREMO

The form was broken. Thus the end was near.
She might pretend that she could play the game
But surely it would never be the same
When rules were ruined and the way was clear

To anything, the hazy atmosphere
Of anywhere, in which the stars became—
In which the stars stayed—distant. Shall we blame
The superannuated sonneteer?

The summer had been emptying its coffers.
The sculptors had exhausted all their quarries.
Statues of lapis laughed. How can you dun

September for past taxes when it proffers
Such a blue morning, such blue morning glories,
Such golden sunflowers, such golden sun?

17. NOTE AI SONETTI 1–16

In Anglo-Saxon beam is masculine
Like Baum in German. Treow, though, like Greek
Dendron is neuter. Yet we need not seek
Far for the cognate drys, a feminine.

Arbor and laurus both are feminine
In Latin. Daphne likewise is in Greek.
Albero and alloro, if we seek
Italian names, we find are masculine.

Italian lauro, too, is masculine,
But though the word may be a bit antique
The laurel is no less fresh, sweet, and green.

Laura, you were so very feminine
And beautiful, in German schön, antique
Though English sciene, our lovely sheen.

18. INDICE

I looked forever to dawn's ancient gold
And found my flight was pointed toward the west,
From which new land the sun slipped off to rest
In an immense sea. I saw only old

Columns, old-world laurels, antique mold,
The sea that seemed to me less edge than nest
For storied scribes of lands storied and blest,
In my mind's eyes. My eyes, you were cajoled

By beauty, beauty, beauty, fresh, clean, bright.
Moon, earth, and sun queued up. The tides grew sheer.
The year would finish soon. The moon was blue.

The city glittered. The gold bridge was light.
Bridge, hills, and ocean rose, descended. Here
The sun set, but the year in Rome was new.

19. BIOGRAFIA

He to the modern was a gold aurora
Gleaming upon another's bright gold hair.
She in late afternoon breathed that clear air
Of dawn as postpostmodernism's aura.

He so loved he could almost be his Laura
And in his voice her voice was doubly rare.
What could she say or be or do or dare?
Could she love if she had to be her Flora?

Francesco, San Francisco glitters. Gold
May glitter and be gold. Behold, oh, rush
To glean the city's sheen hills if not home.

Petrarca, Harvard glitters. Quick, oh, hold
The warm books to your heart. The ticks, the hush
Are ice on Widener's steps. But such is Rome.

20. SOFFIETTO EDITORIALE

Reader, she loved him, for she loved to read
And he read what she read and loved the high
Linguistic hills and stretching word-starred sky
Toward which she stretched. Some hills were thickly treed,

Some trees were silver, some boughs had been freed
From glaciation and would never die
Of ice or sighing, for the verdant cry
That rose among them carried golden seed.

What young Apollo crowns her curls with bays?
What new Maecenas seconds this grand call?
The rhododendrons narrow in the vise

Of January. Janus smiles toward Mays.
Watch the great shadows from great angles fall.
See the great shades from highest peaks arise.

21. FASCETTA

A day in January is the date
On the book's wrapper. Janus, wrap it tight,
If it is bellicose. Night falls. Dawn's light
Shines on rain faintly. Janus, close the gate.

The floods rush roughly. Janus, do not wait.
War's doors must shut. They must be shut. No fight
Is the good struggle. Two-faced double sight
Sees this both ways now. Janus, it is late.

This is not literature or love or life.
Guerra is feminine, Krieg masculine,
And bellum neuter like imperium.

Are passion's platitudes or sex or strife
Grammatical? Out of the flame what jinn,
Out of the flood what Jani ever come?

22. CONGEDO

The little book takes wing and lightly flies
To you, its father, leaving me below
As mortal wives of deities must know
Occurs so that the hero verifies

His half-divine condition. Recognize
Your child. Upon his golden head bestow
Evergreen evergold angelic glow.
Angelic doves may murmur in your skies.

Our skies sustain metallic murderous geese.
You sing in heavenly eternal rest.
I walk where earthly wolves and weasels march.

As you did, I go screaming peace, peace, peace.
Watch how the sanguine sun has splashed the west.
In the east see a rosy rainbow arch.

23. ECO

If the eve of the eve significant
For sanctity and poetry and love
Presented solely gray of cloud above
Yet when the sun went down magnificent

Not gold perhaps but scarlet bars were sent
Up from the set spent splendor not to shove
The clouds roughly aside but just to hov-
Er through and with and in them, radiant

Themselves because the clouds themselves were they
As they became bright clouds and, facing these,
An arc of rose triumphed, and if an eve

Later, late on the eve of Agnes' day,
Not green perhaps but white stripes on the trees
Were pure caresses, won't you find reprieve?

24. RECENSIONE

As yet she does not know that when you pace
Carefully through the rubble as you follow
The pathway to the temple of Apollo
Marked in your books and step into the space

Now closest to the rediscovered place
And undergo the onset of a solemn
Sentiment as you glimpse the single column
Solely restored to rise up from its base

Your feeling suddenly finds its objective
Correlative in something dimly floral
To consciousness as you perceive the site

Not with your eyes alone. You have expected
To see. You do not know yet that the laurel
Blooms there in March. What god grants such delight?

25. SCIENZA NUOVA

And some day will she stroll between the lines
Of laurel arched above the cobbled path
Paved through a universe of highest math
With all its tangents, its cosines and sines,

Its skies horizoned by umbrella pines
And cypresses, its seas the holy bath
Of goddesses in myrtle wreathed, the wrath
Of oak-crowned gods its bursting of confines

Into or out of mountains? Will she know
Which precise sweetness streams from each sweet tree,
Whether from flower, foliage, or bark?

Through that exuberant, austere, clean flow
Of sibylline aroma will she see
Just what light gleams there just beyond the dark?

26. SAGGIO DI FLORA BAUM

Is there a Rome to which the road must tend
Or is desire itself desirable?
What if the brimming pigments could not fill
The canvas, the toccata touch its end,

The purple bud stretch and expand and blend
Itself in paler purpleness until
The perfect palest pinks traverse the sill
And wing into the whitenesses that pend?

What if my author, my authority,
Never steps through the rampart's brazen gate,
Boldly surveys the city with my eyes

Never, and never dons harped liberty
For which my patient sagging shoulders wait?
O Rome, rise up before her. O Rome, rise.

27. APPENDICE: LEONARDO OLSCHKI E L'USIGNUOLO DI COLOMBO

She has to go to hear the nightingale.
Just as the evening star sings to the moon
In those blue halls resounding, just as at noon
The yellow rose beside the bright black rail

Sings to the yellow sun (Bright sun, inhale
The fragrance, grace, and aura of the tune
That rises up the sunbeams through a June
Of yellow rose), just as a first still frail

Dawn sings to dark, it sings. But not at home.
It does not live here in America.
It lives in Europe. To be more precise,

She may just find it if she just finds Rome.
Columbus found it in America.
The nightingale must sing in Paradise.

28. AL SUON DE' DETTI

But was his nightingale our mockingbird
That sings us dulcet death, death, death, death, death?
O live, O last, life, spirit, holy breath,
Be near and be discovered, hear and be heard,

Enduring exhalation and brief word,
Initial, iteration, aleph, beth,
And the great O. O be, she says, she saith,
She cants in accents loud and faint and surd,

She writes in minor and in major letters,
In formal and in liberated verse,
In the most closured antiquarian prose,

In clauses that have cast off ancient fetters,
In sentences now lengthy and now terse.
Troy fell in endless ruin. But Rome rose.

29. IL MIO BEL VELO

The veils of the virgilias of May
Stayed with her spirit. Thus the belle, the bride,
Might recollect the early public pride
And private termination of her day,

And thus the saint, amidst green, white, and gray
Nebulousness that sometimes seems to slide
From the great presence, sometimes to abide
Through deep communion, might in visions pray.

Will we find irises here and Iris there,
Here the purpureal, the aureal,
The candid standards rising from dark loam,

There satin banners floating through bright air,
Her sashes, wings, and veils, memorial
Virgilias here and Virgil there in Rome?

30. FRA LOR CHE 'L TERZO CERCHIO SERRA

It was the year of the virgilias.
Everywhere we walked we found the lace
And fragrance filling, frilling time and space
Frivolously and solemnly. It was

A year of pilgrimage. America's
Flora will not so soon be commonplace.
Frolicsomeness and sanctity embrace
Our maples, tulip trees, robinias,

Our dogwoods, yellowwoods, and mountain laurel,
But above all the yellowwoods. Increase,
Form the third circle, be upon our lips

Virgilias, looked at, loved, supremely floral.
We glimpse the silver boughs, the silver fleece.
We pray: O keep the firebrands from our ships.

31. LAUREA

The thesis possibly comes down to this:
The yellowwood is the virgilia.
What can that mean? Abandoned genera
Are hardly scientific. Does she miss

Old nomenclatures? Is her very bliss
The obsolete? Cladrastis lutea
Will serve or even C. kentuckea.
She studies arbor (arbos), arboris,

And the eponymy surrendered now
To fractured Greek in Latin and a free
Choice among terms in languages more oral.

The yellow wood she calls the golden bough.
Virgilia she feels is Virgil's tree.
Why does she long and long then for the laurel?

32. IN PARTE OV' ERA

Two together! Winds blow north, blow south.
O westerlies, across the western seas
Carry me to the gates of Hercules
And haste me, hero-cradled, to the mouth

Of my great father. Tiber, speak. Not south,
As your words ripple, but against the tease
Of noon and sunset guide me. Harmonies
Of speech and song from the paternal mouth

Must lead me, lone and lonely, to my good,
To my great dawn. Hymns, incense, butterflies,
A golden branch, a golden leaf, a look

Into or out of beech or yellowwood
Will speed me to the spouse into whose eyes
One gazes when one holds the opened book.

VITA NUOVA O MONDO NUOVO

> chiamsi romei in quanto vanno a Roma, là ove questi cu'io chiamo peregrini andavano.
>
> Dante Alighieri,
Vita Nova

1. ROMEA

The vertigo of the virgilias
Was hers, not theirs, and was but momentary,
Shifting to ecstasy. Are you not wary
Of such a claim so soon? The irises

Require long eying. The robinias
Had to be stopped in shock before. They vary,
As we do, as she must. What dictionary
Fixes the scents of the virgilias,

Gives us the ecstasy of ecstasy?
What grammar grants us this alternative:
The pilgrimage to the virgilias,

To each profumed papilionaceous tree
As to envisioned veils of Rome, may give
The pilgrimage of the virgilias?

2. BIBLIOTECA COLOMBIANA

If they who stand and wait may also serve,
The journey is not indispensable.
If armchair navigation, if the will
Of those that sit, may rise above the curve

Of the great world and penetrate with verve
The lands to which the compass is the quill,
The scribe's hand may be just as critical
As the stout ship's. The pilot cries, What nerve!

For you who read at rest beneath your arbor
My heart can feel disgust, disdain, or pity.
The admiral receives my admiration.

But who has watched, beyond the shining harbor,
Among the lamp-lit pages from the city,
Columbus at his task of annotation?

3. L'UCCELLO MOTTEGGIATORE

The mockingbird that sings another's song
Mocked her. But you? Are you the nightingale?
And you? Whose was the question? Does she fail
If she gets query and response both wrong?

And does she fail if all her notes belong
To ancient trees beside an ancient trail
That winds through heights and dips into a dale
Where all those ultrasecular strange strong

Trunks sustain a subtle fluttering
Which might be that of birds and then might be,
If she could study every novel change,

Merely of leaves among which birds might sing
If they should spy, in that vicinity,
Something to draw them from their ancient range?

4. IL TIGLIO

Longfellow's linden lifts into a June
Again. Into how many golden Junes
Has it ascended? What blue afternoons
Have watched the bloom of gold? This afternoon

Has watched and waited and seen very soon
That its blue eyes can read the golden runes
And its gold lips carry the golden tunes,
These new old fragrances. The very swoon

Induced by this bold music in blue air,
Huge as the trunk and tiny as the flower,
Delights, encompasses, and passes on.

Longfellow's sundial is still standing there,
Reading what Dante tells it of this hour:
Think that this day again will never dawn.

5. L'INVITO

Is it Favonius? Catalpas smile.
The lindens' breath is sweeter on the breeze.
I think it must be sweetest to the bees.
Catalpas laugh. Then let's give this a trial.

Let us first walk along the sacred aisle
Under the lindens toward catalpa trees.
The blissful blossoms bless with incense. Please
Be satisfied with incense for a while.

Then let us listen to the lindens' lessons
And hearken to catalpas' canticles.
The clouds are white. The universe is sunny.

The darker weathers and the deeper questions
For these three hours become mere codicils.
The text is wine, meat, greens, fruit, bread, and honey.

6. ALLA SALUTE

On the white tablecloth a vase is set
Beyond the wine, the strawberries, the cream,
And more angelic messages do seem
To emanate from its bouquet. And yet

From lindens' golden wings these lessons jet
And from catalpas' chalices they stream
As from the purple irises that dream
Above the grand white lilies and that let

The one red rose dream over all. The long
Stems carry, with each tune and cup and wing,
The sentence not prevented by repose.

The third is best of wine and sex and song.
So speak the trees. Thus from their vessel sing
The irises, the lilies, and the rose.

7. LA CENA

Here smooth white yogurt, rosy apricots,
Dark bread with raisins, peanut butter ground
Just now, and just-ground coffee all abound.
Time, destiny, or fortune now allots

These terrene happinesses and so knots
Us as with vines to earth that we are bound
Among the sweetest bubbles and are crowned
With grape leaves. Are these benefactions blots,

Like gluttony and sleep and lazy pillows?
Might pleasures that are more than pleasantries
And less than loves and easier than duty

Wreathe us with myrtle here beside bright billows,
Halo with oak? Beyond what deeper seas
Will laurel laud the deathless lust of beauty?

8. LA COLOMBA

Was it the love of beauty or of love
Or of the study of these entities
That sent her stumbling off among the trees
And fumbling into aethers far above

Her outstretched fingers, thinking that the dove
Was distant, when its yearning melodies
Were there beside her, not beyond the seas
Into whose whitened waves she tried to shove

Her small gray boat? Minerva's eyes are gray.
Her step is now impetuous, now measured.
Was it her words that Flora, as she wandered

By the gray ocean, caught? She seemed to say:
Study is love. Love may be studied. Treasured
Beauty may be scrutinized or pondered.

9. O L'INFERNO

Minerva's eyes, like owls' eyes, olive leaves,
Or oceans seem to open to her gaze.
Looking and looking longingly she prays
To see. The pattern that Minerva weaves

Among dove-O-so-lovely grays receives
The white-pink, pink-white roses that amaze
The passerby who passes dazed for days
And equally believes on equal eves.

If you were judge, how would you judge the case?
Was it a child or was it the grown man's toy?
Before the court she saw the prettiest roses.

A scorpion would fix the little face.
It was such fun to force a tiny boy.
Not far from court she smelled most odorous roses.

10. LA VEDUTA

Neither hermetic nor mercurial
Nor prejudiced nor simplified nor too
Brutal, ancient, antiquated, new,
Brittle, sordid, morbid, sexual,

Selfish, or violent, nor fictional
Nor literary was her blinking view
Of hell. It was just literally true,
Just just, just right, and most juridical,

Proven through jury duty. It was not
What she had prayed for. She had hoped to find
Libraries. Life intruded. Was it life

She witnessed through the witnesses? And what
Could she have witnessed to, or was she blind?
Was she the bridesmaid, or was she the wife?

11. IL PURGATORIO

It was the Ides of June, and Virgil said
To Dante as they climbed, and Dante then
Said to the eminent American
Longfellow over whose ensconced bronze head

The monumental label simply read
Poet, and he said, while I held my pen,
Think that this day will never dawn again,
Although they were already with the dead

And I was with the linden and the sun,
And I was with the wind and with the hours.
Song, scent, and sparkle filled the afternoon.

The mockingbird denied day could be done,
And I was with the linden, gilt with flowers,
Grand sample of the everlasting June.

12. IL BIGLIETTO

Another day had dawned. The sun had set
Or was just setting. This day did not die
For us. Black cloths were covering the sky.
The walls were forest green. How could we fret?

The cloths were all of rose here where we met
To try the most unusual or try
The common chicken, common blueberry pie,
By excellence uncommon. Etiquette

Laureled our green words as our green words glistened
For us within our dark-arched history.
We dared to think two poets ate and drank

And talked, we dared to think two poets listened,
Two lauded, loved, two poets' poetry.
This note comes not to praise, though, but to thank.

13. IL LUSSO

Was the famed poet's bust not bronze but wood?
Is not the robin's evening's chief recital?
Was there for all our anguish a requital
In bread's brief or in art's long-lasting good?

Did we pretend our poetizing could
Pay for a luxury that we deemed vital
Even without the ever-echoing title
Confirming our eternal poethood?

We go from luxury to luxury
Living as we do live in lindenbloom
So rich it never needs the rich man's pardon.

We go from ecstasy to ecstasy
Rising as we can rise on every neum
That soars up the cathedral of the garden.

14. L'ALBERO GENEALOGICO

Is Homer or is Virgil my great father,
Is Plato or is Aristotle my
Father, is Dante or is Petrarch my
Father, Descartes or Hegel my great father,

Is Eliot, or is it Pound, my father,
Or is it Longfellow, is it Whitman, my
Great father, or, could it be, Lowell, my
Father, could it be Lowell, my great father?

And if Apollo, chaste Diana's brother,
Should woo me, would deep healing or great fame
Or beauty's music be his gift to me

Or would I call my father or my mother
To save me from corruption or from shame
Or choose to vegetate eternally?

15. DALLA COROLLA AL CALICE

In a catalpa's gold-lined cave I hide
Lying in white between two lines of gold,
Couched there in sweetness, happy to abide
Forever in a flower. Manifold

Delights are pleasures are most heavenly blessings.
Between two dotted lines of gold I kneel
Deep in retreat, for I have signed, my guessings
Become my vows, my hopes become the peal

Of this pure-white yet purple-resonant
And golden-spotted golden-throated bell.
The stamens are the gongs of gold's descent.
The calyx is the chamber is the cell.

The nun is Danae. Am I so small?
Into the pistil's nectarous stem I crawl.

16. DAGLI ALBERI ALLE CASE

I walked among the elms of Harvard Yard.
They rise and widen. Santayana thought
Them scrawny, contemptible. Would it not be hard
To scorn them now? They widen skyward, fraught.

I walked among the oak trees of the grove.
They are not gnarled like Old World oaks. They rise,
Though large-oak-leaved, straight skyward, toward that Jove
Who newly in the New World sky waits, wise.

I walked among the redwoods of the west.
Height is their specialty, their glory, their
Fascination. They rise. They come to rest
Near where the western sun god bends down, fair.

But on my little native island all
Men's dwellings touched the sky. I am that tall.

17. NOTE AI SONETTI 1–16

The bird, the flower, the discoverer
May be discovered in a single line.
The scholar is the deft uncoverer:
Columba (dove), Columbus, columbine

Are one. Italian calice is double:
Calix and calyx, kylix and kalyx, or
Chalice and calyx. Why make all this trouble?
Kl was both men's and bloom's cup's ancient core.

Was the veil verily a revelation?
Is the whole corpus veiled or it is veil?
Is the crown corollary, coronation,
Oak, ivy, myrtle, laurel, grape, or kale?

The cradle fell. The baby was awake
And did not crash, nor did the long bough break.

18. SEMPRE

Did she always feel the air was blue?
Did she always say the day was gold?
Did she think the air was always blue?
Did she insist the day was always gold?

Did she always use the same old rhymes?
Did she always sing the selfsame tunes?
Could she not discover other rhymes?
Could she at least invent some newer tunes?

Did she ever yearn for ancient Rome?
Did her very feet ache for its streets?
Would she if she found her way to Rome
Walk with the Romans in the Romans' streets?

Life must be short, but how long will her art
Be if her life is long enough for art?

19. IL POETA

Bronze? Wood? He had a white chip in his chin.
He was a plaster poet, painted green.
Under green brows green eyes, incised, were seen,
Saw, were incisive. Could we see within

That stare to darkest depths? Did we begin
To feel his gaze, in part perhaps serene,
In part daunting, undaunted, sharp and keen
And penetrating? Did we feel chagrin

Because he saw through us? A photograph
Shows the white-bearded bard before his house.
His chin was burned. The blaze destroyed his wife.

Do his compositions make us laugh?
Have Styx and Lethe flowed through here to douse
The fame that flamed about him through his life?

20. LA POETESSA

The river is not Lethe but the Charles.
The river is the Tiber, my dear father.
Grandfather must be Janus: bridge at Arles
Or Avignon or Brooklyn. Shall I bother

To speak of mothers? Every woman is,
Her mother said, an island. Thus Manhattan
(Algonquian) or (plain Hellenic) his
(Apollo's) floating Delos or the (Latin)

Insula Tiberina might be mine.
Margaret is hers. I wish to glorify,
Not cheat, my pearl although I steal her line.
Grandmother — who is she? And who am I?

Germaine's Corinne, Elizabeth's Aurora,
Emily's Emily, my Julia's Flora.

21. LA VITA

The face turned alien. The words, alas,
Reached home. In fact, their owner had the key
To let them in where they could torture me
In private. Did I see them cross the grass,

Steal up the walk, and peer in through the glass,
As pungent as the roses or the bee
Among the roses? Lilies, warm, soft, free,
Grew by the door through which the words would pass.

My home is not that sort of place. In brief,
I have no home. I have no house and garden.
Have I a window with its bitter view?

I have a hearth, a heart to fire, chill, harden.
The lilies' sweetness is beyond belief.
The lilies live. The lilies, too, are true.

22. IL COLPO E LA COLPA

Was it an earthquake or the beat of hail
That broke my heart? Was it one tiny stone?
The lily is so pure. How can it trail
Such a seductive scent and stand alone?

Was it snow, icicles, the slender sliver
Of glass that blasted mind's bloom and balloon?
The lilies shimmer and the lilies quiver.
The heat, the golden halo of the moon

Do, too. Was it then mind, my mind? What blow
Battered my body, crushed it along a fault
Found on its coast or inland? Lilies grow
Here where the breeze is field-sweet and sea-salt.

Lilies are big. Why was my spirit little?
Lilies are soft. Why was my heart so brittle?

23. LA POESIA

Their home was art. Their life was like a smile
That cheered us. If I said, The thrust of the thrush,
He asked, would it be poetry or mush?
We sat in beauty. Every tint and tile,

Each figure, texture, harmony, and style
Had been thought lovingly. No greedy rush
Or harsh dissension forced a plain or lush
Imbalance or gave proof or hint of guile.

French quiche with broccoli, our native corn,
Our Massachusetts raspberries graced the table.
She served with graciousness. He cleared. The gush

Of song surprised us: something so forlorn,
Luxuriant, wild, artful, sweet, and able
To seem, to be, tears, laughter, sound, and hush.

24. MONNA INNOMINATA

How strange to be a woman made of straw.
How odd to be a wadded Raggedy Ann,
A puppet, pillow, pad, or puff. What man
Or woman ever loved the clumsy paw

Of mauve emotion playing with the haw
Fallen from thorns? What lover ever ran
To catch the puny feather which the fan
Blew from the hot pillow? Who ever saw

The hazy monster lumbering down the coast
Out of the wood along the grains of sand
Far from the woodthrush or the nightingale

And cared? He is beige thought. Then can I boast,
As he proceeds on each foot and each hand,
That I am his? I am his fingernail.

25. QUESTIONI NOMINALI

Call her Rossetti, call her Browning. Call
Her then her brother's sister. I renege.
Call him her brother. Then call him, I beg,
Her husband. And is she Necker de Staël,

La Curchodine, Madame, Baronne, et al.?
Margaret, the dentist said, or is it Meg,
Maggie or Marge or Peggy, maybe Peg?
Mrs. Budenz, she answered, Dr. Fall.

Call her Diana, white in the night's black pool.
Call her Diana, silver in evening's stream.
Call him Apollo, purple in dawn's gray lake.

Is he Apollo, gold on the ocean's cool
Blue afternoon? Call him the moon, bright beam.
Call her the golden sun, long golden wake.

26. QUESTIONI FAMILIARI

Margaret Budenz, née Rodgers (with a d),
Mrs. Budenz, then Ms. Budenz, in life
As teacher, mother, social worker, wife,
Authorship made Budenz. And hence is she

Budenz in book reviews, thus possibly
He for a paragraph, Budenz's wife
In manifold entitlements of life,
Budenz's mother in the mystery

Of my own birth? The exemplary power
Of gods is logic, letters, Lebensraum.
Jove bore Minerva, wisdom, motherless.

Flora could show his queen the small white flower
And Juno was a father. Am I, Baum,
The product of parthenogenesis?

27. QUESTIONI RELIGIOSE

The juniors' mistress always said the same
Old thing. New life, Sister, she always said,
Tracing a little cross upon the head
Black-veiled above the banded brow. I blame

Myself, the junior always said with shame,
Kneeling black-robed, black-cinctured, but I dread
A mental pestilence. If not yet dead,
Mother, my mind is moribund. You maim,

Black death, this runner running to the sun,
This sailor sailing gaily through bright sky.
These feet trod aether and these hands grasped stars.

The mind survives on study. Can the one
For whom I live be death? White, weak, I die
Daily pressed heavily against the bars.

28. QUESTIONI MONDIALI

In the first garden, by the vital tree,
She saw eternal truth and beauty gleam
Beside her as she walked with him. And he
Was real at evening by the mirroring stream.

The second garden stretched above the bay
Up to Parnassus, roseate and gold.
She saw deep waters glitter, leaves array
Truth with the beauty that she saw heights hold.

The beech tree's purple glory calmly glints
Before the portal. Is this then the third
Garden? The Roman fountain nobly hints
Truth about beauty is not so absurd

A notion. Which gate is she gazing through?
Seeking an old world will she find a new?

29. QUESTIONI VITALI

Will she discover this world or the next,
Find a new life or any life at all,
Accept the harsh conditions of the fall,
Hope and still hope not to be ever hexed

By possibility, forever vexed
By triviality, heed a great call
Like that Why do you persecute me, Saul?
Or breathe vitality inside a text?

Is not a vita a biography?
Green willows weep above white lilies' laughter.
Between the long-lost loves and future fears

Is there this moment of hilarity?
Is there a time between before and after,
A space between white smiles and verdant tears?

30. LA LETTERATURA

Do not do sonnets. You are not a man.
Do not converse with any dead white male.
Do not be formal. We have placed a ban
On everything but freedom. Past the pale

Of our poetic is your Greek and Latin.
Tell us of childbirth, name the nameless love,
Leave us your laundry, feed us foods that fatten
Milk but make fit the heart that beats above

The world that lies alive, supine, grotesque,
Present, new, future, muscular, not fat
But slim, sharp, hard. Slim, sitting at his desk,
Roman Catullus knew Greek Sappho sat

Sad at her lyre and sang, down in the dumps.
Shining white lilies rise in giant clumps.

31. TROVARE, SCOPRIRE

Altro è trovare e altro è
Scoprire, Leonardo Olschki wrote.
From the pagoda tree's slim branches float
Green leaflets, float white bloomlets, as the day,

Brilliant in white and green, now floats away
And evening flutters in with its soft note,
Deep-eve-green, high-sky-white. Will I devote
My quest to night-white Dian or essay

Light-bright Apollo? Which one did I see
Glimmer between the boughs? Was it that moon,
Was it that sunshine? Through that lovely foam

Will I love god or goddess, through that tree
Find life, the world, a way, all roads, and soon
Discover something that I know is Rome?

32. ROMA

A noun may name a person, place, or thing.
The person is a lady, bright, divine,
Colorful, fragrant, ever flowering.
Flora she is, the city's self and sign.

The place is now the city, now the world,
Now the world's head, and now eternal life.
Among its hills the winds of history swirled.
Rome is its name, its fame both peace and strife.

What is the thing? It makes the world go round.
It fathers life. It mothers history.
It has a humble and exalted sound.
Love is the name, the claim, the mystery.

I call on Love, call Flora, cry my om:
Rome, Rome, Rome, Rome, Rome, Rome, Rome, Rome, Rome, Rome.

SONETTI PREROMANI

> Or se' tu quel Virgilio . . . ?
>
> Dante Alighieri,
Inferno

1. VIRGILIO

Then are you he? My eyes drop to the ground.
I lift my hands a little. Will I fall?
Can I still see, still breathe? Then should I crawl
Into my hole and nevermore be found

Pretending that the elm can stand proud, crowned
By sun, and, clad by sun, can stand as tall
As heaven's incommensurable wall
Above which suddenly our arms are wound,

If you are he and if, still, I am I?
Then are you he? And are you then a shade
Striding across white clouds of asphodel

As though the sun were striding through the sky?
You seem to shine. I seem to be afraid.
Then are you he? And am I then in hell?

2. UDRALLO IL BEL PAESE

Beyond the Apennines, beyond the Alps,
Beyond the sea, beyond another sea,
On spangled beaches bannered land of the free,
Beyond the monstrous borders of your maps,

Where a new capitol is climbed up steps
Beyond desire and after memory,
Does she desire, remember, Italy?
Your lasting longing recollection helps

Her singing, singer. Is she not one chosen?
Will she ascend a capitol of sand,
Attain the dome of an enormous sootball,

Crash on salt ice of ocean pond long frozen?
Or can she travel? Will that lovely land
Hear her faint name, soft song, and softer footfall?

3. IL ROMANZO DI CORINNA

Fanfares, white horses, high triumphal car,
Virgins in white, escort the poetess
In white and blue, center, descended star,
Crowds' cause, lords' love, sovereign of success.

Later they hurled their traitors from that rock,
But did the maiden earlier betray
Father and fatherland? Did she unlock
Those heights to foes or, goddess, guard the way?

The thirsting hero, like Aeneas, came,
Heroic, from the fire, the storm at sea.
Will, before Dido's diadem or blame,
Napoleon, Charlemagne, and Caesar flee?

The woman crowned upon the Capitol
Is doomed. She climbed Tarpeia's stark stone hill.

4. CORINNA, O L'ITALIA

Italy, land of love and liberty,
Land of my longing, bright place of my praise,
Smoothly my honeyed tongue will move for thee,
My voice mellifluous and dulcet raise

Its undulating part of harmony
Convergent from the then on into now
In springs of song, currents of history,
Fresh as a fresco, ancient as marble brow,

New as the future, eager as gold-tipped bee,
Happy as branches saved from the wind's grim kill,
Slow as the Muses' mother Memory.
Must I address the question terrible?

Is there but one life that can make me free?
Must poet live alone with poetry?

5. CORINNA O PINDARO

The nun must lose the universe for God.
The wife must sacrifice a world for home.
The poet and the poetess must roam
City and wilderness. Cement and sod

Receive their step, welcome those steps that trod
The oldest roads, the blackest pathless loam,
The whitest highways, cut and paved, the foam
Unpavable. Their hands felt, held, the rod.

The poet must not strain and must not plod.
He runs through all existence as his range.
The poet waits upon his lady's nod.

What foot responds to this alarming prod?
What gait, what pace, what journey is so strange?
What lady finds the poetess not odd?

6. LA MEMORIA

Had such a lady spoken for herself,
Christina said . . . What did Christina say?
Or had the Poetess of our own day,
The Great, the happy Poetess . . . What elf,

What goblin, gobbled, garbled, what my shelf
Held of apodosis? She gave away
A golden ringlet. Then she could not pray
For restitution of a pilfered pelf.

With his left arm and hand he cradled me,
Draped as I was in red and fast asleep.
The exegesis has been subtlest art.

Love's right hand raised a greater mystery.
Do not be timorous and do not weep.
Partake. It was his voice. I ate my heart.

7. IL PARTITO

Was she then sad because the dream was ending?
Was it her heart that had been draped in red?
When she was nine and golden-curled what fed
Her unawakened self, with roses blending?

It was the thought that everything was tending
To the great synthesis. Her little head
Could hold that hope. She feasted on that bread,
That fruit, among the blooming boughs there bending.

There would be knowledge, peace, equality.
Each one would give and everyone receive.
Freedom and comradeship would be the toast

And true. Was this abstract? The cupboard's key
Was in her hand. She woke. Would she believe
You can be wrong on that which matters most?

8. IL PARADISO

Utopia at length turned into heaven.
The sky revealed what earth could never show.
She heard eternity. She was eleven.
She saw infinity. How could she know

That music must unscroll itself in time,
That space in paintings bends itself to laws?
She lassoed everlastingness in rhyme,
And endlessness she captured in a clause.

Once there is not none and not always never,
If there is somewhere something still unsounded,
Can the sky not go on and on forever,
The earth not be a piece of some unbounded?

Is what she sees this August's rosy haw
Among the deep green leaves, what she writes straw?

9. IL PATRIMONIO

I must be glad my father was not he,
Madame de Staël said of her mother's beau.
His passion was to study and to know.
Hers was her father, people wickedly

Insisted. Gibbon visited all three
Later — the learned belle Suzanne Curchod,
The banker, their illustrious child — although
Some hated that complacent trinity.

Everything alters. One flames. Each one dies.
The red flamboyance of an August flower
Is not diminished by the brilliance of

Magentas, golds, ceruleans. Hence prize
Father, fame, glory, influence, wealth, power,
Talk, writing, study, knowledge, lovers, love.

10. ROMEO

Suzanne was learned but a foreigner.
Suzanne was beautiful — la belle Curchod —
But when a friend suggested that Rousseau
Suggest to Gibbon that he marry her

Since he had loved her, that philosopher
Pronounced unworthy one who did not know
Her worth. The English father had said no.
The son was scholar, writer, voyager,

The Classic pilgrim, gazing from on high,
Among Swiss heights, with studious discipline
Along the avalanche of truest motion.

The pilgrimage of Italy, which I
(Wrote Gibbon) now accomplished had long been
The object of my curious devotion.

11. SUGGERIRE, ISPIRARE

Perhaps it was not right to say suggest.
Suggestion is too definite a thing.
Rousseau was asked, if Gibbon was his guest,
To praise the woman, not to press the ring.

But Gibbon did not go to see Rousseau,
And neither seemed to be the other's man.
The great can find the fragrant winds that blow
For them and need not be each other's fan.

Is there a breeze all rose-gold from the street
That steals in with the lifting of the pane?
Is there a gust that, if it is not sweet,
Is strong and purple like a hurricane?

The sultry air will stagnate or bequeath
That which will rattle, nothing you can breathe.

12. MONNA NOMINATA

Is monna monkey? Gibbon can be, too.
Is monkey ape? Is ape more anthropoid?
Has anthropos caught name, word, and the true
To rank the multiple, to fill the void,

To recommend the one, to lend desire
Subject and object, drawing down the star,
Finding now light now peril in the fire,
Mingling what may not be with things that are?

Do you love sense or word? Can you feel fame?
How can you touch the sudden demimoon
With precious gold? Why do you taste a name
As if the purplest plum were never prune?

Each rhyme has its significance. Does of,
Which means relation, not chime best with love?

13. CHIARA MATRAINI

She may be named because she is the one
Who names. Distinctions can be very nice.
She is the Adam of her paradise.
She is the sun by which we see her sun.

Commander at the stream of words that run
Between her and her Rome, she casts the dice
Of crossing, not afraid to pay the price
By having judged a prize already won.

Sunflowers by the fence on Sunday night
After September's green-gold afternoon,
Peering like children onto the street's allure,

Pale and confused, though, even with streetlamps' bright
Companionship, without or star or moon,
Shall I be clear or shall I be obscure?

14. TUTTI LI FEDELI D'AMORE

The heliotrope stands straight or hangs his head.
The poet, though discomfited, must try
To stand, endure, survive, respire, not die,
To flourish for the living, not the dead,

Since all his fragrance is in pages read
By the so sensitive if mortal eye
Of not one but the many who will sigh
To breathe and breathe the odors simply said,

Simply or subtly uttered, offered up
To one who lives or has lived like a sun
Solely illumining the day that flies

Like the light flowing, flown, or overrun.
Was nectar or was hemlock in the cup?
The lover lives. The lover's lady dies.

15. UN SECONDAMENTO

The terrible inclemency of death,
The dread unkindliness of destitution —
The one, November's thankless late solution,
The other, January's last chill breath —

Are in September second's gentler truth
Hardly a sliver of insinuation.
Sky's blue, earth's green, light's gold comprise a ration
Not niggardly of fruitfulness and ruth.

The silk tree still filled full of rosy bloom,
The rose of sharon purpling on the lawn,
Peach roses rampant by the picket fence,

Speak to the breezes of no stormy doom,
Speak to the evening of a rosy dawn.
Second them all, September, here and hence.

16. CHIAROSCURO

Out to the sky I flew through golden air
Before the sun could touch the equinox.
Before the sea could break me on the rocks
I broke through ocean's golden road, from where

I could descend, descend below the blare
Of stars' incessant harping magnavox
That played the ancient tune I would outfox.
Did I first catch that brief impassioned clair

De lune so lovely on the silvered waters?
Evading autumn, winter, evening, night,
I would dart farther, deeper, higher, nearer.

There was a realm ringed by the musing daughters,
Darker than darkness, luminous far past light.
There was a self closer than self and dearer.

17. NOTE AI SONETTI 1–16

Must we not welcome any monkey business?
Must we not let in any monkeyshine?
Are we not serious? We deal with isness,
Existence, essence, being, mine and thine

And all the world's and that of all creation
And of the uncreated and the sole,
The little impish bits of decoration,
The last unfathomed grandeurs of the whole.

We love the moonshine and we love the moon.
We love the reference. We love the word.
We love the fragile everlasting bloom.
We love the mocking of the mockingbird.

And we can tell the monkey from the ape
And listen to the nightingale on tape.

18. LO SVILUPPO

The plumpest plum was once the fairest flower.
The Herculean beech tree was a nut
Cradled with others in a husk yet shut.
Do we begin with beauty one fine hour

And grow to sapience, as sweet and sour
As the blue-purple fruit, or do we cut
Our way from truth beyond and, if, or but
To beauty, pearled and purple-verdant bower?

And do we not grow up or not grow old
If we extend our arms and reach and reach
But do not clutch that which we count as naught?

September seemed to us the age of gold.
The plum's blue bloom was beautiful. The beech
Bore food for paradise or food for thought.

19. TRASLATO

Is there an image for this mystery?
Is there a metaphor that represents
This love to tell how deep it is, how dense,
How high, how wide, how taut it is, how free?

Is there a symbol of this liberty?
Is there a myth of this experience
Of intellection, sense in every sense,
Infinitive: to touch, to taste, to see,

Perchance to hear with unsurpassable
Deliberate delight the promises
Of sirens promising Now know, now more,

Know more, to clench the intellectual
Beginning of cognition of what is,
Take the deep breath, and swim for that far shore?

20. LA RICERCA

Intensity, desire, exhilaration,
Yearning, fulfilment, exercise, repose,
Passion, abstraction, vigilance, daze, doze,
Accuracy, distraction, desperation,

Despair, hope, coldness, heat, imagination,
Vocabulary, wordlessness, praise, prose
At most prosaic, most poetic rose,
Recklessness, measurement, and delectation

Are fibers in the feathers of these wings,
Are feathers in the pinions of this flight,
Are feathers in the cap of one who makes it.

Is its success the finding of those things
That ever shimmer in the end of sight?
Is the quest prize to one who undertakes it?

21. L'OCCASIONE

When crestfallen they look every which way
Shirking the skirmish with the covert glance,
We inadvertently will look askance
Upon their tenements, but when each ray

Of fresh celestial yellow renders gay
Each haloed face of gold, a stately dance
Needing no motion happens. In the trance
That happens we are dancing, as are they.

Solemn or merry, planned or accidental,
Painful or plied with earth's unearthly joy,
These meetings mean. What is the casual?

Sunflowers hence are never sentimental
If sentiment is that which must alloy
The sensuous, the intellectual.

22. IL DISCORSO

Do not believe that I intend to preach.
If I appear before you here today
I know that I have nothing new to say.
Do not conceive that I intend to teach.

Muscular, proud, profoundest king of a beech,
Can you be crushed if I mew, bark, or bray?
Can you be crunched in my too swinish way,
Succulent, luscious, lustrous pearl of a peach?

Touching the trunk is drawing smooth gray power
Through flats of hands. The silvers, purples, greens
Color my soul. The reach becomes my reach.

Into my mouth what was the mind's white flower
Goes as the flashy, fleshy fruit. This means
Spirit and body echo through my speech.

23. O VOI CHE PER LA VIA D'AMOR PASSATE

O you who by the way of love may pass,
See if there can be pain like my great pain.
I must be confident I could attain
The object of my love except, alas,

For that hostility of cruel, crass,
And unrelenting agents. Will they deign
To spare, to favor me? Across the lane
One red leaf glowers on the sassafras.

If you are poor in pride you may not climb
Up the entrancing heights, called out grave space
From brooks, streams, rivers, seas around me curving.

And from the tides I heard the shout of time
Turning a stern and elemental face:
If you are certain you are undeserving.

24. IN SETTEMBRE LE ROBINIE DEL GIAPPONE A
    CAMBRIDGE NEL MASSACHUSETTS

Millions of prayer beads on pagoda trees
Were green beneath my fingers as I prayed.
I prayed in Latin, not in Japanese.
The greens were neither emerald nor jade

Nor jaded but alive. Was Latin dead?
I could have strolled the sidewalks of Japan,
But Latin on my tongue and in my head
Lived. I explained: I must pray as I can.

The rose of sharon on the evening's lawn
And morning glories on the avenue
Before gold noon and after golden dawn
Were bluest purple or were purplest blue.

I prayed they pledged the most superlative,
Alleged: Non morieris. You shall live.

25. PIANGETE, AMANTI, POI CHE PIANGE AMORE

The morning glories were the bluest blue
Each morning, but we buzzed by them to work
Ingloriously. Then is to live to shirk
The deepest duty? Is to be untrue

To the profoundest self survival? Few
Live by their life. Life for the lifeless clerk
Expires each day or he must be berserk.
Tears are concordant with the morning dew.

Do not be lachrymose. Do not lament.
The forenoon crawls away. The afternoon
Lumbers along. And life begins at five.

Snatch up the pen, for all the spirit pent
Within the alien will surely soon
Come home again, will surely come alive.

26. DEH PEREGRINI CHE PENSOSI ANDATE

Our world is green. Our leaves and lawns are green.
Our sun sits gold-throned in his azure hall.
Our flowers play the symphony of all
The orchestrated colors ever seen

At a September matinee. The keen
Crimsons, reds, scarlets, oranges, golds, forestall
The foliage and vibrantly enthrall
Eyes with bright freshness, while the sweet serene

Peaches, pinks, whites, and yellows take a part
With violets and indigoes and blues.
Alas, good pilgrims, can you without pain

Forsake all this for distance, have the heart
To drum gray roads to Rome with dusty shoes?
Alas, dear pilgrims, you go, I remain.

27. IN QUELLE PAROLE CHE LODANO

There is a mission. This is it: to praise
Lips that have spoken to the single soul
Alone in solitude and to the whole
Village or continent or globe in days

Long since long gone and in some present phase
Of clear September's brilliant barcarole
Of loss and gain and for some unknown goal
Glimmering dimly through the future's haze.

Love was the author of this lovely true
Romance, of words once uttered in the dark.
I think I understand now what they mean.

Rome called across an ocean just to you.
Her tongue is yours. And so you must embark.
You cannot praise what you have never seen.

28. L'8 SETTEMBRE: LA NATIVITÀ DI MARIA

All the greens gleam and glitter in the sun.
Patches of shadow loll upon the lawn.
The grassy glassy glister of the lawn
Patterned by shadow, silvered by the sun,

Is silver glister glittering in the sun.
Are some greens grassy shadows on the lawn?
The shades are argent rags along the lawn,
The blades argyric glistens from the sun.

A blade will cut, a sword will pierce your soul,
Your own soul, so that out of many hearts,
The hearts of many, thoughts may be revealed.

After a birth a death may make a whole.
Before a death births may play many parts.
Within a thought a thought may wait concealed.

29. POETA FUI

Kisses upon the doors! The houses fall.
The city falls. The women fix the doors.
The doors must fall since all the afts and fores
Are known. The poet told us of them all.

He skitters with the women through the hall.
He strolls in sandals the ensanguined floors.
The women fix their kisses and he pores
Over the silences behind the wall

Broken and left behind. He left behind
The women and the kisses. There they are.
They have not burned. The kisses still are burning.

And has he turned? And will he surely find
Our road for us? For us will he unbar
That gate? He leads us up this hill of yearning.

30. IL 12 SETTEMBRE: IL SANTISSIMO NOME DI MARIA

The poet needs no name, for he is he
Known as the poet. The philosopher
Is the philosopher. Philosophy
Gives him her name. It is not him or her.

Caesar is Caesar. Caesar is Caesar's heir.
He is no king. He rules in Rome and Russia.
He reigns eternally and everywhere.
We have no king but Caesar here in Prussia.

Julius is Julius. Julius is July.
The fifth month is not May. It is the seventh.
Splendid September, nominated by
Seven is ninth. The ninth is the eleventh.

Who is she whom an angel bends to greet?
They say her name is bitter. It is sweet.

31. DAL 13 AL 14 SETTEMBRE

Then did you see her? On this night you died
In the ninth month. O learned Alighieri,
May the pedantic scholar raise a query
To you perhaps now standing at her side?

September rests in all September's pride
Of gold and emerald and ruby berry.
September in New England, quick and merry,
Pops down the acorns that the squirrels hide.

O honored bard, may I, ashamed, uncouth,
Belated, pose my question: Am I wrong
If I suppose my quest can reach eleven?

Was there a truth beyond the poem's truth
Or sunken knowledge deep within the song?
Did you find Virgil after all in heaven?

32. VIRGILIA

Is there a price one finds too high to pay?
If the virgilia once from silver bars
Dangled a million pearls, a billion stars,
Ravishing as the Twins in latest May

Or as their peerless sister on a day
In June when Helen smiles and all war's jars
Grow quiet or as she who loved harsh Mars
In peace and unto peacefulness, but hay

Or straw now hangs on leaden rods like loot
Counted unworthy of gorilla powers
Ravishing earth and sky with guerresque might,

Remember that this precious straw is fruit
Seeded with countless mills of priceless flowers
Shimmering on beyond the end of sight.

FIORI TOSCANI

Cut flowers brought by the Italian girl
Stayed on my table, soft, sweet, bright, composed,
Precise, alive, expansive, and expanding,
As if her words remained, white trimmed with crimson
On long green sentences, as if her phrases,
Gathered in laughing meadows, came and stayed.
Savor them. They are pratal. They are florent.

LETTERA AL PROFESSOR FONTANELLA

> Forse lo stai aspettando
> Luigi Fontanella, "A te Mrs. Jones."

Well, yes, that is correct. Yes, I do wait
For him, or is it it? It is so late,
And what, or who, will sate?

You see you saw my eyes can never find
Rest or arrest. I wind and I unwind
The scarf designed, then signed.

The luminaries in the streets are leaves
Leaving their mansions. No, they are not Eve's
Red and gold fruit. Such peeves,

Much less my casual note and studied loans,
Must not blur laud through soft shades or sharp tones.
Yours, Angelina Jones.

Macaronic

> Quintus ab aequoreis nitidum iubar extulit undis
> Lucifer, et primi tempora veris erunt.
> Ovid, *Fasti*.

Naso, with you I read the ancient skies
And mire the shining Lucifer arise

Out of the ocean February ninth
And call it spring. Shall I then ask these both:

The snowdrops if they flourish in the snow,
Ai bucaneve se fioriscono?

MACCHIATO

> Writers on the history of science often convey the impression that when Galileo pointed the newly invented astronomical telescope at the heavens in 1609 he discovered or "saw" mountains on the moon. . . . Of course, he did nothing of the sort.
>
> I. Bernard Cohen.

If there can be no mountains on the moon
Can they be seen? How could there be a spot
Upon a sun conceived immaculate?
Will not a fire from heaven burn that rot?
Shadows may fall too late or come too soon.
Coffee is stained with milk and milk with dark
Brews for the nighthawk or the morning's lark.
Can our meridians glare upon the quark?
Shadows may fall late or descend at noon.

VIAGGIO-VILLAGGIO

BUON VIAGGIO

White we arise. The library grows gray.
What will you see? What will you have to say?
The pages flapped and flung us on our way.

PARCA-VILLAGGIO

In Honor of Mario Luzi

In March the road to Rome lies through New York.
Manhattan rises white, or is it gray,
Under the great gray wing, or is it white?

Are there three Fates? Then the first Fate lived there
Where the white spire shines silver near the sky.
That Fate became incarnate by the fountain.

Stuyvesant Park, though such a little place,
Held fountain, held small nonna, big bambino
Babbling, the stroller pushed, the water splashed,

A language splashed from grandma to boy baby.

No tongue addressed her thus. That liquid lingua
Was others', theirs, gray woman's, baby boy's.
She, infant, listened to the others' speech.

O native village, O dear little island,
They glimpse you, lifting Romeward as the white
And gray wing tilts. So many years have flown.

The first Fate is a whisper, is a wave
Not yet dispersed in the thick urban air.
The middle Fate, who dwells in Massachusetts

Sibylline, sitting in a cave of books
Wreaking large syllables upon the leaves,
Wresting wide words from well-turned folios,

Routed her through New York. The alate beast
Grumbles addio from its silver throat.
The third Fate waits in Rome, imperial.

She cooed. Huge pigeons flew across the park.

Trans World

A somehow earthier cloud swells in the sky.
What somewhat earthlier white rises below?
What puffs are peaks, what swelling is a cutting,
What massive vapors are what massive snows?
Crossing the Alps thus airily would be
Unworthy if the bird had not first flown
An ocean swelling into the truncation
Of night west of those Herculean posts.

UMBRA-OMBRA

> Cominciai allora una canzone . . .
>
> Dante, *Vita nuova.*

The major shade of altitudes, of mountains
Whose heights hoist, host, harbor a long cadenza
Of shadow lengthily unfurled with evening,
To some is the mirage of sandy fountains,
The rose that is mentition of a lens, a
Mockingbird's luscinious deceiving.
They are discovered grieving.
They are found freighted with anxiety.
Satanic in their fall, like Samson free
In their arising, fierce expansiveness
Of feral force of frightful strength, no less
Immortal if a part,
The natural, of it must die, they press,
Alive, against the encircling walls of art.

Quomodo sedet sola civitas . . .

DIVISION THREE
BRIDGE

Television

He walked from prison as the world looked on.
He spoke. We heard him speaking. If our throng

Can see so far, how can we stay so blind?
If our crowd is so close, how can we find

One free and not cry, childlike, home free all?
How separate a residence so small?

What was your cause so great for seeing Rome?
Liberty, said the slave, and free came home.

Grace

Deliver me from bulk and blood and pain,
Devote me to the good, the true, the sheen,
Love, O celestial, infinite, divine,
My longing and my laughter and my own,
O let me see, let me complete my tune.

Vergil/Virgil

To Virgil the virgilias are true.
Their rods are magical, their fillets white.

To Vergil the virgilias belong,
Verging on bloom as he once verged on song.

You thrill, virgilias, fill with lunar light,
And stand old dangling exquisitely new.

Thanksgiving

Blessed be the beech, blessed be this iron strength,
Green heroism, grand autumnal bronze,
This heir of vernal copper early poured,
This intimated silver, gilded glint,
Full final goldenness Novembrian.
Blessed be the books of blissful bookishness,
Tickets to anywhen, rockets to every wherever.
And can a nascent strand be sanctified?
Hallowed be language, antiquated, fresh,
O language fabulous, Aesopian.

Thesis

The tabulation seemed complete at last.
The shades were measured. Then the die was cast.

I've got that straight, I wrote. Now what line lies,
I said, to vision from the pedant's eyes?

LUCUS A NON LUCENDO

Shall I let pass the chopping of the oaks,
Five from the grove, selected for destruction
Like Jove's vast pillars tumbled for construction
Of edifices edifying folks

To whom these silent drums, gigantic hoax
Of hierarchic preacherly instruction,
Must predicate a damning of obstruction?
Am I the angry priestess who invokes

The thunder from the sudden space of sky
Cleared of its June-green leafiness and free
To rest upon arrest of June-soft grass

Before the earth gapes? Oh, the oaks were high.
The hole will be as deep. Shall I not see,
Or must I beg the guards to let me pass?

October Thirteenth

Release me from this tedium, this rage.
The prisoner slumps. The lioness's cage
Crazes the queen-gold lioness. Assuage
The pain of ice, the pain of fire, the wage
Of stunt, stump, stupor, frenzy, fury. Gauge
The gap: one late-sprung mockingbird on stage
As full choir, one full native maple's sage
And free and regal-ruby-golden age,
And the drab, trammeled autumn of my page.

November Fourth

Were the virgilias, are the virgilias, gold?
In her Miltonic blindness could she see
The dazzling aureation of the tree
Which, here and living, in my heart I hold

With her, there, elsewhere, never to be old,
And with her beech, not gold yet, yet to be
The treasure of November, history
Revisioned, revolutioned, bronze age rolled

Back to first splendor? On this day she left
This gilded shore. She bridged the Styx, I know,
With music, sanctity, and Latin. How

Could she not, there, though here of sight bereft,
See through the darkness, shine through the silence, row
The stream with gleam of golden lyre, fleece, bough?

PONS

Let me allonge along that line that leads to love and life and light

SECTION TWO
QUESTION AND ANSWER

Question and Answer

What is the answer? Yes, perhaps, or no.
What is the question? Will I ever go?

What are the city's names? Love, Flora, Rome.
Why will you go to Rome? For liberty.
What will you do when free? First find my home.
Why will you walk the ways? I want to see.
What will you sit and watch? Height's vast blue dome.

Will what is said be ever what is so?
What is the question? Will I ever know?

Versed Sine

Invenire vim lunae ad mare movendum.

To find the force of the moon to move the sea.
Thus Newton. To invent the strength of the sea
To sway the mind. To find the force of the mind.

To Bruce Bennett, Richard Rorty, Quintus Horatius Flaccus, et al.

> "... pip and squeak."
> Bruce Bennett, "To a Formal Poet."

A. SOUNDS OUT OF SEASON

1.

Then could I, undespairing, hope to be
   Wide-winged and feather-free,
Or is the far-flung flight denied to me,
   Pinioned by history?

2.

Was I air or, devoid of feathering,
   Turkey or, with each wing
Wide, duck imprisoned in the encircling ring
   Or swan about to sing?

3.

Free as a feather, light, oh, as light as air,
   Free, oh, so free from care,
Feeling the spread of my wings, I become aware
   Of what I am soon to dare.

4.

For after reason and the reasoned rhyme
   And reasonable rhythm, time
Himself attends me as I slowly climb
   Into the pantomime.

5.

The silence of the mutest swan may greet
    The silence of the feet
Unshod upon the grass, the last, discreet
Tapping of keys upon machines, the fleet
    Scratching across the sheet.

6.

Vision is out and conversation in.
    Seeing must cease and talk begin.
I saw the ghosts, the angels on the pin.
    Theory, once sight, is din.

7.

Can Janus speak at once from either mouth,
    Or does one voice come forth
To mingle only with the nasty north,
    One with the soothing south?

8.

And when you represented formal verse
    In phrases apt and terse
Was it your guess that plaint, defense, or curse
    Could be at best but worse?

9.

The starlings circled, circled, called, and cried
    That they would be enskied
Far from this winter which their black clouds pied.
    The starlings lied and lied.

B. RHYMES AND/OR REASON

1.

If, wordless and unenvisioned,
The nestlings lifted themselves one by one above my disinterested gaze,
Since I was neither marksman nor martyr,
Neither the artisan nor the artist nor the augur
Of the azure aviary as
The garden's golden goal,
The burnished birdlets and the green lean leaflets must have been,
Must have been
Reality or even merer dream,
Not the average zeal of all alliteration.

2.

Then do I aver that the age,
Which is my own,
Presents its list on the page,
Its menu along the screen,

Of — shall I call them fruits forbidden?
The alphabet begins, care-ridden:
Avocado, beef, and cheese,
Damnation hanging along the trees.

Arboreal ancestors aimed
Not just at apples.
Vision itself has maimed
The rollings, the distant ripples.

3.

O do not clear the sky.
The nebulous — O do not look up into the heavens.

If you were born in a planetarium you must stop the show.
The starry-eyed will bow their heads.

If you grew up in a museum, hurry, unlearn that
Do not touch.

If you have lived in a library, silenced, whisper, vocalize, start to shout.
The books are deafened and disappear.

O do not cry over disappearance.
Well, will it rain? Will you water the grass? Walk on the grass.

4.

When the figure became the figured
She knew that she was standing in the pool.

She should have known from the chill on her shins.
She should have known from the wetness around her legs.

It should not have been from the lying tears
Left from the meres of her eyes.

5.

Draw the curtain. Cry Encore.
What once was will be once more.
Give it just a little time
Out of sight and out of rhyme.

6.

Could it have been, noisily, the monetary, monitory honking of
   the gasoline-gobbling geese, rebounding from brick to brick,
   resounding from roof to roof, reverberating amid the chimneys,

Could it have been, pointedly, this Empire State Building, big
   bibbed baby standing radiant gazing into the companionable,
   companioning, blue-caped, maternal, heavenly sky,

Could it have been, conjointly, that Grand Central Station, bear
   and angel, with cubs of comers, with ghosts of goers, with kin of
   kindly constellation on constellation,

Which taught her, which brought her to learn of, to yearn for, the
   city, the citadel, the capitol, river-risen, hill-built, entraining
   termination, and the head and the empire and the center of the
   western webbing of the welling world,

Could it have been the new in the name of her glassy, glossy
   birthplace hometown that spoke of the old, that murmured of
   the eternal, that questioned whether, whether the essence of the
   future's fortune rested or stretched

Before her

Or had nested before?

7.

At Philippi your wings were clipped
   And so you wrote at Rome.
Of this long afterwards you quipped
   To Julius Florus. Gloom

Will in those early days have gripped
   The Julia Flora whom
You found a cow when she was stripped
   To just my line and chrome.

8.

If it is two thousand years since you were seen
    By fleshly eye, by Florus,
    By one of us, dear Horace,

Can it be two thousand years that you have lain
    With goddess Libitine
    Beneath the Esquiline?

If Cerberus saw and licked the wine-god's shin,
    You, too, saw Bacchus,
    Horatius Flaccus.

9.

If I shall see the virgins
    Ascend the holy hill
Where the deodar burgeons
    There I shall see you still.

C. ROUNDS IF NOT TREASON

1.

Will Julia

Marry Marius the martial
Or possibly Pompey the prime
Or teen-aged merry Marcellus
Or that trusty old Agrippa
Or tearful Tiberius tented like Achilles,

Commit adultery, or shall we call it treason?

Shall we speak of stepmothers, write romance or novels?

If you try to lift yourself on Pindar's pinions
You will give your name to a sea as Icarus did,

By falling.

But, Julus, Horace continues, you,
Since you, he must imply, can fly
With worthiest wing, can sing
Of Julia's father, martial, prime, august.

Julus, the fierce Fulvia's son,
Julus, Julia's father's sister's husband's son,
Julus, Julia's father's sister's daughter's husband,
Julus, Julia's husband's sister's husband,
Julus, Marcella's husband, or shall we call him
Jullus, the adulterer,
Is Antony's dashing, daring, consular, greater-plectrumed,
    epic-scrivening son.

Certainly he could dictate any script.

Why was Antony's name erased from the arches?

Julia's father's name might be changed to Janus.

Might Julia be the philosopher?

May Julia be the poet?

Did the poet, seeing Julia, forever forfeit the sight of Rome?

2.

Will Flora
Find the fig tree in the forum
Big with the living figs
Living with the big and living leaves?

In the evening
Would Julia be seen
By Flora by the statue by the tree?

Around the fallen capitals
Can the acanthus rise?

3.

Which cliff is the Tarpeian?
Has it slipped, slid, slithered down the hill?
Has it rumbled from one summit to another?
Which miss is Tarpeia?
Traitress to father and to fatherland?
Nocturnal savioress of assaulted Rome?
The bolted gate is opened.
The enemy will enter by this track.
The golden shields are piled upon her body.
They lie. She is divine.
The goddess glitters from her shrine.
The city glints. She whispers, "It is mine."

4.

The proofs will follow
Or else the refutation.
The thesis as hypothesis
Will later be the dissertation.
Can I descry, describe, and guide
From this profound outside?
Or can I tell or tell you what is true
When all is in view and nothing is in view?

5.

If tarradiddlediddle is my forte
And whitest marble vision is my goal
Will ocularcentricity distort
My dazed and dazzled journey to the pole,
My crazed half sail half oarage into port?

6.

I will not try myopic telescopes
To call the Calends when the moon unhides
Nor tempt those presbyopic microscopes
To probe the temples lighted by the Ides.

What truth is this that shimmers into view?
O vision, vision, vision! Let me see!
Is this a conversation? Is this you
And you and you and, in this instant, we?

7.

I could be cygneous
Or gallinaceous.
I might be aquiline
Or olorine.

Can you then speak to me?
And will I then resound the mi-
Ra of your gests? Or change my do re mi?

Or change my ABC?
But will I be at sea?
But will I see?

Is that the foghorn, this the ring
Of the air-clear bell?
And then will I tell everything?
And then will everything tell?

8.

And will the grandeur of my wings betray
The grandeur of my gaze, for I shall know
What swans see and what soaring eagles say
To Jove and what old Saturn plans to sow?

9.

Infinite Beauty, render beautiful
The flesh, the intellect, the poetry

Of one who holds the triple miracle
The gift by which thy gift is rendered thee.

Bestow that health which must assume its part
In heady climbs to science and to art.

Even a liturgy thus purged and plain
Fails. Can an unmysterious rhyme sustain

The poem? Does the tulip glare too red?
Will you select the hyacinth instead?

The prayer, the charm, the vow shall bear this shape:
O fig, O olive, O sunned, shadowed grape,

Exist, live, grow in green, in leafiness,
And verdant or empurpled through each small

Expanding orb that adds to mere success
Dazzling urbanity that hazards all.

D. TIMES WITH THE TEASE IN

1.

If you would answer we might well converse.
You spoke, and I replied, and that was all.
I, ever rusty, listened in the fall
To words that March had labored to disburse

Through reams of August into autumn's purse
Which twinkled with the golden coins that call
Their estimates across the urban sprawl
And dwindling fields through which the gilded hearse

Travels the amber track of time. And now
Will winter whiten into that great lie
Burying purple soundlets out of view

(I should say, out of hearing), or, somehow,
Will utterance that must be mine or I
Surge with the snowdrops into yours and you?

2.

But to be worthy of the conversation
Will one have learned the language, played the game,
Stridden along the stage, embraced acclaim,
Wresting the least satanic connotation,

Wrestling the most angelic concentration,
From pit or bleachers, infamy or fame,
Bull's ear, wild curved boar's tail, a sheep's most tame
Curl, or those curling anthems from the nation

Of birds that settle or from birds that pass
As though a momentary note could say
Enough for ecstasies of sun or sorrow?

I hear fine droplets light upon the grass.
Must prized pearls, must praised daisies, win today
The accolade of welcoming tomorrow?

3.

Vendere: scendere;
Vivere: scrivere;

O

To love: to live;
To do: to die;
To save: to sieve;
To see: to say: to sigh:

L'infinito: the infinitive.

4.

To hear or to have heard or else to hope
That from the glitter-gleam of silver speech
Nutlet will find itself gigantic beech
Or, to effect a turning in the trope,

Silvery strands will twist themselves to rope
Both long enough and strong enough to reach
And grip the branch from which each thread and each
Connection linking threads sustains the scope

Inherent in the activated swing
Becomes the subject. Will the finite verb
Convey, although beloved elms were felled

For failing at the testing of the spring,
If others spread above campaign and curb,
The messages which lengths of summer held?

5.

Why do I say what only seems to jar
Those who might want to hear what I might say
If I could sink my silver into gray
Or raise up out of mud a golden bar?

Why does the tree rise proudly as a czar
And reach across the overshadowed way
If those who pass compel the tree to pay
For greenest sovereignty with blackest scar?

Why does the bird lift to the distant star
Cantatas which the sleepy neighbors pray
Will terminate before impatient day
Tethers bronze horses to the golden car?

Why do I love what only seems to bore
Those who might want to glean what I adore?

6.

Listen, Letitia, lover of that breath
That sweeps upon you silently from skies
That offer you, before the body dies,
Balms that desiderate the body's death.

Visions, Letitia, greet you on the path
That climbs to summits where the mortal eyes
Widen like cornets wreathed to solemnize
Instants of sempiternal aftermath.

Morsels of matter let the vision live.
Bits of the earthy dark arise to feed
The spirit's lightest breathings. O, consent

To bend and take the particles that give
Strengths that the highest chiming wingbeats need.
The body is the spirit's instrument.

7.

I said that I would do it. Did I state
I would have done it? Did I then await
A future or a past

Or something that would last
Longer: the future in the past, the late
Lingering tempo, tense with time's strange date?

8.

I beat my breast, I, hypocrite auteur.
I listened, yet I listened just enough
To scrape from erudition's pile the fluff.
O speak more loudly through the veils, ma soeur.

Then is the mea culpa de rigeur
Or may I plead the denseness of the stuff
That intervenes, tied scarf or handled muff,
Between the hearer and the cri de coeur?

If I had understood a little more
Would I have curved my fist around the throttle
Of my response and not crouched here alone

Fitting my phrases neatly to the drawer,
Crushing my clauses deeply down the bottle,
Leaving my sentence on the telephone?

9.

You said this, you said this, and you said this,
And you said this and that, and you and you
Said that. And were there others, more or few,
Who said some other thing, and did I miss

The ones whose contradictions raised a hiss
Throughout the throng? Did someone give a view?
Did one or many tell us what was true?
Did any doom us down the deaf abyss?

We gathered at the banquet on the hill.
We stretched our hands to bread and reached for wine.
We gathered there for better or for worse.

We banqueted till all had had their fill.
We talked. We talked unendingly. Come, dine.
Come and converse with us. Come and converse.

E. BOUNDS THAT LET BREEZE IN

1.

The sonnet sent by electronic mail
Offers itself to its recipient
Perhaps as purely an impediment
To conversation on the sober scale

That holds the future and that must prevail
Over the weights and measures prevalent
In centuries profoundly different,
When convents kept their nuns within the pale.

When castles kept their queens and their queens' daughters
Within the battlements securely zipped,
Would I have held a feather in my hand

For fingered flights across a manuscript
Or scribbled with a pebble on the sand
Or rippled rhythms into ebbing waters?

2.

If from her head they snatched the sacred veil
And if they pulled the pure ring from her hand
Shall we confess that we misunderstand
Their times? Shall we acknowledge that we fail

To read the heart beating beneath the mail,
Compute the mind beneath the miter, and
Inscribe within our righteous reprimand
Our times in paragon? The jealous jail

That holds our sisters holds the holders of
Its key. Did fathers, uncles, brothers bind
Piccarda panting for the chosen part,

Costanza constant to the holiest love,
Her ring the radiant halo of her mind,
Her veil the somber guardian of her heart?

3.

It was an error, for my pious hand
Could not have torn that sweetness from the tree.
I walked with one who robbed that sweet for me.
I held the lilac which that loveliest land

Lifted to us. I held that we were banned
From violation. He maintained that he
Who walked among the blossoms must be free
To take and keep. I held the smoking brand.

The fragrant exhalation which it gave,
No, every scent which echoed in that air
From every branch which flourished into fume,

Was sigh, was sign, was speaking. Could you bear
To lacerate your mother? Does the bloom
Droop? Will the lilac drop into a grave?

4a.

If I should tell you you could not believe.
The forest bristled and the forest groaned.
The black leaves whistled and the white twigs moaned.
If you should snap a branch you could retrieve

A truth. The meaning, if I could conceive
A merest meaning, merely was postponed
As my mind slowly, slowly, slowly owned
What my hand, hesitating, could achieve.

I plucked a twiglet from the trunk. A gruel
Dripped forth its syllables. You could not gain
A knowledge of its words just from my verse.

Through wounds alone could man turned plant converse.
Could the guide master poet then be cruel?
Or did he know that speech is worth the pain?

4b.

She grabbed it with her hand or with her foot.
But if her arms were wings the monstrous claw
Must have evolved on legs to let her put
Her mug into the mass that stuffed her maw.

The ravenous voracity that craves
The ravenous voracity that gluts
The ravenous voracity that raves
Is gluttony that satiates the guts

Aging insatiable. The greed that grasps
At gold is ancient, famed. The holy hunger
That like the newest nestling gapes and gasps
To know is older and forever younger.

Will she hear, see, talk, master alphabets?
Oh, will the sun come out before it sets?

4c.

My feet now stand at last upon the top.
My hands, that helped me often at the start
When, timely quadruped, I bore the smart
Of stubborn steep upon my forepaws, stop.

Only my eyes move now. My hands may drop
Until that aftertime when my hand's art
Will strive to scrive on parchment what my heart
Records here from my eyes. No further prop

Is necessary to sustain the sight
Or the sight's monuments. The purple finch
Dawns on the bough. The budding noontide roses

Warm gold and rose and gold. Fresh violet light
Rings lilac, lavender, last hyacinth.
The vision opens, and the codex closes.

5a.

The pacifist who falls in love with Rome
Is tortured by a passion unbenign
And born beneath the Castors' double sign.
Both Mars and Venus splashed with Tiber's foam

The rosy youth who bloomed in royal dome:
Pallas descending from the Palatine,
Pallas advancing through the battle line,
Pallid Pallas carried as ashes home.

Is there no truce? Is one to be content
To wage or to endure eternal war
Or suffer or enjoy a Roman peace?

If Janus has two faces, one is bent
Upon the world. The other cannot cease
To glimpse the universe of metaphor.

5b.

The persons may be second, third, or first.
The terms may be divergent or the same.
Aeneas may not be the proper name.
I am the Dante whom Firenze nursed.

I am the Dante whom Firenze cursed.
I am the man who went to hell and came
Back from the brightness of celestial flame
Unblinded. Pity once kept my lips pursed.

Connections can be purest persiflage.
The thinker as the scribbler may be weak.
The dreamer and the poet are distinct.

The author and the agent are not linked.
What self indwells the pious personage
Who only speaks to say he cannot speak?

5c.

Will it be Rome if at the swampside shrine
I find the goddess or the goddesses
Celebrated on that narrow line
Where the sun stops? The celebration is

The debt of death, the credit of a choice
Of a great conversation, a conversion
That from the bandaged mouth returns a voice
That from the narrow passage flaunts emersion,

The moral of a more that follows less,
The lessons of December twenty-first,
Concentration and expansiveness,
The dark constriction and the bright outburst,

Angerona and Volupia,
Pain of today and pleasure of, ah . . . , ah . . .

5d.

The first city was not the final one.
We built its walls. Its name endures today
As Aenus from my own. We did not stay.
The bleeding bush exhorted us to run.

Copernicus will send us to the sun.
The center must await the émigré.
We launch, and lands and cities move away.
So might the vision slip from the kneeling nun.

The virgin's veil became the scholar's hood.
The vow yielded the hope that holds in view
The doubtful and the unequivocal.

Poverty is selection of the good,
Obedience submission to the true,
Chastity rapture by the beautiful.

5e.

The mother of my home god has her home
Here. Will examined witnesses prove wrong?
And can her habitation rhyme with Rome,
Where I have never walked? The road is long.

The road has been so long. The twenty-third
Sun of the year's last moon is here, and now.
And now is here. Here is forever heard
Calling afar from near the distant plow

That liberates the city from the marsh
And promises the building of the wall
Which separates the city from the harsh
Regime of Mars. Mother, will here still call?

When the priest calls the Calends from the hill
Will I be there to hear or be here still?

5f.

What is that crash? The narrow room is thick
With forest. From the floorboards to the ceiling
Brusque spines, shoots, shrubs, trunks, trees have sprung, concealing
Wall, window, bookshelf, table, chair. Each stick

Barricades each. Solidity. A flick,
A flicker, is unthinkable. Revealing
The limitations of all thought and feeling,
The supervention, in an augenblick,

Of that vast mind-ear-earth-shattering crash
Suffers supervention. What is that crack?
What is that wild and horrend boarlike strage?

What is that plant ensanguined from the gash?
Who is that person under that attack
Wracking his personhood? I turn the page.

5g.

If Pallas died to give the eagle sway
Can we deny that Dante comprehends
How the long story of Aeneas ends?
For Rome was not constructed in a day.

On the great battlefield the young man lay
Slain by the enemy who made amends
By being slain. Destruction simply tends
Towards its own deconstruction. Far away

Force its fierce condestruction. Reap at home
After the final Twelve the sacred spelt
Sown in Book Ten and watered in Eleven.

If Pallas died to sanction holy Rome
Can we deny that Dante knew and felt
The lit crit and the politics of Heaven?

6a.

Big-bellied, starving Harpies made the rents
With their clawed, clawing feet that let the breeze
Of utterance release disharmonies
For which the lacerations were the vents.

Their necks were human, and their long laments
Were strange but human in the stranger trees.
The trees were human, and their miseries
Wintered civilization's discontents.

There was no path around each brambly patch.
There was no way for any wayfarer.
I recognized the spined amphiboly.

Was I the hunter? I the easy catch?
Was I the pilgrim, stranger, foreigner?
Was I the bird? Was I the talking tree?

6b.

The Latin lamentations of the leaves
Had grown from human throat, and they were mine.
The English expletives around the eaves
Were screamed by harpies of another line.

The Latin lamentations were the howl
Of one who loved the umbra of the elm
But whose eruptions ever were found foul,
Corruptions of the vegetable realm.

The harpy, starving starling, winged debris,
Hooked hands and clawed with feet upon faint fame,
Proprietor or tenant of the tree
Named elm of daydream. Why contest the name?

Landlady Malaprop, despising starlings,
Evicted them but always called them darlings.

6c.

Will there be enemies? Must there be war?
Is it at my own feet that Turnus lies
Turning that supplicant hand, those supplicant eyes,
While these eyes roll and this hand sticks before

Swordbelt and sword determine either-or?
The bad but breathing barrier now dies,
The grand and good and godly goal will rise.
Does the famed savior face the savage boar

In bannered combat, final, fine, and thorough?
And does the fated founder grasp and solve
The problem of the blessing and the curse?

The plow turns at the furling of the furrow.
The roll must roll, the volume must revolve.
The end is not the ending of the verse.

7.

Shall I be silent? Shall I explicate?
Does terror render loud or render mute
The prophetess attentive to the root
From which deterrent phrases sanguinate

And to the boughs that bleed the words of fate?
Blood was the price here of a priceless loot.
Blood is of blood this solitary fruit.
You will devour your table with your plate.

Gathering branches for the sacrifice,
I heard the proclamation of despair.
The term, term of my feet, Rome stayed in scope.

In Rome the terrifying tableware
Could be the crunchy, thick, delicious slice
Of bread that bases banqueting on hope.

8.

Therefore look well, for that way you will see
Things that would make you doubt my conversation,
Said bard to bard. The visive revelation
Kept coming on the feet of poetry

That walks and talks with such as you and me,
Enticing eyes, requiring auscultation,
Taking my hand, propelling your oration,
Rendering Polydore and Peter free

To speak of plantedness. The insite force
Of rest and movement is rush and repose
Of sight and converse. Drink the deeper fount.

Not only whirlpools but that gleaming course,
Not only prickles but this purpled rose,
Not only headlines but a verse may count.

9.

I am ensnared. My words cannot be bought,
But I am helpless. You compel reply.
One whom their francs and florins could not buy
Your utterance alone has called and caught.

The net of text entwined, entwining, ought
To bind. It binds the feet. It frees the cry.
It forces song. It frees the song. And I,
Unpaid and uninvited and unsought,

Tin drummer, brazen trumpeter, I dare,
O ancient mellow ones, O great though gray,
O grand and solid silver, sterling, true,

O great and golden, burnished, burning, fair
Darlings, strong, eminent — what shall I say? —
If I can talk at all to talk to you.

Martial 8.69

Miraris veteres, Vacerra, solos
nec laudas nisi mortuos poetas.
Ignoscas petimus, Vacerra. Tanti
non est, ut placeam tibi, perire.

Professor, you admire the classics only
And praise no poet if he isn't dead.
Professor, please forgive me. It's not quite
Worth it, to make your canon, to expire.

Question and Question

Is there a trail which I must soon discover?
Is there a tale of which I am the sleuth?
Did the doves eat the crumbs of evidence?
How shall I ever reach the Rome of truth?

Shall I begin the grand detective story
In this place, at this time? Is vision dead?
And must I apprehend the murderer?
And must I apprehend? Rome lies ahead?

SECTION THREE
VISION

January

Janus sees both ways. My eyes fixed on Rome
From his high hill.

            Record the hour.

                            The years
Mingle, the places waver, the seasons spin.

Can I remember? Daughters of Memory,
Tell me.

        It was the newest new year's day.
I strolled along the ridge. The plane trees strode
Beside me and the lighthouse looked with me.
I strolled? My feet moved slowly. My whole frame
Was taut. My feet moved slowly. My each breath
Was like a runner's. As I walked I gazed.
I gazed? My eyes moved slowly. My eyes fixed
Upon the seen unseen, the unknown known.

I think it was ten thousand years ago.

                 * * *

Beyond the mountains does Homeric dawn
Walk slowly towards us in her satin gown
Of rose, robed in her saffron mantle, stretching
Her slender arms, her long and slender fingers
Outward and upward towards the eastern slopes,
As yet unseen? And do the Roman ghosts
                                        Retreat

Retreat or do their ruins rise around them
Reconstituted for the festive day
As feline night reluctantly withdraws,
Smooth, soft, silk-soft, upon her leopard paws
Of darkness, of despair, of nullity?
The leopard was not granted even hope,
Yet, from that night of screams, of silences,
A song, not facile, not too easy, lifts
Into the windless air. The poet sits
Scrivening at the desk, then with a shriek
Falls to the floor, then cries, You sleep in peace.
I do not sleep. The poet dreams I sleep.
Must such a dark, a gray, a hoary age
Waken to horror, hope, or holiness?
Will dawn come as the crocus comes in spring,
As, when, as when the fist releases fingers
In minutes, hidden August gold unfolds,
Unwraps itself from clasping bud, expands,
Widens before my wondering widening eyes,
Spreads petals while green sepals, one by one,
Drop back, perceptibly is spreading petals,
Is spreading, stirs in present participles,
Visibly, quickly, palpably, perceived,
Being perceived, is in the act of spreading,
Is spreading, moves, comes up, comes on, comes out,
As stars come out, as city lights come on,
As baby crawls across the rug and grasps
My skirt and stands, pulling with pygmy hands
And pushed by puissant forces from within
That little cuddly stubborn mass, as ticks
Signal the instants, as the indicators
Of seconds slip across an arc of clock,
The evening primrose opens into evening?
Did bees plunge in to plumb sweet amber depths?
Will Venus lull to sleep or lure to waking?
Does everything except the passing pass?
My eyes were made for vision, not for tears.
Twilight, swart night's precursor, is its sequel.

The holiday

The holiday approaches, azure, gold,
Like morning-glory morning, sunflower summer.

On the day named the fifth before the Ides
Of January, January ninth
As counted forward from the month's beginning
Rather than reckoned backward from the middle,
The king of hallows in the king's own place
Offers the offering, the sacrifice,
The host, the victim, the agonia.
How can I speak of Agonalia?
Will the day bear us what we cannot bear?
The sky is cloudless and the twilight clear.
This is not agony but celebration.
The language is the veil, the revelation.

King, do you wake and watch? Wake, watch, O king.

Like pines on Ida choiring to the breeze,
Like ships on Tiber singing to the spray,
Like mermaids calling, calling from the sea,
The girls and women of the sacred fire
Call before sunrise. There are only six.
They live next door. They file along the road.
But can they be the daughters of the king,
And is their residence a part of his?
Which year has opened? Is the king the king,
Or is he merely priest? Like Christmas carols
This chanting in a January dawn
Rings shrill and sweet through air both sweet and chill
Yet mellows into melon melodies,
Yet mellows into melodies of melon
Like luminescences upon Mount Alban,
The shades of dark that are the shades of light
In south and east as igneous day ascends
The unseen slopes and nears the waiting cave,
The hollowing that is the hallowing
Of hills and plains that rest along the river,
Where we must rest no longer. Must that fire
Warm or warn, alarm or comfort us?

Is it, for sleep and silence and the dark,
A vigil's graduated intonations,
First bursts, faint phases, traces, trails, and trills,
Is it the banal strange albanal things,
Persistent slight prematutinal things,
Is it the dinging things, the dithering things,
Is it the ringing clock, the twittering birds,
The birds of dream, of dawn, the bells of churches,
Is it the famous virgins that I hear,
The famous virgins vested in their veils,
The vestals draped, enfolded like the brides
They are, not for an hour or afternoon
But for the decades of the vow that binds?

Something seeps from sleep and wakes to day.

This structure is, according to the sign,
A public house, but it is not a pub,
Just as a bar in Rome is not a bar
At breakfast when you quaff the frothy cup
Of cappuccino and consume the puff
Of the cornetto. Fittingly equipped
With chaplet and with cornet, little hood
And little horn, the soldier and the scholar,
The priest, the prince, the poet may proceed
Into the day, the fray, the yea, the nay,
Strengthened to tread the broad or straitened way,
Fortified by the force of rest and motion,
The swirl and swell, the currents and the curves,
The surges that are still, the pond and mound,
The pool and knoll, the well and hill, the dark
And light, the light and dense, the ropes and ripples,
The bulge that has a beauty and the froth
That has a meaning, spread and fold of foam
And fold and spread of pastry, with the crisp
That is the soft, the strong that is the mellow,
The plump that is the elegant, the rich
That is simplicity, the hot and black
That is the white and mild. One may conclude,
Scooping

Scooping from the cup the dregs of steam,
Licking from the napkin crumbs of crust
Subtle with sweetness. One may terminate
The grace of the collation and begin.

If you begin upon the hill of Janus,
King of beginnings, why not choose my route?
Past the loud fountain, past the yellow rock,
The one a Paul's, the other one a Peter's,
I swung along, and then I picked my way
Descending the nameless irregular set of steps
Narrowly curving towards the road's wide curve,
Where the cars curve and whir and whirl upon you.
Down nameless steps, then down the stairway named
The Ramp of Golden Mountain I descended
Under the locust trees once sweet with May,
Now lopped and low. The wider, white-tipped stairs
Wind to the street wherein pagoda trees
Dreamed over worry beads of August glories.
This street is Godfrey Street, which one must cross
To Lightsome Way, or Motorcycle Road,
Which, followed all its length, led raucously
To Thickets of Transtiber Street, which met
Great plane trees on Transtiber Avenue.
Along, across, the avenue I strode,
Then turned into each Little Longer Road
And passed the Lane of Light upon the left
And passed the Street of Light upon the right
And reached Along the Tiber and that pole
Whereat you pause or perish. You must push
The pulser, practice patience. Then the green
Word was beckoning to cross the street,
Was beckoning at last to cross the bridge,
To cross the river swelling green or swirling
In white and brown, a grander hood and horn,
The Tiber, coffee-brown and milky white,
Tiber, Tiber, swerving bright and gold
In the city of a night grown old,
Curving, swirling, swelling by the banks
                                            Where

Where plane trees surge and flake in white and brown.
Leaving the fourfold Janus at the end,
Or is it the beginning, of the bridge,
I pressed another button and advanced
By triple-templed Janus, Juno, Spes,
A knowledge like a faith, a love, a hope
Spurring me on against, across, the current
That curved along the stream of street and flowed
Along the whirring river of the road.
Thus, passing through the arch of pepper gray
Of the triumphal portico, I took,
Between Carmenta's song and Fortune's call,
Yoking Street and Consolation Way
To the gray gate that waited there apart,
Unmarked, obscure, but open. I went in.

The path was rough with roots and pointed stones
Scattered in mud. I staggered and I stumbled
Along the narrow downward sloping way
Bordered by deeply, sweetly leafy laurel
Above the amplitude of the acanthus.
I passed along the grandeur of the path.
Long-leaved acanthus and the long-lived laurel
Lined the rustic mud and dust that led
To Tuscan Street, Etruscan Street, its slabs
Smooth, large, flat flagstones, Roman paving stones
Of basalt, gray on further dust and mud
There where Vertumnus turned the Tiber's flood
And turned from form to form, from self to self,
A Tuscan god on Tuscan Street, of whom
A statue stood in maplewood, of whom
A statue shone in bronze, both here, for whom
A temple cannot add to bliss, for whom
It is enough to see the Roman Forum.
To see the Roman Forum is enough.

It was enough for me. I pressed ahead
Past Acca's tomb, edged by the ancient swamp
And honored as a people's monument
                                                    To matron,

To matron, patron, benefactor, friend
Of Rome, Larentia, mother of the Lares,
Larunda, celebrated recently
In that near year forever old, awaiting
Distant December's new and distant end.

Brilliant divinities of dim December
I glimpsed on glancing down the old New Road
At Angerona and Volupia,
Protectors of the city's potent name.
But it was January. I had turned
Left onto Tuscan Street, where I could set
Foot on a sequence of existent things,
My very pace on pavement, actual
Step on a stretch of actuality,
Stratum of ancient street, solidity
I saw, I trod, I was supported by.
Could I yet sense the sails, the slosh, the marsh,
The oars, the currents, and the watercourse?

It was so cold the woman could not wade.
The ferryman was shouting: All aboard.
The vehicle that pushed off from the shore
Went where I was not going. I remained.
If the Velabrum was a working stream
Or held a navigable element,
Sometimes less effective, sometimes more,
Sometimes more intrinsic, sometimes lent
More by the river flowing to the sea
And, like some fate sewing a cumbersome
Deviant from an ordinary seam,
Overflowing to fill up this slow mere,
As part at least of its aquosity,
I could embark some other day or year.
The vector of my pilgrimage had come
Into one space from any, every, time.
Day might now break on water or on rock,
On ripples or on furrows, lake or loam,
On landscape drained or river with no dike,
On formless marsh or on a marble form.

Straight and high upon the eastern sky
The triple pillars in white elegance,
The Castors' columns, elegant in white,
Glistened above Juturna's Lake, the pool,
Unseen behind the podium but known
(The visible and the invisible
Mixing in any vision of a whole,
As in Juturna's basin, full or dry),
Finished in marble, fed from living founts,
At which the twins' twin horses drank. I soon,
Having turned left on Tuscan Street, turned right,
Entered upon the passageways of white,
And, climbing up the two high steps of white
(If I remember every step aright),
Traversed the walkway white beneath the white
Augustan Actian Arch, whence, on the right,
Filling the lacuna in my sight,
I glimpsed Juturna's pond, then passed the white
Shrine of fire. This was the circular,
The round, the tholic, and the focular
Temple of Vesta, lately built anew
By Empress Julia the Philosopher.
Even a sacred flame may burn things down.
Even a holy fire may deconstruct.
Even a woman may then reerect
The furnace where six priestesses attend
A center and a focus and a hearth
From which a virgin mother spreads her warmth
And radiance to city and to earth,
Urbi et orbi, east, west, south, and north.

I had come from the west and from the north.

I had come tramping over Roman roads,
Had stepped from stone to stone on Roman streets.

Which stones were moved in eighteen ninety-eight?
Which pavements were remade in nineteen one?

If I were fire, the world would feel too cold.
If I were wind, no flag could ever fly.

If I were

If I were water, oceans would be dry.
If I were god, eternal would mean old.

Were I the pope, lambs bleating in the fold
Would be the piglets squeaking in the sty.
Were I the president, the doves would vie
In violence when hawks were put on hold.

If I were death, no mortal would be dead,
If life, no leaf would green upon the tree.
If I were Cecco, he would go unread.

If I were Julia, as I cannot be,
And all her sentences had gone unsaid,
Flora would say all this instead of me.

Julia existed once, that fly-by-night.
Flora rejoices in ten trillion dawns.

The world remembers me as Flora Baum.
Rome makes me Julia Flora of the Tiber.

But I had crossed the Tiber and the tide.

At the little chapel of the Lares,
Guardians of our city and our homes,
Watchers of our walls and of our walks,
Our ways and crossways, I first hesitated.

I looked down Vesta Lane that slanted left.
I gazed upon the vestals' residence
With entrance quite inviting on the right.
Which way should I select? Then straight ahead
I glimpsed a hidden path beyond the trees,
Beside, beyond, the little laurel grove
All green up to the corner where the gray
Bare bagolaro, hackberry to those
Who know its cousin in the distant west
Beyond the sea, beyond the ocean, rose
Rooting in rock, a spaccasassi tree,
A wintry tree, a city tree, survivor
Of urban worlds of shock and stone and scree.

Where there are two ways are there always three?

Standing above us with your watching eyes,
Discerned above me by my wavering eyes,
O Lares, sacred twins who stand in stone
In your twin-columned shrine, your dog in stone
Faithful, alert, attentive at your feet,
Lares, who wake and watch, who watch my feet,
Lares, who stand before my crucial ways,
Whose tutelary eyes regard our ways,
Guard me and guide me, Lares Praestites.

Where would the vestals exit? Would they step
Forth virginal and ceremonial
Out of their monastery by the shrine
From which the Lares watched? Then should I go
Closer and fix upon the convent door
My earnest eyes, my worrying, querying eyes,
My questioning eyes? Directions old and new
Perplex perception. Regularity
Suggests itself, and yet the grand facades
Stretching north-west, south-east, inexorably,
Inevitably, in massive repetition,
Meet in the east-west walls a contradiction.
Did I expect the virgins to emerge
Out of the first, the old, the literal
Orientation, old, so old, or out
From newer old alignments, lasting, last?
It did not matter. It was manifest
That I must look for something on the right.

King, do you wake and watch? Wake, watch, O king.

I heard the virgins then, and it was dawn.
It was, if not quite day, the verge of day,
Finale of the vigils of the dark.
I caught sight of the vestals to my left.
I saw them on the left, already leaving
The stretch of Vesta Lane for Holy Road.
I glimpsed them in the dimming of the dark.

Veils

Veils glimmered in the glinting of the day.
Their veils and mantles shimmered. Should I follow,
Shivering with excitement and the cold,
Hurrying on behind them down the lane
And onward towards the portal of the king?
Should I not follow when the vestals sing?

Should I, in speed, in eagerness, the equal
Of Juno and Minerva, in the scurry
Of that stern urgency, and in haste like
Iris and Ilithyia, on that mission
To birth, not battle, not death's but life's labor,
Rush, almost run, a scudding dove, a pigeon
Nimble and quick and swift?

                              O wake and watch.

Should I report what I have heard and seen?
Did this occur on January ninth?
It was a certain day, but was it that one?
And did they sing, or did they merely speak?
It was those words. I seem to hear them sung.
It was those sentences. I sense a tune.
It was some day, a day which I remember.
It was one dawn, a dawn which I recall.
I tell what I remember, not what is
Or was. I know I tell what I recall.
I only know I say what I remember.

How did I reach the royal residence?

I chose the shortcut, chose the middle way,
The third alternative, the secret passage,
The private way that is the public path.

Beyond the hackberry and bayberries
That rose among the stones upon the left,
And, on the right, the first compartments rising
In files of brickwork over squares of grass,
The marble of each ornamental pond
Was shining like a piece of moon. I crossed

                                      Between

Between the two small pools. As I approached
The portico of travertine and marble,
The partly columned, partly semicolumned
Arcade, the shafts were turning red, bright red,
The channel as it ran in front turned blue,
Stucco covered travertine and air,
The patch of marble pavement of the porch
Started enlarging, spreading till it slid
Beneath my soles. The jolt was minimal.
I stood on marble, peering down the hall.

I tell you what I saw that day, that year,
Not what was seen ten thousand years before,
Not what the next millennia made clear.
What I observed in nineteen ninety-eight,
What I recall of that which I observed,
What of what I remember I relate,
What you receive of that which I record,
If you exist or if you will exist
Or if I speak to gods and ghosts alone
And if, O spirits and divinities,
My vocatives are pure apostrophes
And you now never you but they or none
And I who was content to be the mist
Exuding living lines, if lines can live
And filter issued selves filling their sieve
And I be they and you encounter one
Who in them speaks, who speaks to you, now give
My life to air, I wonder if you hear.

Antiquity came easily. I came
Close to the stone. Antiquity came close.
I breathed, sneezing, millennia of stone.

The end was apsidal, but to the left
As I went in I found a frescoed nook,
I gathered from the fragments that remained.
The fragments were expanding. Wreathes of laurel
Began to grow in paint upon the walls
And on the emptiness above the walls.

Then I was in the hall, in the great room
That fronted on the western portico.
The apse that rendered elegant the east
One reached upon a dusty, sagging floor
Paved in mosaic, dingy white and black,
Patchy, with pieces gone. The walls shrank back.

The emptiness was empty once again.
Where there was something it was something less.
The stucco, come unstuck from stone and show,
Fell off, evanesced. I looked around
Uncertainly, back towards the travertine
Pavement that stretched west of the portico.

No, that was gone before it could appear.

And then upon this west an extra building
Of which the portico was suddenly
The eastern close rose. It sank. A moment
Put it up. A moment brought it down.

Hence is the portico the eastern end
Of something grand to which my eyes are blind,
Or is it, as it feels, the western edge
Of what I see, of what so long I saw?

The portico that ran due north and south
Feels like a sort of threshold on the west,
And I have felt it with both feet and hands
Like Sisyphus, forgetting what it was
So many years ago, so many years.
Left of the modern pathway as you enter,
The stylobate, the base, a hint of shaft
That once ascended as a semicolumn
And just in front a gutter for the rain
Subsist in low yet solid travertine
Before a row of blocks of travertine
In which that semicolumn is involved,
And on the right the remnant of a column,
This fully rounded, unengaged, will tell
More of the story of the portico.
                              The stucco

The stucco that revested drain and post,
Found in the nineteenth century, was lost
Before the nineteenth century slipped away.
That I remember. What I see today,
What can be seen by any one of us,
Exists as stone, substantial, ruinous.

The nook or service room off to the left
Behind the wall of travertine displays
Fragments of fresco on the orange brick coat
Covering concrete above big blocks of tufa.
The piece of painting on the wall of brick
There in the northeast corner is to me
A thing of red and gold upon the slips
Fitting, as bricks should fit, that fit description,
Awkwardly adjectival as chromatic,
Awkwardly metrical as thus phonetic,
By which a red-and-yellow blend is orange.
I say not well what I have not well seen.
I saw thin bricks. I saw thick bits of art
To decorate this small strange ambient.
The wall was orange and the paint red-gold.

The room beyond is much more satisfying.
It still has pavement and that final apse
Towards which one gazes from the portico.

Peekaboo, exclaimed the little girl
In English. Peekaboo was the reply
Of the young mother. Some walls were so high
Mommy could hide behind them, later walls
Or parts of later walls, imperial,
Straight and rectangular and regular
Or thus perceived because preponderant
And dominating, casting in their slant
The old directions underneath the new.
Which is the truly regular, the rule?
Which is direct and which diagonal?
Inflect a line, wrote Newton. If walls go

Every

UMBRAGEOUS VISION | VISIO | VISION

Every which way, which is the way they go?
Some north-south, east-west walls, republican,
Obsolete, supine, superseded, rise
High enough a tiny child can hide.
This playhouse in the playground of the ruins
Rotting in Rome delights, as once in Queens,
Bit of big city in a fresh republic,
Unroyal borough in a ripe new world,
The playhouse in the playground, light if gray
Beyond the shading elevated train,
Thrilled the little princess there at play.
Peekaboo, she trilled and dodged again
Behind some tufa, brick, or travertine.

Orientation eastward is the best,
Natural, literal, ritual, holiest,
Managed by gods from high bright bailiwicks,
Religion's, heaven's, not man's politics.

East-west, north-south the regal walls once ran.
East-west, north-south the walls now rise again.
Eastward I gaze. The curving bound of brick
Intimates something grand or playful here,
A plan, an alteration, purposeful
Or purely art's. On the straight northern line
Huge tufa blocks suppose the origins,
Before, beneath, whatever bricks may face
The walls and face the viewers of the walls
In space where one must strain to recreate
The stucco and the painted decoration.
Sometimes imagination, memory,
Comparison all fail. I gaze on bricks
Narrow and yellow or magenta-red.
I gaze upon the huge hewn rocks of tufa.
I gaze across the vague unfurnished room.
I gaze around the sloping sagging ground
Graced with some traces that negate the gray,
Patterned in black and white, not light and shadow
Only, as night retreats and day advances,
                                        But paved,

But paved, paved with mosaic, white and black,
Paved with mosaic octagons and squares
Along the oblong portion of the floor,
The octagons of white outlined in black,
The squares of white, black-centered, outlined black,
The squares black bordered white, white bordered black,
The black within the white within the black,
Black squares with wide white frames and narrow black ones,
Or do I find black diamonds in white ones,
Or measure quadrilaterals connected
By straight black lines, or do I recognize
Beehive mosaic, white with black designs?
But in the semicircle I behold
The flowing scrolls of foliage. I quote
The frail and fragile pages of my mind,
The fitful fading pages of my pen,
The pages of the archaeologists,
Who see the more and often say the less.
I feel my wordlessness and worthlessness.
I feel my sightlessness and lightlessness.
I feel my rootlessness and rooflessness.
The roof is azure and the roots protrude
And vanish near the ornamental floors.
Designs in dust and underneath the dust
Unite and separate. I am inside
And never am inside. New Zealanders,
Canadians, Italians, Japanese
Brush by me as I stand and strive to seize
Something by dint of eye, by dint of fingers.
Can one write standing? Can one stand to see?
My previous seats are now fenced off from me.
I shift my stance. I must not get cold feet.
Is it cold hands? My mittens hold the heat
But cannot dissipate the chill that lingers
Under the distant sky, that wintry lid.
This bit of true, real roof is just a shed.
What am I in if not in a museum
Out of doors? Dirt must design the floors.

                Since

Since the exhibits were the living city,
Since the displays were days and nights and dawns,
The passages skirt movement, joy, and trouble.
I pass among the ruins, through the rubble,
Assessing levels, questioning directions,
Feeling upheavals, guessing at connections.

I guess I called it nineteen ninety-eight.
Attention! It is Julius Caesar's step.
The greatest general, the greatest priest,
Maximus, imperator, pontifex,
Consul, proconsul, dictator, quasi rex,
Enters the tiny doorway from the east.
I know his footfall and I know his gait
On the mosaic. No, I do not sleep.
I wake. I watch. I walk. I wait. I wait.

Do I perceive the print of Caesar's feet
On the new-laid mosaic of the floor?
Then he has come and gone. I wake. The dust
Settled so long upon that sagging floor
Rests on the vestiges of priestly feet.

The vestals, for the pontifex next door,
Are sacred neighbors and a sacred trust.

The pavement was relaid in modern times.

It was not Caesar then but Caesar's ghost
Striding one dawn across the figured floor
Like an Achilles crossing asphodel
That was that which I saw. I saw him well
Treading with ancient feet on modern dust.

Did he come after or I come before?
Some things are recollected, some are lost.

Some things are lost. I climb the little stair
To the next room. There is no pavement there
Inside the entrance at the western end,
But dirt, a ditch, a pit. Marvel! Beyond
The cavity,

The cavity, stretching from the far
Wall at the east in which I note ajar
The panels of the small imagined door,
Lies the designed, paved, veritable floor.
Some things the hand, as some the mind, may mend.
Some things the diggers miss and some things find.

The pavement, though perceptibly designed
In white by tiny dice of white, a spread
Bordered in white, centered thus, dotted-lined,
Is still discernible as white on red.
The white is tiny tesserae. The red
Is stucco cover with cement as bed.
My eyes, surprised, not sleeping, open wide,
Staring, and narrow, peering. Verified!
Opus signinum, signine work, they said,
Is that on which your visive feet now tread.

Crosses interlocked enclosing squares
Among their bendings form the meander border
Bordering slanting files that intersect
As rhombuses, as lozenges. The cubes
That constitute the lineation shine
As each direct or inflected dotted line
Marches upon the ruddy firmament
Starred by the neat reticulations ruled
By earth's geometry, a skylike order
Suited to human networks, human cares.

Not stardust but a very earthy dirt
Diminishes the glory of the floor
And fills the space in which the pavement fails,
Gazing above which polyglottous tourists
Pause to decipher, ponder, vocalize
The Latin label shaded by the shed.

The sign above reads Domus Publica.

Domestic I am not. Nevertheless,
If I had been a vestal or a witch

Or genuine

Or genuine befana with her broom
(Since, though I carried the befana's broom,
I was not yet perhaps the true befana,
Not yet real witch, not yet, if ever, vestal),
I would have swept those tessellated floors,
Tending to art, the holy, history,
Doing my duty as a public servant.

This structure is, according to the sign,
A public house, but it is not a pub.
This structure is, must be, by name and fame,
The public house. The label is misplaced
Perhaps. Perhaps that tufa just beyond
Is — is it not? — the famous common wall
That joins or separates the vestals' home
To/from a/the true domus publica
Before effects of princely policy
Create a public house high up the hill
And grant expansion to the convent here.

The sign is posted over to the north,
Above the room half ditch, half diamond,
Half discontinuance, half decoration,
Half pattern, half disruption and despair,
Half past, half present, half not here, half there.

Massive rectangular golden blocks of stone
Dug from Dark Cavern, cut from Grot Obscure,
Compose the rows that rise to build the wall
Edging this northern room upon the east
And hence extending south to bound another.

This southern room is paved in white mosaic
Around the little pool faced with white marble,
The small impluvium set in the center
And bordered by one thin mosaic line
Of black that runs outside it as a second
Runs along the inside of the walls
Which frame the room that is an oddity
Because the narrow bands in black stressing
                                                  The white

The white of pool and room, like pool and room
Show slightly different angles and directions.
The disalignments of the slender margins,
Like the disharmony of room and pool,
Disclose the transformation of a space
Awkwardly restored and reconstructed.
Yet on the eastern wall a painting gleams,
Visible or nearly visible,
With trellises and trees and colored flowers
That flower on the plaster on the brick
Upon those steadfast yellow blocks of tufa.

Is this the common or dividing wall?
Is this the wall that joins or separates
The vestals' residence upon the west
And on the east the dwelling of the priest,
The public house, the palace of the king?

Is this the doorway? Am I in the wall?
Standing in the middle, in between,
At a point not south, not north, not west, not east,
Can I be at zero, can I peer
Around and count the rows of stones and number
The building blocks and measure all dimensions,
The first, then two, then three, then four, then five,
Poised as I am, nowhere or everywhere?

Is it the present? Has it been the past?
What am I seeing? Is it what I saw?
What have I read and what do I remember?
What have I viewed and what do I recall?
Is it my eyes I used or those of others?
Is it their mind at noon, my mind at dawn?
The archaeologists have dug and handled
What I have sometimes scanned and sometimes pawed.

Here is a heavy wall, substantial wall,
Impressive boundary wall in blocks of tufa,
In squared work, quadrate style, opus quadratum.
The north reveals one row in Grot Obscure,

Part of a second row that is the same,
And in the center what was a pilaster
Of travertine of which two blocks remain,
One above the other. On the south
The western side is faced with brick, the east
Displays a trace of plaster. Cappellaccio,
That Roman tufa, gray, of ancient use,
Forms the foundation. Two files can be spied
And lie transversely, sticking out a bit
Below the larger tufa blocks above,
Three rows of grand gold rocks of Grot Obscure,
Layers of great constructed stone, of which
The bottom two are bossed or rusticated.
I contemplate the bulge that is a beauty.
But action is essential to the story.

This is my story, said the father's book
In English. Was will Moskau? asked the German.
Rome — Moskou — Rome, the Dutch intitulation
Proclaimed. And other names from other tongues
Labeled that father's book, that father's story.
The daughter's book is Rome. But must it be
Moscow — Rome — Rome? Yet must it not have been
Manhattan — Moscow — Rome — and Rome — and Rome,
Whether in English, German, Dutch, Italian,
Russian, Chinese, French, Greek, or in that Latin
That died yet lives as Rome that died is living?

The daughter's plot is woven oh so slowly.
Which is her Rome, her Troy, her Ithaca?
Is she Ulysses or Penelope,
Telemachus or Pallas or Iulus,
Camilla or the filial Aeneas?
Must das Behagen be das Unbehagen?
Some science of the earth distinguishes
Rome's strata and the strata of the soul.
Some earthly or infernal or celestial
Art will restore the filaments, she feels.
She feels enfolded by the Roman rose

                                                          That blooms

That blooms as though June bordered January
Until the thorn or icicle or spindle
Pierces the spirit. Did she sleep or wake,
Freeze, bleed, burn, weep, dream, agonize, or act?
City of fiction, universe of fact,
Delved into, built upon, bright, clear, opaque,
Rome is what she was born to see or make.

New York, a town that moves not down but up
Was her beginning. In that north, that west,
It was a rocky isle that gave her birth.
But every woman is an island, wrote
The mother in the mother's story. Soft
And strong that mother was, is, stone and soil,
Concrete, cement, steel, glass, green-bladed grass,
Red-blooded rose, lush, thornless.

       Me an island
Bore like the Cynthians beneath a tree.
Yet was that thrust of verticality
A building built on rock and scraping sky,
The which I scaled, from which I glimpsed great day
A-coming from beyond the granite strand
And forth I flew to grasp a fluid view?
Or was I simply born below an oak,
Beech, maple, elm, palm, poplar, plane, plum, pear,
Peach, apple, cherry, walnut, olive, laurel,
Birch, linden, willow, ash, fir, cypress, pine,
Larch, hemlock, cedar, juniper, spruce, yew,
Or simply tree of knowledge or of life?
Or did a simple singing give me birth?
Was it complexly song that mothered me?
Was it an isle of song? And did a night
Conceive me and a dawn bring me to light?
I took my flight to find a fluid sight.
My father is a river. I have lived
In Rome ten thousand years, and I will build
Or I will sow or plant or tend or grow
Rome and a Rome of Rome.

But as for you,
Julia Budenz, you are not Flora Baum.
Your story is a dying. Mine is life.
Your story is like night. Mine is the dawn.

Day is a-coming. Action is essential.
The action of the story must be bold.
The story of the story must be told.

After Julius Caesar, Lepidus
Became chief priest and thus the occupant
Of the official mansion, public house.
That was in forty-four B.C., of course
(Forty-four B.C.E. as commonly
Denominated with more subtlety
Attentive to potential harmony),
After the Ides of March. When Lepidus
Finally died in thirteen or in twelve
Before Christ or Before the Common Era,
Augustus, on succeeding to the office
March sixth, the day before the Nones of March,
In the year twelve, preferred not to accept
A public domicile but rendered public
A part of his own residence, since custom
Or law demanded that the greatest priest
Live in a public edifice, and gave
The habitation of the king of hallows,
Palace of kings when kings were king in Rome,
Pontifical abode most recently,
The people's property, that special home
Built and extended where the Palatine
Slopes to the Forum by our Holy Road,
This regal, priestly dwelling, to the vestals,
Because, as we are told by Cassius Dio,
It had a wall in common with their own.

Action is essential. I must move
Through the small door, up the big step. Within!
Within at last! This must be it, that castle
                                                  Where

Where I will meet the king. Or did I struggle
Up the big step and through the little door?
Here I am. I stand here. I am sure.

Surely this is securely sure, real, true.

Sure! What is true? My shoes are truly set
Upon this herringbone of brick, my feet
Are really in my shoes, and I am on
My feet, where we the people take our stand,
Here where the flooring seems so ordinary
The public come, hum, shuffle, do not know
This pavement laid two thousand years ago
Is what it is in shape and age and name,
Opus spicatum, ancient, still the same.

How many years in half a centimeter?

The brickwork in the middle of the room,
In spicate style, is just a little higher,
Thus later, than the floorage at the edge
In pounded paste of pavement, travertine,
A ground of white stuck, studded, sprinkled, sown—
What shall we say?—with varied scraps of stone,
Green, red, black, yellow, as the words unfold,
Aquamarine and purple, rose and gold.

My mind eyes white cement and colored stone,
But was it crumbs my eyes eyed when I stood
And looked at triturated travertine,
Crumble from origins or tough time's tread?

Four centimeters is the average length
Among the multicolored ornaments,
But towards the now no longer extant center
The chips grow smaller and the setting denser.

City constructed utterly of sound
Instead of stone, how will your sense be seen?
And when each meter floats far from the ground
How will it matter, what will the measures mean?

Yet I am here, and here I take my place
Upon this floor in this material space,

Within at last! And still I stand outside.
What rootless, roofless, ruthless honesty
Confesses every obstacle? That fence
Between me and the rest of public house—
Is it barbed wire? It is a barricade
And, although green,

                not red,

                              it will prevent . . .

I stood at the green wire fence. I was across.
I loved the place too much to break its laws
Or even to imagine a transgression.
I had a permesso. I was an architect
Employed by the excavators to sketch out plans.
I was myself the archaeologist.
I had become a cat. My coat of black
Gleamed as my white paws paused on each huge block
Of tufa, stack on stack. I was the cat
That moved with purpose and with nonchalance
In smooth observance of the rules of measure
With perfect liberty. I was the bird
That flew with purpose, swerving airily
Down to the courtyard, perching on a pillar
That inched above its base. I was the bird
Down in the courtyard, chirping: Do you wake?
I was awake, and it was not a dream.

I am awake. The whistles do not blow,
Screeching and shrieking, No no no no no.
To enter with the feet or with the eyes
Is the great question. I behold blue skies,
But past the barrier of wire and rail
My feet proceed as some permissive veil
Of cloud that Venus drapes about her dears
Reveals the hero and conceals the fears.

                                            Venus

Venus loved Caesar. Venus loved Aeneas.
Veils are as helms for Vesta, yes, for Venus.
Heroic love is not a single genus.
But will the king come forth to honor Janus?

Reply divinely to my dark, dumb yearning,
Blue fire of night, blue morning star, blue morning.

As Elsie Piddock, skipping in her sleep
Along the top of Caburn, where the fairies
Bestowed the magic jump rope (this permitted
Skips beyond high, sly, featherlike, long, strong,
Slow, toe, fast, double-double; little girls
Watched against trouble; stern authorities
Could not close Caburn when the last skip ended
Because her skipping did not end), transcended
Bounding and bound, no less astoundingly
Have I skipped over space and over time.

I have skipped out from time yet into space.

I am Vertumnus, and I turn and turn
With his vertiginous virtuosity.
If I can find a seat my head will clear.
My head will clear. I plop down on some stone.
I turn my head. I turn my searching eye.
A column is my prop. The day is here.
Surely the king of hallows will appear.

The courtyard has two columns, fluted, white,
At the northern end, which is the southern reach
Of the atrium extending to the north
Towards the vestibule which leads to Holy Road.
I take in quickly what I know so well
From years of peering. All too soon the sun,
Leaping the eastern hills, will daze a gaze
Already weakened or, say, made more keen,
By centuries of squinting scrutiny
And by millennia of wide-eyed wonder.
Upon the western column, facing east,

I am

I am no stylite, for the rising shafts
Have long since toppled. Underneath my feet
Between the columns, or what was the columns,
A white carpet of pavement stretches still
Infixed with little stars or little crosses,
Each made of four black cubes arranged around
A central cube of white, and stretching still,
Or formerly, according to the turn,
As head and eyes or head and mind discern,
Somewhat beyond the columns, with a band
Of spaced black cubes aligned about the edge
To form a border, while upon the east
And south and west, where brick walls rise or rose,
Before the lateritious eastern limit,
Beyond the southern and its passageway,
And, as I twist, behind me to the west,
Beyond the remnants of the western bound,
Within the room through which I must have padded
Or over which I must have flown, the floors
Are of that white cement with colored spangles,
More of those floors of hard, of beaten white,
Scattered, or set, with yellow, black, green, red.

Perhaps you do not care about the floors,
About the colors, forms, or formlessness,
About the formerly, about the still,
About the distyle courtyard, hoary height
Within white distyle courtyard, or, without,
Parietal survival and decline.
When one has hardly guessed, one is possessed,
Must be obsessed, by what is barely glimpsed.
When the hard evidence, exiguous
And accidental, is so hard to touch,
One must amass and judge it inch by inch.
Skip to the story. Skip the limp description.
Skip over ditches gaping all about us.
Sit on the brick brink of a rebuilt well,
Up to the south or down there to the north,
And follow the unfolding of the song.

The day is here, and I am here at last.
I sit upon a pillar while my feet
Fasten on black and white solidity.
Not yet, not yet, not yet, no, never, never.
The well of recollection, memory,
Remembrance, on the edge of which I rested
Once is now distant since the dig is deeper.
I sit beside a pit, beside a ditch,
Ditch, pit, abyss of loss, of the forgotten.

I had forgotten that the place I reached
Had once itself been dug to, was a ditch
That filled with history even as it emptied
A memory that was an emptying
Just as it may have been a recommencement.
How far down must the bucket of recall
Sink to replenish substance and return?
How far down can mind dip into the well?
How far down can hand dig into the ditch?
Did I descend with shovel, spade, or knife?
Can I remember that far, this far, down?
Slipping into the pit, will I find life
Or will no voices wake me and I drown?

My seat is travertine, set on a floor
Nicely designed with figures white and black.
Whatever color covered the white block
Is every bit as nonexistent now
As any verticality that counts,
Above the base, low even for a chair,
The circle on the circle on the square,
Three-dimensional but just enough
To render it a piece of furniture
Usable in a three-dimensioned world.
The pavement is a rather narrow strip
Beside the pit. Is this periculous?
Is this more simply gauged a new dimension?
Which level is the level where I live?
The fourth dimension is the history.
The fifth

The fifth dimension is the poetry.
Does time or timelessness have more to give?

What did I know in nineteen ninety-eight?
What did I know and what should I have known?
Should I have said it was some other year
In which I saw that which I say I saw?
Do I describe the Rome of Flora Baum,
Prized by her eyes, my eyes, for centuries,
Or is it Carettoni's Rome I know,
Or is it Coarelli's Rome I feel,
Or is it Carandini's Rome that starts
To ascend before my startled staring gaze
While I descend into the ditch he digs?
Is it a Dantesque Rome that drags my feet
Down the infernal depths towards hopes of heaven,
Or is it Cavalcanti's Rome that drives
My doubting hand and my astounded pen?
Or is my Rome the Rome of R. T. Scott?
Rome, can I love thee well and know thee not?

O Janus of this day, who face each way,
Can I go backward, forward — which is which —
Back — or is it forward — into time
Already timed, traversed, tapped, tabulated,
Back to the past and to its memory,
Or forward — is it back — into a future
Of excavation, scription, publication,
Into moist shoveled holes, damp patterned caverns,
Down into earthy shafts, to library stacks,
Looking for news, something turned up, turned out,
In with the unseen stones, the unread books,
Down to the darkness of discovery,
Sighing for light as from a distant sky?
Shall I embark, hoping to touch that star,
Or stay until that starlight touches me?
Is it a gleam of evening or of dawn?

In Topsy-Turvy House, which Daddy built
In that new nation where we went to play,
Make-Believe

Make-Believe Land, which he himself had founded,
We stood upon the ceiling or the floor
According as the turn brought up or down
Under our little shoes that rested, skipped,
Skipped, rested as the turn brought down or up
Something to stand on, something to dance upon.
Or in another land our big eyes watched
Two little shoes that scooted off alone
As Mother sent them forth adventuring.
I see them going on before me now
Across the atrium of the Roman house.

I hear the vestals in the vestibule
Or think I hear them, coming through the door
That opens onto Holy Road or else
The door that opens in from Holy Road.
It is a public door in public space
Whether it opens in or opens out,
And through it, at the far end of the hall,
I think, I think I hear them entering.

In deference to their vestality
I rise with reverence. How yearningly
I stand between the columns, listening.
I think I hear them singing to the king.
And do I think that they will sing to me?
There is a song. Is it a song I sing?

Women and girls who know what Rome can be,
I long to tell you what my Rome has been,
Not that I can complete what I begin
But that my mind keeps seething into speech.
This Rome is something that I hear and see
Without and that reflects, resounds, within,
Something I sometimes lose and sometimes win,
Something at hand and far beyond my reach.
And if I do not grasp enough to teach
The meaning of its deeds and of its dreams
I must say how it feels and how it seems.
And if

And if I do not feel enough to preach
Its value, its profundity, its height,
I must communicate its sharp delight.

Puella Romam amat. Love first came
Through what was strange and new yet not absurd
In match of sound with sound and word with word.
Poeta Romam amat. Even more,
Poetam amat Roma. Not mere fame
But over oceans rhythmic winds I heard
Lifted my heart with pinions of the bird
Eager to rise and rise and rise and soar.
Over the metered seas of years of yore
My heart flew pulsing on those double wings.
One is the language, one what the language sings.
Arma virumque cano. From a shore
Farther than Troy's, than Thule's, glides the girl
Armed with her love and dives to find her pearl.

The pearly city was not that above
But that below the sky yet not below
The sea but at a center of the flow
Of waters, at a focus of the stars.
The love that hearing kindled was the love
That vision fed and fanned into a glow
Crowning a slave-king centuries ago
Before the hearthstone of the guarding Lars.
The city of the shepherd son of Mars
Whose brother died that he might be the king
Blossoms when Venus smiles there in the spring.
The city which gave title to the czars
Sees Caesar shrine the Venus of his sires
And ornament the court of Vesta's fires.

That Rome is love December will reveal
When Angerona's bandaged mouth is freed.
Rome's joy will be December's joyous meed
Because Volupia receives her due
When laughter thrills a happy commonweal,
For Janus

For Janus sprinkles January's seed
And Saturn reaps before December's need.
The grass is glistening with virgin dew.
The sky is gleaming with that maiden blue
Above the haggish remnants of the past
Silently crying out how some things last
Linking the oldest old and newest new.
Rome is my joy with or without a reason.
Rome is my love no matter what the season.

Dear song, I know that you may circulate
Among the Romans and the foreigners,
Among the tourists, pilgrims, visitors
Intent on business, hoping for a dole,
Spending or saving, filled with love or hate,
Flexible as the slimmest cat that purrs,
Fixed in the pride of his, perplexed by hers.
She is the girl who glimpsed the high, bright goal
And slipped into the deepest, dimmest hole.
Be that girl's best and, like her, struggle forth
To flaming south and east from west and north
Seeking the dawn before dusk takes its toll.
Walk, watch, wait. It cannot now be long.
Harmonize with the women's waking song.

Is it the dead they wake? Then should I fear?
Have they lived? Will they live? What is the year?

If it was nineteen ninety, ninety-three,
Or ninety-nine, what would the difference be?
Or was it nineteen ninety-eight B.C.
Or nineteen ninety-something B.C.E.
When Sibyl showed the ghosts of Rome to me,
Showed me the souls of Rome's eternity,
Showed me which spirits I would live to see,
Beings whom I would meet in history?

Daddy first showed us these on Sun-Up Hill,
Then sank with them in mist and mystery.

Death is the deadline. They have not yet lived.
Death is the deadline. Sibyl, live and listen.
Death is the deadline. Do not die, kind Sibyl.
I prayed too much. I labored much too little.
O gods, O ghosts, show pious Flora pity.
Is this now day that breaks above my city?
The ground beneath my feet is very gritty.

And still I love. And still I yearn to know.
And still the virgins come. May they not go
Before I hear each name and see each face
And query each about this time and place
And stretch to fathom this beloved space.

The leader of the vestals in procession
Addressed to me a very simple question:
What is love? Then must I give a lesson?

She stood there as the pendent cherry tree
Stands April-veiled in white above the blue
Of the cerulean squills beneath the blue
Of azure skies beyond the western sea.

It was too early. I had much to learn.
But courtesy demanded a return.

A virgin asks me and I want to tell
About a feeling which is fierce and soft
And is so lofty that its name is love.
How many tasks can I accomplish well?
First there is stealing, second steady craft,
And third the proof to what I strive to prove
Within the truth, if not quite of traduction,
Still of tradition, if not with the sound
Of feet that pound along the cavalcade,
Still somehow pedaling through the great parade.
Must I compute how love is a seduction
And a sedition, not on solid ground
But whirled around in gusty dust, not shade
Or sheen but indistinctness, frail and frayed?

Wait patiently, my song, wait for December.
Do not go forth but watch and grow. This edge
Will be the pledge of all you will remember:
Amor and Angerona, Rome and Venus,
Volupia and Vesta, trailing Janus.

Be patient, song. Be patient. Feet that pound
Around the space of January's ground
Will sound at last, at last will sweetly sound,
Will prance at last in the land of the most renowned,
Will dance at last in the city of the gowned.

December is yet distant, dim, and deaf.
This is the dawn of January ninth.

The day I know, the time of day, the weather.
I study calendars of stone, the stones,
The stars. The years go flowing like a river.
The men who gave them names are ashes, bones.
Who lives here now? Who sit upon these thrones?
Who are you with your sweet insistent tones?
Who are we? Are we larvae here together?

Have others penetrated these cocoons?
Have other women come with other tunes?
Catching a sonnet sung by Martha Collins
After a line first chanted by Sue Standing,
I open wide my beak and close my talons,
Like Guido, Cino, Dante in responding,
Snatching a word, a feeling, and a time,
Matching the measures, matching rhyme to rhyme.

I sleep and wake among the ghosts. The gulf
Between this ambient and that where Sue
And Martha sing elucidates a self
Making late music, audible to few

Who breathe the breezes which we breathe today,
Or heard by none at all if all anoint
Stern ears against the bony siren's way
Of uttering a florid counterpoint

To soaring columns of a form surmised
In fragments dug from dust or floorage seen
Figured beneath the vestals' tread. Surprised,
I glimpse a Sue, a Martha, in between.

I wake among the ghosts, for I must choose
This ruin which my sisters may refuse.

And now, among these ghosts, is this the king,
Turning to start the Agonalia?
Turning to show their hopelessness all wrong,
Can these be Guido, Tom, Amelia?

Because I hope to turn again, again,
Ever again unto the Tuscan town,
The Latin city, where the Roman men
Have turned into the people of the gown,

Because I hope, though not a prostitute,
To be a member of the togate nation,
Because I, Flora, hope that flower, fruit,
Tree, garden, realm, republic mean salvation,

Because I hope to build up walls of beauty,
Because I hope to raise up gates of truth,
Because I hope to turn into my city,
Because I hope to turn into myself,

I hope to open doors of verity
Uncrushed by massive mures of agony.

Murification? Is this true despair?
Verity? Is that what I hope to dare?
Verification? If I do not know
What year this is, what people come and go?
I know this is the public house at least.
I know this is the palace of the priest.
O Janus, be the gateway of this day.
We come here not to labor but to pray.

Verification? Janus sees each way.
Is truth not but, both and, or either or?
Is truth not but, both and, and either or?
Is truth not yet, and yet, and yet again?
Verification? Does not only trail
But also after it or does not only
Trail the but also striding on ahead?
Where there are two trails must there be a third?

Will two tracks meet in some infinity
Or last or pass or cross or switch or fork?
For children in the subways of New York
The third rail ran, stretched, gleamed dangerously.

As I peer east before the peeping sun
Blinds with its smile, what lack or deprivation,
What access and what presence dimly fill
That eastern dig, pit, ditch, abyss beyond?
And still, and still, and still. The public house
Was clearly marked behind me to the west.
The public house was dug and published here
Where, having prayed and labored, I wake, wait.
Still, is the public house that third house, there,
New-dug, discovered, published to the east?
Can I remember something from the past?
Can I continue somehow to the future?
Can I be, in the present, where I am,
From where I blink before, behind, between?
The ditches open or the ditches close.
The ditches open and the ditches close.

If that beyond me is the public house
And there the greatest pontiff is at home,
This where I rest so restlessly remains
The habitation of the king of hallows.
I rest a question if the pontifex
No longer enters, and the sacred rex
Alone must be expected if my ex-
Pectation is well founded.

                        Something checks
The meditation. Action is essential.

I leave the columns, walk across the floor,
And join the vestals in the atrium
Paved once perhaps with concrete or cement
Enhanced by scatterings in polychrome
And then with brick of which a bit remains.
Upon which level do the vestals step
And stride and stay? That is, what is the year?

Is it a year of white with colored stone?
Is it a year of red in herringbone?
But no, this is the same geometry
As that which at the pillars set the rule:
Black stars, black crosslets, on white ground, white sky,
Cubes of a negative astronomy
Which is a positive design of joy.
This pavement is so nearly visible
That I am nearly able to descry
What I am nearly able to deny
But to reject which might reflect the fool.

We stand beside the peperino pool.

Fabia, I began. You must be she.
I knew I knew her name. Is this the house
Where I may greet the king who on this day
Will honor Janus? But I was distracted,
Encountering the girls and women there
And counting not the six whom I had seen
Or thought I saw but finding only five.
Oh, one must stay at home to mind the fire,
I almost said aloud, I said aloud.
Fabia nodded patiently and smiled.

If that was Julius Caesar whom I saw
Emerging from this building, I continued,
And if he seemed not as he must have seemed
To Brutus when his spirit walked abroad
And spoke those ghostly messages at Sardis
                                          And at

And at Philippi, mighty yet, yet slain,
Monstrous, some god, some angel, or some devil,
Seen through some weakness of the watcher's eyes,
But rather living, vigorous, and vibrant,
If I recall what he was like precisely
Although that every like is not alike
I know just as I seem to know he seemed
The man he was before he reached his forties,
When he was thirty-eight or thirty-nine
Or halfway in between, just as he seemed
This day, this very ninth of January,
In sixty-one B.C., that is, the day,
If I may clarify the designations,
Called fifth before the Ides of January
In A.U.C. six hundred ninety-three,
That is, when Marcus Pupius Piso Frugi
Calpurnianus, if he should be termed
Calpurnianus, and another Marcus,
Valerius Messalla Niger, held
The consulship by which that year was named,
Is this that year?

    May I identify
Surely or probably or possibly
As greatest pontiff Gaius Julius Caesar,
As king of hallows Lucius Claudius,
Pontifex maximus and rex sacrorum,
Priests on this day, in this month, in this year,
Sixty-one B.C.E., however numbered,
However named?

    I beg you to forgive me,
Virgins, if I am inconsiderate,
If I am impolite and incoherent.

Fabia seemed to comprehend my questions
And tolerate the ways in which I phrased them
Partly for her and partly for myself.

* * *

Lifting my foot to ascend, I hesitate.
Was there something else on the ground floor or out in the garden?
Have I remembered everything? I pause.
Can I recall all I have seen today?

I have seen a number of times a dear little boy
Trying to herd his flock of guinea pigs
At evening into their pen in an orderly fashion
After allowing them freedom all day long
In the little garden where they could scamper at will.
He wants them to march in unison, but one
Runs off in this direction, one in that,
Two others in a third. The shepherd learns
At last to gather them as well as he can.

So with our characters, one comes, one goes,
All act as act they must, and we accept
Their necessary presence and their absence
And their return. We catch them as we can.
We follow if we cannot marshal them.

Thus the great noble poet of the north,
The Roman who would never live in Rome,
The Roman who would never visit Rome,
Citizen of the Italy to be,

Was writing on this January ninth
Of eighteen twenty-three or could have been
Writing just then.

                And thus the vestal virgins
Withdrew before the ferryman, who yielded
To Caesar, who appeared and disappeared,
Passing the action to the king of hallows,
To Janus who came first, to Leopardi
Who came so many centuries after them,
And Leopardi yields now to Manzoni
In the same year and on the very day
When Leopardi sat and wrote in Rome,
Communing as we know with Cicero,

                                          And in

And in Milan Manzoni sat and wrote,
Or could have written by our calculation:
I have seen a number of times a dear little boy.

If Alexander did not date the page
Penned by his hand on January ninth
As Jamey dated his, the northerner
Noted, we know, upon the first and last
Leaves of his volume three in the manuscript
Of the first draft of the famous masterpiece
The dates when he began and when he ended,
Or thought that he had ended, that third tome.

He started on November twenty-ninth,
We see, of eighteen hundred twenty-two
And ended or almost ended March eleventh
Of eighteen twenty-three. The latter date,
Together with The end of volume three,
Recorded when he felt that he had finished
The volume and before he added, after
The word England, a new long paragraph,
He cancelled, and to clarify the text
After the cancellation added also,
There at the bottom of the page: continued.

We know this and from this we calculate
What page he could have written on what date.

Shall we add the vast numbers of library books which he borrowed,
The secondary and the primary sources?

Can we measure repairs to the house, arrangements willed,
Derangements made? Can we gauge the long discussions
Of theology held with a Protestant brother-in-law?
Shall we search the shelves for those volumes of Bossuet
Left in the country and lend one then to Henry
When sending back the Calvinists' catechism?

Do we count the hours of illness, his, his wife's,
His mother's, and his children's? Do we count
Those hours and hours of incapacity,
Those days and days in which he could not work,

                                                        Could

UMBRAGEOUS VISION | VISIO | VISION

Could only walk and could not walk alone?
He walks. He works. We must, we will, work, too.

But who are we and therefore who am I?

Am I not she who knows what she will know
In the future about a past which is this present
Since she remembers what she will have learned
By January ninth of twenty hundred,
Or of two thousand, as we still shall call
That year, still weird, still wild, to mind, to ear?
In this future of that past which is a present,
Settled at my desk I calculate,
Upon the basis of what now is known
By us who study published autographs
And autographs unpublished to this future
In which we know much less and yet much more
About that past than those who called it now,
Who called it ours, who called its present hours,
The place attained, the time required, the pace
To place as actual or possible,
The count that reaches real or virtual
Time, or the factual or fictional
Moments of morning, afternoon, or night.

When we compare the pages and the dates
We find the opening of chapter five
Of volume three a reasonable choice,
A passage we select to represent
That which Manzoni wrote or may have written
In the year eighteen hundred twenty-three
On Thursday, January ninth. We find
Something that makes three sevenths or a half
Along the way we walk from date to date,
From page to page. The hero soon will walk
And walk more firmly into history
And we will walk with him, but first we see
The father who has seen his little boy
Learning to herd his pets. The father sits

Before

Before his personages, as he learns
Their ways and learns the words that guard their ways.
But are we we? Can we be I? And he?
Today I watched him watching at his desk.

The study where he writes is very quiet
Although to me the house seems very full
And seems to me the middle of Milan.
The study, though on the ground floor, seems remote,
Apart. Its windows look out on the garden.
The trees are nearly little Peter's age,
Planted by Alexander when this home
Chosen and bought by him was newly his
Nine years ago. The trees and Peter grow.
The family grows. To me the house seems full.

The house seems very full. There are the servants.
There is the friend who occupies two rooms
Not far from Alexander's study. Fast
Or slow, the family grows, the family grow.
Grandmother Julia now is over sixty
And Alexander over thirty-seven
And Henrietta over thirty-one
And little Julia recently fourteen
And little Peter nearly nine and a half
And Christine seven and a half and Sophie five
And Henry three and a half and Claire not yet
One and a half yet not the baby now:
Victoria is not yet four months old.

Let me restate each sum. Within this year
As it matures, the birthdays celebrated
Will be the sixty-first, the thirty-eighth,
The thirty-second, fifteenth, tenth, eighth, sixth,
Fourth, second (if a cloud around that second,
A cloud yet unperceived, yet unsuspected,
Passes; it will not pass; Claire will not live;
Eleven days before that second birthday,
Alas, our Claire will pass), and last the first.

Pity obscures the listing. Hope endures.
Dark futures hold a not unfutile light.
This ninth of January has not passed.
The list endures. The listed designated
By name and age subsist as fully ten
In number. In completed years the boys,
The sons, are under four and over nine,
One more than three, the other less than ten.

Relentless pedantry can guide to vision.
Not Henry, as this friend, that scholar, held,
Not Philip, of a birth still three years on,
But clearly Peter is the dear little boy
Crossing the page of Daddy's manuscript,
Neither too old nor, like his younger brother,
Too young to be the shepherd of his pets.
I see the children gathered in the garden
Out by the liquidambar and sophora.
I have seen young Peter playing in the garden
Among young sweet gums and pagoda trees.

Does Peter bear his father's father's name?
That is, is Peter named for his grandmother's husband?
Does Henry bear his mother's brother's name?
That is, is Henry named for his Protestant uncle?

Dear Henrietta has, since eighteen ten,
Been the devoted, holy, Roman Catholic.
The nuptial rite was blessed in eighteen eight
By a young Swiss Calvinist pastor in Milan
And in eighteen ten by a Catholic priest in Paris.
As the husband decades later told a friend,
When they were newlyweds his dear, dear wife,
Walking with him one evening in the garden
Of their country house amidst the green and the peace
Of a part of the garden that looked out towards the mountains,
And twining together two tiny locust saplings
Planted by him, said: Thus our lives will live.

Will leaves weave silkily above the windows?
Will blossoms whiten on the locust trees?
Spring will bring ritual or history,
The cyclical, the future, or the past.
May will attain its twenty-second day,
And on the feast of Julia, virgin martyr,
The mother will commemorate her name,
The wife abjure a false church for a true,
The famous son and husband enter heaven
And with the ancient saint who died so young
Celebrate there, when he has died so old,
The birthday which a church can term celestial.

Present in Paris at the abjuration,
Witness and signatory to the act,
Was Julia Beccaria widow Manzoni.
Buried in Brescia was the other Julia,
The saint, received, entombed, enshrined at last
Not far from where the sweet rejected queen,
The faithful fierce repudiated wife,
Once pledge, once bond, of France and Lombardy,
Before the linden tree could bloom again
With the oppressed would rest, could rest at last,
Buried there, too, when she had died so young,
Mourned by the poet who would die so old.
From the majestic cloud surrounding us
Julia was witness to the abjuration.

All of these twenty-second days of May,
One in each year, may mark or may not mark
Or may or not be marked by earth's return
In a unique example of the journey
Annually completed in the sky.
May twenty-second, eighteen seventy-three,
May twenty-second, eighteen twenty-three,
May twenty-second, eighteen hundred ten,
May twenty-second in the seven hundreds,
In the four hundreds, in the twenty hundreds,
In the first, second, third millennia,

May twenty-second as eleventh day
Before the Calends of the month to come,
Named as of June although remaining May,
May or may not be fragrant with the candor
Of dangling and expanding blossoming.

Who can remember May in January
When he must hold November in his hand?

His hand moves as he sits, and on the desk,
As on a map in which reality
Exists and moves and lives, appear, appear,
With mountains, lakes, a river, villages,
With beech trees, mulberries, a fig, a city,
History, language, and a little boy
And a large question, What then can we learn,
And a large space in which these all can be
And we can be with them, in which the hours
That pass so slowly pass too quickly, filled,
Fulfilling, rich, enriching, very rich
Hours in which so spaciously we live.

How did I enter? How did I set foot there?
How did I traipse a perilous terrain?

Opening the book, I read, I read,
And, like the peasant hero from the highway,
Saw the great city, saw the great cathedral.

Much have I traveled in the iron province,
Hunting the summits of the gilded hills,
Fishing the channels of the silvered rills,
Of literary criticism, of . . .
Of history, biography, and gossip.
Janus sees both ways, looks below, above.

Janus begins. I glimpse the fulgent bronzen.

Nothing can dim the splendor of my prophet
Or nip the promise which bright bloom fulfills.
Nothing can come between me and my love.

Let the professors make their proclamations:
Servile we will not be before the masters.
We shall not bow. We are biographers.
We shall not cringe. We are the chrismed critics.
We judge the artist's life, the artist's art.
We lecture loudly, proudly pen and publish
Our subtle studies. Masterpieces fail
Tests of perfection, and the masters fall
From pedestals of hagiography.
What a relief when weakness is revealed
And disesteem is justified. We judge.

I defend you, men and artists. I defend,
Against the arrogant who stand and stare
And point, the lustrous pearl, the poet: man,
Son, father, nephew, uncle, grandson, heir,
Stepfather, schoolmate, neighbor, colleague, friend,
Grandfather, landlord, boss. A thread of fear,
One tiny tremor winds into my ear,
Insinuates itself within my heart,
A throb of sound or sense or sentiment
That rattles through my adamant, my steel,
A question: Is there nothing to resent,
Nothing my indulgence cannot span?
With that resplendent paragon of art
What was the wife's life like? How did she feel?

Did Henrietta have to die so young,
Married at sixteen, buried at forty-two,

Twelve times with child? Her pained and dimming eyes
Lifting in resignation to the skies,
She slipped in silence from stunned, anguished cries

And left bereft eight children and her spouse
And one whose only offspring was this spouse,
Fathered in fable by the dandy lover
Or the dull husband who acknowledged him
As his one son, born to his wedded wife,
Julia, who chose as her own epitaph:
Daughter of Caesar, mother of Alexander.

Julia yet lived, and Alexander lived.
The famous father Caesar Beccaria
Was gone, the lover John, the lover Charles,
The husband Peter, all were gone, long gone,
And Alexander's Henrietta gone.

Julia and Alexander hoped and prayed,
And Henrietta wearied, prayed, and died.

Cecidere manus. His grief was unallayed
By art, his agony unbeautified.

She died on Christmas. Yet nativity
Was imaged in one life. A baby stayed
Behind and, all uncomprehending, cried.
Little Matilda still was only three.

Must there be revolution? Can there be
Freedom, equality, and humanhood,
A hue and cry of speech, of history,
Of mind, of passion passing through the wood
Without a victim? Can that leafless tree
Meet January standing, understood?

Shall we greet every aider and abetter?
In forests, fields, farms fenced with stones of touch,
In kingdoms and republics of the letter,
In types of writing or of study such

As, general or more particular,
Theory, history, or criticism
Or ars poetica or code or prism
That fits together or that splits apart
Civilization, culture, beauty, art,
Literature, prose, poetry, the master
May be professor or practitioner,
Scholar or artist or philosopher,
Or, damned and damnable, the poetaster,
Or laudable and lauded laureate.

I wonder if it matters very much.
Who can tell what is worse and what is better?
Meter facilitates. It does not fetter.
Rhyme is no obstacle. It is a crutch.

Let us be human, natural, sincere,
Unartificial, unrhetorical.
But must we always walk when we can dance,
And must we merely talk if we can sing?

And must our hymns await an imprimatur
And all our prophecies be certified
And all our revelations be insured
And all our miracles be patented?

Slivers of lost theology and hope
And bits of lit crit jostle along the slope
From height to depth where every shifting trope
Might shine, design in the bright kaleidoscope.

The gods that had become so tedious,
Now gone so long, so far, last came to us
So long ago, have gone so far away,
We may be pardoned if a glistering
Glimpsed as a glint between the sun and the sky
Is boldly named. Here Janus gazes, here
The Maiden delicately steps, descending,
As from her veil trail ages of gold.

Yet I will not forget a gift that lasts.

I praise, I praise, the book that grants us days
Of dazzling art, of sizzling sun with shadow,
Muteness with mutual communication,
Doom, tumult, hubris, humor, humanness,
With life's vast dark, with life's vague radiance,
Long desiccation, and a final flower.

I too, through blasts, through blasted branches, hear,
Beyond these forests and below those mountains,
The river edging towards the end of fear.

I cross the Adda. Then I cross the Tiber.
This is not Lombardy. I am in Rome.
The book is still unfinished. This I know.
This is still eighteen hundred twenty-three,
Still January ninth. All this I know.

Still, as I lift my foot to climb the stair,
I sense behind me, closer to the garden,
A poet's ground-floor study with the glow
Of a lucescent torch, the truth, the true
Which his hand grasps, holds, offers to bestow.

Janus looks back and forth, sees old and new.
Janus sees south and north, looks high and low.

* * *

Flora, Florinda, can you be asleep?

His voice, though stern, was sweet, with the austere
Clean sweetness of green laurel leaf in winter.

How can your eyes stay closed? How can you sleep?

Was I awake, or was it all a dream?
It was the truth.

    Only an hour before
I had stood gazing at the great green gate.

This has four sections, two that do not move
And two that move each on a wheel that rolls
Or runs along, in memory, desire,
Hope, and presumption of the actual,
Its semicircular metallic rail.
The movable and the immovable
Portions all soar in twelve green metal shafts
Totaling eight and twoscore verticals
Which lead, beyond five horizontal rods,
To spheres swelling below the heads of spears
          That widen

That widen and that narrow in their wedges
Deictic of sky. The hinges to the right
And left of what can close and open function
From two cylindrical green posts that bear,
On top of each, a fivefold cross of red,
With one large central member and four small
Versions, of which two stand, of which two dangle,
On, from, the major, each in one right angle.
Above the midpoint of the whole, moreover,
Where the two moving sectors overlap,
Supported by an upright beam a lyre
Supports a spearhead rising even higher
Than any other structure or design.

That verdant beam is not arboreal
But fashioned by some man, metallic, flat,
A beam that is not Baum, that is not tree,
Yet lyre and spear emerge as foliage.

I was not looking towards a verdurous forest
But towards swift access or stiff barrier.

My feet were still fixed on the little squares
Paving the public place that lay beneath
Travertine steps that went straight to the gate.
I climbed the thirteen stairs and shook a shaft,
Grasping that elongation of a diamond
That served as handle to a spear. There followed
A subtle undulation, but the gate
Stayed closed.

            That horizontal tube must carry
Electric power to the central lock.

Right of the gate a wall holds labeled bells
Or citophones or intercoms or buzzers,
One for the Knights, a second for the Friars.
At such an hour I dared not try to press
Either. I had to enter by a power
Within me or outside of me but not
Within the gate.

UMBRAGEOUS VISION | VISIO | VISION

     Within the gate I saw
Another set of steps of travertine,
Thirteen again, beyond the little landing
Cobbled in pietrini at the front
Edge of which the emerald rampart rose,
For such then seemed the painted metal portal.
Would I give out, give in, give up, I wondered,
First to myself and then to two black cats,
Sleek, lithe, and lean, with eyes of green, that came
Gently descending to the landing.
          No.
I know, and you must know, that I have suffered,
As I have joyed, in darkness and in light
Solely that I might find the walls of Rome,
Venerable and sacred, whether built
And visible, still visible, or built
Once and yet now invisible, or built
Not yet.
     My mind, my heart, is deeply reached,
Is deeply called, by something that existed,
By something that exists, by something further
That might profoundly shimmer towards existence.
Yet, yet, mine eyes have seen and loved some essence,
Some essences, without a necessary
Verification in some being known
Or knowable to body or to spirit
As actually or possibly existing
But true to mind and heart and eyes and dream
Yet not a dream, a sleep, but vigil, vision.

With infelicitous facility
Both what and that can flicker, fade, and fail.

And yet, I whispered fiercely, almost wildly,
Causing the cats to turn their eyes up mildly,
Let me attain both essence and existence.
Let me attain them. I am agonizing.
But nothing matters. These are mattering.
Let me attain them. Let me see Rome, Rome.

This is the apprehension, the creation,
Both of the whole and of each needed part.

This is the finding. This will be the founding.
This is the freeing. This will be the seeing.

This is the getting there, the getting through.
This is the coming here, the going in.

Why does it matter if you enter or
How you interpret your endeavor? Was
The cats' green gaze a fourfold focussed challenge,
The glint of accusation, or a deep
Gleam of comprehension and assent?
Why should I be? Or why should I be I?

The venture, the adventure, is the quest,
The question. Why is who is what is how?

The green of my umbrella matched the green
Of the tall gate exactly. Would this gift
Of the befana be again my broom
As earlier that evening or more simply
Meeting the physics of a different world
Be the umbrella of a Mary Poppins
Which would pop up and top the tips and quickly
Pop again down? I came to my decision
Quickly. I quickly slipped the umbrella from
Its neat green sheath. Quickly I snapped it open.
Distending eight green panels, it extended
Eight silver spokes and bared the silver pole.
I held the handle, rose, cleared, crossed, descended,
Undamaged by the poised and pointing spears
That for a moment targeted this one
Warrioress or sorceress invading
The citadel which they protect. Clorinda,
Could you have entered here more agilely?
Armida, would your magic let you through
With such dispatch? I dared to glance about.
The gate was at my back, and I was standing

Upon

Upon the sturdy, firm, tough cobbled landing,
Looking through bars no longer, seeing freely
The second set of thirteen steps ahead
And then a level space and then the walls
Holding my goal.

                The night was darker here.

My black coat matched the black coats of the cats
Though it was bulky, armor for the battle
Of January, arrows in the wind,
Spears from the cold, and swords thrust through the gloom.

I climbed the flight of stairs and crossed the cobbles
Of the courtyard bordered on the left by lawn
And on the right and front by the portico
Adorning in an ell two golden walls,
The building's visible walls. Within the dark
A bit of lamplight touched the elevations
Behind and stroked the arches and the columns.
I stepped up one small step of travertine
That forms the portico's edge, traversed the bricks
That form the portico's floor, and stood confronting
The tall black paneled portal. In that black
There seemed to be a tinge of green. The white
Of simple marble makes the frame. The panels
Are four, two larger ones below, extending
Amply over my head, two smaller ones
Above for high-held crosses in processions.
The lower left-hand panel does not join
With absolute precision at the top
The margin of the panel just above it
But meets it with the slightest disconnection
That almost shows a tiny opening,
A separation as a hint of fissure,
Rift, slit, slot, gap, lacuna. Nonetheless,
I recognized my hands could never pry
And widen this slim crack or cleft or crevice
Which offered my one esperance of entry.

                                              What

What could I do? What else was there to do?
Should I lift up my fingers in this chill?
Should I aggressively transform my pen
Into my sword and seek and strike and slash?
A door without a keyhole or a doorknob
Rose boldly and uncompromisingly.
Here was strict closure. This was being shut
Out, locked out, out, out.

                    On either side
Frescoes inscribed beneath with names and letters
Keyed A, B, C, D, E, F, G reveal
Figures who see some vision if not given
In paint yet certainly within the painting
And acting in the painting, in its plane,
As viewers from outside feel, clearly feel,
Gazing within the contemplators' eyes.
The contemplators stay within and see.
Who are they? Closest to the door the writers
And intellectuals, Jerome, Augustine.
I sensed their presences but sensed myself
Outside the paintings of, on, in the walls,
Outside the walls, outside the bolted door,
Participating in that same dimension,
Which nothing from outside can ever open.

I turned, and through two columns and one arch
Of the gray portico I saw the arch
And column of the holm oak past the fountain.
The tree, beneath the arch, between the columns,
That grace the porch, expanded, was contained,
Higher and wider though it stood than that
Which framed it. Drawn, I walked across the cobbles,
Across the lawn, and paused before its greatness,
Its cobbled trunk, its green, its green-black, dome.
Passing beneath the tree, I reached the wall
Of stucco, tufa, brick, that lines the terrace:
Rampart and parapet, high, sheer, forbidding,
Seen from without; protective, ornamental,
                                         Low,

Low, pleasant, seen and seen from, from within.
I turned again and leaned on its support
And looked back through the route I had just followed.
Peering beyond the ilex, I could sight
The black rectangle of the door. A column
Of gray in front exactly marked the center.
How could that center open up to me?
I looked right. The basilica's white dome,
Azury, silvery, golden, white, was shining
In invocation to the Father in Heaven.
I looked left. There the black stone of the temple,
Once white, gold, gleaming, splendid and resplendent,
Had called upon the Father of the Sky.
Whom could I call upon or what invoke?
I paced the soft and bumpy rectangle of grass.
I paced the hard and bumpy rectangle of court.
I paced the hard and smooth rectangles of porch.

Ending the longer ell a frescoed wall
Held two grand sibyls, one in red and green
And one in silver and gold, one having written
And one still writing, both with pen in hand,
One gazing deeply into what she wrote,
One staring straight at me. How strong, intense,
Compelling was their attitude. A pen,
A piece of paper, must do much. I opened
My notebook and pulled out a page to write on.

Jerome, Augustine, intellectuals
And writers, hear my words within your walls,
See them within your vision, and receive them
Along the plane, along the plane, along the
Plane of the painting taking them and me
To and beyond, I wrote. I swiftly swiped
The sheet past that small gap between the panels.
Not automation but a humble sentence
Humbly penned elicited reply.
Augustine and Jerome were gone an instant,
And shocks of bolts unbolted shook the door.
The panels opened in.

                    I stepped through quickly,
Passing that barrier of smooth rebuff
And glad to feel the three-dimensional.
I was no longer out.

              I was not in.
A second door stood sturdily against me.
But this one had a keyhole and a handle,
And I possessed a key and held my hand
Ready to use this gift and all advantage.

I turned the key of Janus in the lock,
Whether to the left or to the right
I seem to have forgotten. Either way
It turned. I tried to lift the golden handle,
Then lowered it. I tried to pull, then pushed,
The right-hand panel of this inner door.
It yielded. It was open. I stepped in,
And with a little click it closed. I listened.
How with a loud dull clunk the outer portal
Shut and the threefold thump betrayed the bolting
My ears were witnesses. I did not look.
Was I inside? I did not look behind me.
Blindly I ventured forward in the dark.

Is knowledge vision? Did I knowing see
Not seeing and not seek an actual light?
To have seen is to know. I knew the site
So well my past became my future key.
This place, though doubly darker than the porch,
Did not force me to make my key my torch,
As when obscurity of eye and mind
Together rendered, render, doubly blind.
Magic acceded to the natural,
And memory could make the miracle.

Yes, memory retained a relevance
Because, because, although?, although?, because?,
Since I had come here many times before,
Before this time unlike all other times.
                                        This was

UMBRAGEOUS VISION | VISIO | VISION

This was a church, and I had entered it
Down through the years at reasonable hours
When it stood open and I did not think
How I got in or how I could get in.
Or if the gate was closed I went away
And simply came again some other day.
This day, this night, was other, utterly.

The church was very dark, and I was tired.
I usually visit Tasso's tomb
Within the backmost left-hand chapel. Now
The church was dark, and I was very tired.
All I desired was rest, relief, repose,
The nearest seat, the closest horizontal,
However hard, however hard to see.
I stood a moment to adjust my eyes,
Stumbled two paces up the center aisle,
Fumbled for wood, the feel of wood, the back
Backing the backmost left-hand pew, and sank
Onto the wooden bench. I put my book
Onto the wooden ledge and put my foot
Onto the wooden kneeler. I would kneel
Afterwards if I could. My legs were wood.
My feet were not of clay. My feet were stone.
Into my stony mind no tinge of guilt
Filtered. I put the other marble foot
Up as unfeelingly or regally
As weakling or as hero on that kneeler,
My footstool. On my knees my hands lay flaccid.

Somehow by memory and touch I had,
As well as setting pen and book together,
Already stored my other precious weapons.
I put the key back in my shoulder bag
And let the bag rest by me on the bench
Next to the hulky, humble, not gloves, mittens.
I put the umbrella on the little shelf
Below the ledge, then moved it to the knob
Below the shelf, musing confusedly

That I

That I could lay my glasses on the shelf
If light appeared before I had departed.
I hardly mused even if I did muse.
I barely moved even when I did move.
Inertia worked to govern mind and hand
And foot and knee and, shall I say it?, heart.
Could I be stirred to motion or emotion?
How could I think of thought or genuflection?

Yet maybe I could kneel just for a moment
To pray now to whatever god might hear,
Some god out of my past, out of my future,
Some present god, the Janus of this hill,
The Jesus of this church upon this hill,
The holy total white light sighted shining
Slight bright light white from height of height to height,
From high to low, and seen in varying colors
By the reflective or refractive mind
Of the diversity of humankind,
Or to those colors felt within the self,
Bits of existence honored as existing,
Or to the nonexisting hues of dream
That have an essence rather than a being,
That have their being in desire, in love,
In admiration, in the ought to be,
Or to vast azures which the child perceived
Throbbing in sapphire skies and in her chest
And resting in her eyes, her brain, her breast,
Or to the first cause that is final cause,
The first, unmoving, moving, calling cause
That is effect, that will be the effect,
The vision written, vision I admit
Trembling I see and write, must see and write,
Must go on seeing, writing, writing, seeing.
Janus sees both ways. I must pray to Janus
Before his day is over, in this dark.

Back down upon the marble floor I set
My marble feet, and with a forward movement
                                                   Remembered

Remembered from some past that, if remote,
Was not yet unfamiliar, heaved my body
Perhaps not gracelessly onto the kneeler,
Which, unexpectedly, amazingly,
Was far from hard, was soft, was subtly cushioned,
Delicate and receptive to the most
Fastidious or sensitive of structures,
Not nun's or gardener's or scrubbing woman's
Knees, rough and tough, inured, well trained, well used,
Used to encounters with the horizontal,
But thin-skinned organs where bone, sinew, nerve
Served high-strung instruments of walking, standing,
Practitioners of verticality,
Vertical search and upright contemplation
Suddenly bent, exhausted, in collapse.
How in my weariness, material,
Spiritual, full, empty, could I kneel,
Let alone pray? I shifted backward, slid
Back to the bench. My knees received my hands.

Well, I was still alive, and that was something.
And it was still the ninth of January
And not yet midnight. Of that I felt sure.
I felt less sure about what year it was
Or what millennium.

      This minute gripped
Rest as sufficiency. The church was still,
And I could sit silently and alone.

Blest be this quiet and this solitude.
But if I uttered lauds I did not hear them.
Yet I might write them.

       Wearily I reached
Out to the ledge and took my notebook down
And laid it on my lap and opened it
And pulled a sheet of paper from the pad
And, having closed the book again, held ready
The page upon the cover and the pen
             Upon the

Upon the page and in the darkness scribbled:

The Church of Sant'Onofrio, St. Humphrey's,
On January ninth . . .

                My hand relaxed,
Four fingers lightly folded on the page,
The pen propped in them like a gnomon slanting
Through digits, lifting up above the thumb,
Below the index, over the middle finger,
The point that could record illumination
Were there illumination to record.

I could not see the whiteness of the book,
The blueness of the pen, the white page lined
With blue, the left hand loosely, fondly, cradling
The corner of the notebook and the paper,
Both ivory in hue at height of noon,
The right hand unconditionally guarding
The cylinder of indigo and azure
Or what would glint such tint at dawn.

                              The book
Was sometimes crimson, sometimes white.

                                The bic
Was sometimes azure, sometimes black.

                              The absence
In the entire internal atmosphere
Of whiteness in a blackness acted and
Annihilated accidents of being.

Anguished as Ajax, Turnus, Solimano,
Breathing as feebly, sensing sinews languished,
Perceiving arteries and veins exsanguined,
Fearing no further battle since the night
Chivalrously suspended day's brute fight,

Hearing in peaceful stillness nothing, seeing
Nothing within that placid lack of light,

                                      Slumping

Slumping my bumpy backbone back and hunching
Towards the back meant to meet my back, fit back
Of the sustaining if uncushioned pew,

Along which sloped that spiny thing grown slack
And then that puny pillar turned to lead
And soon that recurved column had to melt,

I felt my eyes close and my heavy head
Sag like a wounded warrior's.
                                  I felt
Nothing.
            Was the sudden speech a dream?

Flora, Florinda, can you be asleep?

The voice, severe but sweet, resembled breath
Of laurel faintly filtered on a breeze
Telling the presence of the laurel sensed
And not yet seen.
                      How can your eyes stay closed?
How can you sleep?
                    Struggling I tried to raise
My head, to lift my lids.
                      My skull was up,
My eyes were open, and I met a glimmer
Of faintest light resembling faintest fragrance
Of laurel not too far, no, close, no, near.

He stood before me, slightly to the right,
Right in the center aisle, outside, beside,
The pew that was the one in front of mine.

Flora, do you not welcome me, not speak
To your good friend, not recognize your Tasso?

My Tasso? You the you that drew me here?
You of the written gift, the long-drawn song?

Io mi son un che, he began, I am
One who as poet poured into the poem
Breath, blaze, bloom, blessedness, my blood, and who
As man, as human spirit, think and care,
More than you dare imagine or suspect,
About you: you, your fire, your flowering.

The white ruff at the collar and the puff
Above the shoulder of the sleeve, the cloak
Tossed carefully or nonchalantly back,
The scabbard that descended from the belt,
Hinting of glint, were dimly visible.

Am I awake? This glimmer in the dark,
This glimmer of a person in this dark,
Stirred in my sleepiness a memory
Remembering the epic dawn, the Roman
Daybreak of this as yet unended day.
How did I name the Agonalia?
I heard the virgins' voices, glimpsed the glitter
Of their white garments, fainter, fainter, far
Now and yet not so far, just hours ago
And just across the river. I did see
Them, I did hear them, clearly, they did sing,
King, do you wake and watch? Wake, watch, O King.
Janus and Vesta met for a long instant.
That was the ending of the long beginning,
Long dawning of this January ninth
Dissolving in this January night.

Yet not yet ending, yet beginning still.
It is not yet tomorrow's dawn, not yet
Today's conclusive midnight, said the figure
Still standing there above me in the aisle
With that soft gleam about him. But his eyes
Regarded me intently, piercingly.

This is no time for sleepiness or sleep.
This is the time for vigilance and vigil.
Ismeno did not speak to Solimano
Nor golden Gabriele to Goffredo
                                                Nor to

Nor to Aeneas golden Mercury
More seriously than I now speak to you,
For truth and beauty are heroic quests
And pens like swords perform heroic gests
And written cities, liberated, built,
Through suffering, through struggle, won, constructed,
Or merely, if stern Fate should so decree,
Worked for and yearned for — no, of course, not only
Tried for and sighed for, only nearly merely
(Let rhetoric not be the flood, the deluge,
Cataract, avalanche, uprooting logic)
Yet necessarily most earnestly
Yearned for and worked for — may be tale, romance,
Satire or meditation or long lyric,
May be didactic, pastoral, or tragic,
May be the comedy, may be the epic,
May be the fragment or the tattered sketch,
Must, if fair favorable Fortune metes
Sufficiency of making and of saving,
Be both the poem and the dissertation.
The poem is your author's and your own.
The thesis appertains to you alone.
I speak plain speech to reach the pleading mind,
The plodding mind that pants for erudition,
The pedant's mind desirous of the vision,
The city rising, triumphing in light,
The child inheriting the light, the light
Finally in its loveliness enough.

His eyes were blue and beautiful, intense
And yet benevolent, his elegant
Mustache and beard were trim, aristocratic,
Courtly, his fine demeanor courteous
Yet strict, insistent, magisterial,
And yet suave, sweet, and kindly, not distracted
Or superficial but, it seemed, it seemed,
Welling from wells of feeling, thought, conviction.
I even dared believe that it was he.
I even dared believe he cared for me.

There is much more, he added with a smile,
Much to say, see, and do before tomorrow.

He was still standing in the nave above me.
Lifting my pen and notebook from my lap,
I laid them on the ledge. Could Flora Baum
Stay seated while Torquato Tasso stood?
I tried to rise, but, uttering a chuckle,
Making a gesture graceful both and gracious
With a hand large yet soft, yet delicate,
Shaking his head decisively yet gently,
He swerved a little, took a step, sat down.
He sat at the end of the bench before my bench,
Crossing his slippered feet in the aisle and grasping
That ledge which backed his pew and fronted mine,
His handsome and attentive face still turned
Towards me. The high, fine cheekbones visible
In the dim glimmer emanating from
His person were distinguished and distinctive.
Yes, this was he. My breath came quickly. Loud,
Loud seemed the beating of my heart. But could
I demonstrate my reverence?

                        I said,
How can I honor you? How can I thank you?

Flora, he answered, know there is no need.
I recognize your sentiments, their depth,
Their fervor. I respect their truth. I welcome
Your good will. We are friends. Let us be friends
Together in our grand adventuring.

I blushed as I responded, I must be
Brave, bold, audacious, foolhardy, a fool,
To speak to you, to speak of you, to seek
To be with you, to see myself beside you.
I ask your pardon, yet I trust your patience,
Your courtesy, your kindness, your kind caring.

Florinda, he replied, I know you well
And I have known you long. How young you seemed
That summer day!

                          I saw you one July
In a green grove.

                      There is a holy grove
Beyond the Herculean barriers
And past the western sea, reached by a breeze
Blown from the ocean, touched by sun, a sun
Ripe from the ocean, falling through the trees,
Teasing the grass to emerald among
Shadows of forest in a land where chants
Unheard, unknown, in older worlds, worlds known
As old, as older, though this forest be
Even primeval, one in which pines and hemlocks
Murmur to birds of worlds with warblings heard
As new, as other, rise with spring's ebullience
And sometimes simmer into summer, chants
Of blackbirds never black but gray of back
And rusty, rufous, orange, brick-red of breast
Yet, like the blackbird, with those thrush's eyes,
The thrush's large dark eyes that see in shadows,
And slender golden bill for golden song.
And other chants there are and clarions,
Soft lamentations of the mourning dove
For some unknown Patroclus with the fluting
Of wings that follows, or the eminent
Cardinal's scarlet carmina, both his
And hers, or in a blaze of blue the azure
Clang of the blue jay, or the crow's caws, calls
Of brilliant blackness, or the mockingbird's
Music, not gray but flashing white, and flashing,
Refracted in the prism of the song,
All of white's colors, all white's potencies,
All day, night, year, or the continuous
Twittering of the sweet swifts of the west
Blissful above the gentle elms of the west,
Above the gracious gestures of the elms.

You entered with the swifts' first chittering.

Dawn in her saffron gown stepped from the ocean
And into the grove slipped secretly, unseen,
Except that here and there, now there, now here,
Her brow of roses and her feet of gold
Showed in the shadow, shimmered in the shade,
Changing a bit of darkness to a beam
Of light.

      But you yourself were still outside
Though near, though very near, though at the verge,
Approaching from the north and from the west
Of that first eastern region, eastern edge,
That eastern strip of what itself was west,
What was the west.

      And yet you did not enter
There at the northwest corner by the ash
But walked east on the northern border, glancing
In at the trees that flourished near the margin,
The oak, the elm, the maple, as you skirted
The spring you termed the fountain of the youth
And passed the walnut with its nestling nuts
In husks of green among green leaflets, for
It seemed a walnut and it is a walnut.

Just beyond this, two tall catalpas flanked
The central northern entrance. In that year
Of chilly winter, chilly spring, late summer,
They bloomed upon this fifth day of July,
Now raising, elevating, through their big
Green leaves their big white panicles of blossom.

These were the guards, the guardians, of the grove
But more like hosts than sentinels or sentries
Or soldiers. Holding up as vigilant torches
Large lanterns like large candelabra, festive
Decor to light a feast, they held a welcome
Of bell or cup, of chalice or campana.
                              The white

The white campanas rang. On fine green napkins
The chalices stood ready. One descended
Direct, erect, into your outstretched hand
Extended more in homage than in hope
Or in desire below, between, the boles
That rose, gray pillars, to green vaulting domes.

The scalloped chalice, redolent of nectar,
Was ivory, adorned within with regal
Purple of runes, two lines of godly gold
Whereby research divines the goodly goal,
For they have led directly to the well
Of nectar's delectable dregs, which, down in the depths,
Yet spume deliciously as scent ascending,
And mysteries of glister soft and restful,
A glisten brilliant still and pleasant ever,
Subtle and fresh as nectar, as refreshing.

Refreshed, you entered then, a grateful guest,
Between those hosts that were two tall catalpas,
And kept on walking forward, straight between
The two tall oaks, between the two small oaks,
And then went curving, circling, wandering
Among the variations of the shade.
How long did you meander in the grove
That day? You seemed at home among the trees,
Among those trees unknown beyond the seas
Between their world and ours, our common world.

How long did you go wandering among
Tulip trees, redbuds, lindens, spruces, firs,
Locust trees, honeylocusts, buckeyes, beeches,
The trees called bluebeech, hornbeam, ironwood,
Yellowwoods also called virgilias,
Kentucky coffeetrees called coffee trees,
Those hollies truly trees and truly hollies,
And ever elms, oaks, hemlocks, pines, and maples,
Oh, maples, sugar maples, sweet and green
And bright and light and plenitudinous?

                                                      How long?

How long? As long as gaily orange and lemon
Daylilies smiled and laughed not far within
The western entrance where the sundial kept
Its watch between two amicable catalpas
That, sturdy, flourishing, florescent, florent,
Uncompromising in their loveliness,
Kept their watch, too, upon the west, as others
Did on the north and others on the south?

You always called the yellowwoods virgilias.
You savored soft or strong Virgilian rhythms
In all the constants, all the permutations,
Of all the trees. Your glance, stance, dance observed
The dactyls of the elms, spondaic oaks,
Dactyls of elms in the levity lent by their lightness,
Oaks' slow spondees, grave growth, grove's own grave weight,
Concord of word and music through the breeze,
Stiffening conflict if winds whipped wands, wounds,
Alliteration in the little leaflets
Lifting on locusts and on honeylocusts,
Assonance in the aspects, granite-toned,
Of boles of beeches and virgilias
If each is seen, considered, fixed, revealed,
If leaves are written on or lips unsealed,
If utterance of trunks inscriptions yield.

After the trumpets of the morning, after
The drums of noon, all through the afternoon,
Will, can, a golden bough amid the shadows
Above an ocean-roll of rhythm glimmer?

Or were there any Ennian echoes there?
Ask if the ash will crash, burn, turn to ashes.
No, this is a beginning, not the end.
Janus has come already, not yet Vesta,
And Vesta's sunsets are not funerals
But flame of home.

                      The laurel, not the cypress,
Will lighten dusk beside felicious olive
                                                    When

When journeys towards the west of east, turned towards
The occident of orient, throughout
The world of words, the universe of verse,
Out through the loci of both shade and sun
Where figures fashion actuality,
Will free the east that is Hesperia.

You strolled on, cheerful in your reverence,
Through the vast annals of the afternoon,
Of summer's endless Ennian afternoon.

Following in the footsteps of your shadow,
You passed a yew, deep green, full, beautiful.
Although like all yews growing in this grove
It was not arborescent but a shrub,
It was a yew. Depths, lustrous surfaces,
Were the yew's beauty, dark, smooth, flexible.
As you walked by it under late rays of sun,
That rose-hued stem, those ample branchings, rendered
It wide and high, shrub rising higher than you.
It is a worthy yew, and just beyond it
Lived the great elm, still lived on in its greatness.

You stood beneath the grand and ancient elm
Ascending and extending and descending,
The elm content, entire, whole, self-contained,
Generous, stretching forth, empowering,
Long loved, much loved, much sung, long sung, by you
Who took your stand beneath it now.

                              Not far
From where you stood, walked up and down, stood, walked,
Walked up and down, walked back and forth, stood still,
Still in the northern portion of the grove
Under and near the elm, you saw across
The grass and through the trees the temple rising
Upon the south.

                    You knew it well.

                                    To Truth
It had been, it was, it is dedicated,
And from its trees you sought Truth, contemplated
That which you sought, revered the Verity
Which you kept seeking, which you sought to see.

On its facade the fane had three large doors
Gorgeous in black wrought iron figurations
And framed with white solidity of stone.
The third, the right-hand, door was opening.
Behold, before it, to my eyes, to yours,
An I know not what of luminous appears
Which there with beam of silver, flash of gold,
Brightens the shadow. Something, too, or someone —
Was it a statue gold and ivory?
Was it a woman who had just emerged
Out of the right-hand portal of the temple? —
Effortlessly held up that other something,
That gleam, that glitter, gleaming, glittering thing,
Thing of the moonbeam and the lightning flash.
She moved, and to the center she went gliding
Smoothly and statuesquely yet with human
Or grander than mere human stance and tread,
Passing along the platform, through two columns,
And slowly down the high wide gray stone stairway.

Along the path across the grass, between
The oaks and then the elms and honeylocusts,
On that gray path that crosses green, green grass,
Below, between, tall trees green, green, she came
Lightly and lovely in her golden sandals,
Carrying armor through the peaceful grove,
And in her step the goddess was revealed.

She walked tall, slender, stately, straight, and strong.
But was she clad in armor? No, that glister
Of gold was not her helmet and its crest
But golden curls above a crimson mantle
Over a graceful gown as white and peaceful
As Roman stola or as Roman toga.

Yet she was carrying both shield and sword,
Not as for battle but as though for someone,
Perhaps a gift for some great warrior,
Achilles or Aeneas or Rinaldo.
I thought this and I thought you thought this, too.
Watching her you were standing very still.
She kept advancing towards you on the path.

Her gown was white, and were you robed in black
And veiled in black when you came to the grove
This day, or was that ample black your garb
Some other year, some other summer, some
Other July the fifth in that same place?
Yes, I remember, calling up another
Decade, another century, another
Millennium within that holy grove
And seeing you, observing you in black
There with another time's experience
There among other wonders, equal marvels,
Miracles similar and different.

This wonder was her coming towards you now
As, simply dressed in denim, you stood looking.

Her fine white gown was subtly interwoven
With blue, green, purple, silver, black, and gold,
In smooth wool web with intricate inlay
That complicated but did not deny
The candor and the purity of whiteness,
While gold thread glimmered through her purple mantle,
Rendering crimson gleam and golden glister
A play of brilliancies and modulations.

Luminous, numinous, she came to you.
Strength of intelligence, of intellect
Profound and radiant and blazing shone
Steady, unwavering, within, upon,
That face that no less flashed from eyes that laughed
A mobile cleverness, Ulyssean,
Shrewd, humorous, which blended with the flame
Of something serious, severe, and solemn.

With her bright gray-blue gaze she gazed upon you.
She halted and she stood there tall before you.
She held out the enormous shield and sword.

The sword was flashing black, was flashing azure.
The shield was gleaming white, was gleaming crimson.

Like the catalpa blossom, like acanthus,
Either as pure or as empurpled white,
And like the rose, a purple that is pearl,
An ivory of lavender or lilac,
Oh, like the rose as violet as white
Can seem, as white as violet can be,
And like the snow, now white, now mauve, now both,
Now dubitable, now white, the shield was shining,
Its candor, its purpureality,
As crimson as the homefire on the mountain
Seen by the sailor sailing on the sea,
As milky as the moonlight in the sky
Observed by earthlings.

      Sky blue seemed the sword.
It seemed cerulean, celeste, celestial.

The sword was flashing black as starry night.
The shield gleamed white as star within that night.

The sword flashed azure as a sunlit sea.
The shield was gleaming crimson as a sun
Lifting from out that sea.

      The goddess lifted
The arms higher.

     Then there beneath the elm
She set them down before you and you trembled
At the reverberating clang, the clangor.

Yet in your eyes a gleam, a flame, reflected,
Accepted, their bright blaze. Your eyes blazed joy.

Her eyes were flashing as she spoke to you.

These are your shield and sword in time of need
For epic battle; in a time of need
For veil, for toga, or for tapestry
These are your loom and shuttle; in the time
Of gravest, greatest, grandest, glorious need
For gifts that glitter, mirror, and endure
These are your blank book and pinpointing pen.
Hence the historiation of the shield,
The weaving of the wool that makes the text,
The telling of the story of the book,
Are yours to dare. Then dare. Rejoice in daring.
Dare to rejoice. Rejoice to learn, to study,
Study with ruddy Vulcan, forging, flaming,
Sending forth strengths, and learn from me, Minerva,
Standing beside you, by you, with you, shining.
I with these gifts give skill and with this call
Infuse a fire, a light, sonority
Of flute, of trumpet, stamina for war,
For peace, for peacefulness, heart for the works
Of womanhood and of virility,
Joy in the ivory, the ebony,
The polychrome of present meditation,
Broad day, wide night, of present contemplation,
Joy in the agon, past the agony
On to the azured lanes of liberty,
On to empurpled heights of harmony.

The shield and sword are heavy. Do not fear.
Like wings they lift against the weight of war.

You have shunned loom and shuttle. Do not shudder,
For if Camillan or Clorindan fingers
Fumble upon the web my hand brings art
Just as to brush and canvas, just as to
Tibia, tuba, and a staff unfilled.
Like bird on wings the hand and fingers fly,
Skimming the plain, the mountain, and the sky.

The empty book, the ready pen, unstirred,
Wait late. Create with joy each winged word.
Release scenes by you seen, sounds by you heard.

Learn from Minerva. If your shield is white
Recall white-shielded warriors, recall

The white, the bright, shield of Deiphobus,
Son to King Priam and Queen Hecuba,
To Hector of his brothers much the dearest,
White-shielded husband to the white-armed Helen
After the death of Paris, leader, hero,
Whose bronze-topped shield damaged the bronze-tipped spear,
Whose bronze-plated shield fractured the bronze-pointed spear,
Whose oxhide shield shattered the shaft of the spear
Of ashwood which Meriones had thrown
Against him down by the ditch, wall, huts, ships, sea,

The white, the blank, the plain shield of Helenor,
Son of a king and son, too, of a slave,
Whose mother brought him secretly to life
And sent him in forbidden arms to death,
Not willingly, by sending him to Troy
Against the Greeks, because, surviving, still
In his first youth, he passed to Italy
Among the yet untried young Trojans, still
Inglorious, for undistinguished still,
Lightly equipped, with bare sword and blank buckler,
To perish in the desperate encounter,

The pure, the plain, the blank shield of Camilla,
Which, not inglorious, unterrified
Horsewoman, huntress, heroine, the maiden
Dear to Diana, dread equestrian
On foot in fight and with bare sword, displayed,
And Trivia erected and inscribed
After the battle, far from the battlefield,
Above her sepulcher, her monument,
When, rescuing them, in a hollow cloud,
The loving, grieving goddess had conveyed
Her armor and her holy body home.

But if your shield glints crimson, remember sunset,
And if it glimmers crimson, recall the dawn.
The azure sword tells noon, the black spells night.
Shades are at play in the trees and across the lawn.
Glory marks buckler raised and dagger drawn.

Learn what I teach through speech and by my being.
On me you see the gleaming of the shield,
The spear, the helm, the scabbard, hilt, and blade,
While my eyes flash in battle and my cries
Crash like my father's thunder through the skies.
The warrioress must shoulder shield and sword,
Taught by example and by shining word.

If I took off the gown which I myself
Had made myself and dropped it to the floor
To don Jove's tunic and the garb of war,
Arming myself with aegis, helm, and spear,
Juno put on the gown which I myself
Had made her, and she fastened it with care
With golden pins, when she desired to stir
In Jove desire to lie in love with her.
Whether I wear or share what I have made
Or share the lovely power of the making,
From me you learn the beauty of the loom.
Clever Penelope, to whom I gave
The knowledge and the skill to do the most
Beautiful work, to make most beautiful
Works, and an excellence of intellect,
And shrewdness and astuteness, more than all
Greek women of renown before her time,
Tyro, Alcmena, and well-crowned Mycena,
None of whom knew as much or was in mind
Or wit as gifted as Penelope,
Who wove a robe both fine and very wide,
Even in Hades underground remembered
As shining like the moon or like the sun,
Was not, for all her workmanship, for all
Her artistry, her art, her fame, the sole

Weaver

Weaver of something bright and glorious,
For Hermes heard Calypso as he came
Bearing his wand and messages from Zeus
To her as to Aeneas Mercury
Would come with messages from Jupiter
Later and even later Gabriel
To Godfrey came with messages from God,
Or will come, for I speak of future things
With all those tenses that suggest the past
Of heroes hearing messengers from heaven,
Receiving visitations from Olympus,
Or heroines or nymphs or goddesses
Dwelling on earth and heard by gods arriving
As guests whom they in turn must hear, for Hermes
Will hear Calypso singing with her voice
Of beauty as before her loom she walks
Weaving her web of beauty with her shuttle
Of gold. Thus you must sing and singing weave,
For heroes hear, will hear, or will have heard
Circe, enchanting Circe, as she sang,
As she will sing, is singing, with her voice
Of beauty as before her loom she walks
Weaving a web great, fragrant, and immortal
Such as are works which goddesses accomplish,
Fine, full of grace and glory. As she walks
And weaves, the whole floor sounds and sounds of song.
The heroes call to her, and men will know
That she can charm and that she can be wise.

Men call me wise Minerva. If they write,
This wisdom brings particular delight.
To you such joy must come one sunny day
Shining in dawn's or noontide's golden ray
And must not be undone when dusk takes sway,
When darkness rules, but must outlast the night.

Lifting the sword she handed you a pen.
Of blue it was, then suddenly of black.
Your shoulder bag will shelter it, she said,
                                         Or you

Or you will hold it in your fingers ready.
It seemed prosaic yet it gleamed. Your grip
Quivered a bit, then stiffened, then grew steady.

Lifting the shield she handed you a book,
A crimson notebook suddenly of white.
This notebook you may carry everywhere,
This notebook you may cradle on your arm,
She said. It looked prosaic yet it shone.
It will protect you as you it from harm.

A glitter issued from those instruments
As of Vulcanian ignipotence,
As of Tritonian armipotence,
And both within them and around them glowed
The lucence to Minervan wisdom owed.

The book was based in your left arm and hand.
The pen was poised in your right hand and fingers.
You grasped both happily. Minerva smiled.

Thus, Flora, Florinalda, you were given
Gifts from Olympus, gifts from very heaven.

Then Tasso added, No more will I tell,
Because itself this book, this loom, this shield,
Will tell much more. Months roll voluminous.

Memorable Minerva you remember
At Rome in March, in June, and in September,
And in the distant grove July the fifth
Commemorate the giver and the gift.

Still of that grove I must evoke one last
Picture. Within, a subtle dusk gloamed vast,
And, as you left, a nighthawk swept the sky,
Swept, swooped, and swiveled. His insistent cry
Was not the crack of croaks or hollow howls
To you but speech unfolded there on high,
Articulate with consonants and vowels.
Rejoicing though you could not see the bird,

You

You willed to listen as he willed to fly.
I heard you murmuring the word you heard.

This was that granting of a summer's trust
In a far western woodland in July.
I witnessed, too, the precious presentations
Made here in January, in the city,
Here in your world's own center, here in Rome.

When it was given January sixth,
As you have written in your dissertation
With full description and complete narration,
I saw the emerald bow with silver arrows,
Which is the broomstick green with silver bristles,
Which is the green umbrella with its spokes
And pole of silver, graciously bestowed
On you by Luna, Hecate, Diana,
And by the witch of Epiphany, the befana,
In her long silver plait and old green shawl
Among her gray-eyed and her green-eyed cats
And the decrescent piles of her possessions
Where as she slept the bomb left her untouched
Down by the arch of Janus Quadrifront.

I saw you on the first of January,
Just as your thesis lengthily declares,
Receive from Janus by the Sacred Way
Within twin gates that peace or war purvey
What he had promised earlier that day
Beside the fragrant gold of wintersweet
On the Janiculum, the golden key
Which is the little flashlight, little torch,
Fit for your purse, which is the bigger torch,
The fiery firebrand fit for bitter war.

And war, Florinda, there must be for you.
The pacifist who falls in love with Rome,
The pacifist who lives in history,
The pacifist who lives in poetry,
                                        The poet

The poet who confronts philosophy,
The lover of the wisdom that will free,
The lover who has longed for liberty,
The lover who has loved the peaceful home
Home to the good, the beautiful, the true,
Must face the fight of heaven and of hell
And of that vast land, fatherland of grayness.
Ask Trivia, Tritonia, and Janus.
You will see all one day, will see and tell.
To have seen is to know. I know you well,
You see. Now know I wish you very well.

He ceased. He moved his hand down from the ledge,
Which it at first had grasped, where it had rested,
On which it had been clenched or from which lifted
From time to time in emphasis. He placed it
Firmly upon the pommel of his sword,
Then in an instant shifted it and set it
Lightly upon his knee. He ceased from speaking
But not from gazing at me with concern,
Benevolence, a certain tenderness,
Like a good teacher, father, brother, friend.

I reached out towards the ledge, on which my pen
And notebook lay, and held it with my hand
And drew a breath. My gratitude was great,
And I was calm and happy, yet I felt
Inadequate attempting a reply.
I let my hand fall back into my lap.

How can I thank you? How my heart is warmed,
Is brightened, by encouragement, with courage!
My heavy, hesitating heart leaps, knowing
How deeply you have known it, me, here knowing
How well you knew the steel, how thrillingly
Your great quill, light and weighty, flew and soared
Like a great eagle.

            How my heart grows full!

How can I thank you? Can I dread to wield
A sword as futile as an icicle,
A pen as futile as a broken sword?
No, it is not the blade and not the shield
The shattering of which my heart has feared.
I bear the arms. Have I the captain's hand?
I wear the robes. Have I the monarch's mind?
This royal glaive is unavoidable.
Yet all my talk of weaponry, of war,
Is not material but metaphor.

The meanings that are figured are the more
Important, Tasso stated. In our world
There is just so much matter for our speech
Which must be multiplied as figures reach
Regions more swarthy or more whitely pearled.
With writing rise rich opportunities
For opulent dimensions, nth degrees.

Our foe, the greatest of our enemies,
The overwhelming enemy of each
Of us, is our great friend, our greatest friend,
Our self. We struggle on until we touch
The reddest depths, the greenest heights, the much
More complex place of peace, our simplest end.

Let me not oversimplify. On these
Subjects we can discourse one day at ease
If leisure pleases and if we, too, please.
We will not mingle what must be distinguished
And separate what ought to be connected
Nor substitute revenge and violence
And overweening military might
And brutal, brittle, blinkered belief and brutish
Brutality of brash retaliation
And blasting, blighting cycle of reprisal
For reasoning, for reasonable deeds,
For reason, nor, as I may do, replace
Poetry, myth, and song with prose, with logic,
                                         With rhetoric,

With rhetoric, with all this credit, with
This excellence, thus letting certain strange,
Fine, trailing veils and gowns and clouds and comets
And glooms and glimmerings and dazzlings vanish
From sentences, nor, as I may not do,
Replace strong, sober prose with frantic verse
Blithely or blindly, counterfeiting poems,
Nor substitute the combat for the parley,
Substitute wars for words, the mongering
Of wars for worthy words, or substitute
Our easy anger for hard understanding,
Our rigid anger for soft understanding,
Our moralizing for morality,
Our harsh prose for a subtle poetry,
War as abstract for war as forced on me.

Yet let me note that if the metaphor
Or if the vehicle of metaphor
Is not the action but the instrument,
Is not the warfare but the hilted sword,
I must note, too, that with the pen we fare
The farthest, far past battle, past the self.
If sword means pen and swordsman stands for penman,
Swordswoman stands for intellectual,
Swordswoman represents what man has meant,
Swordswoman signifies the woman writing
Her way past selfhood to virility,
Past human personality to virtue,
Past femininity to heroism,
Beyond the woman on to work, the work,
Action again, activity and act,
Act and the act, the art, the work of art,
An altar of the Agonalia,
Arena of ethereality,
Both Vestal fireplace and Vulcanal forge
Refining matter towards eternal form,
Maybe existing, certainly essential.
The scholar and the poet disappear
Into the scholarship, the poetry.
                              The woman

The woman of the sword which is the pen
Even in darkness sparkles. She becomes
The written thing which is the constellation.

Not to a difference of sex, of gender,
But to a shift of species and of genus,
Of situation in the universe,
Are we invited, summoned, when the god
Confers shield, sword, loom, shuttle, notebook, pen.
Having intensely turned into ourselves,
We turn into that which we do, weave, write,
And if two should survive they would be Castors,
And if just one that one is an immortal,
Another I like Hercules consumed
By fire and gone to live among the Muses,
Become that second self which, if a thing,
Is king, god, raised aloft to speak and sing,
A heavenly choir, celestial city, home.
I am Jerusalem. You must be Rome.

And yet I speak too plainly to speak true.
Some day the sibyl will expound to you
The paths of blackness and the roads of blue,
And if one's image is the one one drew,
And whether man is man or woman, too,
And where the gods are many or are few,
And how the eyes of Janus find the view
Both east and west, and which old tree is new.

But once, I countered, when what I had marked,
My shield, my tapestry, my scribbled page,
Was snatched away, was wrenched from me, was gone,
Grief alone lingered, grief alone was left,
And how I wept how keenly I remember:

If I build walls and they are battered down
Or slide like mud or wash away like sand
Or, lost in anesthesiology,
Suddenly dimming consciousness, dissolve,
Will some existences have had their hour
                                        Or certain

Or certain essences have had their play
Or certain eyes been satisfied or some
Faces left vacant for eternity?

Down went the walls of Jericho, Jerusalem,
Down went the famous walls of famous Rome,
Down went the walls which like a toponym
Before the greatness failed had gained a name.
What walls of mine built high and strong enough to last
Forever, in an instant turned to dust
Forever, seen by none? Can they be missed
After a Fate determined: They are lost?

These walls which I must cease to mourn were seen
By none before the close of their short year,
Short week, short hour. If they had briefly blazed
In sun or briefly gleamed beneath the stars
Gazed at by struck admiring eyes or eyes
Attentive or indifferent or hostile
Before they vanished, would the longer loss
Be less? And are the builder's eyes not eyes?
Then was the builder's a sufficient bliss?

Having passed over, Tasso gently said,
Into a godly, into a ghostly, realm,
I ask that you consider, too, ghosts, gods,
Among your watchers and your listeners.

Recall, too, how in epic war Minerva
Restored the weapon hurled and how his sword
To Turnus was returned first by Juturna
And then from Venus to Aeneas sped
Back his spear fixed in the wild olive stump.

Thoughtfully, thankfully, I then responded:
On the eighth day — How grateful I must be,
Am, and shall stay forever! — some kind god
Delivered what I deemed was gone forever,
When I had recognized, experienced,
Suffered, the second death, the perishing,
And not

And not what I had gleaned before, the mere
Perishability, of something made
To last, work fashioned by a mortal hand
Yet work erected towards eternity.

What then of time and timing? When times changed
I queried further: Keening walls unseen,
Shall I bewail the walls of Washington,
Lament the walls that fall in tall New York,
The walls, the wars, the afters, the befores?
Pelion, Babel, yield the gravest rubble
To some, to some the line of sky, to some
The body bags, the body parts, the bodies.
But public suffering is private sorrow
As masses splinter and specks reamass
And probing pokes at vanities untold.

Flaming self-righteousness which cannot face
What I have done that this was done to me,
What we have done that this was done to us,
And who or what is I and who, what, we,
And chains of those emotions which a guess
Presses into one's sense of sailing free
Become lumps, substances which one must trace
Through thought, through sentiment, through history,
One's self, one's country, one's whole universe,
Even that second cosmos, poetry.

My life, too, knew these truths, replied my mentor
With a soft sigh of loss and reminiscence.
But now we must begin our pilgrimage
Out to the oak. The others will come later.
Now we have time and now it is the time
For us to see the tree which saw my grief
And enter next the cell which saw my death
Here in the monastery by the church
And then return to contemplate my tomb
And welcome all the rest.

                           He stood. He looked
Above me and behind me towards the doorway,
And as I hesitated, Come, he said,
Now we must go.
                I twisted in my pew
A bit and peered behind me through the dark.
Then I stared up at him. Who are the rest,
I wondered, who the others? I decided
Not to inquire at present. I could wait.
I could ask afterwards or merely watch
To see what happened. Why not? I would wait.
I was still weary, and he was repeating
Courteously and yet insistently,
Come. He reiterated, Come. He added,
It is still far from midnight. There is time
Before tomorrow's liturgy begins.

He looked so eager I could not refuse,
And in his voice I heard a melody
As of a cello, a tonality
As of a woodthrush or a hermit thrush,
Enticing like a rippling rivulet,
A breezelet from a meadow or an ocean,
A rocky waterfall that piped to me.

Assembling all my instruments with ease,
I rose. We walked together to the entrance.
He grasped the brassy handle, and it yielded.
He drew the bolts, and they obeyed his hand.

We stopped a moment in the January
Blackness and chill. Behind us, I could guess
From noise I knew, Augustine and Jerome
Secured the church once more.
                               The gate had stayed
Locked, I remembered. Locked the gate would stay
Against our exit as it had stayed locked
Against my entering. He was a ghost.
                                       I recognized

I recognized this dimly. He could pass
Straight through the mass. Although I think I seemed
Myself a little spectral to myself,
I was still made of matter. Should I try
Magic once more? He was a gentleman.
He turned left towards the corridor that led
In towards the cloister and some convent doors.
Before the entrance to that passageway,
Under the portico, on a pilaster
Right of the door, he found and pressed a golden
Button (I called it golden) known to him,
To me unknown. A cluck, a click, a clang
Were the reactions, gratifying answers.
Cluck was immediate, was the electric
Unlocking. When we heard it we went striding
Across the cobblestones and sped descending
The thirteen steps. Despite the lightlessness
Outside me and the strengthlessness within,
I felt no need to reach out for the green
Railing upon my left along the stairway.
Upon my right the poet grasped the gate
With his right hand, with confidence, with firmness,
Left of the center. Click was the response,
The signal given by the opening.
Then to the left he drew the left-hand section
Squeaking along the metal of the groove
And with a smile invited me to go
Through and then partly followed me and, turning,
Pulled that left-hand, now the right-hand, portion
Leftward again and to the center. Clang
Was closure.

        Subtler was the undulation,
Pulsation, fluctuation, vague vibration,
Wavering, waving, trembling, quivering.
Then all stood still.

              Then all stayed very still.

We stayed until the wind came up the hill
Long minutes afterwards, those two or three
Minutes, sufficient for plurality
And time.

                But when I started shivering
He started down the second set of stairs.
I glanced back suddenly and unawares.
One black cat at the gate, one on the wall,
Watched us depart and seemed to wish us well.

The arrows of the wind assaulted us
Few moments more, and as they ceased we crossed
The crosswalk from the curb across the curving
And cobbling of the road below the terrace
And reached the pietrini of the path.

Nocturnal, silent, things of night, of silence,
Black into blackness, cold into the cold,
We went.

* * *

Old, wingèd god, whose birth long long ago
Amidst the emptiness is seen to be
An interruption of infinity,
You are so old your step is known as slow,

And yet you fly. My mind, creeping below
The weight of nothing, through the agony
Of blindness in a structure formed to see,
Of blankness in a creature born to know,

Cries to you, time, truth's father. Does she play
High there above white clouds? Could she befriend
My lovelorn age as she seduced my youth?

Go slow, time, as you take my days away.
Come quickly bringing truth before the end.
Truth, be my end. Oh, be my being, truth.

This crownless tree is truthful. Over there
That plant, unblasted, grand, so near, so far,
That dome so holy and so secular,
Sod's coronal, is arching into air,

Tenuous, crescent, full, robust, rich, rare,
Dim, light, white, mighty, shining, rising star,
Dolorous tomb, triumphant sepulcher,
High and refined and elegant and spare,

Mind's whole and yet perfection of the part,
Solid, abstract, complex, pure, simple, line,
Material and mathematical,

Erected by the human hand and heart
And yet angelic, earth's and yet divine,
If not the true at least the beautiful.

Your ancient temple, not so far away,
Down there across the river, silently,
Partly marble, partly memory,
Arises into night, as into day,

Phoebus, like chords which sunny fingers play,
Strumming the columns that could come to be
Part of a summer's noon, the harmony
Of pillars lifted, lyric, sweet with bay.

I saw you and your sister in the sky,
And I was yours, was hers, and I am still,
Now and forever. Could you then seem cruel?

Yours are health, truth, and beauty. Therefore why
Am I ignored and ignorant and ill?
Could I have seen your sister in the pool?

UMBRAGEOUS VISION | VISIO | VISION

The moon is in the pool, is in the river,
Or was when I was there a while ago,
How long a while I fear I do not know.
This night has been so long it seems forever.

This night began. I fear it will be over
Only too soon. Within this dark that glow
Poses the moon. Does shy Diana show
Herself thus nude? And must we strive to cover

Covetous eyes in love with loveliness?
Is existential peril something stranger
Than vision as it quivers here between

Cosmos and comedy? In her undress
The maid was made the beast, the star. The danger
Is not the seeing but the being seen.

Why does the night drip crystals? Are they tears?
Why have the winds the chill
Of fingers fumbling on the instruments
Of leafless trees as though each missing leaf
Alleviated grief
Once whereas now the boughs, stark evidence
Of loss, resound with fears
Whispered by midnights, winds, and winters? Will
You leave me here alone, O honored ghost,
Bereft, beloved guest?

Although my sighs and my laments ignore
The force of what I recognized before,
I know the poet is the poetry.
This is the living man, the mind, the heart.
This is the spirit, this the visitor
From the celestial regions of the sheen,
From universes where bright truths are seen,
Out of the depths of human questioning,
Out of profundities of mirroring,
Abysses which will image altitudes
That rise the higher from the deeper roots
Like trunks, like trees, like beams, like dreams of roods,
Plunges of kettledrums with flights of flutes,
Descents through hells, ascents through purgatories
To peaks of paradise, through all the stories
Of heavens, and through all the allegories
Splendid with luminous and endless glories.
Beyond the prison of our misery,
Beyond the stranglehold of agony,
I glimpse the liberation that is art
And feel the freedom of love's cynosure,
Beauty aloft and radiant and pure.

Which was the subject, which the predicate?
The work and not the person is the pearl.
The other self that lives outside the self,
The made and not the maker, is the jewel.
The king is dead. Long live the king. The poet
Dies and the poet's poetry is all.
Then do not pity, mourn, hate, love, or feel
Anything for the mortal. Read the real.

The lustrous lush autumnal rose sends sweet
Scent past the ends of fall's last gentleness
Releasing exhalations that caress
Faces once patient of the long day's heat

Which now assume rigidity to greet
The first fierceness previsioning the press
Of winter. Reddest edge and depth say yes
To joy before the colorless retreat

Of earth into a universe of noes.
Once all was promise, all green burgeoning,
All a first freshness in the innocent air.

But was the rosebud better than the rose?
And is the lyricism of the spring
A beauty which November cannot bear?

I felt your anguish over every book
That held your precious rhymes, for I perused
Your letters. How each editor confused
Everything, mixed up everything, then took

The profits of those pearls home like a crook
I saw. Four centuries had then abused
These jewels. No new setting could be used.
Hope bloomed alone in one secluded nook.

Fingers would pose a danger to the pages.
The room was only for the really rare.
I almost touched your sonnet with my nose.

The book was musty with the dust of ages,
In artificial light, conditioned air,
But I inhaled the fragrance of your rose.

Were you too logical? Or were you mad?
Were you too moral? Or too insincere?
Too full of arrogance? Too full of fear?
Or too excitable? Or just too sad?

Is it the Zeitgeist? Is it not a fad?
Is laureation only for the bier?
If any overview is very clear
Is it not also clearly very bad?

Only the literary is the true.
There that which opens closes, does not close,
Blossoms, is, is what is, is what is not.

Beneath a distant everlasting blue
We reach the secret sweetness of the rose
Of pearl and gold and peach and apricot.

Since you must know the yew if it is you
Because it is your name and if a name
And that which bears it truly are the same
What you have said about it must be true

If as an undergraduate you knew
Yourself, your trees, the bees that come, that came
And tasted what it bears since you did claim
That from it bitter honey must ensue

And very bitter is the designation
Of all that dulcitude that is your own
Gift to the universe. But now we meet

Here by the oak that bears its appellation
From you, named, famed, for you, for you sought, known,
With your cognomen sweet and bittersweet.

In that infinite distance
Between me and the vision
Which to my mind was sight
And which I faithfully believed I would
And which I desperately hoped I could,
When faith had failed the test of finitude,
And which the fiery might
That is desire drawing the stars all night
Down to the self or lifting
The heart up to the stars should, after hope
Has sunk to simple desperation, grope
Or fly for with success,
I gripped a glimpsed infinity of rope
That reached the limit of the limitless
And guided one across
Without exceeding the accepted norm
Of the selected form,
Without the long unraveling of loss,
As though I held the reins of Pegasus
Through quiet and through storm
In my own individual insistence
Upon the common mission,
Uncomplicated in this single instance,
Of trusting in a turning of the trope
And climbing up, not rolling down, the slope,
But my balloon, captive perhaps, then free,
Rose with an undirected liberty,
And I was simply drifting.

* * *

Am I Aeneas? Can I be Goffredo?
I sing the armor and the heroine.
I am the warrior. I bear the arms.

Am I more fortunate than Alexander?
More than Elizabeth? I must be Tasso.
I am the Homer of the new Achilles,
I the Achilles of the latest Homer.
I will like Gaius Julius Caesar write
Of my own wars.

        I write of my defeats.

I speak of them to you, dear comforter.
Forgive me while my miseries meet yours
Here where your mortal miseries were met
Under its shadow by the vital oak
Still green through April dawns, noons, afternoons,
Here where through night, through winter, we can share,
Pensive, repensive, pain or loss or fright
Under the oaken shadow of the sky.

I rest beneath the tree and then I tread
Again the roads to Rome, the roads of Rome,
The avenues and alleyways of Rome,
Searching, researching, for the walls of Rome,
Those which I must discover, must construct,
Have found, have founded, find, found, fight to free,
Rescuing them from slavery so harsh,
A servitude endured, endurable
No longer, unendurable at last,
The crush of ruination all around
And clutch of pride, lust, anger, gluttony,
Sloth all within me, clustered, cluttering,
Dug, digging, dinning, dunning, dark within.
Insidious, tenacious, terrible
Is the dominion of the double cloud
Outside inside the citadel of light,
The citizen of luminosity,

                                  The building

The building and the builder of the beauty
Of truth, the beauty of the truth, the truth
That is the beautiful, might be the holy,
Is, must be, holy, beautiful, and true.

Is this hysteria? This repetition
Of what I have already often said
Is what I must say often while my saying
Has not yet been mutated into paean
And has not yet been muted into silence.

I tried confronting miles, millennia.
There has already been much too much silence,
Not, as my critics sneer, as I might smile,
Much too much speech.

                And still across the river
Fortuna waits.

                Fortuna waits for you.
Tasso had waited and he now replied
Smiling.

        I love her deeply, I responded,
And yet adversities, yet adversaries,
Have blinded me, have lamed me, yes, have drained
Me of my very blood.

                I think of this.

It seemed an incantation, for the snow
Kept faith there with the lilies and the roses,
And yet the friend became the enemy.
It was a diverse horror. The defender,
Ally, companion of my route, my call,
My consecration, turned a face of stone.
The voice was ice. The arm was fire. The sword
Entered my chest.

              I said I would recover.

Strange now, estranged, before my blurring eyes,
Still high above my head, low at my feet,
The gleaming eagle and the glittering dragon
Circle me, flashing talon, flashing fang,
After the aureate years we spent together,
Squamous with squalid gold.

                    Each scale, each feather,
Might constitute a memory, a pang.

And still there is the future.

                 In the glimmer
His countenance was kind, compassionate,
And reassuring.

           Can I look and walk
In that direction, framed and maimed by dread?

Is it a combat or a sacrifice
Which summons me? Have I been, am I now,
Both the rex regum and the rex sacrorum,
The imperator and the pontifex,
Or am I now and have I always been
The pedes and the aries, authentic
Agonia?

             Will I see action soon?
And is the action or the passion mine?
And is my service warfare or religion?
Beyond the tunnel does the temple lie,
Beyond the labyrinth the battlefield?
Am I the presbyter? Am I the victor?
Am I food for the altar or the vulture?

Beyond the terror does the temple rise,
Beyond the battlefield the paradise?

Crusade and martyrdom have shed their splendor.
Courage endures. Shall I still play the coward
Facing a fate ignoble, meaningless,
And mean?

I still see dragon, eagle, swan,
Sword, shield. I still stand summoned by Olympus.
Whether it is respected or reviled,
My armor will be hanging on this tree
Gleaming into that darkness.

                      Tasso smiled
Once more.

            Dull cloud of grayness threatening rain
Or brilliant radiance may be a nimbus.
Glory may coexist with misery.

Those were his words. I listened less forlorn.

Knowledge can be a victory, he ended
With emphasis, and art is a redemption.

His blue eyes beamed with dawn, with azure noon,
There in that night. Mine shimmered in return,
I gathered from the mirror of his gaze
And from the effervescence of my cries.

Although we fail, the furious fire of fight
And smoke of immolation blaze with light.
Let us remember with our frailest breath
And let us reremember to the death.
The madness of our hope and our desire
Flames fragrant. Struck and fallen, we aspire.
Last ranting stanzas gasp yet with a power.
A beauty flashes from the wounded flower.
Laughter may gush from gashes in that saddest hour.

But the two snakes! I see them back of me—
The two that Cleopatra did not see
Though from the battle she began to flee
Followed in loss and love by Antony.

Gold was the ocean, but its blue spumed white.
The meadows of the sea kept reddening.
A Roman August saw the triple triumph.
But this is January. Janus sees
                            Both ways

Both ways. What does my seeing see or seem?
What does the darkness of my seeing seem?

In the blue bosom of the Albula
Victor or vanquished shall I rest at last?
Can I be ready for that lasting rest?
I rest beneath this tree and soon I must
Move. I must move. I sense the insite vim.
Furrina foams below me in July
Athwart the warmth, the heat, the summer's sum,
From depth of well in close of greens and breeze
Up on the slope of Janus. Janus frees
Hot streams into the lock of January
Beneath the gate to guard the Roman prime
Down where the battle batters Sacred Way
And royal Romulus begins to pray
That Jupiter the fugitives will stay
As towards their Palatine's imperiled rim
Routed in foul flight they all start to climb,
Turning their backs on everlasting fame,
Turning their faces towards eternal shame,
While their king lifts his weapons with his pleas,
Under the blast in which the fountains freeze.
And high above the wind, along the sky,
Darkness and stars suffuse the nebula.
They also serve. Let us at least be merry.
Laugh, weep, watch, sleep, ascend, descend, fast, feast.
In void, in chaos, do, divide, desist.
Be early social late reclusive Proust.
Conquer or liberate Jerusalem.
Our nine one one may summon, number, numb.
A motion and a stillness are the same.

No, no, a massive host is massed against me
To wrest me from my precious ones, from you,
Both from the beautiful and from the true,
From all that has enriched me and entranced me.
They will take Rome from me and me from Rome.
Death will be sweet before that bitterest doom.

Do not lie down and die. Alive, exploit
Night's occult potencies throughout the night.
These means you can effectively recite
And in effecting them you are adroit.
In fallow fields of sleep, in seeding flight
Of dream, in fruitful watch, await the light,
And with the force of morning face the fight.
He answered in stern words and soothing voice,
Lessening my dire dread of the dread dice.

Long, long ago I crossed the Rubicon.
Fortuna will await me into June.
Still January has sought sacrifice.
The host may be exterminating foe
Or saving victim.

              Or may welcome you,
He said, to conversation as I do.

May fate this grace upon me then bestow:
To be the guest and not the parasite.
My shy rejoinder was half laugh, half moan,
My quick response half quip, half orison.

Tasso seemed not to take my sigh amiss.

There is a time to joke, a time to groan,
There is time to repent and to rejoice,
I added in a fiercely cheerful tone.
If Antony and Cleopatra die
And Caesar triumphs over them without them
Is it the little minute of the kiss
That lives or plurisecular victory
Or do the ages weigh them both and doubt them?
By what names is Octavius still known?
How shall I see the seeing of my eye?
Is not romance or heroism bliss?
Did we dream Caesar, dream Mark Antony?
Must my dreams cease before I cease to be?
Or is there something past the size of dreaming?
Why in my darkness is there something gleaming?

Manhattan did not melt into the Hudson.
Rome has not been distilled into its river.
But yet Venilia's and Janus' daughter
Canens, while weeping, lying by the Tiber,
Singing the ultimate song, was fused with water.
The flood in this embrace became her husband
And she my mother.

              Swans befriended me
And set me in their nest beneath a tree.
This story I have never told, no, never.
Is it the truth? What more will I discover?

Your mother's song, diffused into the air,
Is sometimes playing in the foliage
And sometimes echoing from sphere to sphere
And sometimes silent.

              Stifled for an age
Yet undestroyed it will once more emerge
Out of the earth, the moisture, or the fire.

Thus he consoled me, but I found my stare
Bound to the ground and radicated there
Although my thoughts went floating up and over.

High on the Palatine, where she was born,
I feel I hear her phantom and I mourn.

You are her child and you her sacred pledge.

His liquid phrases flowed with empathy
And gentleness.

              You will see more in May,
More in September.

              This much I might say.
The swans protected me until a stork
Offered to fly me over to New York.
But I came back to find my father's bourn
And listen to my mother's lullaby
                                      And seeing

And seeing Rome seek here my liberty
And understand the laurel, palm, and oak
And comprehend each year and month and day
And know my spouse before I grow so old
That this great orb will never know my child.

Have courage. You will learn and learn and learn.
Be brave and love.

     I yearn and yearn and yearn.

Black the nocturnal torrents course and curve.

Flow on, dark river, dark below the hill.
Flow on, blue river, blending with the moon.
Rome has not liquefied into the Tiber
Yet is there here a potent distillation.
Flow oceanic, flow Homeric, flow,
Roam, eddy Ennian and stream Lucretian,
Flow Ciceronian and lift and linger
And lilt and live Virgilian, O river.
Flow on Ovidian and rippling change
And changing shimmer, shift, and stay the same.

Soft, run, strong Tiber, rise, sweet Albula.

I heard you on the first of January
As the gray plane trees witnessed from the shore
Cry Father Tiber while you crossed the bridge
Surprised, astonished, at your recognition.

Are there then guardian ghosts like guardian angels
Or genii that are our closest kin?

Sister, he said, thicker than blood is water,
Thicker than water ink.

     You will be true
Though ruby fumes flare, glare, all through the sky
And ruby fluids glitter in the river
Through all its fluvial currents, all glints red
Throughout the universe of sacrifice,
         Then all

Then all is back to black, black is the ash,
Black is the blood, black is the eye's blind vision
In through existence's infinite victimhood.

Thus began my reaction.

                        It continued,

Black is the ink. I think you will be true.
Blue is the ink. I blink. I will be too.
Forgive my hubris with its garish hue.
My blushing face is pink. I shrink from you.
Shall I not slink away without ado?
Must I not hug myself and sink from view?

Must you not trust your brother and your friend?
Poeta melancholicus, some dub
One who touched joy and, if he may admit
What they insist, touched others with that joy.
But here where over us the oak stands black
Can we not study, love, and trust the tree?

Such was our interchange, if I am able
Both to remember and to render it,
For all our speech was spoken in Italian.

Though I have been unsparing in the labor
Both of recalling and of re-creating
Tasso must suffer much from my traduction.

Just as I trusted him he trusted me,
Unworthy though I was and am. Receiver,
From his great wealth supply my destitution.

Black stands the oak. The night sighs in the sky.
The oak stands steadfast and the sky stays still.

Does the moon move? Does its bland countenance
Fatten each second? Does some grand transaction
Ensue between that moon's pale, brave, grave gaze
And this dark arm, that black branch that the tree
Raises in supplication or in threat?
                                            My arms

My arms black-armored or black-habited
Tend oakward and extend on moonward. Friend
Not enemy, I first address the tree,
To you I stretch the hand that grasps my sword
Not in hostility but in salute.
Not foe but comrade, next I hail the moon,
To you I look with longing as I lean
Holding my shield as mirror not defense.
Why is that white face blank, that black limb blasted?

A tree might be a pillar of a temple,
A moon a flower of a paradise.
Great fane, be builded, be. Be, garden, bloom.

Beam answers beam. But lightning struck, cloud covered,
Thunder had come and had departed, trunk
Was starker far and vault above long darker.

Build, edifice. Plot, blossom. Blossom, bower.
Tower, choir, chapel, shrine, enshrine aspiring.
Be formed, be form, be no less, be more, free.

What frenzy crests? What madness makes me scream
Beyond the flights of steps the temple rests,
Beyond the labyrinth the paradise?

I stare across the river through the blackness.
Rome holds so many temples on those hills.
High in your shrine amid a middle distance
Upon the holy mountain called Agonus,
Health, hear me, heal me for my holy task,
That what I have essayed I may make whole.
Weal, let the work commenced be ended well.
Let me not end before my work is ended.
Safety, Salvation, save me from myself.
O save me for my Rome's sake. Save my Rome.
My Tasso summered in a pontiff's palace
On the hill where your altar shimmered, Salus.
I watched your shrine arise white, blue, red, gold
With paintings by the famous Fabius

On the

On the green height. In white, twin cavaliers
Stand looking on audacious and undaunted
And, by huge horses, still affectionate,
Caring as daring, sharing as aware.
For love of Rome I watched them ride to Rome.
I watched the temple of Quirinus rise
Upon, within, that colline verdancy.
The ghost of Romulus gold as a god
Shone on the avenue. A Julius saw him.
He saw him, heard him, saw he was Quirinus.
This I have seen. Will I see this again?
I have heard Cicero and Atticus
Chatting about another Julius
Turning too godlike in that neighborhood.
Safer it surely is that Caesar's statue
Should stand as a divinity's within
The temple of Quirinus, not of Safety.
Are you not Safety of the Roman State?
I have heard Tully on your festal day
In his own language that is your own Latin
In which your single name expresses all
Hail you, Health, Weal, Salvation, Safety, Salus.
I will salute you in some tongue or other.
I will ascend in Sextile to your temple
And to your festival. That will be August.
But this is January. Let me last.

Tasso, you lasted. Is this mad? You worked.
Is our right work our earthly paradise,
The work that is our play our paradise,
The play that works our madness paradise?
Our madness may be rationality.
How patiently you listen. Do I rave?
Is there a rationality that anger
Advances like a warrior to guard,
A play protected by a pious pride,
A lust that burns for truth, a gluttony
Greedy for feasts of beauty, and a sloth
That is the otiosity of art
                                              And the

And the long laziness of contemplation?
How graciously you listen.

                           Tasso laughed.
Patience is easy in eternity,
But those who live in finite time must try
To finish something fine before they die.

Ghosts then can laugh. But must the living cry?

When I am lying on the battlefield
Or on the altar, soon, I sense, too soon,
Stretched supine, wounded, still, I sense, too still,
There on black soil or on white marble or
On the green grass or on the cloth of gold
Or among little variegated flowers
Blooming on sod or broidered on brocade
As on a garment of the guardian
When Flora in her versicolored gown
Steps bright with lovely godhead through the gardens
Of Rome, the bearer of her sacred name,
Will I have finally found or finally foundered?
And will the foe, the pontiff, or the surgeon
Standing above my barely breathing body
Staring find finder, founder, found, and founded,
Subject and object, noun, verb, participle,
The me, the us, the we, the final I,
Gazing into the blueness of the blue,
Listening to the singing of the sky,
Raising the shining city of the shield
Glistening with its iridescent story,
Knowing a Rome eternal for a moment,
Making Rome universal on a page,
Creating infinite Rome within a cry?

Will I recline upon a gray, frayed rag,
Under stray fragments, tatters, tags of cloud,
Gray rags, gray bags, that are the nebulous?

Will I rest on the sand, a rock, my shield,

                                                Under

Under the golden tassels of the oak,
Under the rubies of the yew?

                    Will you,
Tasso, attend me? Will I go alone?
Is death one of those things one does alone?

Or will my corpse be crushed in with the crowd,
Mangled and mingled with the multitude,

Or noble on my versicolored shield
Not thrown away or captured or destroyed?

I ask not for the ransom of my body
If snared and snatched by impious hostile hands

But for the liberation of my targe
Marked by my figures and my signatures

From gradual and temporal neglect,
From instant and eternal nullity.

Tasso suggested gently, Though the saving
Of what worth saving will have been created
Resides beyond the realm of the creator,
The worthiness must lie within the work.
Like death creation knows a solitude.

I know myself as hermit, knight, and maker.
Yet my religion is democracy,
And everyone is citizen and king.

Is not that handsome Tuscan, Astyr, coming,
Trusting his horse and versicolored arms,
In supreme beauty as my new ally?

But comrade, communism was my first
Religion. Will it also be my last?
Is my communion human or divine?

Why do I love the gods?

                    If I commune
It is with beauty.

                    Yet I would consort
Also with truth if when I court the truth
I could come close.

                    I broider on brocade.

Could the trabeculae unclogged come clear?

Must all this plenitude be emptiness?

Fill in the blanks.

                    Insert between the sobs
Something,
          some sense,
                    some thread,
                              some stem,
                                        some petal.

Thank you for your attention.

                              Yet an answer
Is not demanded.

                    Nothing is demanded.

Is something asked?

                    And is it what or that?

Is it inquiry or request?

                    A question
Of essence or existence?

                    Is it madness?

Pansy or thought?

                    A document in madness?

Can madness keep from speaking, cease from speech?

Sweet song, run strong until my Tiber tires.

What envious sliver breaks askant the river?

Tasso responded briefly, quietly.
The oak stands stiff, stern, sturdy, staunch, perduring.
The willow, flexible, renews itself.
The yew, evocative, from darks of green
Glows sad and happy.

      Slowly I replied,
Sadness makes much more sense than happiness.
Yet instances exist of radiant bloom.
Let one who chooses to be cheerful be.
About tomorrow there's no certainty.
I beg a miracle. I try to ho . . .
The uncompleted word became a wail.
But shortly I resumed my argument.
Some call denial that which I call hope.
What I call miracle some call despair
Or desperation. Choice to some is chance.
Some label life what I beweep as woe.

Tasso said softly, Judgment is most just
When all the evidence has been addressed.

Janus sees both ways. I look high and low,
I sighed, and find no fundament, no rope.
The laurel will be won, worn, by a ghost.
The looming future looms already lost.
I name the planned, mapped battle a disaster,
The scheduled sacrifice catastrophe.
I crave the miracle, the mystery,
That makes me of my sole selfhood the master.

Which fight is won yet lost, which lost yet won?
Felled on the field, what cavalier ensanguined,
Exsanguined, like his dying enemy,
Like his dead enemy stretched out there slain,
Unlike his enemy shall stand again?

Stand, trusty tree, and I who like a twig
Am lying on the river, like a lamb
Am lying on the altar, like a knight
Am lying dying on the battleground,
          Shall

Shall stand and cast my shadow like a sapling
By your shade undismayed.

      I am the seed
Arisen from the river like a weed.
Who slew the enemy? It was not I.
I did not wish my enemy to die.
I only wished to live eternally.
I know no foe. No fight is fine. No war
Is worthy. I must war on war. Bright peace
Must be high prize. Wars, battles, fights must cease.
Words, beauties, friendships must, must, can, will, be.
What must be can. What must and can be will.
Will what is said be dead or equal deed?
Will heart be broad and mind be narrow or
Spirit resist the shallow facile lure,
Persist to density and subtlety
Valid for every challenge, pressure, need,
For life, for scholarship, for poetry?
Can tambourine supplant the grand tambour?
Must the great river shrivel into rill?
What did the crowds stream to the stream to see?
One shaken by the wind? Am I that reed?
Jove, Juno, and Minerva from yon hill
Across the flume look down. My enemy
Might, must, be I.

    We spoke of that before,
Commented Tasso, and we may say more
Later.

  I paused.

      I seek a simple me,
The single self. I always am within
I and another. Must this other be
Other indeed, an other? Which? a twin?
A god? a love? Am I thus one or two?
An I? together with an I a you?

These must be future questions, Tasso said.
Your present quest, your present second self,
Your first, your current, I, first, last, is Rome.
The Roman night is all around you now.
Rome's dawn is in you, memory and vow.
Clorinda may not face a normal story
Nor Godfrey chase an ordinary glory.
Listen! The cry of truth, the call of beauty,
In silence sound. Your love becomes your duty.

It was my turn to smile, a serious smile,
The smile of recognition, of the moment
Of knowing yet again what I had known
When something, when a breath, a bird, an ocean,
A rose, an oak, a gleam, a scrap of Latin,
Told me what I am for, and I awoke
From ivory dreams only to fall asleep
Again and yet again and to awake
And in a second to forget the moment
That I had known and that which I had known
And in a moment or a century
To know again.

        It was my turn to laugh
Thinking about the baby laughing facing
The tiger underneath the tree, or thinking
Of solemn Godfrey chasing anything.

A laugh about Clorinda has the sadness
Of Tancred's tears. A laugh about Goffredo
Is not derision but an understanding
Of the ridiculous within the instant
In which extraordinariness is set
Beside the common. And another laugh
About Goffredo is the swirl of joy
That fills us when we see the angel come
On gold-tipped pinions unto him at dawn
Or listen to the gold-tipped syllables
Of mission which the leader sits unfurling
To the ambassadors before nightfall.

Like everyone, I like, I love, I feel
Sympathy for Clorinda, but, like few,
I like, love, sympathize with Godfrey, too.

That I appreciate, responded Tasso.
And, as I know you wish, we can chat further
About this later if we speak together
Of Godfrey's godliness and humanness,
Clorinda's grandeur and duality,
Rinaldo's specularity, Armida's
Queenship of hate and handmaidhood of love.

I murmured phrases. Faintly, from afar . . .
On sea, on land, in air clear and obscure . . .
Patting the tigress with a tiny hand . . .
Seeing the self, seeing the self aware . . .
Behold the handmaid of a love and be . . .
They shall not laugh nor we let fall a tear . . .
Buried beside our god's own sepulture . . .

But mentor, master Tasso, though you stand
Here as a ghost, as yet I do not dare
To talk with you about theology,
Dark, glimmering, brilliant spirit, fair, fair, fair.

He said, Jerusalem is now my home,
The heavenly; yours, earth's eternal Rome.

I answered, Though unworthy I discern
The slow hot fires that deep within me burn.
Anguish of Tancred, Soliman, Argant
Joins with a joy as vow slips into chant.
Those fires as fierce as those of Vulcan's forge
Little by little, if Vulcan wills, form forms.

The poet's blue eyes blazed as he responded
Like a blue flame warming and luminous.
Infant Clorinda, nursed beneath the tree,
Infant Clorinda, lifted by the river
And driven by the wind to soft, safe shores,
Figures your origin. Let her as hero,
Let her as heroine, of wars and words,
Enkindle

Enkindle passion and enlighten action.
How much we suffer and how much we do,
How much we feel, how much we think, and how
Much of this we can say, how sweetly sing,
Measures our plunge into immensity.

What was that second when my heart first leapt
Greeting the equal wingbeats?

       Did I ask
This also? Did he answer?

        Can you, Muse,
Catalogue every question and reply?

What was that instant when my mind first danced
Glimpsing the gauze-veiled moon above the city
Dimmed amid ruins?

        When the moon was still
Diana's and the sky yet Jupiter's?

Or did I live before that? after that?

But you are not a ghost, not yet, said Tasso,
Smiling that smile I always can recall.

How adequate those wings in their libration!
I was exclaiming now, and Tasso laughed
Happily, saying, That was later, then.
The angel in full splendor came descending
E si librò su l'adeguate penne.
And yet much earlier you gazed with joy
And wonderment and terror as did I
When paribus nitens Cyllenius alis
Constitit.

     I laughed, too. So we both know
How to enjoy as well as to endure.
I pictured Tasso in Salerno, Naples,
Urbino, Padua, Ferrara, Rome.

I pondered Tasso's past and weighed my future.

I asked, reflecting, Will I weave like Dido,
With my own hands and happy in the work,
A cloak of richly Tyrian purple threaded
Finely with Lydian gold to swing and flame
Upon, down from, the shoulders of a hero,
Of an Aeneas in his last brief moment
Of happiness in Carthage, and to lie
As a last gift, a last brief gift, upon,
Around, the pallid body of a Pallas
Lying in youth and death before the flame
Funereal awaiting him in Rome?

Will I like Dido weave? or like Calypso?
Will Hermes or will Mercury come down
And take away my hero?

                      Must my husband
Be no one who is human, who is mortal,
Be none but a divinity or death?

Much, suppliant with supine hands, I prayed.
Did I see blind fires in the crusted clouds?
Have I perceived inanity in azure?

Be sentinel, he said, be carpenter,
Stand tall, travail, illumine, rule, your city,
Under the thunder, mid the numinous blue,
While your hands do not fall, your eyes not fail.

I am, I answered, craving and yet craven.
Was it for this that Venus intervened
In Asia and in Africa to save me?

Let Cloacina rescue you in Europe,
He said, the twin, the other self, of Venus,
Close to twin Janus on our Holy Road.

I clutched the altars as I tottered.

                              Mind,
    Be mindful.
              Body, listen.
                        Spirit, whisper.

O spirit, whisper. Spirit, speak. Soul, sing.

I sang so, long ago. Will I so still?

Is this my soul, my spirit, and my mind,
Alive, embodied, capable of light?
Has my self breath for scent, for sound, for fire?

Is there an incense in this wintry air?

Maybe the angel Hermes, nuncio
Mercury, nunciator Gabriel,
Or Raphael, the sociable, the healer,
Sublime among wide heights where skies respire
Descending went on steady wing until
Touching a mountaintop with purpose he
Plummeted. Thus he touched the spot wherefrom
He touched the pulses of an auditor
And through great space was shaking from great plumes
Heavenly fragrance, vision, wish pacific,
Veda, trishantih, seeing, wisdom, peace,
A golden sweetness as of wintersweet
On the Janiculum in January
Yet, as celestial does terrestrial,
Sweetly surpassing that.

                    Was I there glad?

But here we are, just you and I, and I
Am happy, even in this dark, this cold,
Such night, such winter, to be here with you.

Others will join us soon. Did Tasso chuckle?
Including one at least much better known
Than we have ever been for cheerfulness.

Before they come, I said, may I please ask
Clarification of my trust, test, task?
Must I turn counter to the turning world?
Must I forget the shielding of my shield,
Forget the future of my future child?

Tasso began with, Words entail the risk . . .
But we were hearing something else, some sound
That seemed to reach us from the theater
Suddenly, unexpected, unexplained.

* * *

Was it the sibyls, was it Flora Baum,
Who spoke, who wrote, the Latin sentences
With English rhythms? Were the consonants
And vowels classical or medieval,
Christian or Ciceronian? Jerome,
Augustine, uttered, scribbled, words in Rome,
From, for, the city, for the circling world,
Taking past language, making future speech.
It might have pleased them, fusing sanctity
With scholarship or holiness with learning,
To act as and to be interpreters.
Yet in the script as written, voice that spoke,
Something oracular supposed the oak.
But something personal proposed the person,
Whether the third, the second, or the first one.
Something seemed trivial and something solemn.
The atmosphere throbbed, shivered, and was still.
What did the tongue taste, what lips, fingers, touch?

Hic ramus, radius, vox, odor, aura.
Ecce ancilla aurae aureae.
Hic Flora se dat, dicat, dedicat.

Behold the handmaid of the golden breeze.
Into that breath and in that breath I breathe.

Here is the lover of the aureate air
Shadowed in black.

                    The tree is black and bare.

Into that breath I breathed. Am I a shade?
I have become the shadow of myself.
I think I am a shadow of a shade.

Does a shade have a shadow? Does a dream
Require a sleep?

                  Our eyes beneath the beam,

Though we are beings of a day, a night,
Have sometimes caught or almost caught the gleam,
Gift of the gods, brightness of sky, the light,
The sweetness of eternity.

                  An eon
To some is just an age, to some forever.

To some it is a life. This blackened tree
Lasts. Shall I claim, exclaim, proclaim it lives?

                 * * *

The hymn of intertextuality,
The weaving in and out of history,
The plunge into the past, the grand escape
Out to today, into today, the shape
Fusing with futures wooed, the newly ripe
Chord, its tone on tone, its stripe on stripe,
Its maze on maze, its banquet, its bouquet,
Is, was, will be our play, our interplay.

                 * * *

UMBRAGEOUS VISION | VISIO | VISION

After six thousand years Carmenta came.
I think it was four thousand years ago.
Or were there seven thousand and then three?
Can I remember? Can you count such thousands?
How can you count last autumn's fallen leaves
Left by one lonely oak that leans and leans
Or count the blackbird's notes sung in one dusk?
Can I remember yesterday? She came
After my first millennia, came leaping
Onto the shore. I see her still, still leaping.
I see that very day, the one we called
The third before great Jupiter's great moon.
We named our days by moons then, not by suns.
We measured months. We seemed to feel our years.
How can you count the months in all their thousands?
We numbered months. We counted only ten.

Ben tornata, Cappuccino in Tazza,
The young man said as soon as I appeared
For breakfast on that January morning
After my stint of military service.
The younger, plumper, barman said the word.
The older, gaunter, barman did the deed.
Cornetto Semplice, the pastry girl
Thought if she did not say. And thus I knew,
For fact translated thought, what was for each
My true identity and proper name.

I had skipped down the hill to celebrate
Or, more exactly, start to celebrate
Carmenta's feastday at the best of bars.
The warm cornetto and the hot cappuccio,
Selected just for me among the crowd,
I gulped and gobbled, standing at the counter.
Then I felt good. I had been recognized
And reinvigorated, though my garb,
The bulky-shouldered coat it was my habit
To don each morning like a uniform,
Was black, more like a cassock than a tan,
                                    Tawny,

Tawny, or coffee-colored hooded smock.
Unlike the friar's brown cowl, my cap was white,
More like the moon. My scarf was white and curved
Around my cap. The moon went on increasing.

How many moons before had he decided,
Upon the very instant when I stepped
Out of the summer through his open door
Wearing the broad-brimmed tawny hat of straw,
That I was Cap in Cup, not Cap in Glass?
Was Plain Croissant my simple character?
Simple was my decision, Cup was his.

Now, even now, despite gray sky, gray cold,
Snow had been left far north and farther west.
Definitively winning victory
Over the bitterly inimical
Blitzes of blizzards was a simple thing,
If difficult. It was to get away:
Shovel a path, run, rustle, rush, roar, soar.
Here bits of sweet white glaze and soft white foam
Were lickable upon my lips. The moon
Was growing. I had not yet crossed the river.
The day was growing. But the horns of noon
Would signify the gift and sign the giver.

January. This eleventh day.
The third before the Ides. But when she came
There was no January. Yet it was
This selfsame day. I know, for I remember.

In illo tempore. It was that time.

It was, like January, a beginning.
It was a coming strangely Januslike.

Carmenta came. Or say Carmentis came.
Or call her the Carmentes. Is she two?
Or recognize her with two epithets,
Carmentis Antevorta and Postvorta,
Or say Carmenta sailed with her two sisters,
Porrima

UMBRAGEOUS VISION | VISIO | VISION

Porrima and Postverta, say she sailed
With two companions, Prorsa and Postvorta,
Friends in that flight, through wane and wax of moon,
From Arcady to exile, to a home
Miserable and grand, new and eternal.

I stand before her altar on the slope.
That peak is known as Jove's, this slope is hers,
The gate below is named for her, the swamp
Once oozed there, then a harbor was defined,
Later the trading place where cattle lowed
And merchants showed their credit cards of bone
Scratched with their triple names was bustling there.
Where buses bray, on that solidity
Where motorcycles flow, I walked on water.
I entered through one portal of her gate
And set one foot on each ascending step
And stand before her altar partway up
The hill, above the racket and the stench,
Beyond the bellowing, beyond the bells,
Earth's traffic and the tracking of the sun.

We call this day the Carmentalia
Or, to be more precise, the First Carmentals,
Prior Carmentals, first of only two,
This the third day before the Ides, the other
The third day after them, the old Triatrus.
So many numbers and so many names,
So many ancient strangenesses are summoned
To knowledge, erudition, scholarship,
The pedantry that paws and plods and puffs
And blinks and squints its way to vision, if
Glimpses be given after all, if views
Before which watching feet and walking eyes,
After their halting, halt can open, open,
Most like viburnums sweet and spicy white
In winter air, their January light.

From the Greek ship she leapt to verdant shores.
Green was the river, green the grassy bank,
Wild were the wolves, and wild the ilexes.
She viewed the verdure and she heard the howls.
She looked before her and she looked behind.
She seemed to be a fountain. From her lips
Flowed silver streams of speech. She told the story:
There the domain of Janus, on this side
The land of Saturn lay, both deep in peace.
Learning in each, in each pure poetry
Both flourished. By the green and golden river
The green and golden ages rose and fell.
Warriors sowed red wars, gray devastation.
Then a green grew again, a wilderness.
She viewed the verdure and she heard the howls.
I see a golden city, I discern
Aureate oratory, orotund,
Thundrous above the thunder on the mountain,
Subtler than starlight shining in the flower,
She cried. I climbed the hill to find her shrine.

Did I descend in order to ascend,
Come from the ridge across the river, cross
The river, reach an eastern slope at noon?
The Tiber can confuse you with its curves.
Down, down the steps of the right bank I ran
To greet the steps that met me on the left.

I came down from the west. The yellow river . . .
But is the Tiber yellow, green, or brown?
Yes, it is yellow; gee, it is green; but brown
Might be the color witnessed, witnessed to,
The present word without a precedent,
The current color flowing there, the word
Floating like duck or gull in touch with water
That glides, that gushes yellow, gushes white.
The yellow river slid through years of gold.
The tawny Tiber roared through, leonine.
I came down from the west and crossed the stream.

I stand before her altar, and my desk,
Here at the obtuse angle where, before,
Below me, rock, and, back of me, the path,
Petrine and tiny, both respect the corner,
As does the altar, or, let's say, the desk,
Two-winged, brick-based, and topped with travertine.

Below the cliff the long-leaved oleanders
Rise in their green. I wait above their lengths.
Below the cliff the ilexes rise higher
And deeper in their green. I watch their depths.
Behind me shining patches of acanthus
And golden-beaded laurels spread their green.
My heels are on the cobblestones, my toes
On mud, on soil, edged with a bit of green
(All flesh is grass, this freshness is the grass
Of January), edged with bits of gold,
The living lilting gold of dandelion.

The cat, as elegant as the acanthus,
As svelte and sleek and slippery and soft,
That soft that coexists with prickliness,
With dignity, with mythic glint and rhythm,
Is just as much at home in holy space
Or sacred moment closing, opening.
I feel at home among the chronotopes.

I stand at noon before the altar-desk.
Its base of brick is reddish, yet its table
Gleams white. Or is that gray? or grayish white?
The sky glares grayish white or whitish gray.
The white page flashes answers to the sky.
No blue relieves this noon. Blue flows alone
Through the clear plastic onto blue-ruled blank.
A bloodless offering is offered here
Unless my blood is blue. My hand is cold.
Carmentis asks a bloodless sacrifice.

She landed, I know well, not where they said,
Not by Tarentum, I remember well,
                                           Not by

Not by the terrifying test of dark,
But near the ancient altar of Apollo,
Or where his ancient altar later shone
Bright in the open plot, the precious precinct,
His old Apollinar, and where his temple
Outshone this later still, along a way
That one may choose to take, since there are two,
The route beside or through the greens of Hope
And that around the whiteness of the beams
Of Phoebus as one strides between the river
And the ascent on which they set her shrine.

Apollo was it who inspired her song?
But she preceded Sibyl and Apollo.

She glided up the Tiber. Night and day
Are all the same to her who rows to Rome.
At noon she found the spot. No churchbells sounded.
I noted her reflection in the water,
Doubling the leap with which she reached the soil
As the page duplicates the plane that passes.
She brought the page. She taught the alphabet.

Ah, be, Carmentis, dear especial friend.
Good help in January kindly lend . . .

Whether for record or for prophecy.

But was she merely vatic or divine,
Inhabitant of welling depths of spring
And sanctifier of high holy grove
Or human mother of a human king
Whose humble palace on the Palatine
Hercules stooped to enter? She would sing
The imminence of immortality
Carrying to the skies on fiery wing
Amphitryoniades the son of Jove
And then the sempiternal victory
Brooding above the Trojan from the brine.

Warriors, heroes, lords are forced to flee.
Poets are exiled, prophets exiled, too.
Divinities? She sailed to Saturn's land,
Land of the primal god, the exile prime,
Son of the Sky and genitor of Jove,
God exiled from the sky by god his son,
Driven divinity, denied the earth
Except this central spread, this Latium.
She sought in haste that land of latency,
Land to be lavish, latinate, and lasting.

But was it merely Grecian fabulation
That Saturn suffered such a banishment?
Can I remember what December said?
Saturn, whom Janus welcomed, was the second
To settle here. His era was all gold.

It had begun and must begin again.

Her people were Prelunars, Proseleni,
Arcadians, more ancient than the moon.
And did she, too, exist before the night?
Did she, must she have, come before the dawn?
There was no Sunday, Monday, Saturday.
There was no January then. Was then
There no December? Was there then a noon
Before there was a sunrise? Were the years,
If there were years, or were the months, if months
Had come to count, much more uncountable?
Were thousands millions? Were all numbers one
Before moon was conceived or bright sun born?
She was not foreign to that world forlorn.

The Romans had no special word for million.

He was elected as a Foreign Fellow.
Born, as he was, December seventeenth,
The first day of the Saturnalia,
A.D. eighteen hundred sixty-six,
Thousandeighthundredsixtysix d.C.,

In Villa

In Villa Gaida, fraction of the commune
Of Reggio in Emilia, he was born
Italian. Was he ever not Italian?
After his sacerdotal consecration
And after his scholastic laureation
He even did his military service.

Brilliant though always shy, Giovanni Mercati
Heard the call to be a learned priest.
He came to Rome in eighteen eighty-nine,
Ordained already. Study was his love.
As Tisserant, with him, like him, becoming
In nineteen thirty-six a cardinal
Who wore a beard, uncommon in the west
On any priest, in nineteen sixty-three
Related, eulogizing him, Mercati
In February, eighteen hundred ninety,
Was granted his Vatican Library library card.
Erudite scholar and librarian,
Impassioned pedant, passionate researcher,
Specialist in Greek paleography,
Skilled in patristics, Greek and Latin both,
Where he worked long, worked hard, worked very well,
Yet ranging also past the manuscripts
That were his province into other fields
Adjacent or attractive or commanded
Or vacant, on October twenty-third
In nineteen nineteen he became, was made,
The Prefect of the Vatican Library,
Made notwithstanding all his timid fears.
He later was created cardinal.

In June of nineteen fifty he was named,
Though never was a cardinal named before,
To the Class of Moral and Historical
And Philological Sciences of the famed
National Academy of the Lynceans.
Allusion or periphrasis would render,
If clarity allowed, verse better tamed.

A citizen

A citizen since nineteen twenty-nine
Of Vatican City, he could not be claimed
For Italy. Treaties, laws, are praised or blamed.

Carmenta's priests, at least the two we know,
Were prefects or were consuls long ago.

Carmenta made polenta for the Dawn
When Dawn arrived, wan, pale, with baby clinging,
But Songster, brilliant Song, arrived at noon,
Springing across the flavous Tiber, singing.

If she receives pontifical oblations
Who else but I can be the pontifex?
If the Carmental flamen, clad in laena,
Has rushed to other functions, other fronts,
Who else but I may, turned flaminica,
Observe her sacra and her feriae,
Assure her sacred rites and festal times?
The gods are holy places, holy days.
At noon I made it to the hillside fane.

She spoke to others. Will she speak to me?
Her name bespoke a knowing poetry,
A poetry of knowledge, history
Researched, recorded, with profundity,
Pondered explosiveness of prophecy.

O fortunate to lose Arcadia.
O lucky exile. Not Marmarica,
Not Cyzicus, not Tomis, but the rose
Of all the world received her. This is Rome.
This is the opening and this the close,
Magnetic, central, universal home.

O blessed banishment — apostrophe
Cannot be adequate — that is to free
The seed to root, to bloom, to feel, to be.
O let the lamentation yield the glee.
She spoke to others. They and I are we.

Carmentis, shall I claim you, name you, dare,
Object of my obsessive Roman prayer,
To shove my barbarous tongue through Roman air?

Carmentis, you who know and you who note,
Carmentis, you who see and you who sing,
Knower, knowledge, noter, notable,
Seer, singer, seeress, songstress, song,
Prorsa and Porrima and Antevorta
(Ante), Postverta and Postvorta (post),
Two-way turner, turning, turn, and turned,
Turner of this this way and that that way,
Turning that way this and this way that,
Foreturned and afterturned, to view both versions,
In back, in front, before and afterward,
The past, the future, waxing like the moon,
Chanting, chant, enchanting, incantation,
Incantatory, charmer, charming, charm,
Carmentis or Carmentes or Camena,
Carmentis or, I called you first, Carmenta,

Oh, show me Rome. For my myopic eyes
Straining to get it right may get it wrong.
And let each laden layer grant its prize
Of space as wide and deep as time is long.

Oh, prophesy my Rome. Oh, make it rise
All green and gold, all subtle and all strong.
Let the wild weeds and let the wildest cries
Flame into city, garden, discourse, song.

What funny names, Postvorta, Antevorta,
Those Romans called you by, here on this hill.
Do you turn toward me? Do you turn away?

* * *

Rest now rests, and motion newly moves.
The moon is moving on the wane. Carmentis,
Who looked before, is looking afterwards.

When the third sun looks back on acted Ides
Carmentis turns again. I hope to turn.
Carmentis turns again, returns. I hope.
The second turning is the second chance.
The second chance! I hope to turn again.

This is the best of bars upon the hill.
This is the best of breakfasts on the mountain,
The best on Monteverde Vecchio,
On Old Green Mountain, part of Janus Ridge,
Over the hill a bit, in fact, but not
In connotation, as, in fact, I am
Over the hill a bit, bitch, witch, befana,
Though there's a ten-year-old within the crone
And if one feels one's years one feels the bliss
And anguish of the hag and of the child.
Here any suffering is solaced, here
You savor, to assuage your every pain,
The sweet, the soft, the flaky, yea, the plain:
The succulent cornetto semplice.

The thin-lipped woman at the register,
The blonde cashier who also serves the pastries,
Is always nasty, always makes me wait,
Always prefers the others standing there,
Always regards as having come before
Those who come after me, has always felt,
I always feel, my foreignness, my failure
To be a Roman, though millennia
Have passed since I first ordered a cornetto,
Not even knowing that the one I chose
Was cheaper if you called it semplice
When, fumbling for your wallet and your words,
You asked for cappuccino and croissant
In your most sweet, most clear, most breezy way,
                                    Straight

Straight out of dictionarial Italian.
How did I learn to say the one I wanted
Not because it cost a little less
But simply since it tasted far the best?
How did I learn to get the one I wanted
And pay for that and not some other one,
The more expensive one I neither wanted
Nor got?

    What counted was the name.

                                     It happened
Immemorial moons and moons ago.

How did I understand from the beginning
That you could sit here at no extra charge,
That you could take your roll and cappuccino,
Select a chair and table or a stool
Before the little counter towards the side,
And sit and sip and munch and read your book
Or paper or, yet better, write your words
And phrases and immortal sentences?

The aition awaits a later season.
That will be sung in summer. This was winter.
That will be sung in the summer out under the elms.
This was a time to be in, in out of the chill.

A man sat smoking at the little table.
I chose among the stools along the counter
One at the end and placed my handbag, saucer
With cup and spoon, small napkins, and cornetto
Beside my notebook and took out my pen.

Thus I began the second celebration,
The second festival, the second feast
In honor of Carmentis, readying
Spirit and flesh to turn my steps again.

Again, Carmentis! Then you looked before,
Now you look after. While the white moon grew
Was it the past you saw? This lessening,
Is it the future looming luminous
Somewhere, beyond, behind me, after me?
Am I the post- or proto-Roman?

                                          Now
It feels like January, cold and clear.
I came down from the west and crossed the Tiber,
First by the Cespian Bridge to Island, then
By the Fabrician Bridge with Cicero.
Just as my feet were speeding from the span
Where double double heads of Janus guard
The passage back to Island and, beyond,
To Janus Mountain, churchbells clanged Carmenta,
Carmen, Carmentis, Carmina, Carmenta.
It is the fifteenth day of January.
And was it fifteen minutes after noon
When, having passed through Hope green-grassed, I came
To the same station-study-shrine? Who knows
The very stroke of noon? I know that sun
From the blue campanile strikes my face
As at my feet a sunny dandelion
Shines gold in green and brune and gray mosaic
Beneath noon's roof of blue. Yes, I can stand,
Like Henry James, a lot of gold, a lot
Of gold in all its grandeur, its ornateness,
In its solarity. Yes, I can stand
A lot of azure, lots of sapphire sky,
Blueness of January noon, so cool,
So cold, so clear, so clearly belled, so blue,
So clearly blue, so carminal, carmental.

Cicero said that Marcus Popillius Laenas,
Consul with Gnaeus Manlius Capitolinus
Imperiosus, each a first-time consul
In B.C.E. three hundred fifty-nine,
Or A.U.C. three hundred ninety-five,

                                            While

While he was vested in his priestly laena,
The ancient garment like a double toga
Described by Varro, as he was conducting
The public sacrifice since he was also
Carmental flamen, summoned suddenly
To hurry to the contio to quell
A riot, stopped, turned, left the altar, rushed
To the assembly dressed still as he was,
Wearing the special vestment of Carmentis.
He would be consul three or four times more
And prosecutor in a famous case
And win a victory against the Gauls
Which after he recovered from his wound
Would crown him with a triumph back in Rome.
He must have been a potent orator,
Cicero said, because he calmed the crowd.
Who will conclude or who, I asked, renew
The interrupted homage to Carmentis?

Carmentis was already dead, or gone
To godhead, or she always was a god
Although the mother of a mortal king.
Her son Evander was already old
And had for fifty years been ruling Rome
Or what four centuries later would be Rome.
It was a noon, but not in January.
It was the day before the Ides of Sextile.
What can that be? It was the twelfth of August.
Evander sacrificed and banqueted
In honor of no unknown foreign god,
For Hercules, returning from the west,
Greek though he was, had come to them in Rome,
Had come to them and saved them, and Carmentis
Had prophesied the savior's deity.
But what new hero rises in the east
Out of a city's flames and crosses seas?
He glided up the Tiber. Night and day
Are all the same to him who rows to Rome.
At noon he found the spot. Aeneas landed.
                                                                Troy

Troy had found Rome. The pious hero touched
The everlasting sod sung by Carmentis.

They met at the temple of Carmentis.
Hadrian was dead, and Favorinus,
If Hadrian had hated him and changed,
Changeable as that learned lord could be,
The favor which had favored Favorinus
Into disfavor and converted friendship
Into the enmity of competition
In erudition and, which is not certain,
Finally exiled him, for Favorinus
Certainly wrote on exile, probably
From exile, though, at least to me, despite
My study of the works of Favorinus
On exile and on fortune and the rest,
The declamations, essays, treatises,
Encyclopedias or miscellanies,
The expositions of philosophy,
And my extensive and prolonged research,
For I have read the bibliography,
Not merely all the dozens, all the hundreds,
Rivaling those of Plutarch in their number,
Of books that Favorinus wrote himself,
But volumes of the other sort of source,
Of many men who mention Favorinus
And all the authors analyzing him
With balanced, calm, dispassionate appraisal,
With admiration, with antipathy,
With bitterness, derision, mockery,
Anonymous, Biographer, Compiler,
Chronicler, Cataloger, Diarist,
Dedicator, Damner, Eulogist,
Epistolographer, Epitomizer,
Encyclopedist, Enemy, and Friend,
Fabricator, Faker, Forger, Fraud,
Greek, Grammarian, Historian,
Hellenist, Ignotus, Latinist,
Lecturer and Lexicographer,

           Litterateur

Litterateur and Lexicologist,
Moralist, Orator, Polemicist,
Philologist, Philosopher, Physician,
Physiognomicist and Panegyrist,
Pedant, Rhetor, Rhetorician, Roman,
Scientist, Sophist, Satirist, and Scholar,
Writer and Zealot and Abridger, Author,
Aelius Spartianus, Dio Cassius
(While his own work on Hadrian survived
In his own words), Diogenes Laertius,
Eusebius, Fronto, Galen, Gellius,
Julius Valerius and Lamprias,
Libanius, Lucian, and Macrobius,
Philostratus and Phrynichus and Plutarch,
Polemo, Stephen Byzantine, Stobaeus,
Suidas (whom his lexicon has named),
And all the others whom I have not named,
And as I must have been myself in Rome
When Favorinus came or when he left,
I turn and turn the volumes in my head
Since I must not forget what once I knew
Or must have known but I must try, I must,
I must remember whether Favorinus
Was exiled, though, at least to me, perhaps
Too dark of mind, the evidence is dim,
The evidence is not yet quite convincing,
If I still see with vision not yet dim
That brilliant Favorinus was in Rome,
Was back in Rome, brilliant, shining, honored,
Modest, congenial, philosophical.

Favorinus, the philosopher
From Arles, the Gaul who spoke and wrote in Greek,
Who differed with an emperor and lived,
As it is said that he himself had said
About himself, who was the orator
Two of whose speeches still survive intact
Among orations by his teacher Dio,
Of Prusa, Cocceianus, Chrysostom,
                                    The golden-

The golden-mouthed, the golden-tongued, the golden,
Who was the friend of Hadrian and Plutarch
And Fronto and Herodes Atticus
And Aulus Gellius, and who composed
That essay, treatise, monograph on exile
Written perhaps in exile on the island
Of Chios in the year one hundred thirty
And copied in the year two hundred thirty
Or thereabouts by someone probably
Also in exile, in Marmarica
In northern Africa just west of Egypt,
Who pasted three papyrus sheets together
Into a roll, when they had been discarded
After their use for records by an office
Of the administration of the region,
And thus recycling by rewinding them
Employed the blank backs, now the writing side,
To make his own transcription of that essay,
Doubtless to keep and read for consolation,
Never imagining how he became
Preserver of a work that would be purchased
In his edition, his handwritten transcript,
Seventeen centuries later by a pope,
Erstwhile librarian and mountain climber,
When Pius the Eleventh, with advice
Given by wise Monsignor Giovanni Mercati,
Bought for the Biblioteca Vaticana
In February, nineteen hundred thirty,
The Greek papyrus of the book on exile
Exiled from knowledge yet identified,
Since the beginning and the end were missing,
That is, the title page or colophon
Naming the book and author had been torn,
From the discovered roll, which nonetheless
Could be identified, by three citations
In the anthology that was compiled,
Probably from preceding florilegia,
About four hundred thirty by Stobaeus

With lemmas

With lemmas designating authorship
Although these quoted bits are fragmentary
And lack the title as they lack the context
Of the original, the work on exile,
Of which the name, the subject, the existence
Went unsuspected through the centuries
Before the happy finding and unwinding
Of what survived, the reinscribed papyrus
That came to Rome as Favorinus came
In honor back to Rome, where he might meet
Philologists and other learned scholars,
Happened to meet the mad grammarian,
Domitius, difficult of disposition,
Irascible, outspoken, impolite,
Cognominated mad from character
So strange, so wayward, and so so insane,
If the eccentric is insanity,
With Gellius in the temple of Carmentis.

Now hold on tight, now hold on tight again,
And let the roller coaster of the poem
Sweep to a goal. The sapphired diadem
Must shine above the lonely golden throne.

My sentences make sense and are syntactic.
The diction shifts as moods and models change.
The meter meets the standards for its range.
The commentarioles are prophylactic.

If the delivery is convoluted
Its deconstruction is an endless joy
For each receiver absolutely suited
To a profound involvement with the toy.

I hear your questions and I answer them.
The choice is yours. I say what I must say.
And you are welcome if you choose to stay.
And if you wish to turn and go away
I wish you well. And if some time you stray
Back I will be here, too. The roundelay
Cannot condemn. I turn and turn my gem.

Shall I claim all my facts as factual?
That they are. Or they will be probable.
Or I may offer them as possible.
Or they were facts for some antiquity.
Or they are held for all eternity.
Or they are true to what is true to me.

Even if categories be confused
The cataloger need not be accused
Of having catastrophically abused
Matter and form on which she fitly mused.

The witnessed with its varied visages,
The whispered symphony of images,
The words in all their meanings, all their sounds,
Suppose the cue. Performance knows no bounds.

O let the mortal author have her say
Before the judges and the judgment day.
The thesis is the theater of clay.
The poem is the puzzle is the play.

If she has somehow failed to guard ahead
She may guard afterward, as when the Gauls
Climbed by Carmenta's up the path that led
Through darkness and the geese gave saving calls.

Both Tisserant and Laenas wore the purple
And each was secular and each was priest
And each was orator or each at least
Addressed a crowd or else addressed a circle.

If he related, if he was related,
If he was summoned, if he summoned, if
The simple verb or participle waited
To greet the reader near her on the cliff,
Will the best lector turn, return, with bated
Breath for the ultimate semantic whiff?

She breathes with difficulty, dreaming dreams
Of everlastingness. And will she last
                                            As long

As long as January's slanted beams
Gild this today before this is the past?

Must she become a student of the moon,
Grammarian of air, the scribe of sky,
Hearer and writer of Carmenta's tune?
She, you remember, is the author, I.

Patterns of purple march across my white
Scarf and around my cap. And does a blush
Of carmine cross my face? This noontide light
Is brilliant, wintry, limited, and lush.

The beauty and the truth of text or mind
Are not good sense, are not good taste. The blind
May never see, the seeker never find,
Yet with the endless effort of the grind
Effortless ecstasies may be entwined,
Instants akin to visions now divined
And now or now eternally enshrined.

Carmenta's shrine was where they met that day,
But in those days, when Antoninus Pius,
Pius the First, unless a prior Pius,
Antique Aeneas, is his predecessor,
And if Pope Pius First, contemporary
With Antoninus, gained the papal throne,
Upon the martyrdom of Pope Hyginus,
A little after rather than before
The Antonine succeeded Hadrian,
And if to intromit a second pontiff,
Pius the Second, secondly Aeneas,
Later by thirteen hundred years than Pius,
The First, whichever one, as Prince Aeneas,
First Pius, thirteen hundred years before
Equilibrates the tally, is permitted,
Whereby mild Antoninus shines as focus
Of pious history and pious power,
Prime in despite or light of rival count,
The Pius, nameable alone as Pius,

                                    Ruled

Ruled Rome and what to Romans was the world,
You might have met the famous Favorinus
Standing in the Palatine Piazza
Waiting for the emperor's reception,
Conversing, now in Greek and now in Latin,
With other learned men, as others pressed
Closer to listen in until the door
Opened. Yes, the emperor was ready.
The scholars separated. But you might,
Some other time, have heard our Favorinus
Lecturing from the podium as throngs,
Whether or not they understood his Greek,
Listened enraptured. Always listening,
Aulus Gellius spent whole days with him.
Notebooks at night kept day's bright words alight.
One day, when Gellius and Favorinus
And others of the friends and followers
Of Favorinus all had met together,
A message came for the philosopher
From one of his graduate students, who was a man
Of senatorial rank and from a family
Quite noble. Just a little while before,
His wife had given birth. It was a boy.
Let's go and see the baby, Favorinus
Responded, and congratulate the father.
All went together to the house. The mother,
Exhausted, was asleep, but to her mother
The orator-philosopher discoursed
In Greek on why the baby should be fed
At his own mother's breast. From time to time
They visited the sick, their friends laid up
With gout or rheumatism, and discussed,
With the physicians or the friends themselves,
Medical questions or linguistic problems,
Philology or physiology.
Or at his dinner parties Favorinus
Had books in Greek or Latin read aloud,
Allowing interruptions from the guests

Reacting

Reacting to the argument or style
Or any glint that sparked their intellects
And kindled elocutionary powers,
His above all, for monologue perhaps
Or for the give and take of conversation.
And one day, gazing up at golden horses
Above the colonnades of Trajan's Forum,
Walking while waiting for his friend the consul
Still busy hearing cases, Favorinus,
Together with his followers and fellows,
Interpreted at length the brief inscription.
And towards the end of winter, when the sun
Shone warmish on the courtyard of the baths,
They walked and, as they walked, had read to them
A book which Favorinus noticed scrolled
In a friend's hand, and soon they found themselves
Hot in discussion of a passage. Then
They walked one summer evening by the sea
At Ostia until the lights came on.
They walked. They walked. They talked. They talked. They read.
They read. They walked. They talked. Talk has no end.
They went to the temple of Carmentis.

The temple of Carmentis was the place
Where Aulus Gellius and Favorinus
Happened to meet Domitius on that day
When Favorinus the philosopher
Asked Mad Domitius the grammarian
Whether a certain Latin word could bear,
And did bear in the best of Latin authors,
The meaning of a certain term in Greek.
Domitius, fuming, since philosophers
Concerned themselves with words alone, he railed,
While he, grammarian, pursued the good,
Pondering ethics and morality,
Promised nonetheless and later sent
A book with information on the subject.
Verrius Flaccus gave the definitions
With great precision in his book despite

                                                               Omitting

Omitting instances. Then Gellius
Added examples out of Cicero.
It's good to know that contio can be
Dēmēgoría, or a public speech:
Can be the people gathered in the place,
The place, the speech delivered in the place,
That is, the words belonging to the place.

And what was it that Favorinus said
To the young man who in his conversation
Used words belonging to another time,
Old-fashioned, antiquated, obsolete?
You talk to us as though you were addressing
The mother of Evander.

                    O Carmentis,
May I address you? Can I talk to you?

Thirteen or fourteen hundred years elapsed
Between Evander's reign and Hadrian's,
Or shall we say, thus numbering, between
Pius Aeneas, exiled from his Troy,
And Pius Antoninus, emperor
Of Troy, Mycenae, Argos, Carthage, Rome?
Sixteen or seventeen hundred years elapsed
Between the happiest of human spans
Of history and that historian's,
The span of that historian who looked
Back, or ahead, who watched and saw and named,
Thus famously, unhesitatingly,
The almost hundred years begun by Nerva
And sunned to luminosity by Trajan,
Hadrian, Pius, Marcus. After Gibbon
Gazed upon Rome two hundred years and more
Elapsed. I count not months but centuries.

Carmentis, do you turn now fore or aft?
Is it the past that is in front of us,
Before, and does the future lie behind,
After, all alien to our usual eyes?
                              Before

Before the Ides, Carmentis Antevorta,
Did you catch what has happened long ago,
And, following the fullness of the moon,
Do you, Postvorta, capture what shall be
As the machine of time runs down, runs out,
And ages age? Or do you see the child
Coming to birth, and do the mothers pray
To you to help the nascent on their way
Whether they head or back into the day
Of life? O let my child attain the light
After the labor and before the night.

The altar-desk is double, and it doubles
As the broad double fence-post at the corner
Where the protecting fence edging the cliff
Against Tarpeian leap or flop or fall
Turns at the angle where the hillside turns
Furnished with horizontal arrow pointing
Forward, the wide white prow from which I watch.
Above me and below me figures, few
But felt as figures, saunter, stride, or stop.
Corydon seeks Alexis here at noon.
Corydon seeks Alexis here at dusk.
Here it is men who are in love with men,
Men seeking men with whom to be in love.
The lovers, tourists, archaeologists
Climbing the stairs from Yoking Street that lead
Up to Goat Mountain Road and pausing where
A little path diverges to the right
Along a ledge of that declivity
May glimpse the obtuse angle of the fence
With the odd v that is the twofold post.
Veni, vidi, vici: More acute,
More daring, and more desperately in love,
I make and I discover and I form
The visits and the visions and the versions
Offered by post and desk and altar.
                              Dusk
Offers a second second chance.

The sun,
Unresting in his famous flavous car
Yet never restless, is just just descending
Below the level of my eyes. The glare
Will spare me soon above the west. The blue
That the sky is, that is the sky, is bare
Of blame or taint or tint or hint of cloud.
I call this dusk or I will call this dusk
When the eternal azure of the air
Through feeling the departure of the sun
Deepens into such subtleties of past
And future that eternity seems rendered
Not less celestial or serene or pure
But more complex, its altitude profound
With presence holding moments holding rest.
The cat is motion, the acanthus rest.
Movement and quietude are two yet one.

Have I just come, or am I frozen here?
Or do I come as tourist, go as ghost,
Or understand as student, stand as statue?

What statue stood upon that pedestal?
Was there a statue on that marble slab?
We see a stele and we read a tablet.
This is named basis and termed titulus.
For us the carved inscription is enough,
Must be enough, is, whispers, murmurs, shouts.

And still the story does not start on stone.

After completion of the three-year term
In which he was curator of the Tiber,
About one hundred seven of our era,
Pliny composed a letter recommending
His friend Tiberius Claudius Pollio,
Whom he had met when they were young, both doing
Their military service years before.
He wrote the polished social introduction
To Gaius Julius Cornutus Tertullus his friend
And sometime

And sometime colleague in administration,
Mentioning many merits, benefits,
Endearing qualities of character,
Talents, accomplishments, abilities,
Administrative offices well held,
Friendships well held, a friend's biography
Well written, but the letter does not mention
That Claudius Pollio was Carmental flamen.

Pollio tells us this. A marble base
One meter high and forty centimeters
Wide and thirty centimeters thick
Or rather thirty-five, for measurements
May be inscribed precisely in my measures
Although my page is not his marble slate,
Which is inscribed exactly in his Latin,
Informing us that it is dedicated
By the fine person clearly designated
As our Tiberius Claudius Pollio
To Sun and Moon, Apollo and Diana,
Lists five positions. One is military.
Three are civilian and administrative.
Hence four are secular. One is religious.
Is this distinction licit? This is Rome.
The first two show him as a procurator.
The last two indicate him as a prefect.
The central title cries: Carmental flamen.

Thus he becomes the second whom we know.
The first, four hundred fifty years before,
Lived over two millennia ago
And happened to be named by Cicero.
We open and too soon must close the door
On Laenas and on Claudius Pollio.
Although for each I could add to this core,
Their flaminates are absent from that lore.
This is not fiction. Everything is spare,
Limited to what time does not wear.
Apex and laena were what flamens wore.

In cap

In cap and coat I feel my now their yore.
Do we feel years or feel their numbers more?
Miter and chasuble feel rather old.
I donned my cap and coat against the cold.
O Sun and Moon, invest each marble fold
With verity until the tale is told.

It was a joke as told by Favorinus,
The beardless fellow-intellectual
Of bearded Hadrian, more erudite
By thirty legions when he reprehended
A word used by the scholar and all knew
That he was wrong and Favorinus right.

How do you win, equilibrate, or lose?
To truth what can we offer, what refuse?

What did the Songster offer to the Dawn?
The lemon square, denomination less
Than grainy smoothness or smooth graininess,
Than subtle sweetness, subtle pungency,
These designations of reality
More than the signs by which the real is drawn.

And if my offering is vow and prayer
And if the vow and what is vowed, the prayer
Itself and what is prayed for are the same,
And if the song and singing are the same,
Carmentis, Songster, since your song is sight,
Will you grant sooth and song, grant sound and sight?

O you for whom with both, both foot and hand,
Like Sisyphus I labor if to stand,
Sit, scribble, walk, ascend, descend, stop, look
Is all to roll the stone, to write the book,
O God, gods, ghosts, ongoing generations,
Accept my dedication, dedications
Begun with Janus facing still both ways,
Continued with Carmentis on both days.

Her home, her tomb, her altar, and her temple
Or fane or shrine or chapel all were here.
She was a god when gods were presences,
Such powers subtly sensed and supplicated
That living was suffused and permeated.
She was a goddess when a goddess gained
Such human face and human history
That living was perused and entertained.
And if her nod was power well defined,
Was will uniquely individual,
Her power and her will, her exercise
Of personality and personhood,
Or flickering of foliage or fountain
Diffused along a rumor of the moon,
If she turned human or turned numinous,
Was demythologized, euhemerized,
Anthropomorphized, apotheosized,
If she was exiled or indigenous,
An indiges, or if an immigrant,
If she arrived in time or out of time,
Sang past or fostered future, was or is
Or will be, if she merely might have been,
Who might have been her royal secretary,
Who might become her loyal carmentary?

Carmentis cares for birthings and for all
Things of the future. In those goddesses
Who chant the fates of children being born
And who are called Carmentes we may find
None other than one Jove himself who is
In everything and who is all the gods
And goddesses. Carmentis some believe
To be a moira, what the Romans term
A fate, in charge of childbirth, and with this
As reason mothers honor her, while some
Consider her more mantic and phoebastic,
Inspired to utter oracles in verse,
Since carmen is the Latin word for poem.
Some say Carmenta is an epithet,

More

More a cognomen than a given name,
Because she first was called Nicostrate,
Or, in a different tradition, Themis,
And was a Greek, the mother of Evander.
Why did the Roman mothers fete her twice?

They gave their gold. They gained the right to ride
In cars within the city. Gratitude,
Not greediness, fulfilment of a vow,
Not the desire for recompense, religion,
Not bribery or commerce, were the cause.
They sacrificed their golden ornaments.
In horse-drawn carriages they rode through Rome.

After the long ten Trojan years of siege,
The city, rich and mighty, had been taken.
It was not Troy, not Carthage. It was Veii,
The fortified, the powerful, the wealthy,
The warring and the warred upon, the fallen.

The general had vowed before the conquest
That when he took the city he would offer
A tenth of all the plunder to Apollo.
Camillus captured Veii. Rome was bound
By vow. But there were problems and dissensions.
Should spoils already seized by citizens
And soldiers be returned, and must the land
And buildings be included in the tithe?
When all was settled and the treasury
Had allocated funds, another crux
Threatened disruption. People, pontiffs, Senate,
Camillus even, saw no clear solution.

It was the year three hundred fifty-nine
As counted from the founding of the city,
Or else B.C. three hundred ninety-five
As reckoned by a later scheme of dating,
The year which followed after Veii's fall,
In Rome a year denominated by
Six military tribunes consular.

The tribunes were commissioned, with the money
Drawn from the treasury, to purchase gold.
Gold was in short supply. What should they do?
At last they had the funding, but of gold
There just was not enough. What could they do?
The Roman women organized. They held
Many a session. This emergency
Had to be met. They came to a decision.
They fixed upon a common resolution
To offer to the tribunes their own gold.
Collecting all their precious jewelry,
Stripping it from their bodies and their coffers,
They took it to the treasury themselves.
A golden bowl was made and sent by ship
To Delphi, to Apollo's temple there,
In token of Rome's gratitude and grandeur.
The women kept that promise to Apollo.
The men rewarded them, permitting them
To use wheeled vehicles within the city.
This privilege rescinded, many years
Afterwards, two fifteen B.C., in fact,
When Hannibal, in Italy and victor
At Cannae, seemed about to march on Rome,
A troubled time in which the Oppian Law
Was passed to limit women's luxury,
They held a meeting and exerted power
As best they could by voting to deny
Children to Rome. Their privilege restored
Twenty years later, thus two hundred years
After its first conferral, they assembled
And voted once again, to end their protest,
Welcomed conceptions and nativities,
And rode through Rome in cars. Those cars were called
Carpenta. Then the Senate gave Carmenta
A second festival.

     To celebrate
The second festival I came on foot
Although I was a woman and the cars,
             Or rather

Or rather warranty to use the cars,
Had been bestowed on women.

        When the women
Desisted from their strike the Fathers voted
To hold two celebrations for Carmentis
To help the city by assisting births
Of Roman youths and maidens.

         Will their births
Come with the dawn or come at noon or come
Out of the west at sunset?

       I came walking
Out of the west.

      The Greek historian,
Walking around Augustan Rome, observed
Carmenta's altar near Carmenta's Gate
Below the Capitol.

      I found the place.

Romulus vowed — but was it Romulus? —
That he would set a second festival
For the same goddess, for the same Carmentis,
If he could take Fidenae on that day.

I found the day. I found the calendars.

I do not judge. I do not criticize.
I tell what I have heard, what I have read,
What I remember, what our fathers said.
I do not fudge. I do not harmonize.
And were our mothers silent? Were there lies?
Were there mistakes or errors? Should I dread
The testimony of my honored dead,
Interrogate the witness of my eyes?
In the beginning was it Roman mothers,
Lovingly recognizing as Carmental
The blessing of the choice and of the child,
The liberation from the crush of others,
         The struggle

The struggle to be forceful and be mild,
Who dedicated in this place a temple?

What was their motive when they founded it?
Why do they honor that same goddess now?

Carmentis is concerned with birth and all
Futurity. Carmentis knows the past.
As she looks after persons, places, things
And sees before her what has gone before,
Are there predictions? Are there retrodictions?
Must there be volumes constantly revolved?
Can there be things turned over or turned up?
Will there be digging, sifting, restoration,
Taking apart and putting back together,
Novanticism, creativity,
Making anew, or, flatly, making new?
Her words are heard. Peruse the prophecies
And hermeneuticize the histories.

Yes, I have read the sources, verse or prose,
Prosa, prorsa, straight ahead, or turned,
Verted, versus, verse, convertible,
Or possibly more controvertible.
May there be prose in verse or verse in prose?
Was the Carmental epos metrical?
Is it perverse to show prose is proverse,
Perverted to denote prose as proverted?
Is the provertible invertible?
Inversely, may the vertible — diverted
I turn to something less prosaical
Or less diversely dogged by doggerel.
Carmenta's verses were poetical.

I plod from pedantry to pedantry.
Yearning for learning will I suddenly
Discover how the scholars are the free
And erudition is divinity?
Carmentis lands and hands a golden key
That has been carried here from Arcady
And could unlock her godly gate to me.

If gods are sacred space and hallowed time,
If she is capitolial, hibernal,
Can she exist before, beyond, this climb,
Can they be universal and eternal?
Can I exact her potent sympathy
For births by nature, births against the grain,
Births with a greater or a lesser pain,
Or fix each fact when I ascend to see
Just who her flamen is, just where her fane
Gleams on the mountain through the moon's first wane?

Up and down I walk, not up or down
But on the level. I walk up and down
Between one lively lovely clump behind
And to the left and one behind but right,
Outpourings, fountains, fronds, acanthus splashing,
Laughing acanthus, posted right and left
Behind the double altar. Is there one
Altar on which we offer simple things,
Cakes for Carmentis, cornets for Carmentis,
Croissants, cornetti, or does she have two
That she attends: to welcome our respect,
Hear all our queries, listen to petitions?
How will these births be? Let these births be best,
Be for the best. How will they be the best?

Let nothing dead be here. Is this the sign
Affixed beside the entrance to the shrine?
Or do we read here: Leather not allowed?
Here where we yearn for birth the thinnest shroud
Of death must never enter. Not a cloud
Tinges this day's pure heaven. Do I wear
Or carry leather? Neither here nor there
Enters if here a chapel in the air
Is all there is. There cannot be an in
When there is nothing. What has been has been.

Out in the cold I wear my woolen coat,
Black as the woolen habit which the girl,
Spirit aflame, the woman, spirit blazing,

Senses

Senses descending heavy on her flesh
One hallowed day, one January morn
On which she takes the veil that drapes her head
And shoulders like the cap and scarf which warm
The wintry virgin's vigil in the wind
And the expectant in her expectation.
It will make sense. It almost will make sense.

My black wool coat is less encompassing
Than the black woolen habit of the nun
And yet I sense it as investiture.

My woolen coat is not the woolen cloak,
The laena of the flamen of Carmentis,
And yet it signs me for the sacrifice.

The hearths, pure foci, of the goddess burn
With incense, and the ancient offerings
Of milk and emmer make her chaste libations.
Come to the central hearth, or are there two?
To seek the center, find the focus, found
The city, solve the universe, unlock
All portals far beyond beyond, all gates
Deeply within within, may, must my trail
Be circular or be elliptical?
May, must, I follow or surpass the sun?

The dandelion, sunny in the dusk,
Suffers no sunset. Still it shines, it stirs,
It stirs, and it is still. And still it stirs.
It waits outside the railing, patient, flave,
A yellow flower, not a yellow cake,
In honor of the goddess who may deign
To pay a visit to her ancient fane
Before night claims the daylight which is hers.

I glance out towards the bright green grass of Hope
And further towards the plane trees, leafless, plain,
Tan, tawny lions lined along the Tiber,
Fluvial father tawny now, now green.

           The phases

The phases and the faces of the river,
Invisible from here, are guessed between
Those staunch still guards that stand now tan yet green
After the moons that slowly intervene.

The verdant flow has passed three times today
Beneath my gaze, beneath my feet that chose
Their paths across the squares of cobblestones,
Or are they diamonds? See, they point ahead.
No, they point backwards. Look, they look four ways.
I chose my ways that pointed to this place
Where soil meets stone, where diamonds touch the dirt.

Behind me green of laurel and acanthus,
Before me green of holm and oleander,
Darken, the laurels less, the holm oaks more.
Behind me flowers, fruits, the future, glint
Purple and gold within the laurels' buds,
The greenish yellow pledge of golden bloom
And purple berry, while the verdures darken
And yet behind, above, the bays, the wall,
Tan, almost gold, shines brilliant still with light
Sent by the sun, and, higher still, the sky
Is azure yet undimmed.

                    Yet will she come?

Will she now come? And will she walk on air?
O let me see again as once I saw.
Will she now come? I see her chapel there
Before her altar on the hillside where
The hillside was until, by nature's law,
The edges slipped and slid. And should I dare
Believe that in the shimmer of that space
Between the treetops and the bottom stair
I glimpse the glimmer of a woman's face
Discernible as dim and faint yet fair?

A gull glides by before me. Is the river
Invisible, and how far is the sea?

                                      A gull

A gull glides by. The wings that move, the gull
That glides, the gull that hovers, or the wings
That rest, the gull that rests still in the air,
Are and become.

                Is she still in the bare
Hollow between the ilex leaves that quiver
Fitfully, brisk, resistant to the dull
Immobile quiet that the lateness brings
To vision if invisibility
Fills up the emptiness of light's long lull?

Is she thus come? And is she turned to me?

Is this immobile quiet that is bright
With flickering of golden strands of hair
The void from which divinity can stare
Into the eyes of minds sighing for sight?

Or is there nothing? Was there just the gull
Gilded by sleight of splinter of the sun?
Or is that something? Was that something seen?

As I beheld, if ever, ever, I
Saw something, let me now again behold.

What templed town, candor of marble, gold . . . ?

A templed city, white with marble, gold
With gold is flashed like fireworks on the sky.

When, dazzled by my page as by the sun
Of highest noon, most gold and most serene,
When, throbbing through my throat as though the thunder
Of Jove so close rolled down the Capitol,
I bowed my head and passed my trembling palm
Over my eyes and fixed my flinching fist
Beneath my chin, I caught or thought I caught
The faintest flutter of a subtle hum.

Closer than Jove, near, clear in debonair
Delicacy, the goddess waited there,
Standing on grass. And I became aware
Of terraces in place of vacant air.

What was she humming? Exile need not end
In emptiness. The pen is like the plow.
First we shall read the story of the shore.
Then we will build the brilliant citadel
Which we call art, deep-founded, rising high,
Art and our art, long, long afar, now nigh.

A written city, yes, a city built
By song flashes like fireworks through the sky.

Is it this moment? How the tenses shift.
Is it this instant, this, this twink, this tick?
Was it the last? Or will it be the next?
The grass is green beneath her feet, the heavens
Blue as her gaze. She nods. I dare to speak.

Behold, behold, I, Flora Urania Baum,
Known as Julia Flora of the Tiber,
Make, O before, O after, present vows
Of struggle and of study and of song.

Is there a dandelion like a sun?
Is the grass dimming or does it dissolve?

Good night, goddess. How the green grows dark.
The green grows dark. Now, goddess, now good night.
Now how the holm oaks grow their green so deep
Its evergreen shall steep in borderblack,
Verd verging unto umbrage of niello.
Good night, good goddess. How the dandelion
Gleams. Is a gleam eternal golden bloom?
The blackbird darkens darker through the ilex
As from his small gold beak large golden song
Is sudden blossom, glitter, glimmer, gloam.
How short the song, how faint above the blare
As traffic jangles from the avenue

Curving

Curving below. Good night, the blackbird clicks,
Not warbling dulcet dusk but proud in loud
Whispers reiterating, Night. Good night.
A sweet breeze tingling with pollution pats
The dandelion as it pats my cheek.
My hand is cold. My very page is cold.
The written city, city built by song,
Shall rise around this rock and through this air.
Goddess, inscribe its letters and its score
Over the silent portal while the noise
Is not omnipotent and while the night
Declines to nullify the voice of day.

Was that the merl's first January chant,
First springing singing at the desk of dusk?

If the desk-altar faced in this direction
Was it before, was it behind, the shrine?
Was all this sacred space exactly this?
Was it all this exactly in reverse?

Did I gaze south to her, she north to me?
My altar faced this way before her chapel.

Was it this year and not some other year
When on the fifteenth day of January
The blackbird, merl, or merula, with notes
Most like those notes the robin of the west
That sings beyond the posts of Hercules
Will sing to spring, to signal that late spring
Beyond the sunset, sang to January,
Thus to make vernal the invernal merl,
Thus for an instant hinting winter's limit,
Thus for a moment brokering song's charm?

Was it that century and not some other?
It was that month, that day, that taste of night.

What did I vow? To smile, to stare, to sing.

Let the dark evergreens be evergreen.
Let the bright golden blossom be eternal.
Let the brief blackbird's song be everlasting.
Let endless Rome become and let it be.
Is this a cry, good-bye, or whisper, listen,
Or click, arrivederci, now? Good night.

* * *

February

* * *

Intercalary

> Ti libero la fronte dai ghiaccioli
>
> . . .
>
> I free your forehead from the icicles
>
> . . .
>
> Montale, "Mottetti."

> . . .
>
> visione, una distanza ci divide.
>
> . . .
>
> vision, a distance is dividing us.
>
> Montale, "Ossi di seppia."

1.

A cyclone blown against an emptiness
Is cycled to a mind. What storm of words
Circles about high silent cypresses?
I pose among the memorable shards

Shared with the great now gone. The forum roars,
Shakes, and is still. Are these white miracles?
Are these my bright fiduciary stars?
I liberate your brow from icicles.

2.

Not clouds, not cloudiness, but nebulas
Beyond our grandest nebulosities,
Not nebulas but brightnesses beyond
Our pride of finest finite galaxies,

Not brightnesses, abstractions nameable,
Things thinkable, dark thought, deep feeling, fever
Of faith or hope became an explanation.
There were alternatives. There was some other . . .

3.

Must be some day, some season, and some year.
It is a dusty street with paving stone
In places, lined by lawn and laurel, edged
By temples, edged by remnants of the temples

Of centuries, where what was there is here,
When then is moments on the Holy Road.
My gentle footprint presses dust. Electric,
My footstep, touched by stone, sparks, flashes, trembles.

4.

Your step was there and there, was here and here,
Where mine now tests the stone and stamps the dust,
Meshing our vestiges. I tell the least
Of what is happening, for where you were,

Strolling among your friends — shall I say more? —
Strutting among your enemies — the most
I dare declare — you are, alone, a ghost,
Walking where I walk where you walked before.

5.

Do spirits speak, or am I catching sound
Reverberated from a sentinel star
That caught it when it rumbled from this ground
And thundered through all subtleties of air

Attaining stellar status? If my ear
Resonates to the drumming of that noise
From where the senate met that day, that year,
Is that not this, must this not be your voice?

6.

My pen and notebook dub me cicerone.
My English coronates me as the crony
Of travelers from Egypt and Japan.
I answer every question that I can.

No, Caesar was not murdered here but — buried? —
But burned and praised. The Sabine maidens, married,
On this street stopped the war. I cannot say
Cicero guides me, Varro shows the way.

7.

You, Caesar, will deactivate these tides
Through which I come here daily, counting days.
It is the seventh now before the Ides
That no moon regulates, the seventh phase

Of constant suns that sail away to rise
On our horizon. I seek shade, seek shades
Here in your shrine where one white flower lies.
Your altar stands. Your comet flares and fades.

8.

If there is piercing pain, the agony
Not of soul, spirit, mind, or history
But wounded writhing animality,
Is it assuaged by sitting on this marble

Drum under shielding leaves of laurel near
The street by which salvation could appear
While straining Iapyx struggles to tug the spear
And staunch the ruddy floods that gush and gurgle?

9.

The unclaimed arrowhead sticks in my flesh
Under my skin, borne and unbearable,
Essential, consubstantial with the fish,
Fidgeting, fixed, limp, rigid, wriggling, still,

That Flora is, who used to be a flower
Lifting a limpid face above the pain.
Come from your proximate encircling bower,
Dear healing Venus, Venus of the Drain.

10.

This is the Venus of the Sacred Way,
Our Cloacina in her little shrine,
Glint of a marble circle shining by
The bordering stream, the purifying drain.

Here on the boundary two images
Guard us at home and when we cross the line
Out to the universe. Two Venuses
Enkindle human love and love divine.

11.

The greatest sewer is the simplest brook
Rippling and shimmering along the swamp
Before the river. What grand engineer
Channels the creeks that trickle or that hurtle

Into the golden flow? The simplest look
Of simplest love may rainbow into pomp.
What complex Venus turns the purpling spear
And cultivates the lovely blushing myrtle?

12.

Within a pain so great I cannot pray
I wait. This anteroom is filled with seats
Of marble, hard and hot or hard and cold.
I still have feeling then. The others went

When they had waited. Pain will pay my way.
Can I feel more? I stand. Somebody greets
Me, one of the others, still in his toga, bold
And kind enough to come. The gods relent.

13.

All Ides belong to Jove. Then even these
Are his. The living statue dedicated
To him, chaste festal body consecrated
To him who is, strange holy soul that sees

This holy road from which one scales the rock
To train upon the faithful lightsome sky
Of day, of night, the luster of one's eye
Has deigned to don the pondering scholar's frock.

14.

How may I gain this gown? Beneath it, may,
How may, I be? Throughout the night I dreamed
Two questions which the flamen of the day
Flashed upon evening. As I woke they gleamed

Behind my eyes. My rush is opportune.
I stand before Jove's daughter's marble ring.
Meet me at three tomorrow afternoon
Within the temple of my son the king.

15.

He drew his toga very modestly
About him as he fell. Why then does she
Open my coat? How can a goddess guess
My terror of the cold? But on this grass

That is the shrine's green carpet she may dress
My wound with blossoms and infuse my crass
Material with azure subtlety,
Essence of fire and sky and star and sea.

16.

Is he cold, or am I? A ghost is cold
And human flesh warm-blooded. I am young
And he a hoary twenty centuries old.
But I am just his age provided one

Is ever sixty-three if at one's death
That is the tale of years. My tale is this:
I have been listening so long my breath
Flames faintly from the blaze that once was his.

17.

I hear our Father Jove, whose gesture thunders,
Our Father Tiber's vesture roar, the horses
Of Castors riding, cries of Gracchan forces.
I hear those sons, those brothers, and those fathers

Whose characters are squeezed beneath the lens.
Then Marcus Tully Cicero is one,
And Gaius Julius Caesar and his son,
Both Julias' sires like Louis F. Budenz.

18.

Who comes thus out of season, out of time?
I, Flora, raced to Rome ten thousand years
Before this instant when I sit in tears
By brick once bronze refulgent in its prime.

The roses came and went. The apricots
Flowered and fell. This temple is no tomb.
Here Janus sees a future while the bloom
Is tight and hard, a past that never rots.

19.

This is the place of fathers, orators,
Progenitors of sound. The roof, the sky,
Reechoed as they spoke in, out of, doors.
Bereft of cherished fathers, do not cry.

Forget the vanished ashes, buried bones.
Remember in this space of memory
Dear ones, dear words, dear meanings, dearest tones.
No, hear them. Listen in eternally.

20.

What were our mothers like? Waged by their fathers
Upon their husbands, war wracked Holy Road.
They met to spin the strategy that mended
The infant city fracturing to sherds.

While you are killing over wives and daughters,
Your sons and grandsons live, your life, your node.
They held the babies high. The battle ended.
The place of war became the place of words.

21.

The place of words is the comitium, where
The senators ascend the senate stair,
The people meet, the politicians speak,
The rostra roar around each jutting beak.

The kings did much for us. They drained this marsh.
They built these shrines. Much power made them harsh.
Then for the gods we kept a sacred king
But for ourselves we chose the public thing.

22.

You stand before the vanished senate house,
Pre-Julian like many a vanished item.
Between the rostra and graecostasis,
By you the sudden southern sun is sighted.

Midday: Our great comitium is a clock,
Human and huge, and here, O consuls' aide,
With studious voice alone you tell, toll, strike
High noon for us. O shadows, hear the shade.

23.

It is the sixth before March first, a day
That February never reached this year,
This special day, mysterious and strange,
Named Regifugium, for the king must flee

The forum. He has made the sacrifice
In the comitium. Now he runs away
As quickly, quickly, as he can. The rite
Goes on. We watch. We see the meanings change.

24.

On the fifth day before the first of March
In the intercalary month (the year,
Leaderless still, now fifty-two B.C.)
Pompey the Great was made sole consul. Arson

Had torched the senate house in January
To fuel the funeral of Clodius
After his gang and Milo's met. The mess
Fraught February and Intercalary.

25.

Here is the palace of the scholar-king,
Numa, inventor of intercalation
And founder of the flaminate. The flamen
Of Jove is priest of knowledge now. The strong

Are lords of learning. Looking down on rubble
Far beneath which the ancient residence
Rose in its airy mythic ambience,
I stretch towards erudition, priestly, royal.

26.

Equirria: third day before March first.
Horses are racing on the Field of Mars,
But I stay here near Venus. As the stars
Slowly approach the point at which they burst

Upon our vigil, whistles shrill, the herds
Within are shooed and shouted out, the doors
Are shut. Above the Castors' columns soars
A gull and Vesta's vespers are the birds'.

27.

I sit in sun by Vesta, end and center.
Tomorrow March will stride in, vigorous.
Here is the close before the fire's reblazing.
Here vestal flame glows low. It is the sun.

Motionless on the temple step, I enter,
Sentient, my marble metamorphosis,
To sit forever, white, stone, staring, gazing,
Here where the vision and the I are one.

March

* * *

I have to celebrate the Ides of March.
The garden greens around the aqueduct
Ascending, present, presence of invention,
Permanence of inventiveness, the massive,
The vibrant record of vitality.
The garden greens. The columbarium
Descends, the record of the permanence
Of death, inventive permanence in death,
In death's despite. The laurel, ever dulce
In green, is doubly dulce in green and gold.
The almond has already bloomed, the plum
Is blossoming, the apricot will flower
Out of these rosy promises that glow
Along the boughs. On Julius Caesar's altar
The bud of flame above the small squat glass
That holds the small squat votive candle glows
And smokes and flourishes and bursts and burns
Furiously among the sweet bouquets
And billets-doux. The student from Chicago
Unwraps his offering, his bunch of tulips,
His tribute to a concept of a Rome
Existing, having been, and still to be.
Now he is spending one semester here.
He will come back, he pledges. He is happy.
The path on which the Vestal Virgin climbed
The Capitol is open to the public
After years, decades, prohibitions, fences.
Arrogantly I set my sneakered foot
Upon the first smooth stone. My soles are worn.
I am worn, too. I slip. I grasp the railing
And pull myself up, up, towards Jupiter.

UMBRAGEOUS VISION | VISIO | VISION

High on the hill does Jove's oak wait for me,
True in its treeness? Which far March first saw
Its small green flowers and its new green leaves,
Its gold green flowers and its rose green leaves?
When was that oak last verdured, aureoled,
Fringed, tasseled, with the verdant aureation
Of vigor? In a March where I, too, bloomed,

Exuberant, ascending into breath,
Arising, rising, into fragrances,

Fragments or figments first, then fullnesses,
Breathed into me as I breathed into them,

In bursts of ecstasy and pedantry
Enumerating all the blooming Prunus,

The plum, the almond, and the apricot,
And furthermore the cherry and the peach,

Susino, mandorlo, and albicocco,
And also ciliegio, also pesco,

Prunus, amygdala, and arbor praecox,
Moreover cerasus and persica,

And sometimes for susino trying prugno
Or positing as Roman apricot

Hidden in Martial's gifts and Pliny's lists
Still riddling in my scripts and dictionaries

And glimpsed within the thick arboricultures
Of Columella and Palladius

Armenian plum and also or or else
Precocious peach, a Persian plum or apple

In the particular variety
Of apple called Armenian by Greeks

Who later passed praikokia to Arabs
Who passed them back to Europe, back to Rome,

Where one by one the apricots now blossom,
Where they now bloom, white-petaled, purple-sepaled,
In fivefold flowers, fresh and full, in freshness
Of petals white upon still-leafless boughs,
White on the dark March boughs, the white March sky?

* * *

April

* * *

REPLIES FROM APRIL

April in Rome. Among the leaves of bay.
Is it the poet or the poetry?
Is someone speaking? Does the melody
Of some immortal song suffuse this day?
Something is heard to which one must reply.
Petrarch is art. Can I not be a cry?

Sounds flutter forth, and lest they slide away
I turn the numbers with the usual key
That fate has made the one he saved them by.

And yet. And yet. There always is the and,
And yet, but, or, addition, countermand,
Alternative. The answers always stand

With or without the texts towards which they tend,
Letting the overhearer comprehend,
Whether from one or from the other end.

If verse must speak to verse and mind to mind
In deepest solitude, that which must bind
Must be alone, unique, must most unwind

That which makes one of two and two of three
And three of two and one a trinity.
Who is that other, other one, not he,

One on the other side, not you, not I?

(Reply to poem 16)

He moves huge through the spaces as he came
In human size across more human space
From the closed valley, green and gardened place
Below the fountain surging into fame

Almost Horatian, from the court the name
Of which was exile, Babylon, disgrace
Of papacy and empire, through the race
Of heedless seas and over lands untame,

To feel upon his hooded head the floral,
Fruitful, and circumfoliating crown,
See, speak, be seen, be spoken of, admire,

Become a citizen in this high town.
So, too, I come, pursuing my desire.
We reach our Rome, our realm, our love, our laurel.

(Reply to poem 1)

I hear the sound of sighs, as you expected.
I hear the sound of sighs your very own.
Then neither you nor I can be alone.
Here in this April night we stand connected

By something stretched beyond the soft reflected
Glimmering luminosity on loan
From gleaming regions where that glint is sown.
What is that something, sumptuous, neglected,

Tree of the dreamy leaves of starlight? Art
Itself must die. We shore against our grief
These golden filigrees. Not merely death

But six, no, seven centuries us part.
If as I listen joy gives, takes, my breath,
Is all that pleases here a dream so brief?

(Reply to poem 101)

The sixth of April, thirteen forty-one.
It is Good Friday. Passing through the gate
Into the Holy City Rome, you wait
For pomp of ceremonial begun

Not in condolence for God's only Son
Executed through a human hate
Some thirteen centuries before this date,
Death having been by this one death undone. . . .

You will be crowned with bayleaves, not with thorns.
You are the pilgrim come to celebrate
Not holiness but poetry and learning.

Death is before your eyes, which Love adorns
With tears twice seven years could not abate.
Reason will win. The victor still is Yearning.

(Reply 2 to poem 101)

The best will conquer. That is what you wrote
Of longing and of rationality.
The better thing will win the victory.
Reason, that is, the annotators note.

The reasonable commentators vote
For what all reasonable readers see
As that to which the rational agree.
The last day thunders in my heart. I quote.

I listened, and you forced on me a moral
By what you said on Sunday. This may jolt.
Parnassus yields to yearning. Longing leads

So sweetly, steeply, upward, it proceeds
To peaks of immortality. The laurel
Is proof against the ruthless thunderbolt.

(Reply by the rhymes to poem 107)

A pallid wingless utterance, O my,
Crept from my lips and helplessly began
To crawl along the long blue lines that ran
Across the flat blank pad. It yearned to fly,

Rising on silver pinions towards a sky
Of blue infinitudes within the span
Of aquilinian wings and eyes to scan
Black seas and whitest stars of fit reply.

But all its aspirations fall apart
Like feathers littering its little cage
As its thin throat is broken in the noose.

Somewhere, afar, upon a better page
Scratched with miraculous and alate art
A song is launched. It soars without excuse.

(Reply 2 to poem 107)

Trapped! I feel the fetters, nothing more.
Beaten! I cannot move a molecule
Of muscle. Still I strive and strive to drool
The issue not the causes of the war.

The cause was love. The cause was beauty. Pour
Your scorn upon the Helen, proud and cruel,
For whom the battle raged. I was the fool.
I loved a language. No, I love, adore.

I thread the needle, but I cannot sew,
Struggling to clutch each syllable just wrung
From little learned. The will is not the way.

I tie my mind as I have tied my tongue,
Daring to think no more than what I know,
Able to think only what I can say.

(Reply 3 to poem 107)

The rhythm, rhyme, or reason is an oak
Tossing its golden tassels through the air
Of sweetest spring. The rosy leaflets dare
To meet the breeze with kisses. I awoke.

The tiny opening had been a joke.
My little slit of window was a snare.
The leaves are greening. I became aware
That all their essences went up in smoke.

And the image of them went up so sparkly
A thousand thousand sparklers charged the sky,
Arising, widening, and showering.

Only one golden drop could enter my
Prison, equipped so dimly and so starkly.
Yet that one seed was instant flowering.

(Reply 4 to poem 107)

I sat and read. The sturdy letters strode
Before my eyes and pranced across my mind.
I was immobilized. They were aligned
As infantry and cavalry. They flowed

Over the fields along the lengths of road
On to the city where the plane trees lined
The river and the seven hills inclined
Towards that eternity which often showed

Its features there. There, sitting, night and day,
I did not move. The marching phrases moved.
The clauses and the sentences came thronging.

Suddenly, subtly, summoned and approved,
Through streets and gardens I, I, took my way,
Vague with love, the vagabond of longing.

(Reply 5 to poem 107)

Approved? By whom? Not by the literati.
Not by the poets of our prizes' styles.
Not by the scholars' or the critics' smiles.
Not by the new elite, the digerati.

Not by the listings, legible but spotty,
Of bibliographies. Not by big files
Caught in the brimming net that webs the miles
Of information. By the present? Haughty,

I page the past. I call upon the dead,
Appeal to Caesar. Humble, will I win
Pity, O Petrarch? Is the question moot?

Would you have liked to be Pygmalion?
Had Laura answered, what could you have said?
If you responded, would I not be mute?

(Reply 6 to poem 107)

Twice seven years it will be very soon,
And I remember. What do I recall?
I feel that spring, that summer, and the fall.
The winter will not enter, for my tune

Is all of rose of dawn, of gold of noon,
Of glint of glimpse of azure, of the small
Blue blooming in the huge green field, is all
Of green of leaf, of leafiness. To prune

The oak of recollection when the snow
Has gashed the branches is perhaps a duty.
The laurel must be summering for us.

Shores of some other ocean saw and know
Lineaments of such a complex beauty
That I am simply still complicitous.

(Reply 7 to poem 107)

I wrote to you when I still wrote to Joe,
Yet there was no connection. Did you write
To Laura, pope, and emperor one night?
Was that the night you wrote to Cicero?

Cicero spoke to me. To you, I know,
Homer, known only as one catches sight
Of a friend's hair or distant eye's quick light,
Addressed a letter dated from below.

Joe answered. Then the man became the elm
Whose golden tresses aureoled a fall
Three thousand miles of continent from where

Pacific violence might overwhelm
With azure vasts implicit in its call:
Come, angel, haloed in your golden hair.

(Reply 8 to poem 107)

How many women must I share you with?
Your lady love, the mother of your son,
Your daughter's mother (were there two or one
Mother or mothers?), and your very kith

And kin, dear mamma, girlchild, grandchild, pith
Of the same living tree? Or is there none
To rise beside the vibrant laurel, spun
Of sound, the image, figure, symbol, myth?

Francesca, two Elettas, one or two
Anonymous, and one whose breeze-gold name
Is Love, is Loveliness, is lovely Laura,

Ananonymity, sung wreathing fame
Outliving scribbled beech and vivid yew,
Cannot be fascinated fans like Flora.

(Reply 9 to poem 107)

Silence alone is golden when the sound
Of the great golden song, the golden lute,
Aureate violin, aurific flute,
Chrysostomous Promethean bard bound

As to the brow imperially crowned
Subsides to silence. Must I not be mute?
How can I answer? Do I dare to toot
My hornlet when my skiff has run aground?

What drives the pond to emulate the ocean?
What wind, what moon, had power to arouse
The little ripples? What strange avalanches

Came crashing from the anthills set in motion?
What friend, what beast, lurks deep between these boughs?
Some adversary lured me through grand branches.

(Reply 10 to poem 107)

Can there be grandeur in the amorous
Complaints, the lamentations of self-pity,
The sighings suspirated from each ditty,
The long soft sobbings, or the clamorous

Reiterations? Nothing glamorous,
Glorious, gracious, bracing, gripping, witty,
Weighty appears inherent here. The pretty
Is not our life's willed diagram or us.

The habit does not make the monk. What makes
The poem? Does the subject? Far above
Or far below the matter beats the heart

Of purest form. And still my being aches.
Poet, I love you. What is it I love?
The passionate perfection of the art.

(Reply 11 to poem 107)

The artist lives within the art alone.
Then you were not a man. You could not be.
The poet has no personality.
The poet has no body of his own.

His tear, his smile, his glance, his laugh, his groan
Exist as fiction, phantom, fantasy.
The form, the corpus, of his work is he,
His soul, his mind, his flesh, his blood, his bone.

You climbed Parnassus, climbed the Capitol,
Triumphed. To poetry belonged the prize.
The Muses all applauded, still rejoice.

Fragrance of laurel filled and filled the hall.
Did people hear your sweet strong Latin voice?
Could you have had those soft Italian eyes?

(Reply 12 to poem 107)

Power I hate and power is your mark.
I speak to you no longer. Be now he.
Then they will stop their gossiping that we
Wrestle unequally in this great arc

Of closure closing in through this great dark
In which I live though it is light to thee.
Be thou no longer. I am merely she
Who loves the waves whereon she must embark,

The course where I have come down to the wire,
The waves he made, the very route you chart.
Must I communicate this miracle?

Is he an angel? Is his sword of fire?
My adversary with that marvel, art,
Unveils a heaven and unbolts a hell.

(Reply 13 to poem 107)

I lied. I loved. I love. I will not lie.
There are no battles. There are only tears.
There are no hatreds. There are only fears.
The tree has lived. The tree will never die.

The tree is evergreen. It can defy
Sharp fulminations. Still its incense cheers
Dull desolations. Over us it rears
Large shade against too hot and bright a sky.

We have gone down, deep down, and reached the roots
Of pleasure, of delight without alloy
In single instants of totality.

We know the joy, the joy, the jewelled joy,
Emerald, sapphire, gold, leaves, blooms, and fruits.
We love the light. Into the fire we fly.

(Reply 14 to poem 107)

Was I undone as Dido was undone
Or did I like Aeneas hear the call
To sail away? Could Carthage hold in thrall
One whom the gods have summoned? Does the sun

Sink to a burning like the love of one
Whose love was death, or will the shining ball
Rise over Rome like love that conquers all?
Was it a person, place, or thing that won

My undefended heart? I never guessed,
When I began, that Ama, Vide, Veni,
Meant Come, Come, Come, meant For you is the nod,

The thunder, of the greatest and the best.
Is it, is he, the sky, the sky's great god,
Jupiter, golden, bright, or gray and rainy?

(Reply 15 to poem 107)

Why when my admiration is so great
Was I so querulous and condescending?
Why when my love is passionate, unending,
Invincible, does it resemble hate?

Why does the conversation seem debate,
Dispute, harsh argument, rude rough unbending
Contentiousness and testiness, all tending
To petty pawing at the prison's grate?

Why do the sweetest leaves, that from your tree
Release the sweetest shade, upon me pour
Shadows? And shall I blanch below the rays

Emitted by your solar energy?
Stuttering love must grunt and gasp before
The learning and the art far past faint praise.

(Reply to poem 281)

How many hours I passed with you apart
When Uncle Cicero conducted me
Into the nook where dead Latinity
Lives as the lively conversations start.

How many hours, stunned, felled by the dart
Sped from such potent parle of melody
That once it touched me I was never free,
I struggled, rising up from, by, the art

That took my breath away. The Tiber flowed
Golden through multisecular mauve mud
Where Herculean herds of cattle lowed

And armies blessed by Mars paid what they owed
To Jupiter with fingers rinsed of blood
And on the purple cliff green triumph glowed.

(Reply by the rhymes to poem 282)

O soul or ghost of one who often, torn
From dearest dead delivered from the lent
Temporal swathing veils in which they spent
Their fleshly days and which, changed, will adorn

Their brilliant spirits on that brilliant morn
Of an eternal dawn, gave slow consent
To tenuous nights of vigil that present
Those moments when we wait and watch and mourn

And then beyond these blurring tears may scan
Bright features which for minutes, instants, end
The eyes' long dark, what simple signal can

Have glimmered through this late dim caravan?
Is it the merest hood and wreath, O friend,
Of phantom, ghost, soul, scholar, poet, man?

(Reply to poem 40)

If death or dread distraction does not twist
And tear the very thread with which I weave
That text, not life itself, which I believe
To be my life itself, it will exist.

It will exist and through the thickening mist
Will gleam as silk and through the deepening eve
Will ring as song. Dim distances deceive
Only until the instant of the tryst.

It will see Rome. In Rome it will be heard
As light still pours upon the umbrella pines
And rumblings sound still down among the cobbles.

Let me be clear. It will not be absurd.
It will unfurl the banners of its lines
Whether itself it flies or merely hobbles.

UMBRAGEOUS VISION | VISIO | VISION

* * *

But me Parnassus, lonely, arduous,
Lures with its lonely love. Yet not alone
Over the craggy syntagmatic paths
Must I go struggling on a road my own,
However rugged. Others have ascended.
Up on that splendid summit shall we meet?
I see the reddened pebbles at my feet.
My way is mine. The love is strange and sweet.
As each sighs separately what waits above?
Rock, spring, pond, swan, gull, vulture, eagle, dove,
Olive, oak, laurel? It is a lonely love.
When he and she and you and I have ended
The climb what clarities are aftermaths?
Have I and I unmade or remade us?

* * *

I know this morning, when the bard ascended
Into the land of Adam, where once I
Was resident. Are nine years much to lose?
Nine years, three months, and thirty days I spent
In Paradise. I spent the golden coin
Of youth there, fed on milk and honey there,
Yes, fed on nectar. And the golden apples
Dangled from every tree. The apple blossoms
Scented afresh each year, each month, each day.
I spent the golden flower of my youth
In Paradise.

        Must it be lost?

                Regained
It was Parnassus. Rock of rose and gold
Glowed as I glowed with yearning, with that love
                    Of the

Of the ascent in which the arduous
Answers the ardor, where the solitude
Becomes the company of instruments
Formed by the fingers, built by every breath.

O Pales venerand, a greater strain
Is raised from Paradise revisited.
To Paradise, Parnassus, Palatine
My steps ascended. Was the last the least?
The shepherd's goddess is the emperor's.
I walk with Pales through the palaces.

Ten thousand years ago I came to Rome.

The myth, the mystery, the history
Continue: repetition, increment.
Regret will be review, will be revision.
Rereading, revolution, revelation
Shall interpenetrate and interlock.
The freshest text might be the common place,
Place of refreshment, of amenity.

Why did you come to Rome? For liberty.

And over there there was the golden age,
The golden place where savant Saturn sat
Enthroned, once green, then gold, then green once more.
The slope is sown with poppies. As I climb —
One climbs forever — shaggy Saturn smiles.
We wave across the swamp as Pales laughs
Among the trees of love, the Judas trees,
Blazing above Great Mother's old black stone.

Dark armies march onto the field of blue.
What black clouds mass against serenity?
The ebony are conquered by the gray,
The gray retreat before the white, and they
Yield that field. Celestial glorious
Azure is peace and is victorious.
The Mother's hosts of holm oak, sacerdotal,
Cassocked, cast blackest shadows, dark as dear.
The evidence is sure though anecdotal.
                                        Some shades

Some shades we love and other shades we fear.
The hill blooms purple as the sky blooms blue.
Sun thunders gold. The shade is shade of tree.

Such dread and such delight and such desire
Swirl through the purple blossoms blessing me
Before the cordate leaves. And where the old
Marble acanthus, carved on capitals,
Lies fallen on the grass, the green, the new,
The natural, the real acanthus rises.

That cypress indicates the library.
I stand and gape behind the gate of wire.
Someone is coming — not a shepherdess —
A princess surely, an aristocrat
At least, a Roman noblewoman stoled
In white.

  I wait.

    Who locked the library?

*   *   *

Who was that white-gowned figure by the tomb?

I slid down from the wall beneath the almond,
Ran down the steps, and met her on the grass.
She seemed a little sad. It was that bleak
Sadness through which she smiled. It was her smile.
Was it her melancholy? Was it mine?

After, from golden beak, the merl began
To chant a black-clad angel's golden hymn,
While, like souls screaming, swifts were circling high
Above bright cypresses through blue celeste,
We circled that whole monument in silence.

We walked on then beyond the mausoleum
Towards the unruined dome. She was, I knew,
Julia, in white, among the Easter lilies.

These lilies are most pure, most sensual.
The scent of lilies is a memory
And is a freshness, is a presence felt
As sense. The tilted chalices are drunk
Deep for a knowledge. White light glistening
About the trumpets, precious, rare, within
Our hearing and within our grasp, along
Our line of sight, finer than sighting lines,
Is vision, visionary understanding.
Julia, your gaze is keen, your eyes are clear.
Surely you know this passion. You must know
This deepest love, this highest starred desire.
Once more I recognize the ancient flame.

But she was gone. Was it the antic ban?

The Tiber glides on on its yellow way.
O give me lilies with a plenitude
Against this emptiness, give me a scent
Against this absence, grant a strong and sweet
Unfaded fragrance as memorial.

Julia, if you were Julius would you be
Remembered here where Julia's father built,
Lamented here where Julia's husbands lie?

Flora, you must not weep. The child will see . . .

I turned. Why had I recognized that voice?

. . . Will see the heroes mingling with the gods . . .

I saw the speaker and

        . . . and will be seen . . .

Already I was falling at his feet.

* * *

May

* * *

June

* * *

I, not unwept, unhonored, and unsung,
Not simply suffering the negative,
Not purely patient of passivity,
Not merely lacking honor, under lack,
Under sad deprivation, under un-,
But grimly grinning in the face of dis-,
Dishonored, disinherited, disvoiced,

Have searched for fatherland and mothertongue.

Omnipotent and ineluctable
Fortune and Fate have brought me to this brink
Of sight, of speech. The goddess of all song
And sooth has guided me, the god of art
Has been the author and must be and is.

* * *

Roman Sonnets

A sonnet is a little conversation
With all the sonnets that have gone before.
Will rhyme reply to rhyme forevermore
In a perpetual continuation,

Or might this evening see, seal, the cessation
Of twinklings that a new dawn must abhor
And tinklings that, delight to noons of yore,
Fade to dim irritants of iteration?

The loved and lovely ladies lived and died.
Autumns glowed gold, burned bronze, and iced to iron.
Those roses were the roses of their time,

Those snows the tears of yesteryears that cried
Down all the Alps and into their — no, my — urn.
Catullus kissed and kissed without a rhyme.

We give a million kisses and then give
A thousand and then give a million more
And mix the millions with the thousands, for
Our kisses let us love and let us live

Our little life, Catullus wrote. The priv-
Ilege of art is alteration, or
I have betrayed my trust as translator.
My mood has been a mere indicative.

Give, he commanded. Let us, he exhorted.
I do not push my will or waste my wishes.
Each sun rolls like the penny of brief luck.

Before the Ultimate must come unstuck,
Before Dawn's lucent blossom be aborted,
O Fortune, Fortune, give me many kisses.

Millions of kisses, swift and lyrical,
Measured in Latin meters though no rhyme
Numbered the pulses of their lovely chime
Numbered upon another principle

That rendered them no less invincible
Despite all loss of count, all loss of prime,
All loss of gloss in blossoms out of clime,
Still hold the potence of their miracle.

Pull down the book, pull out the dictionary,
Dust off the grammar, move a finger slowly
Along the letters. Must there be a rift

In twenty centuries? The missionary
Crossing the seas of ages glimpses, holy,
Millions of kisses, lyrical and swift.

If I must sonnetize can I not try
Rhymes that no sonneteer has tried before?
Should I not set my shoulder to the chore
Of chopping down these weeds that ought to die,

Not to rise vigorous and multiply
Through shimmerings of garden? I adore
Poppies' defiant leonine red roar.
I worship lilies' lowing cellos, high

Viols of jasmine twittering, the martial
Chant of acanth along triumphal ways.
One could first read the ruins best near dusk.

There is a resonance in what seems partial.
There is a clarity in what seems haze.
There is a truthfulness in what is fusc.

I asked for answers culled from conversations
With past, with future, with eternity.
Carmentis turned before and equally
Turned after. Janus gained the same relations

By facing each and both of polar stations
In space and therefore by analogy
In time. And even Venus of the sea
At the great drain had two orientations.

Did lief light leave the star, this syllable
Slip from the finch's bill? What fingers clutched
An airy ball that mine have nearly won?

Where is the present? Has the capital
Vanished before the period is touched?
Have my closed eyes enclosed this dazzling sun?

Letitia answered. I must answer now.
Then conversation has a speaking part
In life, in living thought, in living art,
In art awaiting birth. I wait, for how

Shall I explain? I nudge a puzzled brow.
To well, wall, altar, pillar, slow eyes dart,
Regarding all the ancient motions start,
Created in the temple of my vow.

On each eleventh day of jasmine June
We gather in the temple of the Dawn,
Our mother and the mother of the Glister

Of day, of fire arising into noon
As each of us, stoled, veiled in gauze of lawn,
Prays for the little children of her sister.

Sister Letitia, on this holy day,
Day of your birth, dear daughter of the Dawn,
Come dancing light and lovely as the fawn
You so resemble, light and fine and fey,

Frisky and solemn, sorrowful and gay
With that bright gaiety the world has drawn
Up from the wellsprings of the gods, the yawn
Of hollows sought that from the earth convey

Refreshment like the freshness of the sky
When Morning, not in mourning but in gold,
Gracefully rises, graciously partakes

Of what we offer her, these yellow cakes,
Corn muffins which, when Dawn seemed sure to die
Starving, the Goddess Song made her of old.

Twin temples stand here bordering on death.
The swamp is gone, the harbor has been moved,
The buses, taxis, motorcars, unhooved,
Inanimate, exhale their monstrous breath.

What are we to the gods? The legend saith:
The child enlightened, wreathed in fire, behooved
To grasp at grandeur, or the loved man proved
Fortunate through the centuries of myth.

What are the gods to us? These goddesses
Are Fortune, one, and, second, Mother Dawn.
Shall their wells tremble at each growling truck?

A red-lipped poppy gasps yet blurts: Here is
Mater Matuta, one, Fortuna, one:
One, Mother Morning, and, one, Lover Luck.

Was he behooved, or is it only it
That could behoove him? If the OE case
Of him was genitive I must erase
That passive subject person, and the fit

Is no less awkward if my choice has hit
Upon what was a dative, for the trace
Of such obliquities remains a base
For comfortable usage. But who writ

— Milton? — Behooves him now both oar and sail?
And now to cross kilometers of brine
With deviltry or godliness unchecked,

Besides humility to strive and fail
Or leisure or the genius to refine,
Behooves an artificial dialect.

The veriest monster is the motorcycle,
The scariest master of draconian
Awful unlawfulness, anomian
Anomaly of self-made track, yet tribal

In interaction, featly fratricidal
In feel of fact. By that Bellonian
Ruin beyond the hippodromian
Pattern, each dragon challenges survival,

Swerving to sweep through what was once the swamp
Beside which Fortune welcomed bellicose
And pious mortals. Immortality

Gleamed in the hero's eyes and seemed so close
That comic jeers were epic cheers as he
Endured the proud and purifying pomp.

Can I compare this place to paradise?
Who would record the garden when the city
Buds with these muscles, rumorous and gritty,
As sinewed virtue burgeons into vice?

Rome is not Eden. Shall I say it twice?
Eden was never civilized and witty.
But where is piety and where is pity?
Where do the pines and cypresses suffice

To bind hearts to the earth and to the sky
As the late golds, although the shades increase,
Osculate wall and column, trunk and bough?

What is this place? Watch the parade go by
Where Saturn on the hillside promised peace
And Janus looking both ways kept the vow.

Yet Peter countered: What more civilized
Than conversation in the evening air
Can you imagine? And one morning there,
Among the fragrances that harmonized

With motions, tones, and potencies surmised
As flow of dance or song or rite or prayer
Or stream or flower fairer far than fair
Or oriole all red or gold, surprised

I glimpsed, I listened to, a revelation
In which such erudition, art, and style
Flourished beneath such trees with leaves so shady

I knew the urgency of retractation
If Eden held the learned lovely lady
Matilda who could make a Virgil smile.

Smile, little baby, Virgil Sibylline
Sang in the stirring lullaby of longing,
Tired of the century of civil wronging,
Awakened by the pact that might design

The centuries of peace, that could define
An age of Saturn as the hopes came thronging
Like lambs in grassy pastures, cowbells donging.
What did the bard devise or what divine?

Who was this baby born Saturnian?
Gallus the son of Pollio the consul,
Antonia the child of Antony,

Julia the daughter of Octavian,
The Christ who is the Roman of the sky,
The dream, the literary bit of tinsel?

Can we condone a poetry of prose,
A song of statement, or a list in rhyme?
Or can we catalogue in metric time
Its petals and yet never smell the rose

With fragrance that the scent of dawn would pose
If light were redolence that morn could chime
As over distant hills the sun would climb
With stars the birds all ringing in the close

Of night and major music of the day?
The other rose was note of noonhigh sun.
The third was dusky as the evening fell

Upon the garden yet a final ray
Of gold from some horizon matched the one
That was a petal of the golden bell.

The dream, the thought, idea or ideal,
Soared like a tree, but I was digging deep
Below the roots to where the waters seep
Now down, now up, through mud we call the real.

What did the secular recess conceal?
Did I awake the goddess from a sleep?
Her eyes were wide, not such as meanly keep
The secrets which her smile might still reveal.

I held her close though she was helmeted
And once had reigned from high above the shrine
That guarded margins and the marginal.

Was I the muddler? She was made of mud.
Her gritty fist was not inimical.
Her eyes and smile were bright. They were divine.

As over distant hills the sun would climb
So over vistaed hills the sun would fare
And over winning hills the sun would dare
To challenge shadows and, now in his prime,

To ratify the battlements of time
As over willing hills his horns would blare
And over winsome hills his common, rare
Fragrance would linger, lowly and sublime.

Over the seven hills the white-gowned men
Clambered and fashioned and refashioned home
Before, behind, beyond the battlements

Which they outlasted in their eloquence.
Wars became words. Were they eternal, then,
Those moments when the sun saw only Rome?

The shape within the frame rose green and gold.
Was it a picture or reality?
Was it a sculpture? Was it truly tree?
The tree beyond the frame rose manifold.

The tree was singing, and its singing told
Through the black notes a golden history
That merl or merlin moved through mystery
Into new substance. But the tree was old,

No, not so old, not old. The tree was ill.
That song became the sweetness of the swan
Keening itself. Then was the frame the wide

Window upon the square where something died?
Four cypresses were corners. One is gone.
And in the emptiness the song rings still.

Another ruin? Read here files of brick:
A bit of apse. Read standing column: one
Of two that ought to stand there as the sun
Catches at angles though the hedge is thick

And though the alban font that should be quick
With light lies low upon the grass, undone,
Or is it yet unmade? Will waters run
In centuries? So many ages tick

So many gods and ghosts, such exhalation
Of wintersweet, what was as what will be,
The utterly unthought of as the known,

Building in Rome as rite, as respiration,
A green acanthus leaf spread on a stone,
A bird that saunters headfirst down a tree.

The roof is netted with a web of stone
That liberates the spaces which it catches
Within its work of axed, chopped, measured latches
That lock and free the feeling in the bone

Along the fingers, wrists, and arms that hone
The edifice emerging from the batches
Of matter, hard, so hard. Who softly matches
The rock's profoundest essence with his own

At every touching glance, each subtle tap,
Each confident advance, each modest halt,
Each flight of mind that forms stone's silver wing

Waiting to rise from and above its map?
Stone's golden rope sustains the awning vault,
But what or who may hold the golden string?

Honor the poet, four grand poets cried
As Virgil with a breathing bard returned
To gardens where they lived who once had died
To life in time and, timeless now, had earned

Fortleben, fortune, following, and found
Forever everlasting timeliness
That stretches far and farther from the bound
Of town and tongue and trend and track to press

Upon the present, where some stand apart
And stroll apart with them, though so, so late.
What bearers of the banners of their art
Beyond the Acheron still walk and wait?

Who will, among the poets, be the seventh?
Who will, among the muses, be eleventh?

It was one voice which uttered that great name
Heard by the poet of a later day,
But were it four it would be much the same
Since that one voice said what four wished to say

And spoke for all before they all appeared,
Neither exhilarated nor depressed,
Not pained unduly, not unduly cheered.
This is their limbo, their eternal rest.

We may not see them in such happy fields.
That limbo cannot live. They live or die.
Their visitor is with them now and wields
Their subterranean power from the sky.

Honor the poet, cried one voice, and we
Know that they all cry, Honor poetry.

How do you reach the sky? The angel's oar
Begins to sweep the waters where the man
Called by the city of the earth began
The final founding, at the Tiber's shore.

The angel rows the spirits to the door
From which they climb or fly as each one can.
The hero rowed to Rome along a tan
And tawny Tiber. Janus watches four

Visions at once from high above the plain
Where, green, green-edged, the Tiber flows between
Peter's white peak and Jupiter's all gold

And, soaring higher from a deeper vein,
Aureate, marble, emerald, are seen
Bold history and poetry more bold.

Through which side of the twin Carmental Gate
Did I depart when I marched out to fight?
Was it the left? Could it have been the right?
I dread the dreadful never worse than late.

I tremble at the fearful Fabian fate.
Three hundred six strode forth in pride and might,
All of one clan. Three hundred six one night
Near to a far-off stream all were but bait.

Which janus did they choose? The one that looks
Out towards the field? The one that leads us home?
There are two arches and a twofold track:

Exit and entrance? sic et non? Redux,
Fortuna Redux, bring me back to Rome.
Loved Bring-Back Luck, unlock our cul-de-sac.

Did we march out to battle in December?
Barbarian branches bear their barren snows.
Thick heavens thicken thicker to disclose
Their own descent, and how can we remember,

Not blue, not green, but coppery November?
Our paths are all behind us. Our track blows.
Where is my land, my January rose?
Our paths are footprints, frozen, ours. What ember

Of expectation warms the latest slope
In whitest web of wind and sky? We follow
The scent of something faint and far away

Up the green river past the green lawns of Hope
To where the martial field holds to Apollo
Sun-scented redolence of leafy bay.

* * *

If I speak clearly can I kill the song?
If I talk muddily may I omit
Brilliants that make the very life of it?
A stolid ox is standing on my tongue.

Some hippopotamus has lazed along
The bottom and emerges to the lit
Surface that swirls above the whirling pit.
Can I tell right from left or right from wrong?

Can I tell, trusting image, metaphor,
Symbol, myth, literature, how I in force
Distrust the force itself, and without cease

Will I wage war on willing, winning, war,
Plunging both tongue and hand into the source
Soaked with which poets scream of peace, peace, peace?

* * *

The Libraries

* * *

The Myth of Scipio

* * *

Quintile

* * *

Sextile

* * *

September

* * *

September 13

Here is the cosmology,
Here is the ontology,
Here is the metaphysics.

What is here is here,
Part of the real world,
Reality of real reality.

To find what is missing that must be found
Look into the dry pool,
Gaze into the empty sky.

That which is virtual,
That which is ideal,
Is real for the understanding you

For whom it gleams
Behind, around, within
The real that you are breathing from and to.

Here is the epistemology,
Here is the geography
Here is the unwrapped map.

Here is the calendar.
Here is the feast, the banquet.
Here is the mystic marriage and the virgin birth.

The moon shines full upon the Ides
The day will shine in fullest clarity
Or will the lightning, will the thunder, break?

The lunar white discovers plenitude.
The solar gold will find equality.
Will I, all words, track the time for words?

Shall I be abstract?
Shall I be didactic?
Will you sit and listen to perfect or imperfect words?

The third father must be Jove.
The virgin mother must be Flora Baum.
The child must cry. The child must smile.

O mihi tum longae
(Smile little child)
Maneat pars ultima vitae.

September 14

There is complexity in the legend.
There is simplicity in the myth.
Is the relevant real one or two or three?

Time will tell.
If I cannot tell
Let there be time.

September 15

The great games are extended.
The games are extended
And extended.

Let me watch the games.
Let me play
The game.

September 16

Must I ask and ask?
Can I answer and answer?
How long shall I be able to scrutinize?

The first father laughs as May.
The second father smiles as July.
The third father beams as bright September.

Vulcan acts the spouse as May.
Apollo plays the spouse as July.
Jove is here the speaking spouse as September.

Is the child one?
Are the children two?
Hold the book open.

This is the third book.
This is the third father, Jove.
Janus is the mother's father's father.

Is the birth single?
Is the birth double?
The offspring may be sole or gemini.

Hold up the child.
Hold up the book.
Is the true Rome the true?

Once born does the beauty never perish?
Can you infallibly trust the true?
Can you eternally see the sheen?

Must the pools turn dry?
Must the storm clouds shade and shake the sky?
Can I tell you all before I die?

* * *

October

* * *

November

* * *

December

* * *

Do we conclude with shadows or with stars?

The sun is setting, and the year must end.
My white empurpled robe is ready now.
Tomorrow, seen and seeing, I will go
Like a consul to the Capitol.

Begin, my child. Old Janus looks both ways.

And January

* * *

Jove's child opens his eyes.
Jove's child opens her lips.

Jupiter high on the hill stands radiant.
Across the gleaming river Janus gazes.

Eloquent the consul ascends the Capitol.
Silent the virgin climbs the Capitol.

Both contemplate the growing Roman city.
Both comprehend the spreading universe.

The oratory blossoms into vision.
The stillness buds in visionary speech.

Quies et motus
Hold motion and rest.

Here we sing.
Here we see.

Look, Janus, the millennia
Before and after sound and shine.

The Gardens of Flora Baum

Set in 11-point Scala OT, the Open Type
version of the typeface created in
1990 by Dutch type designer
Martin Majoor and first
used for printing
programs at
Vredenburg Music
Centre, Utrecht. The name
honors Milan's La Scala opera house.

Printing: Lulu.com

Book design: Roger Sinnott